OWN THE
NIGHT

Selection & Use of Tactical Lights & Laser Sights

SCOTT W. WAGNER

©2009 Krause Publications, Inc.,
a subsidiary of F+W Media, Inc.

Published by

Gun Digest® Books
An imprint of F+W Media, Inc.
700 East State Street • Iola, WI 54990-0001
715-445-2214 • 888-457-2873
www.gundigestbooks.com

Our toll-free number to place an order or obtain
a free catalog is (800) 258-0929.

Library of Congress Control Number: 2009923232

ISBN-13: 978-1-4402-0371-8
ISBN-10: 1-4402-0371-7

Designed by Tom Nelsen
Edited by Corrina Peterson

Printed in China

Dedication

For Rosemarie –

The one constant in my life, whose unwavering faith in my ability to complete this book kept me motivated and focused, and whose photographic skills and keen eye provided the visual documentation so critical for a work such as this.

About the Author

Scott Wagner is Commander of the Columbus State Community College Police Academy and 727 Counter Terror Training Unit (**www.cscc.edu/cttu**) and a member of the National Tactical Officers Association (NOTA); the American Society of Law Enforcement Trainers; and International Law Enforcement Educators and Trainers Association. Mr. Wagner is also active in the International Association of Chiefs of Police (IACP) and Ohio Tactical Officers Association, and serves as area Representative to the Law Enforcement Alliance of America. He has written more than 30 articles that have appeared in *Guns and Weapons* for *Law Enforcement*, *Combat Handguns*, *The Police Marksman*, *Tactical Gear Magazine*, *Police and Security News*, the *LEAA Advocate Magazines*, *Gun Digest*, *2009 Glock Annual*, and *Tactical Weapons for Military and Police*.

CONTENTS

Streamlight–
www.streamlight.com

Surefire– www.surefire.com

Pentagonlight–
(no longer in business)

Blackhawk–
www.blackhawk.com

Laserlyte– www.laserlyte.com

Insight Technology–
www.insighttechnology.com

First Light USA–
www.first-light-usa.com

Crimson Trace Corporation–
www.crimsontrace.com

Tactical Link–
www.tacticallink.com

Midwest Industries–
www.midwestindustriesinc.com

Inova–
www.inovalight.com

Beretta USA–
www.berettausa.com

XS Sight Systems–
www.xssights.com

Kimber USA–
www.kimberamerica.com

Ruger–
www.ruger-firearms.com

KEL-TEC–
www.kel-tec-cnc.com

Sun Devil Manufacuring–
www.sundevilmfg.com

Nightforce–
www.nightforceoptics.com

T his book is dedicated to all the law enforcement, military and lawfully armed civilian defensive and offensive firearms users to whom it is hoped that the ideas and concepts presented within will help them survive any deadly force situations they encounter, and allow them to truly "Own the Night".

The author would like to thank the members of the 727 Counter Terror Training Unit (www.cscc.edu/cttu) Instructional Team who provided additional tactical insight and the donation of time required for much of the photographic documentation contained in Own the Night. In particular, the author is grateful to Sgt. John Groom, Officer Tim Halbakken, Officer Dustin Mowery, Officer Sean Lingofelter, and Officer John Holloway. Additionally, the author wishes to thank (but cannot name) two other team members who are active in the U.S. Army Special Forces for their training and advice.

In addition, the author gives special thanks to Sheriff Rocky Nelson, Chief Deputy Tom Morgan, of the Union County Ohio Sheriff's Office who gave me permission as a Deputy Sheriff and SRT Team Member, to write this book, as well as Sgt. Lyle Herman for agreeing to demonstrate for photographic documentation of the patrol techniques described in own the night.

Finally, the author wishes to acknowledge the equipment manufactures listed on the left, who provided their excellent products for testing and review and the additional photography of use in the field.

2:30 a.m.

"Honey, I hear something, go check it out."

*I grab my handgun and tactical light and go
to check outside. . .*

**Dominate your area of responsibility.
Move through the darkness, in control of it,
choosing the time and direction of illumination. Own the night.**

In 29 years of law enforcement experience, I've observed an explosion in equipment and technological breakthroughs. Some of these breakthroughs have
benefited law enforcement officers and civilians, while others have proven to
be of little advantage, and sometimes have been downright dangerous to the user.

One of the more recent of the latter that comes to mind was a security holster
that required the user's fingerprint be read each time the weapon was removed
from the holster. Although there was much media hype about this holster — and
how wonderful it was in allegedly enhancing the safety of the officer — it thank-
fully died a quiet death. No one stopped to consider what would happen to the
fingerprint reader if the officer fell in the mud and got it on the holster, if the reader
was covered in snow or ice, or if the officer's hands became dirty, greasy, or bloody
before trying to draw the weapon.

I've always disliked the introduction of products that may have centered around
a good basic idea, but weren't developed with the end user in mind or tested by
people with real experience in the field. In the everyday world, this usually means
that average civilian users are left with products that are worthless, or of questionable use, and end up in the trash or in a junk drawer somewhere. When these
products are purchased by the inexperienced and foisted on a law enforcement or
military department, it can potentially cost lives.

In this book, I'll try to help you select and apply the most reliable and practical
electronic sighting and lighting systems available — the type that will work for you
in the real world.

The areas of tactical illumination systems — both handheld and weapon-mounted — and the application of supplemental laser sighting systems are two technological areas that have seen the most development in the preceding 10 to 15 years.
In target/area illumination for law enforcement, we've gone from using hardware

store-supplied aluminum handheld lights designed for general purpose use to heavy-duty aircraft or aerospace-grade rechargeable lights offering thousands of times the candlepower.

In between those two ends of the spectrum were the old Kel-Lites of the 1970s and 1980s, the first of the duraluminum breed. The Kel-Lite was so popular that the brand name became synonymous with "police flashlight." Although no brighter than any similar hardware store variety, the duraluminum construction was what set the Kel-Lite apart: It was a tough light that could double as a nightstick (much to the consternation of many police administrators). One of my former partners had a Kel-Lite that still functioned after being dented in the barrel portion by a fired .22 Magnum bullet.

About the same time the Kel-Lite disappeared, Maglite flashlights appeared. Maglite used an improved switching system that was more reliable than the Kel-Lite, and Maglite made a great mini-light that could fit on an officer's belt (that light is still with us today as the Mini-Maglite).

The much brighter krypton bulbs appeared at the time and the difference in brightness was distinct. About the same time, Streamlight appeared on the scene and introduced the ultra-bright (for the time) 20,000 candlepower SL20 rechargeable light. Police lighting hasn't looked back since.

New models, features, and systems seem to appear on almost a daily basis. Augmented by electronics for power control and switch operation, the flashlight has morphed from a basic illumination tool into a weapons system in and of itself — or at least a system that supports and enhances the weapon.

Supplemental laser sighting systems are still the newcomer on the block. (I say "supplemental" because a laser sight should not be used without fixed sight support.) They're no longer just toys or Hollywood props. Check out the laser system used in the original *Terminator* movie, which was mounted on an AMT Longslide Hardballer .45, to see how far we've come.

Laser sighting systems are used by many tactical teams, mine included, as a very effective pistol/rifle combat tool, and their use is becoming more and more widespread. An integral laser sight is also essential in the use of the Taser Electronic Immobilization Device, which is the most important tool for subject control developed since the nightstick.

This book explores some of the newest advances in all three supportive illumination systems — handheld tactical lights, weapon mounted lights, and supplemental laser sight illumination devices. It also reviews the proper application and uses for each type of device and recommended techniques for enhancing personal safety and effectiveness.

OWN THE NIGHT

Part I:

Handheld Flashlight Systems

OWN THE NIGHT – PART I

Handheld Flashlight Systems

Illuminate, Identify, Incapacitate. This is the defensive triad of any good tactical lighting system, whether it's truly a "tactical light" (one developed with SWAT teams as the end users) or a patrol-type light for general use by officers on a daily beat. Let's break down the concept a bit.

First, all flashlights are designed to *illuminate*. They help us clearly define an area in total darkness, allowing us to maneuver or navigate safely. Any light can do that

Lumens measure light output at the source. Candelas measure the light that falls on a surface. As the surface area (where the light lands) increases, the number of candelas will decrease, while the number of lumens remains constant.

A Surefire 6P, the light that started the tactical light revolution, along with a Smith and Wesson .38 Special Model 67 Combat Masterpiece. When the 6P was introduced, the .38 Revolver was still in regular use in duty holsters around the country.

The Defensive Light Triad

ILLUMINATE

IDENTIFY

INCAPACITATE

to varying degrees, and that's what most police patrol and civilian flashlights are designed to do at a minimum.

The next "I" of the triad is *identify*. Here the flashlight concept becomes more specialized because we're talking about threat identification. Are we looking at friend or foe? It's this area in which previous generations of incandescent lights with halogen or krypton bulbs fall flat. They simply don't have enough lumens and candelas to do the job.

Lumens and candelas are the more modern terms used to define light output, as opposed to the older measurement of candlepower. *Lu-*

mens measure light output at the source, while *candelas* measure the light that falls on a surface. As the area of the surface increases, the number of candelas will decrease even as the number of lumens remain constant.

The beams from the old tech lights can only identify a small centralized viewing area, allowing the user to see possibly only the face and hands of a person, and not necessarily both at the same time. Even with the best of those ancient generations of lights there was a lot of shifting of the beam from hands to face during any type of confrontation because you couldn't see what you needed to see —the face and hands at the same time. With modern lighting systems, that technique is no longer necessary.

The final "I" is *incapacitate*. The concept was pioneered by the Surefire Corporation in the early 1990s: Use the light as a part of the com-bat arsenal to incapacitate a suspect through disorientation.

Using a light to disorient a suspect was first used with the Surefire incandescent xenon gas bulb 6P lithium battery-powered lights. The strategy is now applied to the latest generations of patrol lights.

The understanding of this concept is critical. In the old days, the best we could do was illuminate and identify our opponent. With today's more powerful and flexible lights, we can use the light system to disorient and stun the opponent. If we don't bring enough light (an update of the adage "bring enough gun") to "stun" our opponents, they can use our illumination source as a target to shoot at.

Let's look first at the definition of patrol and general utility service handheld flashlights and some available options.

13

Patrol/Utility Lights

T he basic patrol and utility light in its new format is a series of upgrades that have been applied to the original police Kel-Lite. Constructed of duraluminum or increasingly of some form of polymer, these lights are full-size models based with the capacity of four or five standard D cell batteries. Traditional patrol lights can only be temporarily carried on a gun belt with an adaptive holder, and must be grabbed as you exit the vehicle.

Properly configured patrol lights can accomplish all three of the defensive light triad components — with one big addition. The light can also be used as an *emergency impact device*, serving as a baton when an officer comes under attack and there is no time to use another weapon. My standard night traffic stop approach is with one of these lights held atop my left shoulder. The light provides incapacitating illumina-

tion and a wall of light to stand behind. Held at that level, the light is also ready to be swung down on a violator's gun hand.

Police administrators have long frowned on this once common use of the flashlight. There used to be an old joke about always keeping a toothbrush handy in your police locker to clean blood and skin off the knurling on the handle of the Kel-Lite after such use on a suspect. The added weight of the flashlight batteries makes it heavier in proportion to its size than a baton and increases the impact effect, which — in the reality of combat — is a good thing. However, many administrators, even when they allow the policy, are concerned with bone breakage and skull fracture of suspects, which is understandable from a liability aspect.

Administrators have addressed the issue of flashlights that can inflict too much damage while ensuring officer safety through two different policy routes. The first is by issuing full-size poly-

Streamlight SL20 XP, one of the best and most popular handheld full-size patrol lights, shown with ASP handcuffs and CRKT Tactical Knife.

OWN THE NIGHT – PART I

POLYMER LIGHTS ARE ALL BUT UNBREAKABLE AND CAN DOUBLE AS A STRIKING WEAPON IN AN EMERGENCY.

mer lights (the polymer Streamlight SL-20XP is one example), which are lighter in weight than the aluminum models. The Streamlight rechargeables have 30,000 candlepower/200 lumen incandescent lamps. A hybrid LED model is also available. It has the same standard halogen lamp with the addition of three 30-lumen LEDs for navigation or when less light is needed for some basic tasks. The polymer models are designed for firefighters and other public safety personnel. Since batons are also made out of polymer, the lights are all but unbreakable and can double as a striking weapon in an emergency.

The second policy method is opting for smaller patrol lights that provide the same level of illumination and utility, but are so small that they cannot be effectively used as an impact device. These compact lights are exemplified by the Streamlight Poly-Stinger DS LED rechargeable model.

Beyond size and the additional bonus of being an emergency impact device, the patrol/utility light is distinguished from the true tactical light by a physical feature. The primary operation switch is located in the "traditional flashlight position" — just below the lamp head. All modern, quality patrol lights (Streamlight, Maglite, and others) feature a momentary off/on component in their switches, plus the full push-to-on function.

The momentary on/push-to-on function is essential when holding the light in a relaxed patrol position during open door building searches or initial traffic stop approaches, where light is needed for short-term use. The function is also useful for long-term illumination such as crime or accident scene examinations, area search, or other patrol needs.

In the relaxed patrol position, the officer holds the light in a convenient position for long-term use — in the weak hand (always the weak hand unless swinging it as a baton) with the thumb on the lamp head switch pointing in the direction of the light beam, and knuckles down. Here the light is being primarily used in the illumination mode. In the tactical mode, the light is held knuckles up in the weak hand, with the thumb pointing to the rear, opposite the direction of the light beam.

Patrol officers have a wide range of non-tactical work where these lights are handy, such as entering a bar fight or disturbance. A solid patrol light in hand is about ideal for effectively dealing with the in-

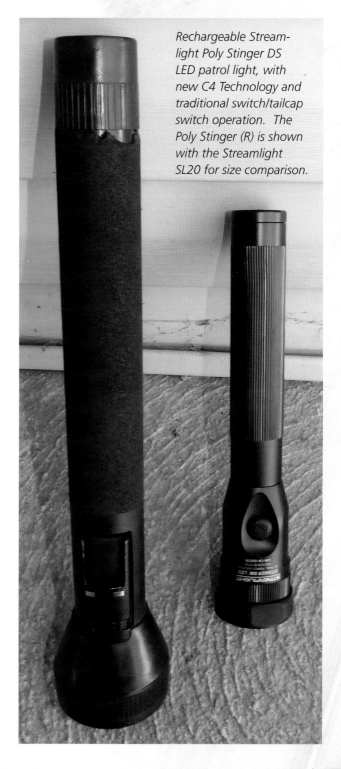

Rechargeable Streamlight Poly Stinger DS LED patrol light, with new C4 Technology and traditional switch/tailcap switch operation. The Poly Stinger (R) is shown with the Streamlight SL20 for size comparison.

cident. TigerLight makes a full size patrol light that combines high lumen/candela output (600 lumens in its newest LED version) with a selection of standard police OC (oleoresin capsaicin, a.k.a. pepper spray) canisters that can be sprayed directly from the tailcap of the light itself. When the need arises, the officer can simply shift from pointing the lamp at the suspect to inverting it toward the ground and aiming the spray tailcap at the suspect. The surprise element makes the OC spray much more effective — the suspect doesn't have time to prepare to take the burst as he would if he saw an officer pull an OC canister from the officer's belt. The TigerLight is a high-quality product that would serve well with patrol officers, security officers, and private citizens. Several models are available, including several tactical-style models.

Streamlight

Modern compact patrol/utility lights, such as the aforementioned Streamlight Poly-Stinger DS LED rechargeable, feature a wider range of features than ever before. With the new C4

technology, the Stinger DS LED system uses an advanced ul-tra-bright LED with a peak output of 18,000 candelas at 140 lumens. The parabolic lamp assembly keeps the beam focused tightly for long distances while providing an adequate illumination corona for navigation and observation.

Part tactical light, the Stingers feature the traditional flashlight switch position and a tailcap switch normally found on tactical lights only. This allows the light to be held in either the relaxed patrol position or in a tactical combative position. However, as with many things that tend to be a compromise, the use of the Stinger as a dedicated tactical light is not its forte — it's simply too large.

Since the Stinger uses LED illumination technology (even at a previously unheard-of 140 lumen output) it draws far less energy than a xenon incandescent bulb. Thus a fully charged LED light lasts much longer than a xenon incandescent. Most will handle 100,000

Note difference in light quality between the pure white LED Polystinger Light in first photo to the yellowish light cast by the Xenon lamp in the Stream-light SL20.

21

hours of use. That's 2,500 40-hour workweeks with the light constantly on. (I'm sure that the light would melt from continued heat, leaving the still-working LED behind.)

In high-end models, one other aspect of LED lights that cannot be underestimated is the quality of light. The piercing quality of the pure white LED beam cannot be downplayed. It isn't even a fair fight against an equally rated xenon lamp.

When I was a third-shift patrolman and xenon lamps first appeared in rechargeable lights like the Streamlight SL20, they appeared to be devastatingly bright compared to the C or D cell krypton and halogen incandescent bulb lights that I had been using. It was like the sun came out when you fired one up, and the illumination advantage over the old standard police lights was also not even close. The xenon lamps possessed the same quality of light that the previous versions of incandescent light bulbs did — the light is a natural yellow. It doesn't pierce the darkness like the pure, radical light quality of the LED. The color is essentially the same as the white light produced by the carbon arc lamps used in WWII searchlights and in the projectors of movie theaters. In those projectors, the high horsepower models were pure white. You couldn't look into even the side of the lamp for long when they were burning. It was like looking directly into the sun. The quality of the LED light is the reason they're used now in holiday light bulbs and police and fire emergency light bars.

My guess is within two to three years incandescent handhelds will be gone from the marketplace. There simply won't be any de-

mand for them. The only remaining advantage they have over LEDs is higher lumen output (up to 500 lumens in some of Surefire's tactical handhelds), but this advantage is continuing to decline. Incandescent bulbs still burn out and break, LEDs don't. Most LED system allow for the use of different levels of light output (most LED systems have this) depending on the user selected setting. Runtime for the Stinger DS LED on a full charge is 1.75 hours of at full-power setting, 3.5 hours at medium light setting, and 6.75 hours low-level light setting.

The Stinger DS LED has been issued to my fellow deputies at Union County Sheriff's office as a backup light system, since it is compact enough to be worn on a gun belt full time. It's also being placed with chargers in all our cruisers in lieu of full-size Streamlight and Maglite flashlights, so our deputies always have a fully charged light available to them.

Strobe Effect

The most interesting feature of the Stinger DS LED is, like a number of tactical lights, its strobing feature. This highly useful but underutilized mode is activated by a quick double-tap of either the standard or tailcap switch. The value of a strobe pulse in a potentially combative situation cannot be understated. The strobe effect causes physical disorientation, especially in near total darkness.

To understand the effects, try this experiment. In a totally darkened room, stand in a fighting stance and have a friend shine a bright LED light, such as the Streamlight or a tactical light like First Lights Liberator or Tomahawk light, in your face. Have him push against you. Even with that much pure white light (120 lumens) you should be able to maintain your stance and footing. Then have him switch to strobe and push you again. Be prepared to catch yourself, because you'll find yourself very off-balanced and disoriented. The test will convince you that a strobing light makes it easier to take your opponent to the ground.

I'd use the strobe when entering any fight-in-progress call, particularly a bar fight. The strobe doesn't affect the person carrying it, only the participants. It causes a sudden "what the hell" moment, allowing you to gain the upper hand.

The strobe effect is also very easy to shoot behind and does not interfere with your low-level light shooting accuracy. This year our deputies qualified behind their strobing Streamlights for the first

time during the low level light pistol phase, and their shooting scores were just as good as they were without the strobe effect.

Speaking of qualification, keep this in mind when you are at the range, regardless of the light you're using. Make sure that as you fire the requisite number of rounds, you and your people keep the light beam focused on the face or at least center mass of the target. Too many times I see officers and police cadets shoot while allowing the light beam to fall everywhere but on the face of the target, and sometimes it's completely off the target. A million lumens and the best strobe available won't do you any good if that power is not focused into the face of the opponent.

Using the strobe light might also be a good icebreaker when approaching a carload of suspicious individuals on a late-night traffic stop. Disorient them for a few seconds while getting a look at their activities, then switch to standard lighting. It should be confusing at the very least.

Inova

A relatively new compact rechargeable patrol utility light is from Inova. The brand is not currently well known in the law enforcement tactical patrol light field as it doesn't have the expansive product line that companies like Streamlight and Surefire do. However, Inova was one of the early innovators in the development of tightly focused LED beams.

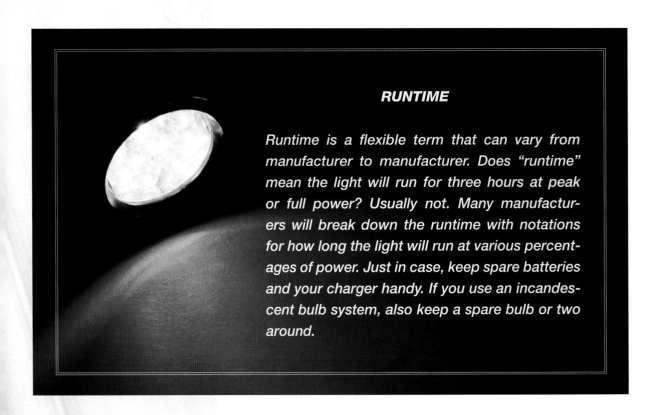

RUNTIME

Runtime is a flexible term that can vary from manufacturer to manufacturer. Does "runtime" mean the light will run for three hours at peak or full power? Usually not. Many manufacturers will break down the runtime with notations for how long the light will run at various percentages of power. Just in case, keep spare batteries and your charger handy. If you use an incandescent bulb system, also keep a spare bulb or two around.

The early version of the Inova T1 light it is one of the first single-element LED lights that I ever handled. In fact, I still have and use it. It has a very thick lens system, reminiscent of old automotive timing lights, to focus the beam. This early version did not have a tight beam with sharp edges, but it is sharper than the other lights that were available at the time. Since then, the light has transitioned to a standard lens system with improvement in the LEDs.

There are two models of Inova lights suitable as patrol/utility lights. The first is the T4. Measuring a mere eight inches in length, this is the smaller of their two rechargeable duty lights. It features the lamp head switch position with a powerful 175-lumen output (the highest lumen LED patrol light that I have seen) with up to two hours of runtime per full charge. No strobe feature is available at this time, but the T4 is a solid, well-crafted light.

One step up from the T4 is the rechargeable T5 light. Only one inch longer than the T4, the T5 bumps the LED output up to a remarkable 200-lumen output with up to three hours of runtime per charge. The power level gives the T5 an effective range of about 400 feet. Either light will give good, solid service to its user, and one cannot feel slighted about the power output.

Maglite

Other patrol/utility light options come from Maglite. The company has been around since the beginning of the tactical lighting revolution, and its product line covers a wider segment of the utility market. It's the only U.S. manufacturer that I know of to offer patrol type flashlights in the original 2, 3, 4, 5 and 6-D cell and 2, 3, and 4-C cell configuration with standard incandescent light bulbs.

Before I got my first Streamlight SL20 rechargeable, I carried a now discontinued 6-C cell Maglite on the street while patrolling on third shift. For its time, 6-C cells provided a good amount of light. Moreover, the C diameter was nearly the same diameter as the standard straight Monadnock polycarbonate baton I also car-

25

ried. That Maglite provided an illuminated baton that was used when my baton was not available.

These lights are still viable in their incandescent lamp form for basic security, patrol, and utility work. Although not terribly bright by modern standards, Maglites are very durable (shock- and water-resistant) and are still constructed of duraluminum with quality machining throughout. Maglite does not make polycarbonate models. Basic Maglites are good to have in home emergency kits (keep those batteries out until you actually need to use the light, they last longer and won't bleed out acid into the light if you fail to check on or use the light on a regular basis). A nice touch is the spare bulb in the tailcap assembly — very handy at 2 a.m. when that incandescent bulb finally burns out.

3-C cell Maglight with Kryton bulb. At one time, a police standard for duty use on the street.

By the way, most convenience stores don't offer spare light bulbs, and they are getting harder to find in stores at all any more as the transition to LED lights advances. Pricing of these old tech lights is very reasonable compared to the new high tech styles and models.

For years Maglite has also offered an excellent rechargeable patrol flashlight with 30,000 or more candlepower and the size is about that of a 5-D cell light. We've been using these rechargeable Maglites in our cruisers mounted in DC chargers for a number of years with excellent service. It's a much cheaper way of issuing lights: Provide for common use of the main patrol light rather than individual use. That said, I prefer to provide my own duty flashlights, since then I know they'll be in proper operating condition.

Maglite also continues to offer the police-quality backup flashlight, the Mini-Maglite. Operated off two AA penlight batteries

Rechargeable Maglight full size patrol light, a long time police standard in duty lights.

27

Backup Lights

Every patrol officer should always have a backup flashlight on their duty belt or somewhere on their person. Furthermore, everyone should carry a small high power flashlight on their person at all times, whether you carry a gun or not, for emergency use. Let me tell a story which illustrates why a backup light is important.

One night at Union County, I was working patrol and made a traffic stop for DUI. I grabbed the common-use rechargeable Maglite from its holder in the cruiser and made my approach to the suspect vehicle. We work in the dark out in the country — there are no streetlights. All you have are headlights, spotlights, and your flashlights.

As I walked up, my light grew increasingly dim until it was totally dead by the time I reached the rear bumper of the vehicle. I did a quick transition, stuffing the dead flashlight into the back of my gun belt, and grabbed my backup Streamlight Scorpion Lithium Xenon. Now armed with plenty of light, I finished the stop, made the arrest, and did an inventory search of the car. I turned in the bad light, which had been bright when I checked it at the start of the shift. The rechargeable cell had finally used the last of its life.

If you work during daylight hours as a patrol officer, you'll often find yourself in buildings during a search — maybe an alarm drop on a residence — and you'll need a flashlight. But oops

— you left yours in the car because it was bright outside. So you either go back or do without and try not to forget the next time. Or you start carrying a quality tactical light as a backup.

A quality backup light should be powered by long-life lithium cells and should not be rechargeable. I've seen officers who don't use rechargeable backup lights on a regular basis forget to charge them and end up with dead lights. Rechargeable batteries won't store their juice for 10 years without use like lithium cells do.

(the AAA versions are way too small for backup use in terms of light output), the Mini-Mag was easily carried and worked well for many patrol officers as their backup light. The main downside to the Mini-Mag was it required two hands to operate, as you had to twist it on and then find the proper focus point for the beam, which is infinitely adjustable from spot to flood. Even with this downside, the Mini-Mag was far superior than the el cheapo low-power penlights that were the only other game in town.

Maglite has also introduced an excellent LED version of its basic lighting system. Currently available in two Mini-Mag configurations and 2, 3, and 4-D cell patrol/utility styles, the LEDs offer true patrol-usable light output with pure white LED light — a vast improvement over the krypton incandescent versions of the same light.

The LED Maglite is actually the only standard battery flashlight I would be willing to use while performing the basic patrol function these days. Priced at about $15 more than the standard bulb models, these lights represent an excellent value for the officer at a small department who may be cash-strapped and have to provide their own gear. The LEDs are not available as rechargeables as of this writing, but I would expect that to happen soon.

I've only found only one minor police-related problem with any Maglite — the adjustable spot-to-flood feature of the lamphead. For police work, you *never* need a wide flood beam. Everything can and should be viewed off a tightly focused central beam and the corona that is projected. You need that tight beam to focus into the face of your opponent in tense situations. When the beam is set in the flood mode, there is a dark spot right in the center of the beam that eliminates the light as a part of the weapons system — you lose the incapacitation capability and the rest of the light is diffused. But what position do you always find the beam when you twist a light out of a common holder? Some variation of flood. Then you have to spend time turning it back before the light is effective again. Maglites are all infinitely adjustable. There is no stop setting to lock it at different levels. This can be easily fixed with a bit of electrical tape to hold the head into place in the spot mode, which is what I did when I carried a Maglite. Not a huge issue, but I found the pre-focused lamps of the Streamlights to be vastly superior for police work.

Patrol/utility lights fill a distinct need that cannot fully be replaced by tactical light systems. I see the trend toward smaller patrol/utility lights like the Streamlight Stinger LED as technology continues to improve and liability of lights as emergency impact devices continues to provoke administrative concerns.

PLEASE DO NOT EQUIP YOURSELF WITH JUNK LIGHTS. IT DOESN'T MATTER WHAT KIND OF GREAT PRICE YOU PAID, OR HOW MANY DOZEN YOU BOUGHT FOR ONE PRICE. IF YOU ARE BETTING YOUR LIFE ON A LIGHT, BUY ONLY THE BEST.

CHAPTER 1: PATROL/UTILITY LIGHTS

Tactical Handheld Flashlights

Here's my definition of what constitutes a true tactical flashlight:

1. It should be made in the U.S.A. to ensure quality.
2. High candela/lumen output with LED light is preferred.
3. It should be equipped with a tailcap switch.
4. Solid construction is a must.
5. Power should be provided by lithium cells.
6. It should be adaptable to being attached to a lanyard-type device.

The design of tactical handheld flashlights is really for direct combative use and not general utility, although they are used that way. There are many good

models out there and some unique systems. Let's look at a few, starting with the most unique of the lighting systems.

First Light USA

First Light USA came on the scene with the introduction of the Liberator Hands Free tactical light in 2004. Marking a radical departure from the standard tubular lighting systems, the Liberator attaches to the weak hand across the palm with an adjustable quick release strap. This allows the weak hand to grip anything else: bike handlebars, K9 leash, or support side of a pistol or rifle.

When I handled one of the first samples of the Liberator on the market around 2005, I was less than impressed. The lamp was xenon as I recall, and the operation of the switches seemed unnecessarily complicated. Further, there was no holster available to carry it on the gun belt.

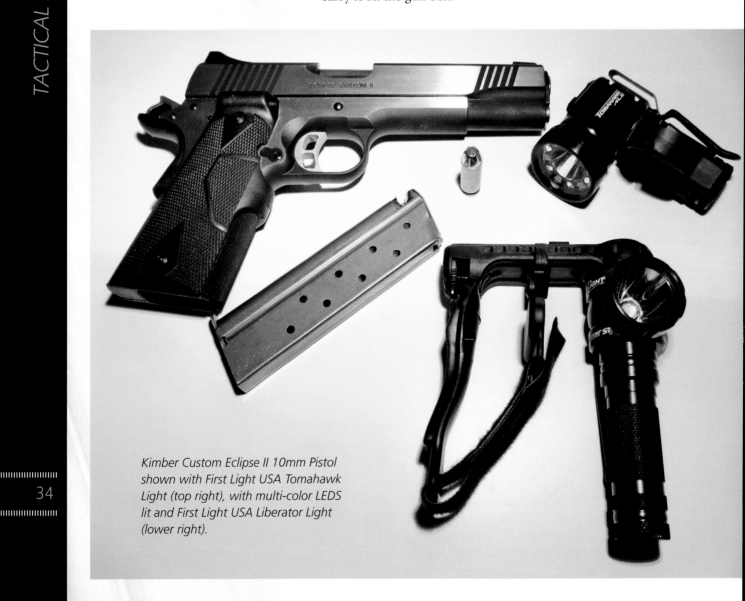

Kimber Custom Eclipse II 10mm Pistol shown with First Light USA Tomahawk Light (top right), with multi-color LEDS lit and First Light USA Liberator Light (lower right).

34

But time and product development has altered my opinion. The Liberator STT resolves all of my earlier concerns about the system. The now almost standard LED illumination system puts out 120 lumens of piercing pure white light. The switching system has been simplified with controls that allow for locking the light to avoid accidental activation. There are several modes: momentary-on, constant-on, and strobing.

The strobing mode on any tactical light is a valuable option that offers improved temporary incapacitation ability, whether used on dynamic entry or when disorienting a carload of suspects on a nighttime traffic stop. The only problem I find with the strobe switch on the Liberator is that it's difficult to reach when the head of the light is rotated for weak-hand pistol or rifle support. However, when the head is turned in the same direction as the handle of the Liberator, the strobe switch is easily reached. The switch should be modified slightly or placed elsewhere, such as on the side of the switch area rather than on top, so that ac-

Author with First Light USA Liberator light in proper two-hand shooting position with FN Fiveseven 5.7x28mm tactical pistol.

35

Author showing one-handed FBI-style shooting position with Tomahawk light and FN FiveseveN pistol. The Tomahawk is an excellent choice for this type of shooting position.

cess is easy when the light is in the weak-hand support shooting position.

A nylon duty belt holster is now included with the Liberator STT, which does a better job of securing the light on the gun belt than the built-in belt clip.

The 120 lumens from such a compact light source is a blinding amount of output — almost double of some of the initial LED systems of just a couple of years ago.

The Liberator system has made great sales strides. It's been adopted by U.S. Border Patrol K9 units and K9 and bike patrol units across the country. I believe this light has tactical potential in entry situations and will continue to work with it on my SRT team and while on routine patrol.

I think the First Light product that stands to gain the widest acceptance and versatility, however, is the Tomahawk Tactical Light. Reminiscent of the old angle-head Boy Scout and military flashlights, the Tomahawk is much smaller, versatile, powerful, and much more durable.

The first thing that draws your eye when looking at the Tomahawk is the finger loop attached directly under the head. This hard plastic loop is adjustable for right- or left-handed use, and two are included with the light so the proper size for your finger can be selected. The loop allows you to retain control of the light with essentially one finger while leaving the rest of your hands free to perform other tasks.

You can use the Tomahawk with a partial two-hand shooting grip on your pistol, although I feel that this grip is more solid with the Liberator because the only thing in the palm of your hand is the main strap. With the Tomahawk, you have the cylindrical battery compartment (two one-lithium 123s) and the belt clip in your palm, which takes up room for the pistol grip, making a two-hand grip more difficult. Where the Tomahawk really shines, so to speak, is in one-hand pistol techniques. The angle head and loop design makes it far easier to utilize the FBI technique than a standard straight tube design.

There are several versions of the Tomahawk available. The one I received for testing was the Tomahawk MC. This, like the Liberator, is a 120-lumen LED light with several features. The most prominent feature is the red/blue or red/green LEDs that ring the main lamp. These color LEDS, like the main LED, have three levels of brightness. The red/blue model that I tested allows you to use the red light to save your "dark adapted" eyesight. You can also use the blue light for that purpose if you prefer, or it can be used to help in identifying crime scene trace evidence such as blood. The green LED is useful for nighttime tracking opera-

Author shown with
Surefire M3 225 Lumen
Combat Light.

OWN THE NIGHT – PART I

tions, as it shows crushed vegetation better than standard white lighting.

Three control switches at the top of the light select the lamps used, power output, and strobe function. The LEDs can be selected in various combinations. On my sample you can select red only, blue only, and blue and red together. All are available at three different power levels. The main lamp can also be set at three power levels, with a momentary and constant-on setting. By pushing the momentary switch and selector button with your thumb simultaneously you get a momentary strobe function. Like the Liberator, the light can be locked to prevent accidental operation. The Tomahawk can be strapped to your vest or clipped to your belt. It's also small enough to carry in your pocket. Both lights are built to the highest quality standards.

Surefire

Surefire has long been the leader in the industry and was responsible for the tactical light revolution with the introduction of the two lithium cell 6P light, which I first saw on the belts of patrol officers rather than tactical officers. Originally available with only an incandescent bulb, the 6P is still available with an 80-lumen LED or a 65- or optional 120-lumen xenon lamp.

In addition to the 6P, Surefire currently offers 41 different handheld tactical flashlights. Most of the models are lithium cell-powered; 22 of the 41 have incandescent bulbs, and many of those have the 225-lumen output. The Devastator model has 350 lumens of output. The Guardian and Dominator each puts out an eyeball-scorching 500 lumens of power.

Surefire 8X Commander rechargeable light shown with spare battery cell and charger.

For tactical team use, I've used the Surefire M3 three lithium cell Combat Light with the 225-lumen lamp in place. All I can say to that power output is "wow," and it's only half that of the Guardian and Dominator.

I've also been working with one of the Surefire rechargeable handhelds, the 110-lumen 8AX Commander. Much larger than the 6P, the higher output 8AX features a tailcap switch, and a "twist to constant-on" mode operated by twisting the head of the light into position. In the other Surefire models, the tailcap is twisted to "on." Also, unlike many rechargeable lights, the Commander comes with two battery cells, so there is always a fully charged cell available. The cell has to be removed from the light and charged separately — this is not a drop in charger-type light. To access the battery cell, the headlamp (rather than the tailcap) has to be unscrewed.

Other models from Surefire feature belt/pocket clips and lanyards, and a couple have the crenelated strike bezel which increases the defensive capacity of the light for civilian users. For you coppers out there, please don't use the light like this unless you have some sort of department-approved training and certification for the Strike Bezel light in place. These "teeth" certainly seem capable of ripping the hide off of someone, and without department approval, your hide will be gone next. For civilian users who don't have the same worries, this option is excellent.

Surefire is also producing models with multi-color LEDs for various specialty applications, stealthy navigating, tracking, and dark adaptive vision preservation.

The only complaint I have about Surefire lights is the twist-to-on tailcap feature. Like the Mini-Mag flashlight, this is often a two-hand or awkward one-hand operation. I definitely prefer a push-to-on tailcap switch with momentary on feature. Obviously Surefire would not be the leader in tactical lighting with its own training institute if this was a huge problem.

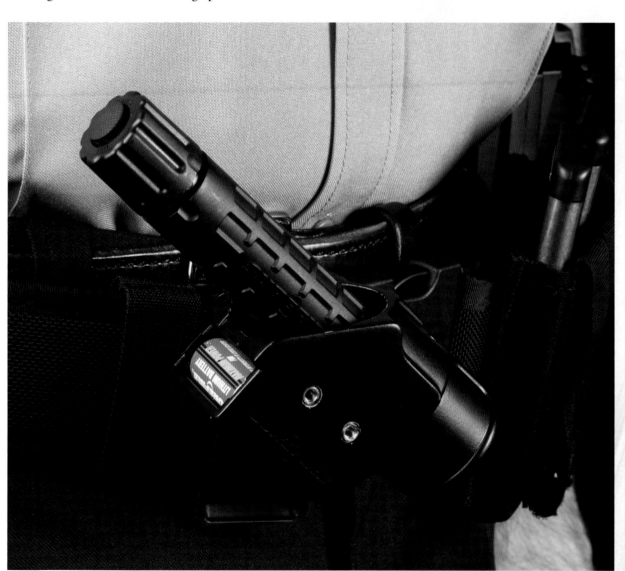

Carry a Light at all Times

I mentioned earlier the need to carry a light on your person on a daily basis. Here's why I have since about 1998. I was in my office at the Columbus State Community College campus one summer afternoon when there was a power outage on campus — an area construction crew didn't do the "check before you dig" thing. Emergency lighting normally makes this a non-issue. However, on this day, the building generator did not operate and there was no lighting of any kind. People couldn't go down stairwells to get out of the building, and with the summer heat made we didn't want to stay inside too long.

I volunteered (without a flashlight) to walk down the pitch-black steps from the fourth floor and prop open stairwell doors and light the way so others could exit. Inching along in the dark was a bit unnerving, and a very slow process. I vowed that day to never be without some sort of flashlight.

Initially the lights I carried were compact LEDs, such as an LED keychain model made by ASP. I soon realized that if I was going to carry a light it might as well be a real one, so I have been carrying some form of pocket-size lithium tactical light ever since. Not only is it good for emergency walking-in-a-darkened-hall tasks, it comes in handy off-duty while out on the road.

Wouldn't it be nice to have a good tactical light if you stopped to help a fellow officer on a nighttime felony traffic stop? How about for an active shooter event — might it be helpful to have a light there as well? Not all active shooter incidents will take place in well-lit shopping centers during daylight hours.

In another real-life example of the usefulness of carrying a tactical light, one of my best friends Tim, an officer from the Columbus (Ohio) Police Department and conditioned martial arts expert, was closing his dojo one summer night when

he witnessed a suspect rob a couple of Jewish rabbis that were closing their office in the same shopping center. Tim gave chase through a darkened residential area without a flashlight (it was in his car). He closed on the suspect at the rear of a back yard. Tim had just leapt to tackle the suspect and didn't see the low, decorative wrought iron fence. His feet got tangled in the fence as he twisted and fell with the suspect to the ground. Tim didn't just dislocate his shoulder, nearly all the interior connective tissue was ripped away.

For a moment Tim held onto the suspect, who soon realized that Tim was in trouble (his left arm/hand was useless as his shoulder was hanging down near his left nipple) and broke away. Tim valiantly gave chase until he realized that he was in tremendous pain and no longer in a position to hold on to anyone.

A major operation, about six months of rehab, and Tim's extraordinary conditioning has brought him back to full function. But I wonder how it would have worked out if Tim had a pocket tactical light.

The Stylus Pro by Streamlight was developed for multiple tasks by professionals and sportsman for single-handed use in any given situation.

CHAPTER 2: TACTICAL HANDHELD FLASHLIGHTS

Streamlight

Streamlight has also become a big innovator in tactical light field with the introduction of the Super Tac tactical light. The Super Tac is Streamlight's brightest, most powerful LED light. Running at a peak 135-lumen output at 30,000 candela, the long range targeting beam is nothing short of incredible — especially considering it's powered by only two lithium batteries. The light is somewhat unusual looking; it has an oversized bell-shaped head and a standard diameter/length tube section.

Streamlight Super Tac shown with included nylon sheath. This is one incredibly bright long-range LED light, also ideal for use by outdoorsmen and women.

45

The Super Tac is also easily adaptable as a rifle-mounted light, and Streamlight included a vertical forend for just such a purpose. There's also a belt clip on the light; it's probably not necessary, as the large lamp would off-balance the light if clipped on a belt, and the lamp is certainly too big to put in a pocket.

The Super Tac is one of the longest-range lights of this size I've ever used. It shows how far LEDs have come in a few short years from the days when all they could put out was soft, diffuse light. I remember thinking that these LED lights would be great if they had a tight focus and a reasonable range. Well, now they do. I live on a six-acre plot of land in the hills, which is a great area for testing lights, and the Super Tac's tight central focus area makes its range far longer than any of the other lights I've been working. While other lights do have a tightly focused LED, this one is extraordinary.

Whether handheld or mounted on a rifle, the Super Tac would be a great light for use in rural patrol areas with wide-open spaces. When rifle mounted, the light should be devastating on entry into a darkened room; when handheld, it would be ideal for searching a large dark indoor area like a warehouse. The utility for a rifle mount would be enhanced by the availability of a replacement remote pressure switch.

The Super Tac comes packaged with a nylon belt holster with a loop large enough for a duty belt. I'd also like to see a lanyard attachment and a strobe switch added to really round it out, but it is a great light as is.

Streamlight offers an expansive product line. I counted 115 products on its website. Streamlight and Surefire are the only two manufacturers that are allowed to supply independently purchased equipment to U.S. Army personnel for duty use. (Streamlight notes it as Team Soldier Certified Gear.) There is no limit to models or styles that can be purchased to meet a soldier's needs.

One of those Army-approved lights is the original Scorpion — the first backup tactical light I used for years at the sheriff's office. Available in both xenon (78 lumens) and LED (120 lumens), the Scorpion has only one problem — the adjustable spot-to-flood feature. However, it was less of a problem for the Scorpion than I found with Maglite products. It seems harder to twist the lamphead, but rarely has it been out of focus. There's no need for this feature on a tactical light, but I think it exists on the Scorpion because the batteries load from the lamp end of the tube, which requires the lamp head to be unscrewed (there is no removable tailcap switch).

In addition to the Scorpion and the Super-Tac, Streamlight makes eight additional handheld tactical lights. The Night, Night Fighter, Strion, and TL series range in power from 78 lumens to 211 lumens. Others include the tactical styled Task Lights and Twin Task Lights. The rest of the Streamlight offerings are patrol lights and various forms of utility lights.

Inova

Inova produces a few tactical style lights in its X series. Available in silver or black, the XO and the XO3 have some good basic features with 4.8 and 5.8 watts of LED power output.

One innovative tactical light, the Inforce Color carbon fiber light, weighs only 4.5 ounces (1.4 ounces lighter than the simi-

Officer uses Inova light with blue led to examine for trace blood-spatter evidence.

lar-sized Inova T3), and the carbon fiber construction results in a light body that's about 40 percent stronger than aluminum. Carbon fiber also dissipates heat better, and the Inforce features venting behind the lamp to allow for even more heat dissipation.

Designed for military and law enforcement end users, the Inforce features a 125-lumen primary white LED with tailcap push-button operation and tailcap twist function selection. The Inforce is constructed to MIL-STD 810 and is available with a remote tailcap and 1913 rail mounting system for use on rifles. It's rated as waterproof to 66 feet. A lanyard can also be attached in the notched area under the pocket clip.

The Inforce features four separate LEDS in the mildly crenelated lens bezel, which is much less sharp than some competing aluminum light designs and may be better suited to police pain compliance and control tasks. The LEDs are all low-power, specific-purpose lights, and this is one of the few lights that have all four color choices: Red is for dark adaptive vision preservation, blue is for fluid detection (useful in crime scenes to help find blood or semen), green is good for map reading (but what it is *really* good for is tracking suspects across crushed vegetation), and white is for low profile navigation.

Even though there is only one LED for each purpose, they are more than adequately bright. Here's how the light functions are selected by the tailcap position: With the light pointing away and the tailcap turned all the way to the right, the light is in one of

Inova Inforce carbon fiber light shown with green LED illuminated. This light is available with remote pressure switch and mounts for installation on an AR-15 rifle Picatinny rail system.

LED COLOR CHOICES

RED:
Dark adaptive
vision
preservation.

BLUE:
Fluid detection
(useful in crime scenes
to help find blood
or semen).

GREEN:
Map reading, tracking
suspects across
crushed vegetation.

★ **WHITE:** Low profile navigation.

two push-to-on modes. Pushing the button on and releasing it fully, the light stays on at full power. Another push turns the light off. Pushing the light switch in and holding it in, then immediately pushing again, reduces the power through two levels. (Nice feature, but one I wouldn't use a lot.) Twisting the cap one stop to the left sets the main lamp into a momentary on mode, which probably should be the first position of the endcap. The next position to the left allows you, with each push of the button, to select your LED color of choice. The next turn of the tailcap to the left gives you a momentary on mode for the LED you selected. The final stop position gives a constant-on for that same LED. I have been carrying it in my pants pocket for several days and have found that the tailcap has stayed in position and fixed on the setting.

The Inforce seems to be an excellent light system, with multiple applications and a minimum of complexity. It's a good backup light for patrol officers, a good light for crime investigators, a good light for military personnel, a good basic tactical light, and, at 125 lumens, a good powerful light to mount on an AR-15. In my position on our tactical team as team sniper and as-needed entry position, I'd use the Inforce as, at the very least, a good backup light. The switch positions are easily learned and intuitive and overall operation is very simple.

Blackhawk

Blackhawk, the internationally-renowned purveyor of all things tactical gear-related, provides a fine line of tactical (not patrol) illumination tools/flashlights of the highest quality — even though it doesn't make its own lights.

My first experience with Blackhawk lights was with the Gladius Night Ops, produced by Insight Technology. It was the first tactical light I used that had a strobe feature. The main feature of the Gladius is the unique tailcap switching system, which has been picked up by other companies. The system has five modes and is operated by twisting it into the proper position, then activated by pushing the tailcap button. The modes are momentary on, constant-on, strobe, dimming, and lock-out. The light has six volts of power.

The original Gladius is rated at about 65 lumens, and has been upgraded to 120 lumens and marketed as the Maximis. The light is easily operated and comes with a lanyard. I received a Maximis for testing and comparison against the original Gladius. There is no difference externally between the two lights other than the marking on the Maximis. The color scheme is the same (black as tested), as are the controls.

One visible difference is that the central element of the LED on the Maximis is about twice the size as the one on the Night Ops, but you have to look at the lights side by side. The real difference, of course, is the light beam. The light heads and beams are the same size but, at 120 lumens, the Maximis gives a much whiter light beam. It is sharper and has a tighter, better defined central portion, and a wider corona than the older model.

The tailcap functions are the same. The tailcap must be put on the light when adding or changing batteries, and a pin in the

tailcap must be aligned with a notch in the main body to operate properly (otherwise you risk damaging the light). Blackhawk has added a notice to this effect on the main body under the cap. While that part is marked better, it's still hard for me to see the pin inside the cap, as it is very small and sits high inside. It'd be nice if there were alignment marks on the exterior of the light, but that really is a minor point.

The Gladius Night Ops, and now the Maximis, is my light of choice for dynamic entry when using a pistol, with the lanyard looped onto my left wrist and operated in strobe mode.

The Gladius Maximis is a very solid light and not a gimmick. It's one of my top picks for a handheld tactical light. My only complaint for pocket carry is the tailcap, which features four protrusions ostensibly designed to aid in holding the light when using odd techniques like the "syringe." These protrusions make the Gladius somewhat uncomfortable to carry in a pocket and are hard on fabric. The designers could consider a round grip area for use of the syringe technique, or eliminate it altogether. There are also two lanyard attaching points for some reason. In spite of these small annoyances, I highly recommend this light.

Syringe technique, favored by some, but not by author. Requires too much delicate hand positioning and is not a forceful way to control the light.

Lockout Mode Mode

A lockout mode feature is essential on any light system, even LED, and not just for battery preservation, but for safety. Lights get hot, even LEDs over extended use (LEDs produce less heat than incandescent bulbs but can still get hot). If the light turns on accidentally in confined spaces where heat can't dissipate, the batteries heat up and the entire flashlight gets hot. I've had this happen in pocket carry. In certain lights with no lockout feature the whole light can get too hot to touch. This can, under the right conditions, result in fire.

Recently after a mission, a central Ohio SWAT officer put his AR-15 (with weapon-mounted light) back in his unmarked department-issued vehicle. The light either didn't have a lockout or he didn't use it. In any event, the way the gun was cased and positioned caused the pressure switch of this very powerful light (probably 200 lumens of output with a xenon bulb) to activate. The result was the SWAT vehicle and all its equipment went up in flames. This example illustrates the serious safety risk of not locking out or disabling the power source when storing these powerful illumination tools.

Most tactical lights have some sort of lockout feature because this genre of lights is relatively small and they are often packed in confined spaces for storage. Other lights recess the switch into the light body in lieu of a lockout mode. Some weapon-mounted lights, such as those from Surefire, have a separate on-and-off switch in addition to the pressure switch to disconnect the power supply. Make sure that you use it whenever the light is not in use.

PentagonLight's 60-lumen X2 shown with the Blackhawk Sentinal light and the 110-Lumen Ally.

The Blackhawk Night-Ops line also has several traditional hand-helds with the latest technology. I tested the Sentinel PL3 XTR. This is a latest generation LED lighting system, and is a compact yet powerful light. Powered by a single lithium cell, this mighty mite produces 65 lumens of white light with three volts of power.

Billed as the most powerful light of its size, the Sentinel features the CREE LED, standard aircraft aluminum construction, momentary off-and-on tailcap switch (I love not having to twist anything), glass lens for clearer light over plastic, a pocket clip for bezel-up carry (handy for a tactical vest, not as much for standard the pocket carry), and a crenelated bezel. To put lumen power in better perspective, the packaging says that this one-cell light has the equivalent light output of a standard 6 or 7-D cell flashlight — amazing.

While field-testing the Sentinel, my girlfriend and I arrived at her home late one night late. Earlier in the day she had been deposed in a divorce case against her husband who had some questionable business ties. I had just pulled into the driveway when another car pulled in right behind me. It was pitch black and we weren't expecting anyone. I couldn't see anything but the headlights of the vehicle, which appeared to be an SUV.

I quickly stepped from the truck, conscious that my gun was strapped on my ankle, drew the Sentinel from my pocket, and raised it into an FBI hold (shining it into the driver's side windshield) as I approached. I was able to see one white male behind the wheel. I asked, "Can I help you?" The startled driver said that he had just pulled in to tell me I had no brake or taillights.

He was just a good samaritan doing me a favor, but I didn't know that when he pulled in. I felt the need to take the offensive and use my light as my initial contact weapon, just like on a traffic stop.

Another light carried by Blackhawk is the Ally PL3 XTR. It has the same construction and features of the one-cell Sentinel, but has a more aggressive gripping surface in the center barrel of the light. Instead of the diamond pattern surface of the Sentinel, which doesn't have much purchase area, the center of the Ally features distinctly raised rectangles that allowing for better gripping. The bezel head is the same for both lights. The lumen output is 110 at three watts, equivalent to an 11-D cell flashlight.

The Ally is a very compact light for its power output. For size comparison, I have one of PentagonLight's two-year-old 2-cell handheld LEDs, rated at 65 lumens. The PentagonLight is larger in diameter than the Ally and nearly an inch longer, making the Ally and many other 2-cell lights much more accommodating for pocket carry — and they pack a much greater punch.

The Ally was involved in a field test just a couple of nights after the incident with the good samaritan. It was one of those "Honey, I hear something, go check it out" moments at 2:30 a.m. I grabbed my Smith & Wesson 332 and the Blackhawk Ally and went to check outside. When I turned on the Ally, it was like total daylight in the hall and living room. I then blasted the light out through

the picture window out onto our car in the driveway. I saw the car and surrounding area perfectly. Nothing had been disturbed. I was confident that, had I encountered someone in the dark, they would have lost their night vision unless they had a light of equal power and I would have won any gunfight that might have ensued.

That was a clear demonstration of "own the night." I was dominating my area of responsibility. Rather than turning on lights, I moved through the darkness, in control of it, choosing the time and direction of illumination. Certainly beats the old Ray-O-Vac by the bedside.

One thing missing from both lights is strobe capability, but it's certainly not a deal-breaker on lights like these. One or the other will find its way into my pocket, or tactical vest, quite often.

Insight Technology

Insight Technology, the manufacturer of the Gladius for Blackhawk, has its own version of the light: the H2 Typhoon. The Typhoon is mountable as a weapon light with a ring adapter for 1913 rail systems and is available in three colors.

Insight also offers a new line of handheld lights, the X-series LEDs. The three models —X120, X150R, and X200 handhelds —

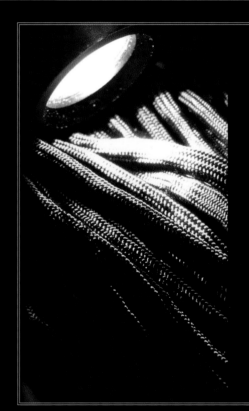

A word of warning for law enforcement types: Unless you are in a life and death struggle with no other tool available than a crenelated bezel flashlight, don't use it as a defensive tactics tool unless you have been departmentally trained and approved to use it on duty. With the exception of the InForce from Inova, the crenelations are just too sharp and will tear skin. This cautionary note doesn't mean you shouldn't purchase these designs or that they don't have defensive tool application. They would be great to carry on aircraft for use in say, thwarting a cockpit takeover. Another non-defensive use of the crenelated bezel/tailcaps is for breaking tempered auto glass.

can be considered as upgraded Typhoon lights with some of the same light features, but with a simplified tailcap operation. There is no twist adjustment of the cap required to select operational mode. It's all done by pushing the tailcap button.

Here's how the X-series switching works. For momentary on/off, press the switch in halfway. For constant-on, push the button down until the click set is reached. To activate the strobe feature from the off position, double-tap the switch within a half-second. For dimming mode, click and hold for four seconds. There's no lockout mode, as the switch is recessed lower and requires more pressure to push than the Typhoon light switch.

Manufacturers should consider just how much pressure is required to operate their lights. I have tested some prototypes recently that require way too much pressure, and I have relatively strong hands. Manufacturers need to be aware of needs of smaller officers, female officers, military personnel, or civilians. This is not a problem with the X-series lights.

The X120 is the smallest of the three lights, providing an amazing 120 lumens of LED light with power provided by only one

Utilizing bedside cover with light and laser sighted Glock 32 .357, with Surefire X300 pistol light. Glock is additionally configured with XS Big Dot Tritium Express Sights

lithium cell. Previous generations of LED lights from all manufacturers of one-cell lithium designs were in the 40 lumen range, so the power output of the X120 is a huge development.

The X120, X150R and X200 all feature digitally managed circuits to control heat output. Insight wisely removed any Typhoon/Gladius protrusions from the tailcap, making these lights easy to pocket, a function particularly effective with the X120. A pocket clip and lanyard come with all three lights.

You have to have lanyard capability if you're using any light in a true tactical situation. Your light is not something you want to drop in a drug house in the middle of a raid.

The second largest light in the X series is the X150R. The X150R uses a rechargeable lithium ion battery system that provides 150 lumens of LED light. Tailcap switch operation is the same as the X120. All X lights also have crenelated bezels and tailcaps and all three can be attached to a long gun using the Insight ring mounting systems.

The X200 is the top of the X line. This non-rechargeable model puts out a blinding 200 lumens of light from three lithium 123 cells, the highest LED output I have seen.

Insight is very specific in terms of runtime for their lights. The Proxima will run for 90 minutes on full-power setting, while the

X200 and X150R run for two hours. These lights represent outstanding choices for the serious user and are affordably priced compared to some of the competition. Insight is also heavily invested in laser and optical sighting systems, making some very high speed low drag equipment clearly defined for military special forces and law enforcement tactical use. Most of its gear is available for civilian purchase as well.

Example of bad technique: the bright central beam should be aimed directly at the suspect's face to effectively disrupt his dark-adaptive vision.

Tactical Handheld Flashlights Summary

In closing for this section on tactical handheld lights, remember, these lights also need a backup when carried as part of a tactical team. As an example, while on entry, I'll use a strobing Gladius light coupled with my pistol and also keep a Surefire M-3 Combat light stuffed into my vest for easy access. A second or third light, if the mission is long and you rely on lithium power, is an absolute must. Always check your lights before the mission, like you would check your weapons.

Chapter 3

Handheld Flashlight Tactics & Principles

N ow that you have a wide selection of lights from which to choose in both the patrol/utility and tactical arenas, let's talk tactics.

What I hope to provide are some basic operational principles that can be applied across a wide variety of situations, positions, and conditions. The techniques I teach as a firearms and defensive tactics instructor are first and foremost intuitive. They're grounded in the concept of natural movement — your body will gravitate to them instinctively since they are comfortable. These are techniques you may revert to when you are under stress — like while getting shot at. I say *may* revert to because you never know what your mind will tell your body to do in these situations even when you pre-plan.

When I was going through the shotgun instructor segment of the Ohio Peace Officer Training Com-

mission Police Firearms Instructor Training class many years ago, we had a high-stress competitive drill at the end of the course. The drill was this: Three hostile targets were placed seven yards distant. Six friendly targets placed in front allowed only a partial view of the hostiles. We had to fire one round on each hostile target with a shotgun using buckshot, then transition to our handgun and fire two more rounds each on the same hostiles without hitting the friendlies. The time limit for the entire drill was 10 seconds.

I watched the first couple of shooters work the course and decided what I would do when it was my turn: Fire the three shotgun rounds, transition the shotgun to left hand, and with my right hand (strong hand) only, engage the three targets again with my handgun. I rehearsed it several times mentally before it was my turn. I fired the course clean and under time. Not everyone did, so I was feeling pretty good. My buddy, a good shooter who didn't clean it, congratulated me. I said (puffing out my chest mightily) I found it really easy to do clean the course by shooting it one handed while holding my shotgun in my left.

My bud looked at me with a puzzled expression and said, "That isn't what you did." Returning an equally puzzled look, I said, "Yes, it was." "No," he said, "what you did was drop to a kneeling position, set the shotgun down, and fire two-handed." Then my memory rebooted — that *was* what I did.

There are two major lessons to be learned from this experience. First, you never quite execute in real life what you trained to do in practice. It may be close, or may be very far from it (like throwing your gun away as you run from a fight crying like a schoolgirl). However, the more training reps we do, the closer the real-life response will be to the practiced response — *unless* what we are training to do is so far from natural instinct that the mind refuses to use it.

In my case, I only had some mental rehearsal beforehand. There was no chance to practice it. If I had a chance for at least one repetition, I probably would have used the technique I had mentally planned on.

The second point is just as critical. You won't remember your actions in a high-stress event exactly as you performed them, and will be unable to immediately and accurately recount them. I was only under a mild amount of stress. No one was shooting back or striking me. I was warm, dry, uninjured, and light was adequate. The distance to the target was known and exact and I had been firing from that same 7-yard line all week. All of these factors kept this from being a traumatic event, although not one that was completely stress-free: I was surrounded by other police firearms instructors, all of whom wanted to see who would do the best and which loser would shoot a friendly target. On top of that, there was a tight time limit so the adrenalin was pumping, and when I shot it, I experienced a mild amount of tunnel vision. No one wants to jack up a shooting drill under those conditions. The drill produced only a fraction of real life street stress, but it was enough to prevent my recollection of the event until my partner recounted it to me accurately.

I learned then and there to never immediately relate the detailed portions of a high-stress incident such as a shooting to investiga-

tors without some time passing after the event. I had been told that in two separate police academies I attended for basic training, but had never experienced anything quite like it. There's no doubt that decompression time is needed following a post-shooting event to allow the juices to stop flowing in the brain so the reconstruction of the event is accurate.

There are a lot of flashlight/firearm techniques that are just ridiculous. They might look pretty in a photo or out on a static range under controlled conditions. But they're dangerous to use on the street and are so intricate and require such delicate movements to pull off that you won't revert to them under stress. That kind of stuff is what I avoid. Why teach a technique if it won't be used at all or if it's dangerous to attempt?

Also understand that these techniques are not the only ways to shoot with flashlights, lasers, or weapons lights. They're the foundations that I *actually* used on patrol, on SWAT, and while off-duty. They work the best, at least for me. Practicing consistent foundations that work in a variety of circumstances allows for the best performance when the rubber meets the road.

At our 727 Counter Terror Training Unit at Columbus State Community College, we teach an Advanced Tubular Assault Class covering bus, passenger trains, and aircraft. Our foundational principles for how to deal with each of those platforms remain the same, with minor adjustments. The positions taken, weapons used, and assignments are all essentially the same, regardless of the platform we are working in — school bus, transit bus, single and double-decker train cars, Lear jet, and Boeing 727. Learning and performance by trainees is simplified and enhanced by using these consistent foundations.

The IFS Stance

First, let's talk about handgun shooting stance and positioning, since the pistol or revolver is what will be used with a hand-held light. In academy and sheriff's office training, I teach what I call the "Interview, Fight, and Shoot" stance (IFS). As an officer, you should not be worrying about making major adjustments in foot position when your situation changes from that of writing info on a note pad to throwing a punch, or from throwing a punch to shooting your handgun.

Using the IFS stance, there is no stepping from this position – where the strong foot is back and the weak forward in the interview position – to, say, an isosceles shooting stance where the feet are placed shoulder-width apart and the arms come equally together in front to form an isosceles triangle shape before you can shoot. Why waste the time?

Further, feet placed directly across from the other and shoulder width apart is not a solid defensive tactics position. You can be knocked to the ground with little effort. It's an okay position on the target range, but not so nice when used on the street. Just draw the gun in the interview position and shoot it. Ball the fist and strike with it. Draw the baton and swing with it. The only foot movement should be stepping offline and getting out of the way, or retreating if substantially outnumbered. There should be no additional step (no pun intended) added to the process that requires a foot reposition in order to engage a weapon.

An officer using the IFS technique has his hands and shoulders already in position to fight with hands, a stick, spray, Taser, or a gun. Isn't that what we're teaching — to "fistfight" with a gun in

Police officer/firearms instructor demonstrates proper shooting grip with semi auto pistol. Left hand support thumb is locked over right hand grip thumb. Note how this position keeps the hands well away from the moving slide and slide release lever.

65

Officer demonstrates proper foot positioning in IFS stance. Strong foot back, feet shoulder width apart. If not for the hands extended in a shooting position, this would be an ideal boxing position.

hand? All of this is very natural. So this is our first foundation: a solid, practiced, yet relaxed IFS stance.

Practice Using One Hand to Shoot

Next, if we are using a hand-held flashlight, that means that the lighting hand is occupied and we will have difficulty doing anything besides holding the light. This is why pistol-mounted lights were developed — to allow the user to have both hands on the gun while shooting.

However, pistol lights shouldn't be used for any other flashlight illumination purposes, such as routine door shaking, checking in the rear, or approaches of misdemeanor suspects whether on foot or in a vehicle. Their use should be strictly limited to activities such as dynamic entry, which will be discussed later. The only hand-held lighting exception is the First Light Liberator, which is a hands-free light. The Liberator leaves the light hand free to perform other tasks, like supporting the gun shooting hand. So if you aren't using a Liberator light, you have to shoot one-handed.

HANDHELD LIGHT TACTICS

Principle #1:

When training to shoot with a handheld flashlight, learn to shoot your gun with one hand.

Officer demonstrates a two-hand "Harries" shooting position using the full size patrol flashlight during a search. Note how the officer's body is in danger from incoming rounds if the light is fired at.

Officer utilizes the Harries technique during an entry. Flashlight used is the Blackhawk Gladius Maximus. Note lanyard keeping light secure.

So the first foundational principle is this: When training to shoot with a handheld flashlight, learn to shoot your gun with one hand only.

It seems that accurate one-handed shooting is almost a lost art. I believe that this is the case in part because of today's use of high-intensity rounds for police duty, like the +P+9mm, .40 Smith and Wesson, .357 SIG, the .45 GAP and the .45 ACP in its high performance plus and hollowpoint versions. There was a reason that the .38 Special was the premier and almost universal police service cartridge for nearly 100 years in this country. The handgun, after all, was designed as really a "one-hand" gun. In the days when most police firearms training used one-handed shooting techniques (as exemplified by the "FBI crouch" position), the .38 Special cartridge was ideal as a duty round.

The low-pressure recoil of the 158 gr. round nose lead bullet at a sedate 750 feet per second velocity, coupled with the heavy all-steel Colt and Smith & Wesson revolvers that were the only game in town at that time (and even when I started policing in 1980), made it easy to attain hits on the target *and* the bad guy. The only problem with those hits with the marginally powered .38 Special

Author demonstrates the traditional FBI crouch position, which was designed for strictly one hand use. Note the low crouch, fully extended shooting hand (pistol is .40 caliber Smith and Wesson M&P). Weak arm is drawn up in a fighting position and, in pre-body armor days, as a makeshift shield over the heart to protect against incoming rounds.

69

was that they were sometimes only moderately damaging. Things improved greatly with the advent of more modern hollowpoint bullet designs, but the guns were still limited to six shots.

The advent of crack cocaine in 1985 provided a massive power infusion to the small number of street gangs. With that came a switch in the gang weapons of choice — from the switchblade, zip-gun (home-built single-shot handgun), to UZI subguns and the Glock handgun. The police were overwhelmed by the new bad-guy firepower. An arms race ensued, and we began arming ourselves with Glocks and other high-capacity pistols like my personal favorite, the Beretta 92 9mm.

Today, due to our current gang situation, the war on terror, the active shooter phenomenon, and the use of illegal soft body armor by criminals, we have lightweight semi-autos with polymer and aluminum frames for duty use loaded to the gills with high-pressure, high-intensity, and highly effective defensive cartridges that are sometimes highly difficult to shoot with one hand.

The recoil is challenging. Even though we don't practice enough to become truly proficient with one-hand techniques, what technique do you think you think an officer or civilian in a high-stress training encounter or real-life shooting situation will revert to when suddenly placed in these situations? One-handed technique

A similar reciprocal arms buildup occurred in the 1930s in the Dillinger era. At that time, our predecessors armed themselves with Thompson submachine guns, the Browning BAR fully automatic .30-06 caliber rifles, and, in 1935, the Smith and Wesson .357 Magnum revolver cartridge and Colt .38 Super automatic pistol cartridges. The pistol cartridges had been designed specifically to penetrate through gangster automobile hoods and into the engine area to disable them. The .357 was touted as having the ability to crack an engine block. Specific rounds were developed for the .357 Magnum and the .38 Special such as the sharply pointed "Highway-master" metal penetrating bullet.

70

is the natural response. Unless you're already in a two-handed stance, there simply isn't time to bring light and hands together before shooting. You simply start shooting with the hand the gun is in.

Hopefully your weapon of choice has tritium sights. I worked with plain black sights on my guns for the first 22 years of my law enforcement career. Take advantage of all the technology available to own the night. Use Crimson Trace Laser Grips or a comparable sight system on your weapon, because if a flashlight becomes an afterthought when the shooting starts, maybe the sights and lasers will too. Instinct will rule and you'll be directing fire, as much as you can, on the threat until the threat stops or until you run out of bullets.

If you watch police cruiser cam videos of officer-involved shootings, you'll see a lot of one-hand shooting techniques. Once the action slows or stops, the support hand comes up to join the gun hand. I've seen this occur time after time in force-on-force simulations and during training — especially when a flashlight is added to the equation.

One-hand shooting positions are commonly used even when most training involves two-handed shooting techniques. The mind, when the body comes under attack, says "Stop the threat! You have your hand on the gun! Shoot! Shoot! Shoot! Don't wait for that other hand! You don't have time!" You go with what you've got.

Say, for example, some really big guy is about to tear you apart. You find a pretty good-sized stick on the ground to use as an equalizer. You can grab it in time to start laying wood to the attacker before he can twist your head off. However, the stick isn't large enough to absolutely ensure that you will be able to beat him into submission. Several feet away is a large piece of oak that can most assuredly do the job. Do you drop the stick in hand and try to get to the bigger one and risk being grabbed, or do you start whaling with the stick you have? If your answer isn't the latter, be prepared to think "I wish I woulda …" as you lose consciousness, thanks to the big guy.

Had you started with the first stick, you could have bought some time to make it to the second stick to finish the job if necessary. Same thing with shooting for life and death. You start shooting with one hand when you're surprised and crunched for time because that hand is ready to go — it isn't waiting for the second hand to catch up. Your brain is trying to maneuver things around to save your life. As the action unfolds, the second hand will catch up to stabilize things, and fire will become more precise and deliberate after that.

We have to train to fight with one hand only, and must develop the skills needed to buy time to bring in the second hand or end

Officer demonstrates the "traffic stop ready" position. Full-size patrol light is up on weak side shoulder and can be used as an emergency impact device to create distance or to disarm a suspect while drawing your own firearm. Light used is a Maglite Rechargeable.

the fight fast. This will require more practice with the modern, heavy-recoiling "two hands required" handgun configurations that we now use.

In fact, during qualification, I no longer allow our deputies to use a Harries-type flashlight technique (where the weak hand holding the light supports the shooting hand) to qualify during low-level light training. They use their light in a traffic stop or building search ready position, and shoot entirely one-handed. Traffic stop ready, by the way, is having the patrol flashlight light raised up in the weak hand with the tube end resting on the weak side shoulder. Also, the state-mandated "hip shooting" qualification phase of the annual qualification and basic training course requires officers to draw and fire two rounds with each command from a holstered position, strong hand only, with the weapon tucked in close to the side, reholstered on command.

Recognizing the need to teach and accommodate the natural stabilization to a two-handed shooting position, I have long had our deputies and basic police recruits — after shooting the mandated two rounds — step back and move to a two-hand high cover-and-scan position, which is what one should do after firing rounds and taking the suspect down. More precise shots may be needed and more opponents may be encountered, but the initial contact starts with one-handed shooting. This exercise simply reinforces and practices what would be a natural response in that situation.

Training for one-handed shooting should be practiced not only at close range, but at longer distances and especially with flashlights. What is the average distance from a patrol car to a suspect vehicle, for example? An officer will begin his approach to a vehicle with a light in the weak hand and a hand on the duty pistol — an officer should always make a traffic stop approach in a ready draw position. What distances will he cover? We've done drills to simulate a traffic stop or suspicious person walk-up by having deputies exit cruisers at the range, with the light bar going and flashlights on. As they approach the targets, at some point they will be given the command to fire. No person I saw going through these drills moved into a Harries shooting technique when they advanced to the firing point. They all shot one-handed.

Another drill is a "flashlight failure" (or a failure of the officer to hold onto the light). The officer starts with the target illuminated by his flashlight. On command, he has to let his light fall to the grass in front of him and shoot with ambient light only. I want them to learn to engage in the gunfight with what they have in hand (their gun, ready to use) rather than bending over and picking up a light while being shot at. Getting an officer to learn to not depend totally on his light is an easily accomplished task,

73

Officer demonstrates improper positioning of light, so that gun and sights are illuminated, rather than the target. Notice shadowing on the target from the illuminated hand. This obscures a good part of the illumination field that could have been used to the officer's benefit, plus it puts the light directly in front of the officer's face to draw fire.

especially these days with the almost universal use of night sights on police duty weapons.

Another natural inclination, besides letting your light cast off target, occurs while holding your flashlight in the weak hand. Many times shooters hold the light in an improvised two-handed grip so it illuminates the sights of their gun. I assume this happens for a couple of different reasons. One is that they're attempting to pull the light together with the pistol while shooting so there's some semblance of a two-hand shooting technique. This causes them to inadvertently illuminate the gun.

The second reason may be that they're attempting to see the sights while shooting. When a shooter lapses into this position for whatever reason, a couple of things happen that are both bad. First, the gun and hands cast a shadow directly into the center of the target, removing the light incapacitation capability. Second, this position illuminates you. Some of the light is reflected off the backs of your hands directly into your face, so the suspect can clearly see you.

This brings me to the second foundational principle of hand-held lights: Use the light sparingly.

Use the Light Sparingly

|||||||||||||||||||||||||||||||||||||||||||||||||||||||||||||||||||||||

Light should be used sparingly except when doing routine things like searching an area for discarded evidence, searching an impounded car, or other safe tasks. Leaving your light in a con-stant-on mode when dealing with a potentially armed suspect merely gives them a readily identifiable target to shoot at.

Limit the use of light, turning it on only for as long as you need it. When you're confronting a suspect, use it to take out his night vision and incapacitate him, if only for a brief time.

This is a difficult concept to impart to the new combat pistol/ri-fle trainee. Try this experiment at the range next time you qualify. Shine the brightest light you carry directly into the eyes of a fel-low officer while he's off the line and when it's totally dark around him. (Never do this kind of horseplay stuff when folks are trying to actually shoot on the line). You can even use your strobe. Then see how long his dark-adapted vision is screwed up. That's about how much time you'll have to gain an advantage against an opponent in a gunfight.

Also consider this: If you're facing a dark-adapted opponent who's adrenalin-charged and ready to kill you, you get an extra advantage. The adrenalin and other chemicals working in their fight-or-flight mode also cause the pupils of their eyes to dilate. Maybe nature set this up to give us the best advantage possible in pre-supplemental-lighting caveman days.

But here's the flip side of the coin. If you didn't take out your op-ponent's dark-adapted vision at first contact and your light merely illuminates them, guess what he's going to be shooting at? Your light, which may be held right in front of your face.

To show how tough their lights are, Surefire and other compa-nies use lights that have taken bullet strikes from bad guys in their magazine ads. Bullets striking flashlights or handheld lights is not uncommon in policing and certainly in the military. Heck the mil-itary actually tries to shoot out the lights of opposing forces. And in the policing world, aren't suppressed .22 caliber pistols, rifles, or even high-powered airguns available to shoot out streetlights? So why wouldn't a bad guy send a bullet racing toward your flash-light, they only thing they can see? It happens all the time, particu-larly in patrol work, where we tend to have our lights shining for longer periods of time as we conduct business.

Leaving the light on and using it too much is something I see regularly when conducting basic training drills in our police acad-emy. During building search exercises, which come before basic firearms, cadets use flashlights and simulated handguns for the first time. I've given them the basic rules for searching a building

HANDHELD LIGHT TACTICS
Principle #2:
Use the light sparingly.

in class, but have not shown them detail on how to do it or given them dry runs. They go in to search a two-classroom area knowing there's a suspect inside they must find. It's interesting to watch how they handle it.

Year after year, the same errors are made. Cadets leave their lights on too long, they use the lights in a semi-dark room when they don't have to, and they regularly illuminate their partners from behind. They also talk too loud, bump into stuff, bunch up, and the like. It takes some work and explaining to get them to rely more on their own dark-adapted vision and limit their light usage because it's natural to want to see everything with 100% clarity all the time under conditions close to sunlight.

The average person, unless sleeping, wants to be in sunlight as much as possible. Most people fear darkness and avoid it. We may have the ability to deal with it, but that doesn't mean we have to like it. This is why the "shadow warriors"— people who operate in darkness, including special ops detachments — are so feared. What's scarier than being attacked in our sleep? Why do we avoid dark alleys and streets in questionable areas? Survival instinct. Darkness hides danger.

Case in point. During my tenure with a central Ohio police department as a full-time patrol officer, I relished working our 5 p.m. to 3 a.m. late second shift. That's when the bad guys came out to play, and I was getting paid to play with them. It had become my working environment of choice even in the old-tech flashlight days.

We hired a new officer one summer who had worked for a city street department. He was put through the Ohio State Highway Patrol Basic Academy and performed well enough. He had been on third shift with his field training officer only two weeks when they encountered his first open door on a small warehouse. They did a basic search and, finding no one or any evidence of unlawful entry, secured the door. Searching that dark warehouse was way beyond the rookie's ability to cope, and he went back to his street department job the next day.

That kind of stuff doesn't happen often, but it illustrates the point. Dark is scary. That's why our military coined the mission operative phrase "own the night." We've overcome our fear of the night through training and advanced technology. We own the night against opposing forces in Iraq and Afghanistan, and we use it to our advantage. We have been working toward that end since the earliest introduction of radar and sonar during the Second World War, and later when night vision equipment was put into regular combat use during the Vietnam War. Nazi scientists developed the "Vampire" night vision system by the end of WWII, but it didn't get any real combat usage. And since night vision is not really advanced enough (yet-give it five to 10 more years) to use on a constant basis, we still must rely on flashlights.

Using light sparingly is an unnatural response to a natural situation that has to be trained into the individual operator so he or she can incorporate the concept without fear. Operate your light sources (hand-held or weapon-mounted) with the momentary switch, move your position if you can, then use it again. Under totally dark conditions and with a powerful light (120 lumens or more), you can position yourself behind a wall of light and keep your exact location unknown.

But that will only be of benefit if you follow foundational principle number three: Don't hold your flashlight directly in front of you.

Don't Hold Your Light Directly in Front of You

||||||||||||||||||||||||||||||||||||||||||||||||||||||||||||||||||||||||||||||||

The FBI had it right almost 75 years ago. If a bad guy (or a good guy, for that matter), can't see anything else to shoot at in a totally black area, he will shoot at the light he can see. Yet in the quest to shoot a one-handed gun in a two-handed stance at all costs, we have developed flashlight techniques that require the shooter to acquire some semblance of that all-important two-handed shooting grip.

These techniques are good for use at the target range and for getting a perfect qualification score in static courses of fire. But when you use them, you've positioned yourself directly behind the flashlight. Regardless of what two-hand technique you use, it causes you to put your face directly behind the light — right where the bullets are heading.

Remember how flashlights survive and continue to operate after being struck by incoming bullets? The light survived, but where did the pieces and parts of the bullet travel? In the pictures I have seen, the bullets don't go into the light. They bounce off and go somewhere else, which is why the light still works. Tubular aircraft aluminum is pretty tough stuff. So if the bullets don't penetrate the light, where did they go? And where would you rather have them go, into your hand, wrist, or arm when holding the light as far away from your body as possible; or into your eyes, nose, mouth, or brain, which is where they'd go when you hold a light front of your face?

When you hold the light at your side, either high or low or somewhere in between, make sure you hold it slightly forward so you're standing behind the wall of light, not in front of it.

HANDHELD LIGHT TACTICS

Principle #3:

Don't hold your flashlight directly in front of you.

||||||||||||||||
77
||||||||||||||||

When is creating a wall of light preferred to working the light in a momentary fashion? The following are some specific situations. It all boils down to this: *Momentary switch use of the flashlight is for locating potential threats. Creating a wall of light is for taking them down.*

Modified FBI one-hand stance (high officer) vs. two-hand Harries stance (low officer). Illuminated light is the Surefire 8X Commander. Unlit light held in Harries position by low officer is the Streamlight Super Tac. Note how Harries-positioned officer will draw incoming rounds right towards his face, while officer using modified FBI stance will have rounds travel (hopefully) past his head.

Momentary on

Dynamic entry

Basic building search

Supporting K9 track

Initial approach to a suspect on foot

Initial approach on a traffic stop where the cruiser is used to create the wall of light as the officer maneuvers around

Pursuing suspect on foot

Wall of light

Approach a suspect on foot in a totally dark area with no existing ambient light

Engaging a suspect in a gunfight (trying to take out adaptive vision)

Breaking up a crowd situation, such as a bar fight (strobes helpful)

Approaching the vehicle on a traffic stop to make contact with the occupants

Felony traffic stop takedown

Felony takedown of suspect on foot

Image shows author not utilizing Surefire M3 Combatlight as a wall of light. Below, image shows wall of light created by using Surefire M3 Combatlight. Note shadow of authors Kimber 10mm just to the left. Light must be held off-center to avoid drawing fire to center, or used sparingly if it doesn't take out opponents night vision.

In Summary

When a threat is placed directly in front of a person, that's what the mind, eye, body, and responses focus on — stopping that threat. When we talk about a light being presented to the bad guy, along with the "Police, don't move" command, the light is the threat. They can see nothing else and it is the best and only target available.

By holding your flashlight out to the side, away from your body and especially your face, the incoming bullets pass right by you, while your bullets produce a devastating effect on the properly illuminated and incapacitated aggressor.

This is pretty common sense stuff and is all borne out in practice. Find a good quality handheld light for patrol or tactical use, back it up with another light or two, and practice shooting with that light in one hand.

OWN THE NIGHT – PART II

OWN THE NIGHT
Part II:

Weapon Mounted Lighting Systems

Weapon mounted lights fall into three basic categories, although there is some crossover with a number of the models. The three main categories are:

- Dedicated pistol lights designed primarily for use on pistols via Picatinny (named for the former Picatinny Military Arsenal) M1913 rail systems.
- Dedicated rifle lights designed for mounting on rifles, primarily AR-15 variants via some sort of rail mounting system.
- Handheld lights adaptable to mounting on a rifle.

Pistol Light Systems

Before you select a pistol mounted light, keep a few things in mind. First, any pistol light you get should be 110-130 lumens in power. Second, it must use an LED and not a xenon lamp system. Third, the locking/mounting system must allow for easy and rapid mounting/dismounting of the light. Fourth, the overall size of the light must be compact (unlike the Glock labeled/marketed model which is massive) and fit in a wide variety of holsters designed to accommodate pistol lights. Finally the pistol light should be of duraluminum construction (the carbon fiber INOVA INFORCE being an exception) not plastic. There are a lot of different models out there and not all lights are created equal, so let's look at a few of the best pistol type lights available today.

Picatinny-type rail sections shown on FN FiveseveN 5.7 and Bushmaster Carbon 15 AR-15 with Midwest Industries quad rail allow for solid mounting, and most importantly, repeatability, i.e. you can remount the hardware on the same exact place on the rail after it has been dismounted.

Blackhawk

Blackhawk has introduced a pistol light system designed in part around their SERPA holster system. The Night Ops Xiphos NT is the only polymer pistol light system that I would actually use, with a number of features that make it worthy of consideration.

The first is polymer construction. Although the other lights mentioned in this chapter are constructed of duraluminum, which gives them a solid feel, there is nothing wrong with polymer when done properly (think Glock). The Xiphos has a solid yet somewhat lighter feel to it than the other lights mentioned here, so there should be no concern about using it for the life and death stuff.

But the polymer construction isn't what makes it different. While it works fine with most other conventionally-shaped non-SERPA light bearing holsters, it's designed to work properly in their SER-

Blackhawk Xiphos mounted on Glock 32 .357 Sig, author's polymer-framed duty pistol. Note the offset of the light which accommodates the Blackhawk SERPA holster.

85

PA holster system. The SERPA requires special positioning of the light because of the clamping lever that keeps the weapon secure. The clamping lever, which sits midway on the main body of the holster, holds the weapon in place until released by pressure on in from the index finger while conducting a draw. It must be pushed in to release.

If there is a pistol light in the way, that isn't happening, so Blackhawk has to provide its light with what appears to be a permanent mount to allow proper operation of this holster. The mounts come in three models – right, central, and left.

I received a right-hand light for testing, although I don't have a SERPA to test it with. (The manual says that the Xiphos will work with certain conventionally shaped light bearing holsters.) This one is set up for a right hand SERPA, so the light body is offset to the left (away from the clamping lever) about ¼ inch. The light is marked with an "R" on the operating switch. For the left handed

SWAT sergeant trainer uses a Glock 34 in solid two-handed grip with Xiphos light mounted.

SERPA user, the light would be off-set to the right and is marked "L". While these models may work in some holsters other than the SERPA, to make sure, they have a center mounted light marked "C" designed to work with all holsters.

The Xiphos is rated at 90 lumens using the new CREE technology that is used in Blackhawk handhelds. It's very bright, but that is about 20 lumens less than the Surefire X300, 35 lumens less than the Insight Procyon, and 45 lumens less than the Streamlight TLR.

However, that 90 lumens of brightness is produced using one lithium 123 cell instead of two, which gives the light less width than the other side-by-side two-cell models. That's what is really keeping the weight down, not the polymer construction. It also might save you some money on batteries.

The Xiphos has a slightly different ambidextrous switch operation than the other three lights, as its switch is only "mimicking" a momentary-on mode. Constant-on is obtained by tapping the switch forward only once, from either the right or left side. Momentary-on is mimicked by rapidly pressing the switch forward on either side in a rapid double tap which I find a little odd. If you ever do any real life searching for bad people with a pistol, rifle, or handheld light, you know you are popping the momentary-on quite a bit to search, which means you are tapping the light twice as much as you would with a real momentary-on switch. This takes some extra work and training to use properly. And you would definitely have to train with it, since only one tap leaves the light on.

The third mode is the strobe mode, which is activated by tapping the switch rapidly three times. When you do this, the strobe stays on until you tap it again. I like the constant-on part for the activated strobe. I'd like to see the order changed to one tap for momentary-on, two taps for constant-on, and three taps for constant strobe. This would be an important change, since out here in the field we are all used to a single tap on any light for momentary-on.

It would also be great if the light mount could be interchangeable, with adaptors for the three positions needed to accommodate the SERPA system.

As far as performance goes, the beam on this light is very tightly focused, as are the beams on most of the pistol lights out there, with a light but well-defined corona area.

Surefire

||||||||||||||||||||||||||||||||||||||||||||||||||||||||||||||||||||||||||||||||||||||

Surefire's X300 Weaponlight for pistols (also now for rifles because of their new and very cool rail-mounted remote pressure switch) features a solid-state, electronically regulated LED that generates 110 lumens of tactical-level (meaning incapacitating and concentrated) light.

Surefire has been the leader in pistol mounted lights for a long time. The X300 has the now standard 1913 rail attachment system, designed for quick and solid mounting.

The X300 incorporates a special TIR (Total Internal Reflection) lens which creates a tightly focused central beam (the weapon part of the light) and a wider corona (the illumination part of the light). The corona projects into the area surrounding the central beam for use in slow searches.

The solid construction of the unit is evidenced by the fact that the unit is waterproof to 22 meters. The on and off switch is at the rear of the unit and has a momentary-on feature (push forward on either side lever towards the front of the light) as well as a standard on position activated by rocking the lever either all the way up or all the way down. I found that for my use the switch position comes up a little short, which forces me to use a thumbs forward grip on some pistol models to operate the X300.

Midwest Industries/Sun Devil mid-length gas ported custom AR-15 with Surefire X300 and rail mount pressure pad. Traditionally a pistol light system, the X300 is now usable on a rifle. Note how little room the entire package takes, and how there is no vertical foregrip required. This tiny light still projects 110 lumens of power.

CHAPTER 4: PISTOL LIGHT SYSTEMS

The High Thumb Grip

Nice for Pistol Competition, Not so Nice for Real Life

Unless you are using a thumb forward or high thumb grip to facilitate operating that pistol light, don't use it! That grip was developed by IPSC shooters who started using it in competition in the 1980s and 1990s to make it easy to release the thumb safety of a cocked and locked 1911 pistol. It works okay for that but it isn't necessary and, in fact, it is dangerous to use outside of competition.

When you put your thumbs up high on an autopistol, you are putting your thumbs in contact with either the slide or the slide release lever, and two bad things invariably happen. Since the slide of the pistol needs to operate without obstruction in order to cycle properly, see what happens when you touch it just a little bit with your thumb while shooting. Likely you'll experience slide lockbacks.

Another problem that I've seen emerge over years with a high thumb grip relates to accuracy. This grip may work well for competitive shooters who practice many thousands of rounds a month. For the average cop or military personnel who shoot much less, the weak support hand will weaken even more in the area between the thumb and forefinger.

Author demonstrates high thumb position on Glock 32. Note how dangerously close authors thumb is to the slide and slide release lever.

This means that the pistol, an object dominated by the laws of physics, will seek the path of least resistance as it torques while being fired. That means towards that weak area created by this grip style. For a right handed shooter, almost universally the shots will drop down low and left. For a left handed shooter, the shots will tend to be low and right.

If you hold the pistol the right way, weak thumb locked low over strong thumb, the weaker area is slightly toward the backs of your hand, and the pistol torque will be straight up and back. The shots, in absence of trigger jerk or flinch, will be well centered.

I currently carry the X300 for mounting on my FN FiveseveN pistol for use on our tactical team. For rifles, the rail mounted pressure switch replaces the battery compartment floorplate thumb switch that comes standard mounted on the X300, and pops smoothly and easily onto any standard AR quad rail. I mounted an X300 on my custom Midwest Industries/Sun Devil AR with mid-length gas system to create a minimalist rural patrol gun. The X300 is the only accessory besides an Aimpoint Comp II and Tactical Link single point sling that I have mounted

Author shown with Glock 32 in a proper two hand shooting grip.

Surefire X300 mounted on .357 caliber Glock 32, author's night fighter pistol. Pistol is equipped with XS Big Dot tritium sights and 1st generation Crimson Trace Lasergrips (without master cutoff or frontstrap mounted switch). Author is using a forward thumb shooting grip solely for the purpose of activating the light. Note that thumbs are nowhere near the slide release or the slide itself. This is why the author prefers a handheld light for primary use with a pistol, so that a solid grip is maintained. A pistol light can always serve as a backup.

CHAPTER 4: PISTOL LIGHT SYSTEMS

Pistol-mounted lights aren't just for pistols. They are also useful on less lethal weapons, such as the double-barrel Kimber JPX Jet Protector OC gun. The JPX puts out two large globs of OC at about 242 mph, making a tremendous impact on the suspect. Featuring a Picatinny rail, the JPX allows for mounting of lasers and lights.

on it. It is very small, very bright, very lightweight and located directly under the boreline of the rifle. The pressure switch is mounted on the left side of the rail and is activated with my left thumb as I don't have a vertical foregrip installed on this particular weapon, again, to keep it minimalist, so the X300 setup is ideal for its purpose.

Surefire also makes the X400, which is basically the X300 light with a integral laser light. A number of companies produce integrated light and laser systems. A good overall feature, but one that also needs to be practiced with. There is a lot of activity going on up there, perhaps too much to be truly effective when the user is under high threat.

Insight Technology

||||||||||||||||||||||||||||||||||||||||||||||||||||||||||||||||||||||||||||||

The Insight Technology XTI Procyon presents a generational leap forward in pistol lights by incorporating an easily activated strobe feature. Insight added this feature, pioneered in their Typhoon/Gladius light, to the Procyon and, at 125+ lumens, it outshines many other pistol light systems.

The Procyon's activation switch is easy to reach. I had no problems manipulating it, and saw no need to obtain the remote switching option that is also available for the X series. For constant-on, the independent operating switch on either side is pressed up. For momentary-on, either right or left side switch is pushed down and held for as long as the operator desires. No problem with index finger operation and no need to break the grip.

Officer with FNPS90 5.7X28mm tactical carbine and Streamlight TLR2 (laser combo), traditionally used as a pistol mounted light, in this case mounted on built-in optical sight (with backup irons on either side) frame assembly.

Insight Technology Procyon mounted on Beretta M9A1 (which has updated features specified by the Marine Corps).

Now for the cool part: By double tapping either right or left switch down, the strobe effect is operated for as long as it is held. Release the switch and the light is off. Push down once and you have the standard light again. If you want a constant-on strobe, push the momentary switch on and off for the standard light mode, then push either switch up into the continuous on position, and the strobe stays on.

Insight's laser/light combination pistol lights are the M6 and the subcompact size X2L, which was designed for subcompact rail autoloaders like the Springfield Armory XD. They produce a total of eight different pistol lights to accommodate various models of pistols and rails.

Streamlight

Streamlight has upgraded their TLR-1 Rail Mounted Pistol Light with proprietary C4 technology which has been infused into nearly all of their current light line. Now operating at 135 lumens at 7000 candela and a long range targeting central beam (illuminate, identify, incapacitate all fulfilled here), the TLR-1 also fea-

TLR-2 is Streamlight's laser/light combo version.

tures ambidextrous momentary/off-on switching. It easily latches on and off pistol rails.

The TLR-1 switching is slightly different than the Surefire and Insight lights. Pushing down on the right side toggle switch locks the light into the on position. Pushing up on the right side toggle gives momentary-on. Pushing down on the left side toggle switch provides momentary-on, pushing up gives locked on. It could be a little confusing if you are using different lights. Just practice with it and be consistent. The increase to 135 lumens of power is a great development without an increase in size.

The TLR-2 is Streamlight's laser/light combo version. Like the other companies, they merely extend the size of housing to accommodate a laser below the light.

While the units from all the makers listed here are solid and reliable, a potential purchaser should try them out a their local shop to decide what switching system for both elements is the most intuitive for them. That said, I really think that the best setup is a separate light and laser, like any of the aforementioned lights combined with a set of Crimson Trace Lasergrips. However if Lasergrips aren't made for your particular railed autopistol, one of the combos lights may be a viable option.

Safariland

Safariland, known more for the holsters that accommodate pistol mounted weapons lights than the lights themselves, introduced the RLS (Rapid Light System) a couple of years ago. As I

This photo sequence shows officer mounting the Safariland RLS on a Glock 22. Starting in the open position, the mount is slid onto the rail of the pistol. In the mounting position, with the light hanging down, there is less chance of the hand being swept by the pistol muzzle. Once the mount is in place and latched, the light is swung up to the left or right. The pushbutton tailcap switch is activated by the weak hand thumb. Officer then acquires two-hand shooting position with his light active.

CHAPTER 4: PISTOL LIGHT SYSTEMS

said before, there are some pistol light systems that are adaptable to both pistol and rifle, or from handheld to rifle, but this is the only one I know of that is designed to go from being a handheld light to a pistol or even a rifle mounted light.

Carried in a holster on a duty gunbelt, the RLS, by means of its special mounting system, is designed to be a quick on and off

light. One of the advantages to the RLS is that its design keeps your hand out of the way of the muzzle when attaching it to the rail. Once the mount is slid onto the rail, the light is swung into place on either the left or right side of the pistol, depending if the shooter is right or left handed.

The light is a traditionally-styled tactical light that can be used as a handheld light with the mount in place, or the light can be removed from the mount entirely. Interesting idea, but one I found unusual from a company making light-accommodating holsters.

The current 65 lumen rating is not only half as bright as most other tactical handheld lights, but is only half as bright as most of the current smaller pistol light systems. Also, even though mounting and dismounting this light is apparently easier than most of the more compact systems, it *must* be dismounted to holster the pistol – a step I'd rather skip if confrontation with a suspect is changing from deadly force to physical force.

According to my friend Tim Halbakken of the Columbus Ohio Police Department, who has been issued an RLS for field testing, the system is truly rapid with a little practice, but it cannot be operated with one hand only. Also, the light is noticeably dimmer than many of the current ones available, but he still feels it can be a good system. In my opinion though, I want to be able to holster my pistol with one hand only while drawing other weapons such as the Taser, or using my weak hand to deliver a strike or some other defensive move.

The RLS light was adopted by my campus police department at Columbus State Community College for use with Glock 17 pistols, but it is not one that I would have selected for them. I don't believe that any pistol-capable light is for general patrol issue. There are too many better and simpler options available. The RLS remains a little too gimmicky for my taste.

Pistol Mounted Light Tactics & Principles

So let's talk about some foundational principles of the pistol mounted lighting systems. The first foundational principle when working with these lights is: *Don't shoot a hole in your hand when mounting and dismounting the lights.* This is best accomplished via two routes.

CHAPTER 5: PISTOL MOUNTED LIGHT TACTICS & PRINCIPLES

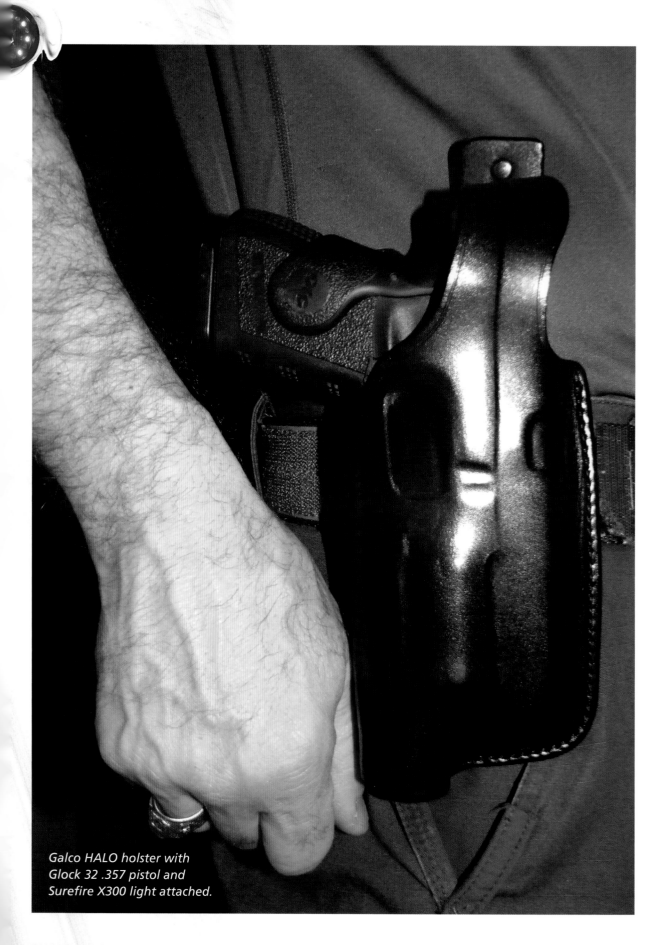

Galco HALO holster with
Glock 32 .357 pistol and
Surefire X300 light attached.

Don't Shoot Your Hand, Part 1: Use the Right Holster

First, get holsters that are designed to carry your pistol with the light attached, so you don't have to take it off (or use the Safariland RLS, which minimizes the risk). After all, reducing the amount of times you have to perform a potentially dangerous task generally decreases the risk of being injured by it.

For example, if you never have to take your gun out of the holster while working at the police department, you probably aren't going to have an accidental discharge with it there. Those bullet holes you find in various areas of any well used police department? All of them have to do with some facet of removing weapons from holsters, vehicles, or weapons lockers, or loading and unloading them.

Galco, among others, is even making a plainclothes/off-duty holster for pistols with lights mounted on them called the HALO. The HALO would certainly come in handy for street crime attack teams or any other type unit that works in low profile clothes such as blue jeans and raid jackets. All the other major manufacturers of duty belt holsters also have models to accommodate pistol mounted lights.

Our SRT duty holster is currently the Safariland 6304 tactical thigh holster with ALS (automatic locking system). A couple of our guys use the excellent Blackhawk SERPA holster system for their SRT rigs. Like the duty rigs, the SERPA is now also available in its off duty or plainclothes guise to accommodate flashlight mounted pistols, and is very intuitive in operation.

Whichever holster you get, whether or not you are mounting a light on the pistol at all times, make sure it has some form of retention and is not an open top design. You are much more likely to need to keep your pistol *in* the holster during a fight with Conan the Barbarian than to draw it at lightning speed to take out Ike Clanton. The more retention the better, and this goes for civilians too. You can't resolve every issue with a gunfight, that is why these lights make a great intermediate force addition to your weapons system.

Other than the increased size to accommodate a pistol light, the Blackhawk and Safariland holsters totally replicate our standard duty holster in function and form, making training time minimal. In fact, I use the SERPA mounted on my armor to carry my FN 5.7 pistol while carrying the Glock 31 in the thigh holster with light mounted.

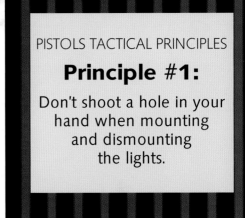

PISTOLS TACTICAL PRINCIPLES

Principle #1:

Don't shoot a hole in your hand when mounting and dismounting the lights.

103

Pistol Lights from Xenon to LEDs

||||||||||||||||||||||||||||||||||||||||||||||||||||||||||||||||||||||||||||||||||||

Pistol lights have come a long way. The early Xenon models did not stand up well to the shock of repeated firing while mounted, so to preserve bulb life they weren't often mounted during qualification courses. Not a good idea, but necessary to preserve the light for when it was needed most. They also weren't very bright, drained batteries, and actually seemed more of a novelty or gimmick when first introduced rather than a useful tool – much like the first models of the Taser.

Fortunately, as with the Taser, good old capitalist determination persevered and the lights continued to develop. What really boosted their popularity were advances in LED technology. While the LED was a nice development for the handheld light arena, it wasn't essential to the survival of the breed. After all, you can do quite nicely with a good xenon tactical handheld light system if just have spare bulbs available. For pistol mounted lights it really was essential. The development and application of the LED allowed the lights to be smaller, brighter, draw less power and almost totally resistant to the shock from cartridges fired from the pistol or a rifle.

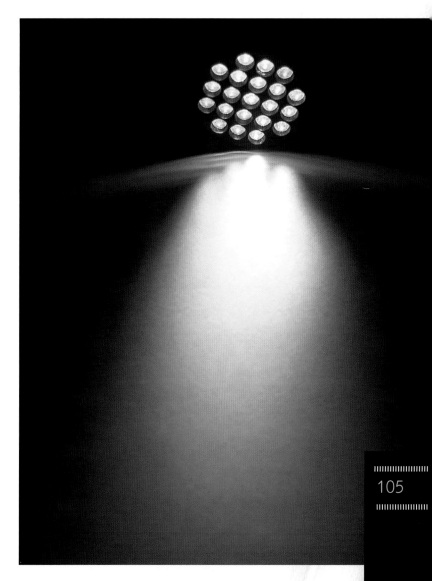

At one time I was pretty skeptical about pistol mounted lights. In fact, to save money for the sheriff's office, I turned down the issue of a pistol mounted light and new holster, preferring to work with a handheld. Then I started working with these lights for an article for *Tactical Gear* magazine. A light bulb went off in my head, while working with the Insight Procyon in particular. There just might be something to these things in limited applications.

In my opinion they are clearly *not* for general issue to police patrol officers, but are great for tactical team members and anyone who wants to use them in civilian home defense. I found this part out about the civilian home defense application at my home one night. I was awakened by my dogs barking in the middle of the night in the house, which is not a common occurrence. I grabbed my Glock 32 compact .357, which has Crimson Trace Grips and XS Big Dot Tritium Front Sight with white rear express sight and, because I had been practicing with it, the Insight Procyon. A real night fighting pistol indeed!

Since the dogs had stopped barking and come back to the bedroom, which told me "false alarm Dad, go back to sleep," I walked into the living room to check the area rather than taking a position of cover and analyzing first. I found that I quite naturally activated the Procyon and that it vastly simplified searching. I didn't even grab a handheld light. I was now a convert, and sheepishly asked my SRT Lieutenant for the new Safariland holster to use with the Procyon. So now I had the right holsters to go with the light.

I have also found another advantage to the pistol mounted weapons light. The extra bit of weight on the muzzle end helps to attenuate the recoil of our .357 caliber Glock 31s when mounted, making for smoother shooting.

Don't Shoot Your Hand, Part 2: Use Safe Gun Handling Practices
||||||||||||||||||||||||||||||||||||||||||||||||||||||||||||||||||||||||||||||||

Holsters that accommodate mounted lights are only half of the equation for preventing injuries from mounting and dismounting the lights. By using them you reduce time on target, i.e., the amount of time that your hand will spend in front of your own pistol muzzle. The second part of the equation will prevent trips to the emergency room and avoid a lifetime of harassment from the troops. Simply put, it is this: Use safe gun handling practices.

It is nearly impossible to *not* put part of your hands or fingers in front of the muzzle when mounting or dismounting a light. It is a basic fact of life that, with the 1913 rail system or most other proprietary systems, the light has to slide onto and off of the rail

Officer demonstrates hasty (yet safe) mounting of Surefire X300 on a Glock 32. Step 1: Reach over top of pistol and hold it slightly (1/4 to 1/2 inch) out of battery with the weak hand. Step 2: While holding the pistol out of battery, attach light to front of rail. Step 3: While still holding slide out of battery, lock light into place. Step 4: Release slide back into battery and clear weak hand away. Check to make sure the pistol is fully in battery before use. Note that this is not a manufacturer approved technique.

CHAPTER 5: PISTOL MOUNTED LIGHT TACTICS & PRINCIPLES

from the muzzle end for rapid mounting/dismounting. Herein lies the problem.

Pistol light manufacturers advise the purchasers of their products to only mount/dismount them with the pistol totally unloaded (magazine out, chamber empty, and slide locked back). While this may be the ultimate safe way of doing things, it isn't always practical when lights need to be mounted and dismounted quickly.

There is another way (*not* manufacturer approved) of safely mounting and dismounting the light. It's pretty simple, although of course not as safe as working with a fully unloaded pistol.

Holding the pistol light in the weak hand and the loaded (yes, loaded) pistol in the strong hand, place the thumb of the strong hand under the backstrap of the pistol and reach over the top of the slide with the fingers of the strong hand, covering the slide.

Next, pull and hold the slide slightly out of battery, about a ¼ inch or a little more, and hold it there. The gun won't be able to fire if you should somehow contact the trigger.

Then, mount the light and allow the pistol slide to move back into battery. Make sure that the slide is actually fully back into battery. It shouldn't be a problem if you didn't pull the slide back too far and start the cartridge to actually eject.

Just to be completely clear, the *safest* way to mount and dismount lights is to fully unload the pistol. However, there is the real world out there, where cops and soldiers must operate with expedience as a priority. But there are safe ways to be expedient.

Use the Light Sparingly

The second foundational principle of pistol mounted lights is the same as the same as the second foundational principle for handheld lights: Use the light sparingly.

Pistol mounted lights are for one purpose. They exist to take out the vision of an identified threat directly in front of you while you are rapidly advancing on their position (read that emergency dynamic entry). It is not a searching light, a signaling light, or an illumination light. Using it for those tasks, even carefully, will lead to pointing a hot pistol at something you may not intend to shoot and destroy. Remember that basic safety rule: Never point a firearm at anything you are not willing to destroy with it.

The pistol mounted light serves or should serve only one purpose, and that is as a weapons light. It is, in essence, a confrontational light. Granted, the light can be used in a searching mode during a dynamic entry when the action slows a bit but the scene is still active and not fully secured, or maybe during a standard building search, but remember the problem here. The light is mounted directly under the pistol, and if you are using the light for longer term tasks, guess where you are directing incoming fire to: The same place that you do when using a handheld light in the Harries type position.

Many years ago, when Crimson Trace came out with the most practical and reliable handgun laser sighting system to date, one of the biggest complaints by naysayers in law enforcement at that time, and some today, was that lasers would draw the fire of the bad guys directly into you as you were sighting in on them. These were some of the same folks that were okay with a pistol mounted weapons light. Just don't add a laser to it.

In fact, the pistol light does the same thing as a laser when the laser is left in the constant-on position, only worse, since the beam is casting about over a much larger area than the tiny laser dot, making your general position easy to locate. In reality then, the weapons light is much more likely to draw fire to the user than the laser, when used improperly. The weapons light, when it shines on a suspect, says "I can see you now." The laser dot on the same suspect says "I can shoot you now." Big difference in the impact on the decision making process of the bad guy. An old Crimson Trace T-shirt sums up this concept: "Crimson Trace, helping bad guys make informed decisions."

PISTOLS TACTICAL PRINCIPLES

Principle #2:

Use the
light
sparingly.

Rifle Mounted Light Systems

The primary difference between rifle weapons light systems and pistol mounted systems is size. Most rifle systems are larger, heavier, and have larger reflective lenses, thus putting more candela and lumens downrange.

Rifle and shotgun mounted lights were what we saw first on police weapons systems. The shotgun light was developed first because that was, for most police departments, our only long gun. Those early lights were large incandescents that used standard D cell batteries. They either replaced the fore-end of the shotgun or had the shotgun modeled around them in a bullpup-type configuration.

High Standard Bullpup

The first of that type was the High Standard (HS) Bullpup which was introduced in the early 1970s. An odd looking weapon, it had an AR-15-type carry handle with a standard flashlight molded right into the handle. I never had the opportunity to fire one, but noting how the receiver was hooked to a flimsy curved/hooked plastic buttstock at a small central attachment point, it probably smacked you so hard that your momma said "ouch" when you fired it.

At that time, the flashlight was only minor help in terms of illumination and maybe identification; no thought was given to using it for incapacitation. That was what that 12 gauge shell was for. It did answer that age old question of "how do you search in a dark area with a shotgun in hand when you are by yourself?" It always required at least one other officer with a handgun and a flashlight and you sticking close by. Not a good arrangement.

As you can imagine, in any of these old HS shotguns that I encountered, the flashlight never worked. The bulbs available at the time simply couldn't take that much pounding, so I'm sure that a keeping a good stock of replacements was critical. After all, one would hope you only needed the light for a couple of shots anyway in a combat situation. Ultimately, this early attempt at answering the light question was not satisfactory, so the HS was a very seldom seen weapon. In fact, the only place I have ever seen them is in police storage lockers.

AR-15

Enter the AR-15. At first, the civilian/police versions of this weapon, made available in the late 1960s and 1970s only by Colt, were in the same boat as any other rifle that may have been used previously in small numbers by law enforcement, such as military surplus M1 carbines, but never fielded on the street. There was no thought given to mounting any sort of light on the weapon, partly because there was no adequate light source available and partly because our forefathers mostly fought in the daytime. Nighttime operations were very limited, performed only by the most elite, small groups of troops.

Conditions remained static for a long time until the expiration of Colt's patent rights on the AR system and the explosion in not only the popularity of the AR system by other manufacturers, but also in aftermarket parts for the system. Notable was the development of the Picatinny M1913 rail system and removable carry handle on the shortened M4 carbines by the U.S. military.

The rail was first developed for mounting their emerging weapons sighting equipment such as the Aimpoint optic on these guns in lieu of standard military iron sights. This system became limited issue, operational at the time of the Battle of Mogadishu in 1993, and was deployed by special forces operational units like Delta. You can see some of the first M4s in the hands of Delta Operators in the movie "Blackhawk Down."

As of this writing the M4 is our battle rifle standard for all services except the Marines, who want the ballistic superiority and accuracy of the full length AR-15 platform. It is my understanding though that there is a move for the Marines to begin acquiring an M4 variant.

As most of the world's battle areas are urban, rather than huge and sometimes purpose-dedicated open fields, the compactness of an M4 in door-to-door fighting becomes a major asset and even a requirement. Question though: How did our guys in WWII do it in the urban fighting in the major European Cities with no rifle lights and a very long rifle like the M1 Garand? Answer: Sheer guts, a lot of learn-by-doing (WWI was still an open field war, very little house to house action there), and also some substitution of better house-to-house weapons when possible. The M1 Carbine, Thompson Submachine Gun, and M3 "Greasegun" all come to mind for use here as superior close quarter battle guns of that time.

As the Army developed the M4, civilian manufacturers took notice and, in combination with the sunset of the 1994 Clinton Assault Weapon Ban in 2004, ushered in the boom era of the AR-15 rifle and the M4 carbine in particular. The first iterations of the civilian M4 available were sans collapsible stocks, flash hiders, and bayonet lugs to make them compliant with the law. When the ban was lifted, things changed. Back came flash hiders, collapsible M4 stocks, and the all important bayonet lugs.

These first new guns had the standard military round forends and A2 carry handles. Next came the removable A3 carry handles and optics rail system. However, there was still no ability to mount a light on the weapon without use of the policeman's secret weapon, duct tape. Actually, electrical tape works as well, at least in the U.S. environment, and it comes in the requisite tactical black color. I simply took a Streamlight Scorpion handheld light and taped it to the forend of my M4 so it could be activated by my left thumb. It worked okay as long as the light didn't get banged around, and with the brightness of the Scorpion was better than nothing for entry use.

Then came a new M4 with a quad rail forend and vertical foregrip. Actually that M4 is one of the best, but sometimes underappreciated Bushmaster Carbon 15. The Carbon 15, for those not familiar with it, is a traditional direct impingement gas system

M4 with a twist. The upper and lower halves are constructed of carbon fiber, which is 40 percent lighter and 40 percent stronger than aluminum. It possesses a natural lubricity quality that I have found, after many thousands of rounds fired through it, enhances reliability. It seems to need less attention to interior cleaning as the steel parts slide against carbon, not aluminum. Also, the carbon dissipates heat much faster than aluminum, so the receiver halves remain cool after extensive firing even though the barrel gets hot.

Having worked with this particular gun for a number of years now, I felt that it would be an excellent replacement for the current M4s. If the military didn't want to go to a piston driven operating system, it might be the next best thing. While working with this gun initially for an article for *Tactical Gear Magazine*, I obtained a drop-in quad rail from Midwest Industries and a vertical foregrip. To this I added my first dedicated light system from PentagonLight, their Stealth Assault Model with attached laser aiming module.

As an old guy and traditional rifle shooter taught by my dad and developed further in the Boy Scouts, I initially had no use for the vertical foregrip. You may have noticed by now that it sometimes takes me awhile to realize the value of certain items that in retrospect, should have had obvious. I hope that this tendency also gives me time to observe and see if these new developments are actually a good idea or not. Anyway, I first tried a vertical foregrip on an M4 belonging to one of the other guys on our tactical team and I thought, "this is cool!" It totally changed the feel and control factor of the gun, and I had to have one. The Carbon 15, with its light weight, was the perfect weapon to mount one on. Let's look at some of the light systems available for rifles.

Surefire

||||||||||||||||||||||||||||||||||||||||||||||||||||||||||||||||||||||||||||||

Surefire has introduced their new Vertical Foregrip Weaponlight for Picatinny rail mounting. For me, this is a great improvement over their innovative dedicated forend weaponlight. Due to its smaller size, it allows for greater mounting flexibility and utilization of other spaces on a quad rail. This was a great system before the development of the universal rail system. It was really the only way to mount a high power light on an AR, and it still

Surefire M900A mounted on Bushmaster Carbon 15, with Nightforce NXS compact precision rifle scopes mounted on flattop rail. Note uncapped LED maneuvering lights (inactive) just aft of front sling mount.

marketed. It is just a little bit cumbersome, and if part of it went down the whole forend needed to be replaced, which was a pain. The Vertical Foregrip Weaponlight addresses that issue.

Two models are available, the M900A that mounts with an ARMS throw lever mount (the type I favor) and one that mounts with dual thumbscrews. The test model M900A that I received came with the MN11 125-Lumen Xenon Bulb system and two red LED navigation lights mounted on the side. Also included was the 225-lumen lamp assembly. While I think that overall the LED rep-

Tactical team with Midwest Industries/Sun Devil AR-15, Aimpoint Comp 2 and activated Surefire M600C Scout Light.

resents the superior illumination system due to its dependability and long life, the brightest one I have seen to date is only 135 lumens. Very bright indeed but 90 lumens short of the eyeball-scorching 225-lumen xenon lamp. Three lithium 123s power this unit. I mounted it on my favorite AR-15 "test mule," the ever reliable Bushmaster Carbon 15. The unit locked into place simply and securely via the throw lever mount.

The M900A features a lockout tailcap to prevent inadvertent activation while stored, which is good since the heat from the xenon lamp would probably start a fire if activated while stored in a case. The momentary-on pressure switch on the sides of the vertical grip is easily activated and there is a constant-on switch located at the rear of the light itself for long term operation. The red navigation LEDs are activated by a pressure switch at the top rear of the grip, and can be covered with tethered rubber covers should the need arise.

In a more conventional style rifle light, Surefire has introduced the M600C Scout Light LED Weaponlight. Compact in diameter, this 120-lumen LED light mounts to any Picatinny rail with a thumbscrew locking system. The Scout Light's reduction in size will be welcome on any AR where multiple accessories will be mounted. If I wasn't already using the X300 on my rural patrol rifle, I would certainly use the Scout Light, but it would probably work best with a vertical foregrip, which I wanted to avoid.

The Scout Light is equipped with interchangeable pushbutton and remote tape switches.

Streamlight

While Streamlight doesn't make what I consider a true, dedicated rifle light system, they have made the Super-Tac mountable on a quad rail system. They also have remote tape switches to use on the TLR-1 and 2 should you use them on a rifle. Another really cool option for the TLR-1 and 2 is a vertical foregrip that allows mounting of the TLRs on either the right or left side of the foregrip just by changing the rail position from right to left.

The TLR mounts sideways on the rail, allowing operation of the standard TLR pistol switch by the support side thumb without

Author with Bushmaster Carbon 15 with Streamlight TLR1 mounted on their rail accessorized vertical foregrip system.

having to change to a tape pressure switch. I find this to be a superior way of mounting a light. Using the TLRs without a pressure switch means that there is no wire that has to run anywhere on the weapon itself. That is a problem with most of the standard rifle light systems, there is a remote switch and wiring that must be protectively secured.

Another exception to the requirement for using a remote pressure switch on a rifle is when you mount a light like the SuperTac, Inforce, or any of the other handhelds via a ring adaptor to a rail

mount. Actually, most of these lights will mount using a scope mounting ring. You merely use the pushbutton switching that comes with the like this vertical foregrip and the advances light without changing anything. With accessory equipment like remote tailcap switches available from all the major manufacturers for their pistol lights, it is really turning them into multi-weapon lights (they aren't just for pistols anymore).

Purchasing a pistol light for use on a rifle is a viable option and makes a lot of sense. After all, 135 lumens of LED light is nothing to sneeze at and really is more than adequate for most tactical usage. Pistol lights are super compact and don't clutter up the gun, which I really like. If you want more power from Streamlight for your rifle than the TLR-1 or 2, then mounting the SuperTac on their vertical foregrip would make your AR a great open area search weapon. The beam may be just a little too tight for best use indoors. Its pattern is very reminiscent of the old 6-volt lanterns that mounted right on top of the battery, but you can make that decision. After all, you can never have too many lights or guns! The TLR-1 or 2 in their new upgraded brightness versions should serve well for most entry situations, although without the power of other dedicated rifle light systems like the Surefire 900A Vertical Foregrip Light.

Blackhawk
||||||||||||||||||||||||||||||||||||||||||||||||||||||||||||||||||||||

Like the system for the Streamlight, a Blackhawk Xiphos pistol light can also be mounted on vertical foregrip or rail system on a rifle, but I am just a little hesitant to do that. Why mount a 90-lumen light with strobe when you can mount a 130-lumen light with strobe like the Insight Procyon? (Unless I need just a little less light for, say, hunting coyotes.) If you already have one for your pistol and don't keep it mounted all the time, you can certainly put it on your rifle. It should work fine. I am just a little bothered overall by the Xiphos switch operation. It is too easy to accidently leave it in the on position when you only wanted the momentary position.

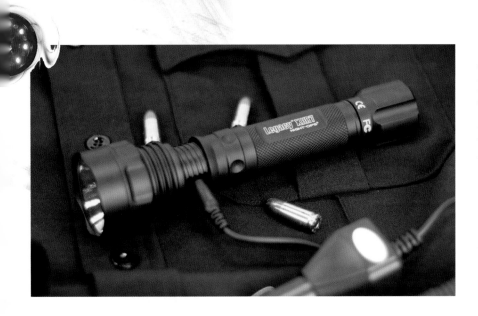

Nearly all the aforementioned manufacturers have handheld or other lights that are adaptable to rifle mounting, so I won't cover those again particular options again. Really, nearly any handheld light can become a rifle light with the right mounting system. It is just a shame that one of the best tactical lighting manufacturers out there, PentagonLight, is out of business. They made some of the most innovative products on the market, and competition always brings out the best in manufacturers.

More is Not Necessarily Better

Foundational principal number one for gear for AR-15s or other rifles is this: Don't hang too much junk on them. Every cool gun magazine, including the ones I write for, loves pictures of AR-15s with every conceivable accessory and device on the planet hung on the quad rail, the vertical foregrip, the rail upper, the

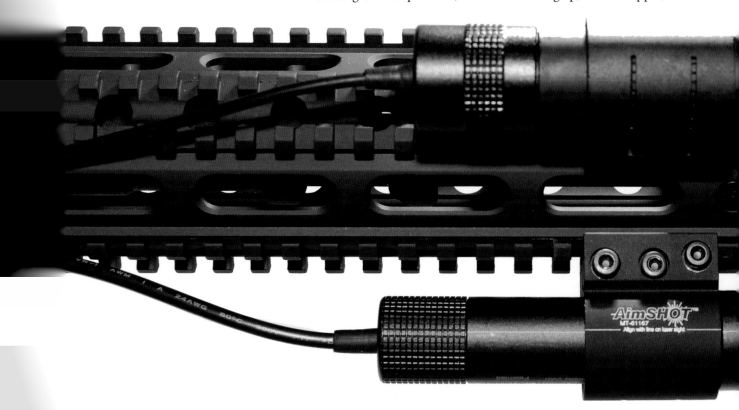

stock, the pistol grip etcetera. Combine these items with bipods, cinched magazines or 100-round drum magazines, and sound suppressors that take the 16-inch M4 barrel and turn it into a 20 inch barrel, and you have just created yourself a crew-served weapon. You aren't going anywhere, at least not in a hurry, with that thing.

For gun magazine and book editors this is a good thing, one picture with one gun and a bazillion gadgets on it right there on the cover. Talk about getting the most bang for your buck! The problem with this imagery is that we all want to be cool tactical guys, so we start putting all that stuff on, hoping the chicks will dig it and we can have a gun just like the one on our favorite pub cover. The real deal is that few of us need all that stuff, at least mounted at the same time.

I have the privilege of working with some very qualified special forces operators who are our lead instructors at the 727 Counter-Terror Training Unit. These guys are the real deal, one is a Sergeant Major and one is a Master Sergeant. The Master Sergeant is enough into ARs (the Sergeant Major hates cleaning them) that he does some custom work and repair on them on the side. He has on his personal AR a light and a Trijicon optical sight. Besides his baked-on camouflage paint job, that's it. Good enough for him, good enough for me. So I believe in avoiding the clutter (with all the extra weight, switches, wires, batteries, and stuff to get hung up with) unless you have a special purpose gun, such as a sniper rifle that needs night vision, a big scope, IR illumination, a suppressor package, a bipod, and on and on.

RIFLE GEAR

Principle #1:

Don't hang too much junk on them.

The minimalist concept is especially true for the M4 configuration of the AR. The gun was designed to be fast and maneuverable. Don't ruin it if you are really going to use it for that purpose.

If I am going to tote a 10 or more pound battle rifle around, then it's going to be my M1 Garand with some real .30-06 caliber battle rifle ammunition, or a Springfield Armory M1A with some almost as good 7.62mm NATO battle rifle ammunition. Like I said, that's *if* I wanted to tote a rifle

like that around. But having to lug a M1 Garand-type battle load around is why the original M16 was developed.

The military, actually the Air Force, turned to Eugene Stoner and Armalite to develop a lightweight battle rifle that could be carried by airfield security personnel in Vietnam all day long in tropical heat, without undue fatigue. The concept was so enticing that the Army soon figured that if they issued their troops the M16 and a boatload of ammo, it could be humped long distances all day long, with a far larger number of rounds available in a battle load at the same overall ammunition weight. Not bad, but unfortunately this original concept was lost to the military with their next generation of M16s, the heavy barrel generations M16A2. Equipped with longer buttstocks, heavier more durable handguards and beefier rear sights, the once lightweight M16 weapon system went from a svelte six-pound rifle to the more portly M1 Garand weight range of 10 pounds. What were they thinking?

The ultimate in lightweight, minimalist, reliable firepower: the Bushmaster Carbon 15, paired with the carbon fiber Insight Technology Inforce light system mounted on Midwest Industries quad rail forend.

Try to avoid thinking the same way. Why lose all the fast handling capabilities of the original M16A1 or especially the M4 carbine and make it too sluggish to swing? You have to be able to bring it to bear and swing it quickly to be effective with it in combat situations. With all the junk attached, you can't use it for the very role for which it was designed.

Admittedly, some competition ARs are heavy, with special barrels and weights and gizmos to negate whatever recoil one feels from the 5.56mm round, but that stuff is a game. It isn't like going up a flight of dark stairs or narrow hallway where there are bad people, instead of judges with timers, who are waiting to hurt you. Notice the competitors aren't wearing helmets and 30 or more pounds of armor or gear. They are also not fighting to save the lives of their loved ones from unknown dangerous intruders in their homes, nor are they trying to es-

DELTON AR-15 A2 with Midwest Industries front sight mount and Surefire M600C Scout Light and remote pressure switch placed on standard AR forend. Note use of electrical tape to help secure pressure switch to forend. Great trunk-stored rifle for emergency situations.

123

cape gangs of thugs and looters while trying to bug out of a Katrina disaster.

To be clear, I am not knocking competitive shooters. Competitions are the best way to stay tuned up, and I shoot in steel plate competitions myself. You are shooting at these events, right? Trigger time is all good time. We just have to be careful what we take from the competitive world into the real world. There have been a number of good things, many in fact.

Competitive shooting, at least the gaming type, should be thought of as the Detroit Auto Show where the concept cars are unveiled. They look really cool and slick up there on a controlled platform, but they really wouldn't do well running on the street, if they actually run at all.

Two years ago we received at our sheriff's office several M16A1s with the original triangular handguards, and shorter A1 buttstock from the Department of Defense Law Enforcement "Lend Lease" program. The M16A1 is actually a very fast-handling gun due to the lightweight 20 inch barrel and the shorter A1 buttstock. The original length stock is about as ideal as you can get for all users, and works well even while wearing heavy body armor. The old A1s shoot and operate great here in the sand and jungle humidity-free environs of Ohio. I would be content using them on entry in addition to their regular patrol duties, with a light attached on a front sight mount and an XS sight up front. The very few malfunctions I have seen on the range with the guns have been caused by the use of some very old magazines that were not the ones that came with the guns.

The length of the A2 barrel is really not a huge hindrance to maneuverability; we are talking about only a four inch difference. I think the bigger hindrance is the overly long A2 stock. What makes the M4 better suited is the ability to shorten its stock for more precise fit. Still, our Marines mostly use the full length less lively A2 rifle for combat missions even today, including house-to-house fighting, and they are still effective. Our soldiers in Mogadishu acquitted themselves very well in that battle against overwhelming numbers in house-to-house street fighting while equipped with the M16A2, but remember, we are talking about the box stock gun. No add-ons other than the occasional optical sight bolted to the carry handle. Once you start adding on, the A2 easily becomes a 12 pound rifle, and we don't want that unless it's some sort of SDMR (Squad Designated Marksman Rifle).

So, what if you are not going to use your AR-15 for dynamic entry or other SWAT duties? Maybe you want it for home or ranch defense or just for fun. If those reasons are what you want your AR for, then weight additions from equipment are less consequential, unless you are planning on just throwing the gun in the back of the

Jeep, John Deere, or pickup truck where all that fancy stuff can get banged up. If so, get a nice plain jane full length A2 like the ones made by DEL-TON or, better yet if you can find it, an old Colt A1 rifle with nothing additional added to it maybe other than a light at the front sight mount. The bottom line is, do what you want to make yourself happy. Knock yourself out. That has been part of the fun of the AR revolution along with all the accessories and individual customization and making the rifle exactly what you want it to be at any given time.

However, if you are looking at your AR as a truly effective, combat-capable arm, rein yourself in a little.

Choose Quality

This brings me to the second foundational point of the rifle and its lighting systems, which for these purposes also includes the sights. It is this: You are using a military, Mil-Spec (hopefully) battle rifle or carbine weapons system. Don't hang non-Mil-Spec garbage on it. Those $19.95 red dot sights that you get on special in catalogues or your local gun emporium belong on a nice Weaver railed or tip up grooved .22 rifle, or on a shotgun designed for hunting such non-threatening species as turkey. It doesn't belong on a quality battle rifle that you are planning to stake your life on.

I still see guys doing this on serious guns. It is like buying an $800 handgun and holstering it in a $19.95 holster. Don't do it. If you are short of cash, wait awhile and get Mil-Spec gear for your rifle. You want to look like a pro? Get pro gear. Don't stake your life on junk.

On the other hand, there are some things out there that are unnecessarily expensive for what they do and how well they do them, so it is not necessary to got to the other extreme. If you want to spend a lot of cash and the item in question is quality, then go for it.

Optical Sights

Now that I have set out some basic parameters for your consideration of the AR, let's talk specifics. If you are in the 50 or better age range like your's truly, consider a red dot zero magnification optical sight like Insight Technologies ISM-V (with co-aligned integral laser sight) or an Aimpoint Comp II, III, or IV Sight. While I can still use irons on ARs, I like to update them with XS Sight Systems tritium big dot or tritium stripe sights.

I hate to admit that. Reading articles from fellow gun writers lamenting their aging eyes, I used to think, "Come on guys, suck it up. It can't be that bad," until I was about 47 years old. Then I realized those sights were not as sharp anymore and I needed a little assistance. Those guys weren't kidding about sight focus,

ISM-V mounted on .450 Bush-master carbine with collapsible stock. Laser sight is active in the straight-on image and can be seen just to the left of the red dot front objective lens. With a larger capacity magazine, the .450 could be a formidable special purpose law enforcement weapon.

especially as light grows dim in the evening. It is a problem, but it can be compensated for.

XS Sights are a big improvement, and I can work with them just fine, especially in rapid fire situations. They would be great for a home defense carbine, especially in the big dot configurations. They do work great for me as backup sights, but as the primary they don't work as well as the glowing, electronic red dot.

Why a red dot? Simple. It's the best no-brainer reference point for high stress use in the most intense situations. Look through the

glass. See the red dot. Put the red dot somewhere on the threatening target along with a laser if you have it. Pull the trigger. Pull the trigger again, as many times as needed to stop the threatening target. Reload and be ready for more threatening targets.

Notice in that sequence there was no, "Gee, do I put the top of the chevron thingy on the bad guys chest or head?" Or, "Hmm, what part of the concentric circle around that little dot is the bad guy falling in and what distance is that?" Or, "Is the red dot perfectly centered along with the cross hair that runs through the middle of it on the bad guy target?"

Now, I am not knocking the other systems out there. Some very experienced hands like them, and they are also very admittedly cool, but boy, do they clutter the field of view and confuse things, at least for me. One of the earliest perceived advantages of the red dot optical sights was that you didn't have to align a front and rear something or other to get an accurate sight picture. You just looked at that one little red dot. There was no parallax effect, which means basically, you don't have to look directly through the rear of the optic to hit with it. If you can see the red dot on the target, you can hit it. Another advantage was that as long as you had a fold down front sight you had an uncluttered field of view. No crosshairs, circles, or anything else. Why would I want to add extra lines or circles or whatever the newest gee-whiz reticle design there is to a that?

One of the big things in confronting suspects, criminal and non-criminal alike, is watching their hands and looking for what is in them. I also believe in watching the suspect's face at the same time. Their eyes give away a lot. The pre-attack 1000-yard stare, the furtive looks glancing at your holstered or unholstered

gun targeting it, looking to see if you have other assistance or for an avenue of escape, showing cold iciness that indicates previous prison time, nervousness when concealing an illegal act or sometimes, just sometimes, a willingness towards compliance. I want to see all that as much as I want to see what they have in their hands.

Imagine you're a cop, covering a suspect who is now in the surrender position, not shot, you just have him in a felony type takedown position. He's either standing (for the moment until you can get him down) with hands up, kneeling, or proned out. Maybe your suspects are still seated in a vehicle. If you are watching them through an ISM-V, you maybe even have them illuminated with the co-aligned integral visible laser too. With that, or any, red dot sight, the only thing in the sight window that obscures a full view of him is that little red dot, which even at 100 yards only obscures a 4-inch-diameter circular area. With this large, clear field of view you can see what is in their hands, or the expression on their face and the look in their eyes as you cover them.

My advice is to stick with the red dot for real world use, and save the other reticle types for competition and fun. Of course, if you want to lay down precise longer range fire out of a full length rifle, then go with a more traditional type of scope and reticle.

Night Vision

Some of you may be wondering, "What about night vision equipment?" Unless you are going coyote hunting or looking to kill some other nighttime beasties, ask yourself if you really need it. While I would say that you truly can own the night while using it, I would also venture to say that the answer is probably no, that you don't need it. But needing and wanting are two different things.

One of the problems is that the earliest Generation 1 and 2 NV equipment, while being of inferior light gathering capability, was also bulky compared to the newer Generation 3 stuff, which is sale restricted and quite expensive. Get it if you want, skip it if you don't want to clutter and weigh down the gun. In any event, an examination of night vision gear is well beyond the scope of this writing.

Define your purpose

|||||||||||||||||||||||||||||||||||||||||||||||||||||||||||||||||||||||||||||||||

Since I will cover laser systems in the next section, lets move on to the lights. Since I already described a few of the different types available, you can make your decision thusly: What are you going to use the rifle for?

Are you a tactical team guy who will use it on dynamic entry?

Are you in the military purchasing approved off-the-shelf equipment for personal use in combat?

Are you someone who has the gun for dedicated home defense where you won't need to lug the rifle around for long distance?

If the answer to any of these questions is "yes," then by all means, a light like the Surefire M900A Vertical Foregrip Weaponslight with the 225-Lumen Xenon Lamp Module would be my top pick. As I said before, this is real eyeball scorching power.

Using the M900A would also be a must if I lived on a ranch or large land area in the American southwest, where I might have to protect myself, family, and property against illegal drug traffickers

Officer maneuvers in low light using the Inforce red LED option mounted on Bushmaster Carbon 15.

or other border-related threats. I would want to have the most powerful light available to cast over my property, and yet be able to still maneuver with the low power LEDs as I changed position. The Surefire M900 would work well or it might just be the starting point. If my property was very wide open, with limited tree cover, I would even consider mounting the Surefire Guardian or Dominator lights on my AR for 500 lumens of power.

However, if I want my rifle to be a real life, day-to-day general purpose, do a little of everything, hump over long distances AR, any of the standard, aforementioned dedicated rifle lights would work fine. I like the Surefire Scout Light, or the nice lightweight Inforce handheld mounted with the INOVA rail adaptor. The Inforce would also give you four different color options in the auxiliary LEDs.

Remote Tape Switches

If you want to refine the definition even tighter for the general purpose AR, go with the dedicated pistol light from Insight, Streamlight, or Surefire, mounted either on the rail or on the vertical foregrip. Try to set it up to run without using a remote tape switch. If you do use a light with a remote switch, check two things. First, make sure the wires don't touch any "hot" part of the gun, like the barrel. This may sound like a no-brainer but sometimes one loses attention to detail.

In 1997, when I took the required training to be a certified law enforcement "Assault Weapons" instructor through the Ohio Peace Officer Training Commission, I was shooting the course of fire alongside an officer from an area police department who was equipped with an M16A1 and one of those new-fangled, yet el-cheapo, laser sight things designed to mount on a rifle. His A1 had the pressure switch for the laser taped to one of the flats on the triangular handguard and the sight was mounted on the front sight triangle. The cord to the switch, a coiled affair like an old telephone cord, at some point due to movement from the shock of recoil or improper positioning, came in contact with the barrel and in very short order burned through it. He was done with the laser. I really didn't get to see any of the laser sight actually being used, it was toast on the second day of class when we began live fire. I have to admit though, that I thought even then that the concept of a laser sight on a rifle was way cool. However, the Crimson Trace Laser Grip that I had mounted on my Colt 1991A1 Commander functioned perfectly. I saw then there was potential for rifle mounted lasers, just maybe not with that arrangement. I mention it now because the same thing can happen with remote switched lights.

Don't wind cords through the openings in a quad rail, because the aforementioned will, at some time, happen. Also don't tape

them to the receiver, it gets hot too. Make sure the wire is secure in addition to being out of the way of heat. Try and get a system with the shortest cord possible and tape it to the rail and/or vertical foregrip so there is nothing dangling. Don't let the excess hang free or it will hang up.

Tight Central Beam or Broad Coverage?

With that being said, there is no cleaner mounting solution or system available than the use of a pistol light without a remote cord. I particularly like the Insight Procyon in this role due to the fact that it is currently the only pistol light with strobing capability. If strobing is not for you, or you don't feel that it is necessary, then any of the other pistol lights that I have mentioned will work just fine. Just make sure that when you set them up on the rifle that their operation is intuitive and natural and that the light being cast meets your needs.

The new LED pistol lights I have been working with, along with the LED handhelds, all project a very tight central beam with a light corona. In comparison, the Surefire 8x Commander Xenon at 110 lumens paints the light with a broad brush if you will. There is not tight spotlighting effect.

LED pistol lights won't always be best for entry, as a xenon light like the Surefire 900A puts out a much wider cast of its beam. Again, because of its incandescent nature, the beam is not precision focused like an LED. There is no sharpness to its edge. The LEDs as currently produced won't cover as large an area at close range as most xenon bulbed systems. Remember, all the development work with LEDs was done to produce a much tighter beam than was possible in with the early multi LED lights that cast a very soft wide glow over a very limited distance. Also I am sure that the other part of the goal was to have one central LED do all the work, and not a multitude of them.

Beyond this, another factor limiting the coverage area with a pistol light is that the lamp head assembly on a pistol light will never be as large as the one on a dedicated rifle light, whether LED or xenon. It has to be of reasonable size to holster and to save weight. The PentagonLight Stealth Assault Lights were a case in point. Their light output started out in the 65-lumen range, ending up at the 120-lumen level before they had to close up shop. But their larger lamp head cast a much wider beam, and they did, and still do, work extremely well. In fact, PentagonLight concentrated on rifle mounted and handheld lights only. They never produced a pistol light, their handhelds *were* their pistol lights. If you are lucky enough to have one of these lights, hang onto it and take good care of it, especially the Weaponsights with the integrally mounted laser sight, which was operated by the thumb of the hand holding the vertical foregrip.

I had one of the most powerful weapons light systems, built by Pentagon-Light, mounted on one of my Systema Training Airsoft Guns at the Counter Terror Training Unit. A prototype model, this "tubular assault light" was designed for the lead runner to use in aircraft takedowns to take out the dark adapted vision of everyone in the aisles.

The wizards at PentagonLight had mounted two xenon assault lights together in tandem at 200 lumens each, so when activated then there were 400 lumens of incandescent light produced. What was unusual about the light system wasn't the amount of lumens that were produced, since units by Surefire produce 500 lumens. What made the system cool was the separation of the lamps. They allowed the light to be more diffuse and project over a wider, yet somewhat overlapping area. Both lamps were activated by the same pressure pad switch, and one of the lights had the integral laser aiming module on it.

Why didn't this design go forward? Simple. It was too heavy and made the gun slow to move. The lights were fairly large, and they increased the width of the weapon, making it difficult to get through crowded aircraft aisleways. But

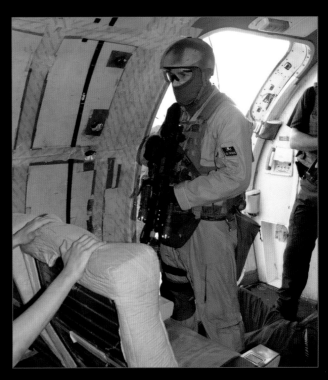

Student in advanced tubular assault class with Systema Airsoft gun and tandem light system developed by PentagonLight. Student, a U.S. Marine, keeps watch over secured passengers following breach and assault role play.

it sure did make for an overwhelming wall of light to come in behind. I think it is still a doable concept, if we had a manufacturer that was willing. With smaller lights like the Surefire Scout Light, kept in tighter, it might very well work. The pressure switches would just have to be linked into one. This could also work using pistol lights by linking two of Streamlight's TLR-1 pistol lights for example and working them off a single pressure switch. Then you would have wider area coverage for entry.

This "issue" of a decreased coverage area when using pistol light mounted on a rifle rather than a dedicated rifle light may be much ado about nothing when considering the type of AR we are building. Remember, original but updated concept, light weight, minimal stuff hung on it to keep the weight light. This is a multi-purpose, do-a-little-of-all-things AR kind of gun. The pistol mounted light may not be ideal, but it will work and is certainly better than no light at all, and the modern pistol light is better than most of the older low power models.

In talking with some of my coyote hunting buddies, they tell me that lights like this would be a good on their coyote guns. Not too powerful and very compact and lightweight. Coyote hunters are often walk-around hunters, so they need to keep their guns reasonably accurate and lightweight. They need just enough light to illuminate the eyes of the critter in question at a distance where the .223/5.56mm is effective.

Slings

So what's left for this concept AR that we are putting together? One thing: a sling. What kind? I like the single point quick detachable slings from Tactical Link. Simple, strong, and fast. With the rear attachment points of the single point, there is little danger of getting it hung up in the lights and other equipment on your AR. Also, the method of carry when slung in front of your body is more protective of the devices on the rifle. With a military sling, carried off to the side, there is a much greater chance of stuff getting hung up on tree branches, buildings, fences, etc. and tearing the attachments off of your gun. They are much more protected when carried on the body.

Tactical Link slings are now even quicker to attach to the stock with a new mounting system that clamps over the M4 collapsible buttstock near the receiver. The older version required the removal and replacement of the mounting plate on the AR receiver with a replacement one that had the quick detach swivel on it. This, system at least when I put it on another gun, resulted in the loss of springs (temporarily) that hold little things in place, like the firing/safety selector. Of course, I didn't really read the directions before mounting it. With their new system, this is no longer an issue, and the stock does not need to be removed to attach the Tactical Link.

We have been using the Tactical Link system on all our Systema Airsoft M4s at the 727 Counter Terror Training Unit, as well as on a number of our live fire weapons, and have found them to be an elegant work of simplicity. These work fine for all kinds of purposes, particularly if one of your purposes is real life tactical operations. I don't like the less expensive bungee slings, triple point slings, or slings which need to be named after people.

If tactical operations aren't on your activity list, then you might consider a standard carry sling. Single points aren't necessarily comfortable for long term carry over distance. They also can't be used in a "hasty" arrangement to give you a locked-in position for distant, carefully aimed shots. They would work and do work great on that rural patrol rifle that is only sporting the addition of a light for example. We have just the standard carry sling, military issue nylon, on all our M16A1s. But the military slings are lousy for tactical team use.

State trooper during aircraft assault with Systema Airsoft rifle equipped with PentagonLight laser/light stealth assault light, Aimpoint Comp 2, simulated taser, and tactical link OD green single point sling.

CHAPTER 6: RIFLE MOUNTED LIGHT SYSTEMS

Rifle Mounted Light Tactics & Principles

There seems to be far less controversy concerning the tactics involving light usage on AR-15 or other rifle systems as opposed to tactics and principles for handheld tactical lights or pistol mounted lights. There really is less to get worked up about. There is little or nothing to do with hand positioning or mounting/dismounting lights or any of the like topics, as the light is positioned well to the rear of the rifle's muzzle. However, there are still some areas of commonality here. So, the number one foundational principle for tactics is this (again): Use the light sparingly.

Use the Light Sparingly

The gun is in front of your face again. While you can perhaps better take out the vision of your opponent with a more powerful rifle light, you may actually draw more direct fire if you leave it on too long because the rifle light is a larger target. So shut the light off as quickly as you can.

Just like the with the handhelds or the pistol mounts, keep moving and changing your position while using it, and then move after deactivating the light if you can. Or at least maintain your position of cover or tighten it up some more.

RIFLE TACTICAL PRINCIPLES

Principle #1:

Use the
light
sparingly.

140

Choose a Safe Stance

The second foundational principal involves your physical stance with an AR-15-type tactical rifle. Unlike the hold you generally use for accurate shooting of the rifle in target stances (with your elbows out) keep your elbows locked in for moving while shooting, especially in close quarters. You might end up using your AR to search your home and may be moving through tight hallways, around obstructions, or up and down stairways depending on the construction of your home. You certainly don't want your wings poking out as you enter a room to check it.

Your basic standing position should come out of the IFS stance that I described earlier for use with the pistol. Keep it all the same for consistent operation. You should also use, where possible as you move, a good solid kneeling stance behind solid cover.

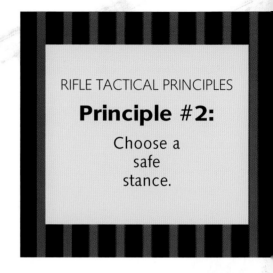

RIFLE TACTICAL PRINCIPLES

Principle #2:

Choose a
safe
stance.

141

et's talk about solid cover for a bit. Cover is actually a fleeting concept. It really should not be permanently counted on or any length of time, as it can be rapidly destroyed in many cases by the right type of incoming fire. The right type can be either very high volume of fire, or very high power of individual rounds.

Many years ago, I participated in a demonstration of that principle. At a Boy Scout Camp Shooting range, we did a law enforcement firearms demo for the Scouts. A police officer from another department brought along an American Arms 180 as part of the demo gear. Developed somewhere around the 1970s, this amazing full auto submachine gun looked just like a Thompson submachine gun except for the drum magazine, which contained 500 rounds, yes 500 rounds, of .22 LR (that's right, .22LR rimfire ammo) mounted horizontally on top of the gun. Rate of fire was nine rounds per second, and continuous firing of the 180 sounded like one loud "brrrrrpp" with no individual shots discernible in the firing string.

Now, a single .22LR round striking a cinder block will only make a mild pockmark on the surface, and you are pretty safe behind it for quite a while. With the American 180 set on full auto, we demolished concrete cinder blocks at 50 feet in about two seconds per block, leaving behind an unrecognizable pile of rubble. That's because all the impact energy was dumped on it as about as close to simultaneously as possible.

Speaking of cinder block, you also know that cinder block wall will stop most standard velocity .38 Special or lesser rounds, again, leaving a small divot in the surface when fired directly perpendicular

to the surface. But how long will cinder block last when hit by a 5.56mm round or larger? Answer: Not very. One round of ball ammo will crumble it at close range. The second part of a double tap will make it to you.

And there is no comparison to the 5.56 when you hit cinder block with a 7.62 NATO, .30-06, or larger caliber like a .300 Winchester Magnum. Cinder block will also not withstand much in the way of .357 Magnum or .357 SIG rounds. I have shot cinder block with .357 Magnum rounds, and it takes it out in one shot.

So as it turns out, most material and structures that we consider cover are actually merely concealment. Brick walls, cars, trees, all of it can be degraded when hit with the right ammo.

We did some testing awhile back on a junked Pontiac Grand Am to see how our 55 gr 5.56mm

Hornady Tap would perform on it. We were impressed, as the round went through the driver's side door, through two cardboard targets in the seats, and landed in the inside of the passenger side door, making a dent visible from the outside. When the serious work of data collection ended, I unleashed my M1 Garand, loaded with 150 grain FMJ ammo and shot through the driver's door. The rounds went through both sides of the car like a hot knife through butter and blew up huge chunks of dirt from the backstop on the far side.

So be ready to move, and move quickly, anytime you announce your presence to a bad guy or bad guys through illumination, gunfire, or other means, no matter what you are hiding behind.

Prone positions with the rifle should generally be avoided in most urban police work and military operations. It is too easy to take a round in the face if you expose yourself slightly while laying on the ground.

Bullets do not react like pool balls on a pool table. Pool balls hit the cushion and bounce out at the same angle that they came in. But bullets and shotgun pellets are different in terms of what they do when they strike a hard surface. When fired at a hard surface at a 45-degree angle or less, they will strike the hard surface (asphalt, concrete, packed earth and water (which becomes "hard" in relation to the velocity of the projectile, which is why you never shoot at water because it causes ricochets)), move six to eight inches off the surface, and travel parallel to it until all its energy is expended or it strikes something. If I am going to have something struck by a bullet, I want it to be something easily repairable, or maybe even expendable like a foot, or ankle, or knee, which is what might be exposed to bouncing bullets, especially if your cover is only your police car door. If the rounds are coming in perpendicular to that door, get out of there to the rear of the car.

Save prone positioning for sniper (er, precision marksman) shots behind good cover and concealment, keep your position hidden, and make that shot count.

Avoid Leading With Your Muzzle

Also don't expose your location when using the standing, prone, or kneeling position with your gun barrel. This is my third foundational principle: Avoid leading with your muzzle. When you round or prepare to round a corner, don't advertise and give away your location by sticking the muzzle out there beyond it.

It is easy to keep a pistol tactically tucked in but still at the ready, pointed in the direction of the threat while still maintaining illumination capability and visibility. Not so with a rifle. Slicing the pie on the corner or at a doorway takes a bit more maneuvering even with that 16-inch short M4 barrel.

It takes extra care to keep a position of engagement in the area of the anticipated threat. That's why certain AR systems are ideal for this task, like Sun Devil Manufacturing's exquisite 6.5 inch barrel AR upper. Also the MP5 PDW subgun, or even better, the FNP90 5.7mm PDW would excel.

In fact, in all likelihood you will have to lower that M4 into a tactical tuck for rifle as you maneuver, thus taking your light out of the picture at least momentarily. This also happens if you are on a tactical team and in an entry stack. You can't point the rifle mounted light ahead of you then either. It is exactly for this reason that I don't take a rifle in on entry anymore. I have the Blackhawk Gladius Maximis or the Surefire M3 Combat Light with lanyard, and a pistol light on my Glock 32 with its Crimson Trace Lasergrips. I have full confidence in the ability of the .357 SIG round from my Glock in dealing with any threat I may encounter, and I don't really feel the need for the 5.56 mm round indoors at close range.

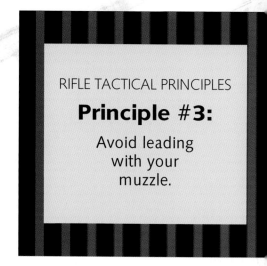

RIFLE TACTICAL PRINCIPLES

Principle #3:

Avoid leading with your muzzle.

Close-up of Sun Devil 6.5" barrel 5.56mm short barrel custom rifle. For real life use, author recommends an optic other than a Tru-Glo system, unless the weapon is going to be used only for plinking.

146

I would rather save the AR for longer range shots on the perimeter or in the open. I would take the Sun Devil AR for entry into aircraft or train assaults, and maybe larger bus assaults, simply because of the longer-range straight-line shots that may be needed. And if I do, my elbows will stay tucked in. If you have ever ridden AMTRAK and seen how long the train cars are when all the intervening rail car doors are open, having an AR in there will definitely be a consideration.

I also prefer the AR for use on felony traffic stops, open area searches, and certainly in active shooter situations where an encounter at any range is possible. But for that close quarter, awkward position hallway and closet fight, I'm fine with the pistol.

Practice With and Without the Lights

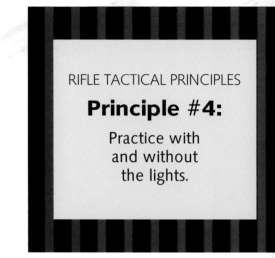

RIFLE TACTICAL PRINCIPLES
Principle #4:
Practice with and without the lights.

Foundational principle number four: Make sure you practice with and without the lights, under true darkness conditions, and include failure drills in your practice regimen. This goes for rifle and pistol. The lights can go down, right?

Even with a 10 year shelf life on lithium batteries they can fail, and here is the rub with many LED systems. Remember all I have said about them is good – long life, relatively unaffected by the cold, extreme white brightness, and total reliability due to the shock resistant nature of the LED itself. All good stuff. The only problem is that, unlike incandescent bulb systems, there is often, depending on the particular brand, little or no warning that it is going to go down. You can be using it at what seems to be full power and then suddenly the light is *gone*.

The manufactures of the new systems want to insure that you always have as much lighting available to you as possible, so the circuitry keeps the LED at near full brightness until it's dead. That never happens with an incandescent. Since their light output isn't computer controlled, they start to fade and warn you that it's time to get fresh batteries.

The LED handhelds I have used from PentagonLight *will* grow dim in their power output, so I do get a warning – but they grow dim quickly. This was on older models that weren't tuned to give full output until dead. Now that I think about it, full output until dead is a good operational theme for us in individual combat.

So here is the deal. 123 Lithium batteries are cheap now, especially when purchased in bulk. Keep tabs on them. Test the light before use and keep track of roughly how long the batteries have been used, then replace them. Always keep spare batteries and spare lights, and always test the spares too.

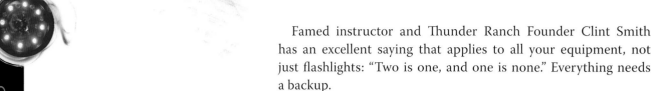

Famed instructor and Thunder Ranch Founder Clint Smith has an excellent saying that applies to all your equipment, not just flashlights: "Two is one, and one is none." Everything needs a backup.

There are some nifty M4 stocks out there and even AR pistol grips and vertical foregrips wherein spare lithium batteries can be held without adding any bulk or changing the configuration of the weapon. If you don't have a way to secure them on your rifle, keep a couple of spares in your vest or equipment pouch.

Train to Shoot in Total Darkness

And then practice plan "B": Train to shoot in total darkness.

When I was just starting out in law enforcement, working second and third shifts, my duty weapon was a Smith and Wesson Model 19 in .357 Magnum caliber (although I had to use .38 Specials in it), with a 4-inch barrel and plain black, Smith and Wesson Patridge front and Micrometer rear sights (state of the art for those days). No orange front sight inserts back then. Flashlight? I'm not sure as it was a long time ago, but I think I used an old Ray-O-Vac aluminum 6-D cell light that had belonged to my grandpa. It wasn't until I started full time policing as a municipal police officer that I joined the Maglight revolution. Anyway, we had to qualify back then in low level light and almost totally dark conditions on an indoor range.

The targets were the old NRA B27 all black silhouette with central 10 and X rings. The result? The other deputies, trainees, and I all hit the target. We used the muzzle flash from the first shot to better locate the sights, quickly locked them in place together and continued firing, using the muzzle flash to observe all the subsequent rounds, adjusting as necessary. The first shot was sometimes off just a tad, meaning it would still be in the nine or eight ring (you would be surprised what you can do when totally dark adapted) but the other five shots would be in the 10 or X. It is still a technique you want to train with and become proficient in, even with the advent of night sights.

Night sights are very bright until you fire that first shot and the muzzle flash disturbs your night vision. Their glow is not as apparent, since you have wiped out some of your dark adaptation, so you are back to working with muzzle flash to obtain alignment. This phenomenon varies with the amount of muzzle flash your particular load generates. The same holds true for rifle use. Even with a muzzle hider and or brake attached, the M4 in particular with its short barrel and high pressure 5.56mm cartridge generates flash.

You can see how well flash hiders work when you fire a 5.56 out of a Clinton Era 1994 Assault Weapon Ban-version without one

148

CHAPTER 7: RIFLE MOUNTED LIGHT TACTICS & PRINCIPLES

next to one with a flash hider and the same ammunition. Yikes. Same effect when firing the great Ruger Mini-14. Definite difference, but one that actually can assist you with the alignment of the sights since there is more light available to reference by.

What also helps is the addition of tritium sights for the AR platform. XS Sight Systems is the best choice here bar none. I favor only using a tritium front, although they do make a tritium rear with a dot on either side of the peep aperture, which replaces the original military one. I don't think it really helps in sight alignment when using ghost rings or peep sights, and I worry just a little about putting my eyeball so close, even for limited periods of time, to two vials of radioactive material. I may be overreacting, but I also don't favor a crotch-carry holster for a pistol with night sights.

Whether mounted on a pistol or rifle, I no longer like tritium rear sights, especially when you are talking about three pistol sights in which all the sight dots are the same size. I get all those same-size, little green dots confused when the action is fast. Too many choices for me. That's why I use only the tritium front big dot on my Glock 32, with the plain white stripe express rear. For pistols, how much more do you need to see than that big round glowing front sight in a close quarter gunfight? Just follow that big bouncing front ball and put it on the target.

For the AR-15, XS offers two sighting choices that will mount on either a fixed front AR sight or on a folding backup iron sight (BUIS) front. For most M4 applications, the guns used in closer range home defense and genuine tactical use, I would select the big dot tritium front.

Let me also mention here that the tritium vial in all XS sights is surrounded by bright white, almost ivory polymer in order to really bring the sight to the forefront, regardless of lighting conditions. This makes it easy to pick up in daytime lighting conditions, which is something that is lacking in most of the three-dot configurations to a large degree. In fact, the dots are so hard for me to find for anymore (as apposed to plain white three dot configurations) during the daylight, that I treat my Glock night sights as if they are plain black and use the tried and true standard of aligning the top of the front sight with the top of the rear, holding the front in the centered in the rear, with an equal amount of light coming through on both sides. I don't even use the dots for alignment, even on non-tritium sights.

It doesn't happen this way with the XS, whether on rifle or pistol. On the rifle, that round big dot front sight is clearly distinguished and is great for ranges within 100 yards. Beyond that, the nice big round dot begins to obscure too much of the target. If you are making your rifle more multi-purpose, to accommodate a

wider variety of distances and circumstances that you anticipate shooting from, the XS Tritium Vertical stripe post front sight will be the better choice for you. With it, you still have the tritium for night use, the white outline to enhance daylight pickup, and the fact that the sight is a square post that can be used with standard alignment methods for aperture or peep sights. It is the sight I have mounted on my Bushmaster Carbon 15, a multi-purpose rifle, and it works well. If my weapons light goes down, or the Insight Tech ISM-V loses batteries, I have still have the strongly defined front sight, and that's all I need.

XS Sights are absolutely top of the line gear. I don't like the fiber optic color tube-type sights like the TRU-GLO, available in red and green configurations. I am not knocking them for use in plinking or hunting guns – they are a fine product and also a great way to train new shooters, especially kids. Describe sight picture by alignment of color so the new shooter can grasp the concept of sight alignment more quickly. I just don't think that fiber optics, unless they are some part of a Mil-Spec combat optic like Trijicon, belong on guns whose ultimate purpose and use may be to save your life in mortal combat.

I like tritium. I like white. That's all you need on your irons.

Have a Fallback Position

Have some fallback position to go to in case each, any, or all of the weapons systems components (for purposes here, illumination and sighting equipment) fail you. Practice shooting without the weapons light. In a real life encounter, you may not even have the time or thought to turn it on. Maybe you forgot to turn on the master cutoff switch and you have no light, so continue to conduct shooting training in total darkness.

Let's say you are training with your light system, starting a string of fire. The light doesn't go on or fails, and you can't get the light system to operate with one try. Go without it. That's the purpose of my patrol flashlight drill with the pistol where I have shooters drop the light to the ground first when they get their fire command. They have to start firing, regardless of how well or poorly their target is illuminated. I don't want them trying to pick up a light that might be of dubious value when bullets are flying. And if the light is damaged by gunfire you can't use it anyway, so go without it.

This is also where having a backup flashlight light comes in. For failure drills on your optics like the Insight Tech ISMV sight, or an Aimpoint Comp II, III, or IV or some other system, practice with it turned off, shooting through the glass using the backup iron sights. You need to know if you can see through it enough with the red dot off and still get some sort of sight picture with the irons, which is also where the XS big dot will help.

You may have to practice activating the BUIS first, as they are, after all, backup sights and will probably need to be flipped up before shooting.

A failure drill could consist of something like this. Fire 10 shots with the electronic sight on, immediately shut it off, flip up the BUIS (without shooting yourself or anyone else) and fire another 10 rounds. If your accuracy is not acceptable due to the electronic sight mounting position, look at it and see if there is anything that can be improved. If not, practice removing the sight after the first 10 rounds, and fire another 10 without it. You may need to do this in a real life encounter anyway if your optic has been damaged by incoming fire – you may not be able to see through the broken glass. This is another reason why I believe in quick release mounts for any type of battle optic.

If you are using BUIS or a folding front rear/sight combo, practice some emergency return fire drills with the sight folded down. That's right, no sights at all. Figure out what reference point you can use off the gun to at least approximate the location your bullets will strike.

A number of years ago, a good friend of mine, a probation officer from Ohio, Michael Skeen and I went to compete together at our first NRA Action Pistol Shooting Competition. Mike was one of the best shots I knew at the time (until I got better, of course) despite being blind from birth in one eye. I was shooting an excellent Ruger Security Six .357 revolver with adjustable sights, while Mike was shooting a Colt Officers Model .45 ACP with an electroless nickel finish. He had just gotten the gun and was doing very well with it, considering neither he nor I had shot the course of fire before.

After he fired his very first shot string at the running man phase (which he shot well), he announced that the front sight had popped out of its dovetail, and we looked for it for awhile in the grass to no avail. Mike fired a couple more of the stages after shooting the running man phase and actually was beating me. Finally near the end of the competition he was offered the use of an AMT Longslide 6 Hardballer .45. He actually did worse when using it, despite the fine target sights, on the last phases of the course. He said the increased mass of the extra long slide threw him off a bit.

Mike didn't need the sights, and you should practice without them from time to time as well. Some nationally recognized trainers conduct point shooting programs where they actually tape over the sights or remove them entirely so the shooter must shoot without them as reference. The results seem to prove that this can be done, at least at limited and controlled distances.

As final part of failure drills, make sure you can load your AR, clear it, and charge it in total darkness, just like your pistol. That includes malfunction clearing. By limiting use of the flashlight, you avoid illuminating your gun and position, taking out your own dark adaptive vision, and getting distracted from the potential threat. If the AR gets to where you can't clear it and get it up and running again, *dump it*. Get to your pistol and finish the fight.

Check Lights and Sights After Firing

Foundation principle number five: After shooting an AR-15 for any period of time, check your lights, optical sights, and laser sighting systems, especially when using cheap ammunition.

Since it is so scarce/expensive, many individual users and agencies have resorted to using ammo manufactured by China or Russia. Their ammo is packaged in steel cartridge casings, many of which have zinc washing or other types of coating for feeding reliability. Even U.S. manufacturers have been using this format for their practice lines of cartridges to make the ammo affordable, since brass is so expensive and scarce. Hornady was the first U.S. manufacturer whose steel case practice ammo we tried, and it worked fine. Winchester also has a steel case practice line which I have used with some success, so steel cased ammo can function (although I still worry about all that steel on steel banging around in the AR action during firing). The main problem is that the Chinese and Russian stuff shoots dirty. And since most lights are mounted near the business end of the rifle, especially if you are using a light mounted on the front sight frame, it is absolutely bound to get dirty.

When cleaning your AR after firing, make sure the lenses of your flashlights, optical sights, and lasers are not covered with soot from the ammo. Use something designed for cleaning eyeglasses and optics. You don't want to scratch lenses on your lights any more than you do on your optics. Most of the high end lights these days use optical glass for lens construction to enhance the capability of the light system, making the light sharper and brighter than light systems that use polycarbonate lenses, although polycarbonate is tougher than optical glass in most cases.

To make full use of the light power behind that lens, don't clean it with napkins, handkerchiefs, or some other rag, and make sure you are careful when spraying solvents. You may actually want to dismount your light and optic. Bausch and Lomb makes individual eyeglass cleaning packets that contain wet cleaning wipes. They should work fine for the light lenses.

Check all the wiring connections if using remote switching, and make sure that your pressure pad is still secured to the vertical foregrip or rail. Never rely on just the Velcro strips that come with most remote pads to hold them in place. They simply won't stay secured in place under any kind of rough use, like turning the light off and on. I use electrical tape at the top and the bottom of the switch to hold it in place. It stays tight and secure and for this purpose I prefer it over duct tape.

As your final check, make sure the main switch to the light is off when you are done. If you are using a pistol light mounted on the rifle and it has a standard rear toggle switch, you may have to pull the battery cover off the light and remove the batteries. This is a critical step to avoid ruining your light or burning your car to the ground.

Remember to check and change your batteries as often as needed, and check your mounting system as well, especially if your lights mount using thumbscrews or another non-locking arrangement.

Very little other maintenance is needed. Most quality pieces are waterproof and, in the case of LEDs, shockproof.

If you are still using a xenon lamp system, you can keep another bulb available, but you can't change it on the fly when in the middle of an operation. My recommendation: Upgrade to an LED. There is no reason to still use xenon bulbs on a high pressure operating system like an AR-15. That way you don't have to worry about your light going down because your bulb burned out. (You can still worry about it going down because you forgot to change the batteries after long light use.) This is not a big issue for handhelds, since you can carry two handhelds and transition quickly. Here we're talking about weapon-mounted lights. Rifle and pistol lights are not so easy to replace and transition in an emergency.

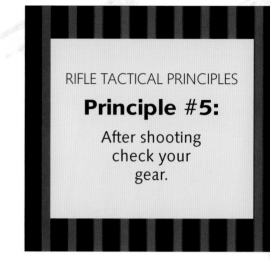

RIFLE TACTICAL PRINCIPLES

Principle #5:

After shooting check your gear.

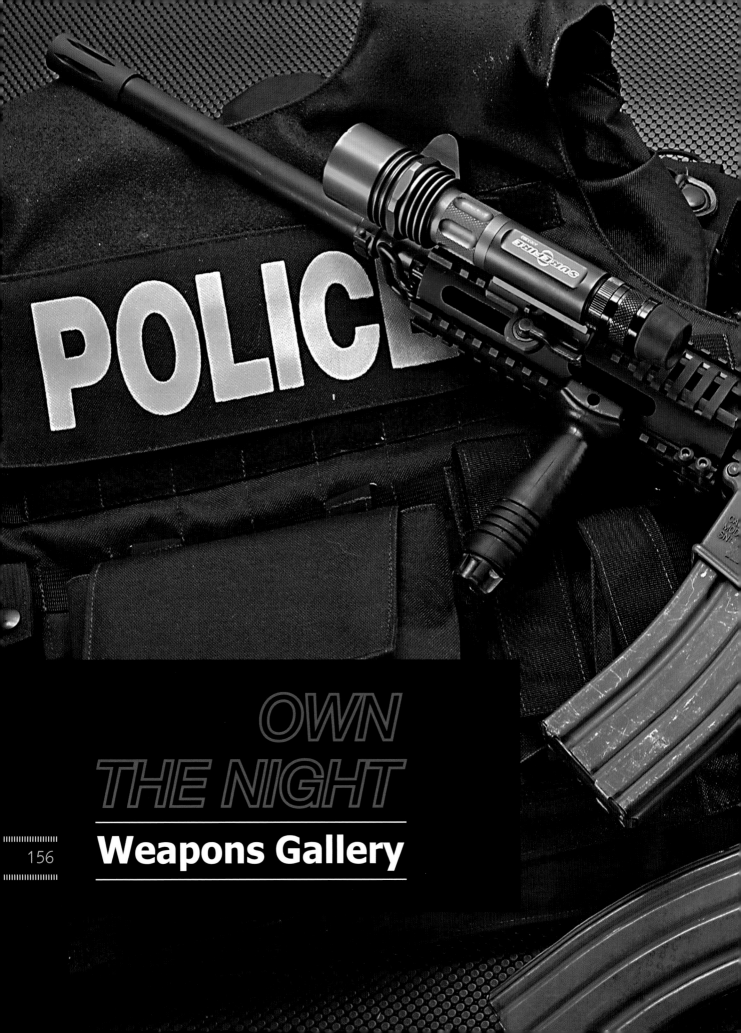

OWN
THE NIGHT

Weapons Gallery

DPMS A-15 in 5.56 with Surefire
Weapon Light, CTC LaserGrip
and full tactical entry rig.

OWN THE NIGHT — WEAPONS GALLERY

Opposite page: Duty-Ready Kimber Stainless Pro Tactical Light Rail II with a Surefire X200 mounted.

Right: Off Duty-Ready Kimber Ultra Covert II with digital camo and Crimson Trace grips.

CTC Combat Trio – Beretta 92 with Crimson Trace laser grips, Smith & Wesson 1911 with Crimson Trace laser grips and AR-15 with CTC Vertical Fore Grip.

Off Duty-Civilian defensive array, Kimber full-size (oppositie page), and Kimber Compact .45 ACP 1911 Pistol (right), Kimber Pepper Blasters, Surefire X300 combat light, and CRKT folding knife.

OWN THE NIGHT – WEAPONS GALLERY

Outstanding combo, Springfield XD full-size in 9mm with Surefire X300 pistol light, Crimson Trace LaserGrips and KA-BAR Combat TDI knife.

OWN THE NIGHT – WEAPONS GALLERY

Different pistols with various Crimson Trace designs– CTC grips for Glock mount on trigger housing pin at rear of frame, SIG 239 mounts off grip screw, SIG Pro mounts off frame pins.

168

Opposite page: A Pair of HK P2000 compact pistols and Streamlight TLR2 with laser module.

Above: Kimber Tactical Entry pistol with Surefire X400 light and laser module.

Opposite page: Battle-ready Beretta 92 with Crimson Trace LaserGrips, M4 A2 carbine with fixed handle and Crimson Trace sight designed for mounting off carrying handle.

Above: Glock 17 9mm in desert tan frame and Crimson Trace LaserGrips.

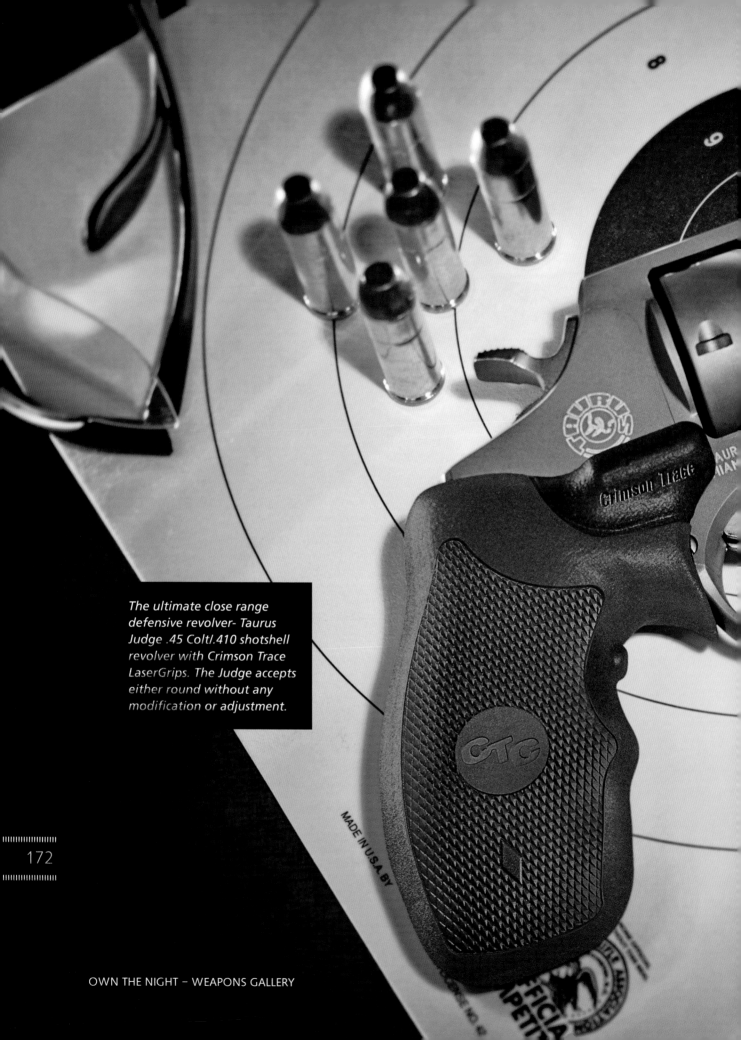

The ultimate close range defensive revolver- Taurus Judge .45 Colt/.410 shotshell revolver with Crimson Trace LaserGrips. The Judge accepts either round without any modification or adjustment.

OWN THE NIGHT – WEAPONS GALLERY

Above: Smith & Wesson CTC factory equipped 1911 pistols and Airweight .38 Special revolver.

Opposite page: Top- Smith and Wesson - M&P 9C Compact, 9mm with Insight X2 tactical light. Bottom- Nighthawk Custom Tactical 1911, Enforcer in desert tan with Insight M3X Tactical Illuminator.

OWN THE NIGHT – WEAPONS GALLERY

Crimson Trace's newest vertical foregrip and weaponlight combo – the MVF - 515.

A pair of excellent Surefire rail-mounted weapon lights on AR-15 rails - never leave the light control cable dangling as shown. Remember to secure it properly with electrical tape.

OWN THE NIGHT – WEAPONS GALLERY

OWN THE NIGHT – PART III

OWN THE NIGHT

Part III:
Laser Lighting Systems

181

Laser Lighting Systems

T he other component of owning the night, besides seeing, is targeting the bad things that can hurt you. One of the best ways to do that – available to civilians, law enforcement, and the military alike – is through the use of auxiliary laser sighting systems.

Lasers aren't just for Terminators anymore. However, laser sighting technology has been slow to gain acceptance in law enforcement circles. The reasons? Lasers, outside of their use in speed measuring devices, have been considered merely as interesting toys when applied to sighting systems for cops.

Officer with a .40 caliber Smith and Wesson M&P and Crimson Trace Lasergrip activated.

A litany of complaints about laser sights for law enforcement have slowed, and continue to slow, their acceptance as a standard issue tool for practical use on the street. These complaints come primarily from administrators behind desks at the station, who usually no longer come out on the street to experience what is really going on. If they do come out, they are often afraid to function fully as a cop, so they never get an idea what it's really like to work with the tools that they issue to others. They also have no idea what tools might really be useful and beneficial for those who are doing the dirty work. The list of objections looks something like this:

- Lasers are toys, they really don't help.
- Lasers are too expensive for the benefit received.
- Officers will become laser dependent. Those lasers will go down when needed most and the officers won't be able to hit what they are shooting at.
- Lasers draw incoming fire to your location.
- If multiple officers are using lasers and are all covering a suspect, how do you tell which dot is yours?
- If we get lasers, we will have to get new holsters to go with them.

"Lasers are toys."
||||||||||||||||||||||||||||||||||||||||||||||||||||||||||||||||||||||||||||||||||||

Lasers sights are not toys. They may have been at one time. The little laser pointers you can buy at the truck stop on key rings are toys, but the laser sighting systems you would put on a combat weapon are of the highest quality and designed for serious use. They are effective when encountering dangerous suspects, and do several important things when applied to a threatening human target.

First, they let that human target know that they are a target. That dot, centered on their chest or forehead, tells them without question where the bullet is going. This has resulted in many people giving up – I have experienced this firsthand – without the officer having to fire a shot. It is very disconcerting to have that red dot appear on your body, even with an unloaded or simulated weapon. Isn't it preferable to get a suspect to surrender rather than having to shoot or tase them?

The second benefit is that the officer knows that they are targeting properly and will hit what they are aiming at. They may wait for just a split second longer before pulling the trigger because they have targeted with confidence, allowing the suspect one final chance to surrender.

The third benefit is that the officer, when using a laser, is able to shift their focus off the rear and front sights of their weapon. This allows them to see the offender's face and hands. The officer can make positive identification of what they might be holding or what they might be thinking about doing, while still maintaining a target hold.

There is no comparison between laser sights and iron sights, especially on a pistol, for that kind of observational ability. Is that a cell phone in the suspect's hand or a gun? An officer using a laser may be able to see that it is a cell phone before they have to pull the trigger, and avoid shooting an unarmed person.

What if an officer is knocked down, and in a weird one-hand position on the ground, and they are able to

X26 Taser shown fully charged and ready to fire with LED illumination and laser sight active. The laser on the Taser system has proven to be a real attention getter. Laser is positioned between the LED diodes, and is activated automatically with the right setting on the Taser.

sight using their laser when they shouldn't or couldn't use the iron sights in time, and they shoot the suspect and stop them before they themselves can be shot or killed? Do these circumstances sound like anything that you would use a toy for? It sounds to me like these situations are the result of employing a powerful supplemental sighting tool, not a toy.

At the 727 Counter-Terror Training Unit, we found that laser sights really excel in rapidly-moving, close quarter battle situations where there is a need to identify friend from foe with people packed in tight spaces. You operate much more effectively in those situations, especially where lighting is dim, when using a laser sight. The dot sweeps across passengers with your eyes, as you rapidly move down aisles to secure the plane (or school or passenger bus or passenger train). You clearly identify the folks you are dealing with, while still ensuring that you will hit what you shoot at.

"Lasers are too expensive."

Considering the consequences of the circumstances described in these pages, it is easy to conclude that lasers are not too ex-

Author shown in downed position with Glock 32 with Blackhawk Xiphos pistol light and Crimson Trace Lasergrips. The laser allows a person in distress to acquire the target and fire without getting a picture with the iron sights.

pensive for the benefit derived from them. For multiple officer purchase, most weapons systems, lasers like those from Crimson Trace (the best on the market), are priced in the $250 range or less. Yes, that does add up to significant money if you have a large agency, but how much does it cost when you shoot someone, even without a lawsuit? What is the amount of dollars and value lost when an officer is shot? Considering those costs, $250 looks like a pretty good investment.

"Lasers draw incoming fire."

Improperly used pistol, rifle, or handheld lights are much more likely to draw incoming fire than lasers. In fact, I can't think of a single advertisement for a laser sighting system where they show how tough their laser sights are when then take a bullet – like the light ads show. Laser sights simply project too narrow a beam, from too small a diode source, for too short a time, to draw fire.

"Officers will become laser dependent."

Next objection: "Officers will become laser dependent. Those lasers will go down when needed most and the officers won't be able to hit what they are shooting at."

The essence of this objection is simply a training issue. Have your officers qualify with and without lasers during your qualification course. That way they will practice using all of their tools. Practice a failure drill, as well as a daylight operation drill, since the red lasers are not easily seen in bright sunlight.

As far as lasers breaking down, these new systems and latest generation devices are as reliable as flashlights and are highly durable. Breakage is not common.

"How do you tell which dot is yours?"

First point: If you have four officers with lasers pointed on a suspect and you look at the suspect and see four dots nicely centered on the torso, who cares whose dot is whose? All are going to result in hits unless the shots are jerked off target, which can happen with or without lasers.

Second point: You can tell your dot from the others. I learned this in a training class put on by Crimson Trace. We had four to six officers put their lasers on a target. Because you are standing behind your own individual laser beam, what looks confusing to a bystander is not confusing to you. Based on your own variations in movement, you can readily tell which laser dot is yours, no question. Try this at a range yourself. It is simply not an issue.

"We'll have to buy new holsters."

Quad team using lasers makes entry into a storage area (opposite page). Finding a suspect, they illuminate him with their active lasers, three red, one green. All dots are very easy to distinguish.

Final objection: We will have to buy new holsters to go with the lasers. This is only a partially valid argument, and depends on the system you use. If you buy a rail mounted laser, you will likely need a new duty holster. Also, if you have holsters for pistol mounted flashlights, and decide to upgrade the light to a laser light combo, because it is larger you will probably need a new holster. If you buy the huge Glock branded pistol light or laser light combo, good luck in finding a holster at all.

The single best answer to the holster issue is to equip your pistol with Crimson Trace Laser Grips and a separate dedicated pistol light, if you must mount one. In most cases, Crimson Trace requires no change in holsters, and is now made to accommodate nearly every duty pistol out there, even the new Smith and Wesson M&P, in an unobtrusive manner.

There are a lot of laser and light combos out there for pistols, but they just start getting too bulky. Also, if one part breaks you lose the whole thing to repairs. There also gets to be too many switches and gizmos there. Crimson Trace is simple to operate with momentary hand or finger pressure depending on the grip model (unlike most other manufacturers) and it allows you to maintain a more solid grip on your pistol, since you won't have multiple fingers up front pressing on various buttons operating momentary lights, turning lasers on and off, turning lights on to the constant-on position etc. This is *the* setup for pistols.

187

Laser Systems: Available Options

Let's look at some of the latest laser technology on the market.

Crimson Trace

Crimson Trace Company (CTC), the premier name in pistol laser sighting systems and developer of the Lasergrip, continues to produce new models for popular pistols and long guns. They are converting their standard pistol grips over to Mil-Spec configuration. The first Mil-Specs were for the Beretta 92 service pistol, and the progress continues.

I received the newest version of grips for 1911 pistols, which I mounted on my Kimber Custom Eclipse 10mm pistol. The original 1911 Lasergrip that I tried nearly 10 years ago featured two sepa-

189

rate grip panels. The activation pad, light, and components were on the right side of the pistol, and it was designed to operate by pressure from the middle to rear portion of the right fingers. It wasn't the easiest switch position to use but it worked with a little practice. Their newest version features grips attached by a centerpiece that contains the switch, which is now positioned on the frontstrap of the frame. Pressure from the middle finger operates it now.

Also included was one of the newest versions of Lasergips, (this one is not really a "grip") for the new Ruger .380 LCP, the Laser-guard. This unit fits from the rear of the trigger guard where the pressure switch sits on a small part of the frontstrap forward to the laser module which is situated directly in front of the triggerguard. This centers the laser directly under the bore, which eliminates the windage offset effect of the laser module on standard grips.

CHAPTER 8: LASER SYSTEMS: AVAILABLE OPTIONS

If there is any downside to CTC, this is it. For windage, the laser has to be dialed in at the distance you desire, from right to left to where it will intersect the bullets flight path and match the iron or scope sight alignment. This has to be done with elevation as well, but that is true of all laser sights. The windage is only an issue for CTC or any other laser mounted offset to the bore.

Crimson Trace also plans several new Laserguard models for many of the smaller and concealable polymer pistols available on the market today. The Laserguard family includes a master cut off switch which, while featured on most models, was not a part of the Glock series of Lasergrips. CTC now includes Laserguard models for the Kel-Tec P3AT and P32 (Model LG-430), the Kel-Tec PF-9 (Model LG-435), the Glock 26/36 (Model LG-436), the Kahr PM9/40, P9/40, CW9/40 (Model LG-437), and the Ruger LCP (Model LG-431).

192

Adjusting Laser Sights

When you adjust laser sights, the direction to move the sight so that it moves the shot to the correct target location is *opposite* that of traditional iron sights or scope sights. Traditional sights/scopes operate in two focal planes, where a laser dot is in a single plane.

With traditional dual focal plane sights, you move the sights in the direction you want the shots to move. If the shots need to come left, move the rear sight left.

With lasers, you move the dot the opposite direction to where you want the shots to go. In other words, if you need to move the shots fired off a laser sight to the left, you move the sight direction right. Moving left would just move the sights further to the right. If the shots need to go up, you need to move the laser dot down. This is because of the single focal plane of the dot. You are aligning only one part of the gun – the point from where the beam emanates – and not a front and rear sight together.

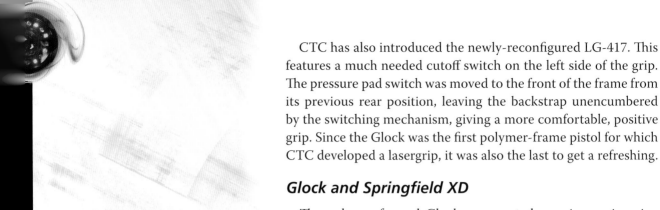

CTC has also introduced the newly-reconfigured LG-417. This features a much needed cutoff switch on the left side of the grip. The pressure pad switch was moved to the front of the frame from its previous rear position, leaving the backstrap unencumbered by the switching mechanism, giving a more comfortable, positive grip. Since the Glock was the first polymer-frame pistol for which CTC developed a lasergrip, it was also the last to get a refreshing.

Glock and Springfield XD

The polymer-framed Glock represented a major engineering problem for CTC, as their initial grip designs all centered around pistols with removable grips. Then along came the popular Glock, with a one piece frame that was not easily modified.

The first solution was not the best, but it was the only game in town. The problem was that it required permanent factory modification of the pistol, thus voiding the factory warranty. They attached a laser diode to the front of the trigger guard and ran wiring through the inside of the hollow guard, into the frame, and installed a pressure button from inside the grip to the outside by drilling a hole through the frontstrap. It worked, but it was not popular. Outside of CTC displays at trade shows, I never saw a Glock thus equipped.

Eventually the CTC developed the pop-on, rear button activated grip for the Glock and it worked well. It just lacked a master cutoff switch.

When the polymer-framed Springfield XD became popular, CTC went to work to accommodate that model. The issue with developing a CTC grip for the XD like the one used for Glock was the fact that the XD has a grip safety located right where the rear pressure switch for the Glock is positioned. So that was a no-go. The engineering team soon revamped the design for the XD, moving the pressure switch to the front of the frame and leaving the backstrap area open. In that design they also installed a master cutoff switch. That design was adapted for the Glock series. The new system is a lot like the original CTC Glock concept in terms of setup, without requiring permanent modification to the pistol.

So far, the new "grips" are available only for the 17, 19, 22 and 23, and I would assume for the 31 and 32 as well since the frame is exactly the same size. It looks to me like CTC has perfected its own design for the Glock series at last. The larger frame sizes, such as the .45 Gap and .45 ACP pistols, will undoubtedly have the new model lasergrips available in the near future.

AR-15

Crimson Trace also makes models for the AR-15. On models that accommodate fixed carry handle ARs, the laser element itself runs up the left side of the receiver so it's equal in height to the rear sight and in the same sighting plane.

In the VF-302, for flattop ARs where the sighting plane is much lower, the laser element is embedded in the vertical foregrip like the standard Crimson Trace Lasergrip.

Brand new for 2009 is the MVF-515 (Modular Vertical Foregrip). The MVF-515 is a generational jump ahead of the VF-302 and it is also CTC's first foray into the tactical lighting field. This new vertical foregrip, which mounts on a MIL-STD 1913 rail system, contains not only the laser of the VF-302, but a 150 to 200-lumen LED flashlight. The adjustment for the power level is the lens bezel, which is given a ¼ turn to select the power option. The big news about this system is that Crimson Trace is the first out of the gate that with an LED system that is not only in the 150 lumen range,

which is in itself a big leap forward, but they have raised the bar to 200 lumens for a light of this size.

One of the best things about the VF-302 and MVF-515 laser foregrip systems is that there are no wires dangling. There is no separate pressure pad switch that has to be taped on. As much as I like (or liked) PentagonLight's Stealth Assault Light system with its integral laser, the light had to be activated by the remote switch while the support hand thumb operated a momentary switch located on the rear of the laser diode element. CTC's vertical foregrips, like the Surefire 900A, keep the area clean and clear of external wiring.

In addition to the fact that the light is incredibly bright and may remove any advantage that xenon lamps still have over LEDs (at least in a light of this size), CTC also added a strobe mode for the LED. Both the laser and the light are powered by a pair of lithium 123 batteries, which reduces any logistical concern about needed to keep spare CR1032 watch calculator batteries around for the laser.

The light has a claimed operational burn time of two hours, which I would assume would be at the 150-lumen setting, while the laser will run for 40 hours, which I would also assume means without any drain from the light itself.

As currently configured, the laser pressure panel is on the left side of the grip, while the light pressure panel is on the right. The modularity of this grip means that it can be taken apart rather eas-

ily (while still being very durable) and separated into the laser half and the tactical light half. There is an infrared laser option available for military and law enforcement users. If other options, like a green laser, became available in the future, they could easily be popped right in to the existing setup.

The MVF-515's significance cannot be overstated. I believe in keeping a clean configuration for the AR-15, and the MVF-515 certainly does that. If you are a believer in lasers and are setting out to configure an AR for combative purposes, or you want to reconfigure your old AR and upgrade it, I would highly suggest the MVF-515 as your light/laser option. In any event, when looking for a CTC laser for your AR, make sure you purchase the right model, as the difference in the distance from the laser element to the sighting plane for each model is significant.

Ruger

Finally, CTC has partnered with Ruger Firearms on the introduction of their LCR (Lightweight Compact Revolver), Ruger's first foray into the lightweight revolver field. While Lasergrips have been available for the Ruger SP101 for some time, the SP101 hasn't been at the top of the hit parade as far as concealed carry revolvers go. It is an old style Ruger, reliable and very solid, with its forged all stainless steel construction. On the market for a long

time, the exposed hammer SP101 really never came to the top of the list as a pocket carry gun.

Enter the 5-shot LCR in .38 Special +P. The LCR features a polymer grip frame, which houses the fire control mechanism and attaches to the working frame of the gun. It is a forged aerospace aluminum frame that Ruger "synergistically" hard coats. This is the component that houses the cylinder and barrel and is the real support for the actual firing of the cartridges. Weighing in at 13.5 ounces, this design represents what I call the new Ruger line, and was launched right out of the gate with CTC grips as an important component of the gun as a defensive weapons system.

Crimson Trace continues to hold the edge in laser sighting systems due to their easily accessed, momentary-on switch system, innovative designs, and adaptability to almost any quality firearm on the market.

Officer takes aim with a Smith and Wesson .40 M&P equipped with Surefire pistol light and Laserlyte FSL attached to the rail.

199

Kel-Tec P9S with Laserlyte FSL attached.

Laserlyte

Laserlyte offers a number of laser products. The original Universal Pistol Laser Sighting system is a very good buy for those in the home defense market wanting to equip a gun with laser sighting at a very reasonable price.

New for 2008 is their Kryptonyte Laser bore sighting system, which uses an extremely bright, green iridium laser that works out to 25 yards in daylight. In overcast or shadow conditions it is visible to 100 yards or more and is superior to red laser systems. If you have never seen a green laser, they are very impressive. Using one in a bore sighter is an outstanding idea, and I look forward to working with this product.

Laserlyte's new FSL ultra compact laser sighting system offers a universal setup for anything with a Picatinny rail. It features a left side activation switch (constant-on, no momentary feature) and an attachable bottom rail segment that allows a tactical light to be mounted directly to the laser module itself.

For testing, I mounted the FSL on a Kel-Tec P9S, which has a single rail notch molded into the front of its very small frame. The rail mounts to the pistol via a small slotted thumbscrew that locks it in tightly. With the FSL mounted on a micro pistol like the Kel-Tec, it takes some readjustment of your hand position to activate the switch, and I find it works best using (I can't believe I am saying this) a thumb-forward grip, with the tip of the left thumb extended forward to activate it. The hand position is tight due to the tiny size of the Kel-Tec.

Mounting the FSL on a more standard-sized Glock 32, I found I could maintain more of a standard shooting grip and activate the laser with my left index fingertip.

The Bushmaster Carbon 15 with Laserlyte FSL mounted on Streamlight railed vertical forend ultra light. Tactical light is the Insight Inforce carbon fiber light. This is a an ideal setup for a female or small statured shooter due to its light weight.

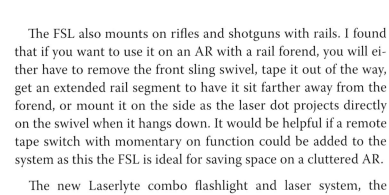

The FSL also mounts on rifles and shotguns with rails. I found that if you want to use it on an AR with a rail forend, you will either have to remove the front sling swivel, tape it out of the way, get an extended rail segment to have it sit farther away from the forend, or mount it on the side as the laser dot projects directly on the swivel when it hangs down. It would be helpful if a remote tape switch with momentary on function could be added to the system as this the FSL is ideal for saving space on a cluttered AR.

The new Laserlyte combo flashlight and laser system, the WHYTE LYTE FLASHLYTE WL-1, is a 25-lumen pistol light that runs on four A76 watch batteries that power three separate white LEDs. This tiny light is half the size of most other pistol lights and will fit all subcompact rail pistols by itself or mounted on the FSL. The trade-off here is the light output, and the company knows it, telling you in its literature that there is just enough light "to see and target in a room or garage." I always appreciate honesty.

This light is really for illumination and identification, not target incapacitation, and it is designed to fit on very small pistols like the Kel-Tec, so it covers a niche market. I would definitely want to back up this light with a larger hand held.

Another problem is bulk, believe it or not. When you do stack it with the FSL you get a system that hangs down below the triggerguard, even on a full size pistol like a Glock. This is just a little too much for me, and if I was going to stack something on the FSL, it would be a more powerful light. I like the concept of the tiny size of

the FLASHLYTE, but would like to see it with a little more "oomph" in the lumen department before I consider it for duty use.

Insight Technology

||||||||||||||||||||||||||||||||||||||||||||||||||||||||||||||||||||||||

There is another laser sighting system available from Insight Technology, the ISM-V. While optical sights are not really the primary focus of this book, the ISM-V as a red-dot sight system bears inclusion and needs a more detailed, separate description as it is in a separate category of sighting system.

Insight's Integrated Sighting Module-Visible (Spectrum) – the ISM-V – is a combined red dot and laser sighting system. An infrared version is available for military/special ops units. A compact system, with an appearance much like a mini-camcorder, the housing appears to be constructed of the same type of rugged fiberglass that is used in the well known heavy duty Pelican cases system, and should provide long service life without a hint of corrosion. This also keeps the unit lightweight. The entire unit is powered by a supplied Lithium 123 battery.

In addition to the red dot sight optic, the housing also contains a visible spectrum red laser that can be activated directly off the housing, or with a supplied remote cabled pressure switch, which is a necessity unless you plan on leaving the laser on during your operation. The main off and on control knob, easily accessed, has four settings: "O" for Off, "P" for program, which as the manual states, is reserved for future development, "RD" for Red Dot optic only, and VA for visible aim, which allows for use of both the laser and the red dot.

The separate, soft rubber large laser activation button, located on the left side of the housing (from the sighting end), activates the laser momentary on with one press, continuous on with a double tap. The remote switch does the same thing, but allows for much more convenient operation. If fact, I would find it very difficult, if not impossible, to run the laser in actual shooting use without the remote pressure pad switch. The switch clicks into place firmly, but could be pulled free if caught on something during normal slinging of the weapon.

Also note that the rubber cover for the switch port is small and not attached, and may be easily lost (which I almost did while unpacking the system on my couch).

The red dot sight, activated by pressing and holding for approximately two seconds the plus and minus dot intensity buttons located on top of the unit, has an infinite adjustment range rather than using clicks.

The rear objective field of view (the part you are sighting through) measures 7/8-inch in diameter, as compared to the full inch wide objective on an Aimpoint Comp II.

Attachment of the unit is accomplished via the standard Picatinny rail system and is locked and held in place via a slotted thumb screw. I don't like this arrangement anywhere near as well as I do an ARMS or SIRS locking type system or the locking system on the Aimpoint Comp II. It will loosen over time and under full automatic fire. However since few law enforcement and civilian users engage in extended full-auto fire, it is certainly less of an issue for them.

The ISM-V represents a very interesting departure from the stand alone red dot optic sight. The infrared laser version would prove very useful when operating with night vision gear.

Laser Devices

Laser Devices is another company making high-end laser systems for military and law enforcement end users. An interesting concept that they are marketing is the EOLAD laser and holographic weapon sight.

In a cooperative venture with EOTECH sighting system, the EOLAD (EOtech and Laser Aiming Device) is a combo device much like Insight Technologies' ISM-V, except in a more compact format.

The EOTECH is available in a variety of configurations, utilizing a lower power visible-read laser, an infrared pointer/illuminator for use with NV equipment, and a new high-output green laser that gives up to 20 times the visibility of a red laser. When the lasers are combined with the infrared illuminators, they are stacked over and under like a shotgun. Like the ISM-V, the EOLADS are operable with remote cable switches.

Laser Devices also makes the DBAL-A2 (Dual Beam Aiming Laser Advanced-high power) combo laser system-with choices of red, green, and infrared illuminators and aimers. This system, clearly designed for high end military and tactical team users, has no optical sighing system and is designed to be mounted on the AR quad rail.

In addition, the ITAL-A and OTAL-A (Inline and Offset Tactical Aiming Lasers-Advanced), a smaller single function unit, are available in green, red, or infrared. These units have the provision and availability of mounting a Docter micro red dot sight on top of your M4.

The ITAL-A is designed for flat top ARs devoid of fixed sights. The OTAL is designed for ARs with a standard fixed front sight, and the laser beam projects just to the left of the front sight so the beam is not obscured.

Laser Devices has a number of other AR systems available which are pretty standard systems. Interesting are their laser sights and

CHAPTER 8: LASER SYSTEMS: AVAILABLE OPTIONS

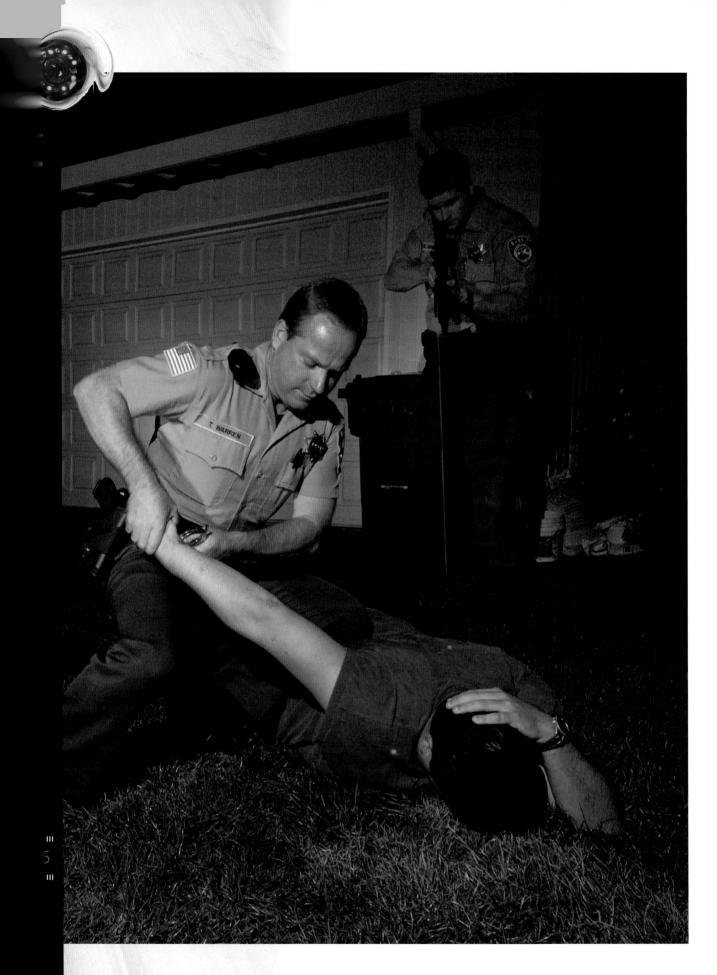

mounts for the HKMP5 and G3 submachine guns. The MP5, once the darling of high end tactical teams and operators, was once available for a limited time in .40 Smith and Wesson and what I thought would have been the ultimate SMG caliber, the 10mm. Anyway, the MP came out at a time well before the Picatinny rail systems and actually relied on iron sights. When the 5.56mm caught on as the ultimate CQB cartridge with the introduction of quality expandable bullet rounds like the Hornady Tap, the MP5 fell into disfavor.

Further complicating the problem is the complexity of the MP5 and its operating system. While highly reliable, it is clearly not set up in the same modular fashion as an AR-15. The proprietary German parts also caused a problem, and there are no critical aftermarket components for the MP5. HK is sometimes difficult to get parts from. One of our area SWAT teams uses HK pistols for their operators due to their reliability and operating system. However, there have been, in the past, problems getting parts. It is now rare indeed to find teams in our area at least, still using the MP5 as a primary entry gun.

All that being said, it is one of the great guns of all time, but succumbed to less expensive, competing designs. It is rare to find a company producing a laser sighting system for a weapons system that has become somewhat passé. That doesn't mean that the MP still isn't in use around the world and it is still for sale in five basic variations from HK, its just we aren't using it over here as much.

The good folks at Laser Devices make three different systems for the MP5. The laser systems are the MP5K Foregrip Laser, where the laser mounts below the barrel, and the MP5 single and dual beam lasers that mount just below the front sight above the barrel. This system is operated by remote pressure switch, with the foregrip laser has an actuator button on the front. Options for the MP5 systems are limited to the red laser, and infrared laser and illuminator.

In addition to the MP5 system and all the rifle mounted options, Laser Devices markets the MOLAD (Multi Operational Laser Aiming Device) designed for mounting on pistols. A rather large unit that wont find a home in a lot of current duty holsters due to its size, the MOLAD features a 95-lumen xenon tactical light (much larger in size that the newest Streamlight, Surefire, and Insight Technology generation lights). The light is mounted with the choice of red laser, IR Pointer/IR illuminator, or IR illuminator.

If the MOLAD is too large, or you don't need all the options, there is the BLAST 2 laser and tactical light combo. With a choice of a 95-lumen xenon bulb or a 150-lumen LED lamp, the BLAST 2 is much smaller than the MOLAD, but still represents a larger light system than the aforementioned ultra compacts.

All the Laser Devices equipment is top notch quality, and most is built to Mil-Spec.

Laser Uses, Tactics, & Deployment

Laser Applications

There are applications for lasers other than as weapons sights.

Training and diagnosis

A great use for lasers is for diagnosing shooter flinch or trigger jerk. It is sometimes hard to see if a shooter is yanking on the trigger, rather than smoothly bringing it straight back. You can certainly guess by the fall of shots, but it can be made easier to detect by the shooter, trainer, and onlookers through the use of the laser.

The dot drops low out of sight when the trigger is mashed and jerked, and then is brought back up on

target for the next shot. The dot should move up slightly with recoil above its sighting position when the trigger is pulled properly.

This side benefit of a laser sight is particularly useful if you are using a system of partner coaching, where the coach may not be all that experienced in the nuances of accurate shooting. They certainly can see the dot moving down and back up, and clue in the shooter that they are flinching or jerking the trigger. You don't need a special system for this training and correction, the weapons laser sight on your pistol or rifle will work just fine, and can be used as an informal part of the shooting training.

Officer takes aim with his AR using a JTEC green laser mounted on the rail of his AR-15.

Another training facet is for dry fire handgun training via the Beamhit Electronic Laser Target System, which is now offered by the MPRI company. Beamhit, which is used by civilian, military, and law enforcement shooters and competitors, has advanced well beyond a simple system with electronic target. The Beamhit 190 is now a self contained system with the target in a plastic case, and is easily transported and stored. It hooks into any Windows-based computer system for operation and scoring purposes.

The Beamhit uses a laser insert for your pistol or revolver that is operated off the vibrations from the firing pin hitting the plastic portion of the insert, triggering a laser shot. The original model I have shows the effects of the advances in technology, as the laser module itself that protrudes out of the bore is too large to allow for holstering of the pistol. The new models, with the more advanced laser, allow for full holstering of the pistol so more advanced shooters can practice drawing and shooting.

When the laser fires and hits the electronic target, the laser flash shows up on the target and gives visible feedback on where the shot impacted the target. The shot is also registered in the computer (that you provide) along with total elapsed time, time between shots, and a visible target display on the screen that shows the cumulative shots in a running tally. A hard copy printout of the target, times and scores can then be generated.

This system, at its lowest level, is designed to train new shooters in basic trigger management skills. It can also help a shooter to enhance their skills by precise trigger management practice through safe dry fire training that is documentable and repeatable.

The Beamhit 190 system is a very reasonably priced product at its basic level, and allows for some very precise and safe, indoor dry fire training. Dry firing can be boring for some, at least over extended periods of time, but dry fire practice is one of the best ways to maintain proficiency. The Beamhit 190 is a great way to conduct that practice, and it does one thing that standard dry fire practice can't: It documents your progress.

Laser bore sighting

Another non-combat laser use is manufactured by the weapon sight maker, Laserlyte. It is their Krytonyte Green Laser Bore Sighter System.

Laser bore sighting is not a new concept. A bore-diameter rod with laser sighting head is inserted into the bore of a pistol, rifle, or shotgun. The laser dot is then placed on the target at the distance you want the bullet to impact, and the sight, scope, or adjustable iron sight is adjusted to coincide with the laser dot. The bullets should impact pretty near the point of aim, with only some minor adjustments needed while firing.

in these conditions within 15 feet.

Considering the fact that most police shootings happen in dark or dimly lit conditions, this hasn't been a huge disadvantage to the traditional red systems, but it is a limiter.

erate, rather than a couple of CR2032 or smaller watch and calculator batteries. It is not the laser portion itself that is large, it is the power supply.

Lasermax has produced a much smaller green laser system that uses a much

smaller battery back. I have no idea how long the batteries last in the Lasermax system, or its brightness level when compared to a larger green like Viridian, but it does show that the technology is shrinking the overall size.

One other potential problem area for green is that, due to the different way that the beam is produced, they apparently don't operate quite as well in cold weather. Green lasers are also more expensive right now than red ones, at least $100 more in similar systems per copy. And with the exception of perhaps Lasermax, very specialized holsters, large and ungainly, are needed to accommodate the green laser-mounted weapon. This makes green laser technology only a rifle mounted proposition for law enforcement use. In fact, it is really not ready for civilian use outside of the home defense pistol, as there is no concealed carry option for a pistol-mounted laser other than in some type of carry bag. It is going to be a while before this new technology is good to go in our duty rigs and concealed carry holsters.

These issues will likely be short lived. If you recall, originally red lasers were huge, required and drained huge supplies of batteries, were not able to be holster carried, and were cold sensitive. The visibility advantage of green laser technology cannot be denied. In two to three years from this writing, green lasers will likely be the color of choice and replace the red dot applications in all but the least expensive systems.

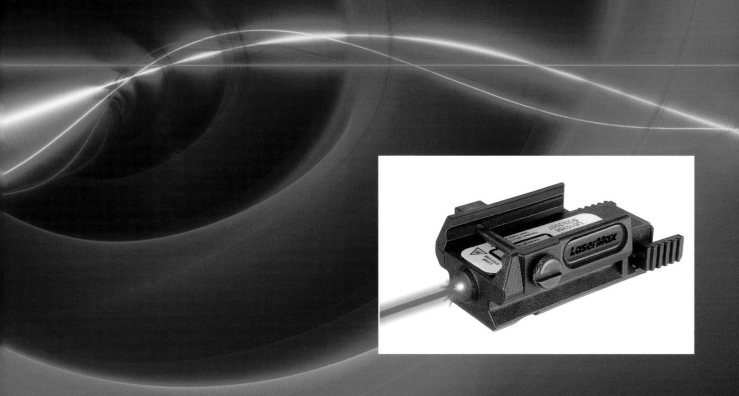

The only problem is that the laser dots have been red, and that means that the distance that you could sight in with outdoors was limited by sunlight. Red laser dots rapidly wash out in sunlight. You had to either boresight in at a range that was close enough to see the dot, or you had to wait until there was an overcast day or shoot at dusk.

Enter the Green Laser. Laserlyte has harnessed green laser technology for the Kryptonyte Bore Sighter. Green is incredibly visible in all lighting conditions, which means that you can use Laserlyte's system at any time or any reasonable distance for sighting in. For rifles that usually means 100 yards or less.

Laserlytes bore sighter now makes the use of lasers practical for this purpose. Laser Devices is also marketing a similar bore sighting system.

Auxiliary Sighting

I have long been a proponent of auxiliary laser sighting systems. I say "auxiliary" because while it is used primarily, it should not be relied on as the primary sight on the weapon. That job goes always to the iron sights. Lasers and other electronic sights can break and run out of battery power (eventually) in the middle of the gun fight. The switch can be in the "off" position when you needed it "on." The irons should always be there. If they have been destroyed or broken, then it's probably time to find a new gun, and maybe some additional friends to help you out of your situation. This is true whether your electronics are on a pistol, rifle, or shotgun

Tactics and Deployment
||||||||||||||||||||||||||||||||||||||||||||||||||||||||||||||||||||||||||||

Laser sights, as mentioned, are auxiliary sighting equipment. Although they do not replace iron sights, they are often used as the primary sighting system. It is the natural thing to do where lighting is limited – either low level late afternoon light outside, or standard lighting conditions or less inside with the action moving quickly.

In those situations, nothing is faster in allowing you to *illuminate* the suspected target (you see the red dot in the appropriate location on the bad guy), *identify* the threat (your vision focuses in the same plane, and you can clearly see what the suspect has in their hand or the expression on their face), and then, if necessary, *incapacitate* (shoot them, or deploy the Taser Cartridge if that's the source of the laser dot shining on them) if they do not comply with your demands.

These are the same operational principles as those used with the tactical lights, just a slightly different application. I guess when

A Laser Moment

One night while driving home, I was startled by what appeared to be a red laser light flash across my rearview mirror and through my car. After my initial "what the hell…" reaction, I looked in the mirror for the laser again, and noticed that it emanated from a ragged out 1960's Ford Econoline Van. I also saw that it was being pointed across other cars on the freeway as they were driving.

Fearing that this vehicle had a gun attached to the laser light. I knew I had to report the vehicle and intended to follow it until I got some marked local police vehicles to stop it. I called in on my then new-fangled cell phone and got the 911 operator, and started explaining what I had.

I started slowing down to let the perpetrator go around me so I could get his license number. Well, he was having none of that, and began to slow down so I could not get behind him. I slowed, then he slowed, and the next thing I knew we were stopped in the middle of I-70 during late, dark rush hour. He started to get out of the van with a crazed look on his face. I grabbed my S&W 638 (with CTC grips) and got out to meet him.

As he rounded the back of my car he was reaching under his shirt. At that point I lit him up with the laser and said "STOP"! He saw my laser dot on his white shirt in the chest area. His eyes got big and he pulled out . . . an empty hand! He said, "What, are you going to shoot me?" I said something like, "If I have to."

He got back into the van and took off, heading east on the freeway. I got back in my car and pursued, er followed, him, using that cell phone thing. He exited and head out into the country. I got in touch with that county's sheriff's office, who vectored in two cruisers to our location. They got him stopped and found a laser pointer in his car.

They took a report, and their misguided county prosecutor didn't charge him with anything, not even disorderly conduct. This was back when there was a laser pointer issue and talk of banning civilian sales of laser pointers or laser sights. Here was a genuine misuse, he could have caused a crash on the freeway, he was almost shot since it was possible he had a weapon, he diverted police resources to deal with him, AND he made me mad. All that and no charges against him. I guess the moral of the story is "Don't bring a laser pointer to a laser sighted gunfight."

I was hooked on lasers at that point. Up until then, the laser had been a theory. But this night, the laser stopped this clown (suspect) dead in his tracks. It allowed me to clearly see what was in his hands (nothing) while knowing I would hit him dead center mass.

Author takes aim with his favorite combat pistol, the Beretta 92, with Crimson Trace grip activated. Note use of iron sights in conjunction with lasergrips.

you think of it, the laser also is an incapacitation device in and of itself, as it does cause people to stop and think about their next action.

Care and Maintenance

The tactics are not complex for using laser sights on pistols or rifles, or for that matter, shotguns. However, there are a few operational concerns.

First, monitor the systems for physical damage, especially after they are bumped or banged.

Next, keep track of battery use. Some of the current red lasers will run for 48 hours continuously before going down, which is a lot of duty and, of course, play time. Remember the greens will use a little more juice, at least at the time of this writing. If your laser system operates off of standard watch calculator type batteries, and not lithiums, be aware that long term exposure to cold will affect them.

Finally, and this is probably one of the most important points, keep the laser lens clean. The laser lens is a small opening, but you'd be surprised what can kind of crud can accumulate there. Some of the worst offenders are cleaning solvents and oil, especially in the case of Crimson Trace grips. Most officers tend to over-solvent, over-oil, and slop this stuff everywhere. After all, if some is good, a whole lot more ought to be better, right? This is especially true when using some of the very effective spray degreaser solvents. That stuff gets everywhere.

The problem, if it is one, is the location of the Crimson Trace laser diode itself. It is right at the top of the grip. Instead of pulling the laser grip off the pistol prior to cleaning, some clean around it.

It is also possible, on older grips that were not Mil-Spec, for solvent to get inside the grip panel from inside the magazine well and affect the laser. That was a little more serious of an issue, but not anymore with waterproof Mil-Spec models. Since Crimson Trace always stands by their gear, it is almost a non-issue, other than being without your grips a short time while they await repair or replacement.

If the lens gets dirty or oily, it will still work but you will get a "spider web" or cracked glass effect around the laser dot. The dot becomes less distinct and actually changes shape, becoming almost oblong, as it shines over distance. This ruins some of your precision, as the dot is getting too large. This is why CTC provides, with all their grips, a set of very tiny cotton-tipped swabs for cleaning.

If you follow cleaning directions and still have the spiderwebbing problem, the diode might be cracked or failing. This is a rather rare occurrence though.

To avoid this headache, do three things.

- First, oil sparingly. If you weren't aware of this, after cleaning there should only be five drops of oil placed in appropriate locations on your Glock, for example.
- Second, watch the use of spray solvents and cleaners around lasergrips. The fine airborne mists can land on the lens even if you keep it out of the way.
- Third, remove the grips while cleaning, or maybe cover the laser diode lens with a strip of electrical tape (don't touch the glass of course) during cleaning. It just requires a little extra care.

Use Your Iron Sights

Employing basic methodology with lasers, whether red or green, makes them more efficient.

First in any bright, overhead sunlight conditions, red lasers are useless and even green lasers take a second or two to pick up on. This brings me to the first foundational principle for laser tactics, especially with pistols: Use your iron sights first to reference the laser dot location.

When activating a laser on a direct threat, you should not be tracking it across the floor and up the pant leg of your opponent as if it was a fleeing mouse. If you are going to cover down on the person, cover down with a reference sight picture with the irons (tack the front sight on them) and then activate the laser if necessary.

This eliminates two issues. First, if you target with the laser this way you are still using the irons to gain the initial sight picture. If the laser fails, you still got the iron sight picture. Second, if there are indeed multiple laser equipped officers targeting the same individual, you will instantly acquire your own dot on the subject, rather than perhaps momentarily mixing it as it runs across the floor. A third advantage is that you will be in a full ready shoot position. If the suspect moves, reacquire them with the irons (the reference is faster), then the dot, or both together. When using the laser on a pistol in bus, train, or airplane assault, I move through the area using the reference iron sight picture in the background (out of focus) to keep track of the dot. The two systems should not work independently of each other.

Use your judgment

There may be times that you don't want to put a laser dot on a subject. Sometimes you don't *want* them to know they are a target, so that you don't change their actions. Examples of this would be hostage or barricade situations.

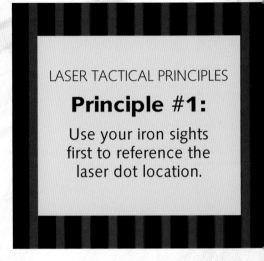

LASER TACTICAL PRINCIPLES
Principle #1:
Use your iron sights first to reference the laser dot location.

A couple of years ago I was on a call with our tactical team on a drug warrant. The suspect was known to be armed and had been working out of a nice house in a residential neighborhood. This was a joint mission with the city PD, investigators, and tactical team.

We secured the outside area of his house and hid, knowing he was not home. Our surveillance vehicle followed him to his house and when he got into the driveway we took him down without incident.

He was brought into the house after we cleared it. We informed the detectives that we had found some handguns which were secured, but we didn't do a detailed search. Our mission was just to clear the house of bodies.

The suspect was brought in handcuffed and sat at the kitchen table for questioning. I notice something odd about his demeanor. He had the 1000-yard stare and was very despondent. A pretty

220

good sized guy, I figured he might have the potential for trouble. The tactical team was told to stand down and we secured. I was driving home when I received an emergency call back to that location and given the radio code "10-44" – officer needs help.

I made a quick u-turn on the interstate and headed back up. I called dispatch to see if anyone was hurt. At this point no one was and the suspect had barricaded himself in the house with a loaded handgun, threatening to take his own life. How did he do that? When I left, he had been handcuffed behind his back.

I arrived at the location and was given a perimeter position outside. He was holed up on the second floor in the master bedroom with limited movement. We had two of the PD SRT guys on the porch roof with the hallway window busted out, one with a 9mm COLT SMG and the other with a bean bag launcher. They were not going to let him out of the bedroom.

I learned that a well intentioned officer wanted to provide the prisoner more comfort as they interviewed him and worked the search warrant. They had already found a quantity of cocaine and guns. In order to facilitate his comfort, they re-cuffed him in front, with two hand cuffs linked together cause he was such a big guy. The city K9 officer, who had been watching him, had put Lassie back in the cruiser and was there by himself while the detectives continued to search the split-level home.

When the officer's attention was momentarily diverted, the suspect ran up the stairs, with the K9 officer sans K9 chasing behind. Apparently the officer fired his Taser at the suspect, but only one probe hit and that was in the arm. Before the officer could try and make a better connection with a drive stun, the suspect reached between the mattress, and pulled out a loaded Smith and Wesson pistol. Fortunately, rather than shooting the officer, he took *himself* hostage.

At that time, we did not have laser sighted duty weapons, even for the SRT team, so those did not come into play.

One of the narcotics detectives assumed the mantle of hostage negotiator behind a body bunker at the top of the second floor landing. The suspect was inside the doorway in the bedroom to the left and was contained there. He had been told that if he left the threshold of the bedroom door, which would endanger our negotiator and team guys on the stairs, he would be shot by the myriad of weapons pointed at him. He apparently was agreeing to the rules as he stayed in the room, with the gun to his head, finger on the trigger, hammer cocked back into single action mode, and a Taser probe sticking in his left forearm with the wires dangling.

I was rotated to a position at the top of the stairs by the negotiator and asked to try another Taser shot. Let's see, one shot

LASER TACTICAL PRINCIPLES

Principle #2:

Use your judgement. There are times when you should not use the laser.

failed for whatever reason, the guy holding a gun to his head with finger on trigger was desperately saying that he didn't want to go to prison, and two sets of handcuffs may interfere with a probe striking home. Not a good opportunity. Plus, he was facing us and the best Taser hits are in the back. I was less than confident and the stakes were high.

All this time watching the suspect, I noticed that he never turned the gun towards us, which still made him a good candidate

to try a less lethal force option. I passed my Taser back and asked an officer to switch off both the targeting laser and LED light. I would try to deploy it if the opportunity arose, but I did not want to warn this suspect that it was coming and cause him to retreat. I also wanted a shot at him when his arms and handcuffs weren't in the way. I targeted him with the Taser light and laser off. He didn't notice, and that was the point. Unfortunately, he didn't get into the position I wanted, nor did he ever take his finger off the trigger.

I told command that I couldn't get a Taser shot and was given a 12 gauge bean bag gun. The bean bag gun would allow me a clean shot *if* the suspect would take his finger off the trigger just for a moment. I didn't want to risk the shot as I felt this guy was close to pulling the trigger, and I didn't want to do the job for him by making him involuntarily jerk.

After about another 20 minutes, the suspect laid the gun down and agreed to give up. However, before he did he started to reach for the handgun. He was popped by the bean bag gun at a distance of about 10 feet and dropped like a bad habit. When we pounced, he said, "Boy that blank gun sure hurts."

The point is that you may not want to use the laser each and every time, whether it's on a pistol, rifle, or even a Taser.

With Crimson Trace, make sure you practice your grip tension so you don't activate the laser at an inopportune time. The same is true with any rifle mounted laser.

Don't Lead With Your Laser

Far too often in slow search training, I see officers operating with the laser beam active while searching in darkened areas. I played a bad guy during one or two of these exercises and could see the team coming, led by the magic red dots. The movement and track of the dots coming down the hallway told me where the guys were coming from. So the third foundational point is this. Leave the laser off until you need it, and don't lead with it. Save the dot for actually targeting an individual. By leading with the laser on, you let everyone who sees it know that you are in the area and where you are looking.

For laser sight systems that don't use momentary switching, but are of the push-to-on variety, like the Lasermax guide rod laser system, be prepared to turn them off at a moment's notice. This takes a more conscious effort than relaxation of grip pressure with lasergrips.

Can You Shoot Around a Corner?

The next tactical concept is this. With the laser, you *can* shoot at odd angles, one handed, without accessing the pistol's sights.

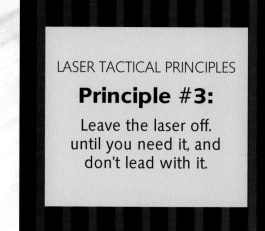

LASER TACTICAL PRINCIPLES
Principle #3:
Leave the laser off. until you need it, and don't lead with it.

223

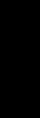

Yes, you did just read about the need to always use the iron sights as the first reference point for the laser dot, but that it is a concept for use in most situations, when the situation is not moving to "out of control." Exceptions to the "use the sights" guideline would be when you have been knocked to the ground and may be limited to one hand use, when you need to target someone from or inside of a confined space, or when you are carrying a ballistic shield. Let's examine each of these situations.

First let's look at a situation where you've been knocked to the ground. Here, the need for a backup gun is underscored, since you may have lost your primary duty weapon in a scuffle. The backup gun is an *ideal* platform for a laser sight, especially one of the lasergrip models from Crimson Trace.

My backup gun is the same as my primary off-duty gun, the Smith and Wesson 332. My rationale is this: If I'm using the backup gun, my stuff is in the wind. I don't want an accidental magazine dump or a failure to cycle. I want a gun that can fire from inside a jacket pocket, *will* fire when I pull the trigger, can make contact shots without jamming, is lightweight, that I can conceal in my left front pants pocket, and that can be fired even upside down with that laser dot on the target without concern. That leaves the revolver.

With Crimson Trace grips on that Smith and Wesson (or the new Taurus 6 shot .38 snub revolver) you have the perfect backup package. If you are on your back, side, or stomach and need to shoot, trying to use the sights may not be practical. You may need to fire that gun with a broken arm or dislocated shoulder. You can do it with laser sights without bringing the gun fully up into play.

In academy training, I demonstrate CTC laser grips on a Beretta 92. In just enough lighting conditions to barely see the target, I back off to 50 yards and standing, holding the gun at hip level with two hands, I squeeze off six or so shots. This demonstrates two things. First, that you can use the laser in the dark at long range and target an aggressor when you really can't see your sights and hit the aggressor and, second, that you don't need to hold the gun in a conventional type hold and stance to get hits.

Part of your training regimen with the lasers then, should be shooting (safely) from odd angles, in grounded positions, without using your sights. If I can fire from the hip in these conditions, I can fire and attain hits without a conventional grip if my arm is broken or otherwise compromised.

224

A second point about limited hand use: If your backup is in your weak-side pocket, you'll be drawing it with the weak hand. You may have to emergency fire it with your weak hand, since there may not be time for a strong hand transfer. That laser dot makes the shot much easier.

While shooting out of or in confined spaces, you may be in such a position of cover that you really can't get into a good shooting position, for example, behind obstructions or behind the wheels of a car. Shining that dot out of those confined spaces may be the only way to target an aggressor with your limited view. In a scene from the movie "L.A. Confidential," one of the lead characters sees the bad guy walking around outside the shack he is hiding in. All he can see is a lower leg, and he shoots, striking the bad guy. That is an example where a laser would assist, and one that a homeowner,

secure in their hiding area when dealing with an intruder, is likely to encounter.

The biggest use advantage among these specialized situations is the use of the laser when behind a ballistic shield on a tactical team. There is some controversy about this. Columbus Ohio SWAT training sergeant and founding partner in the 727 Counter Terror Training Unit, John Groom, believes that the shield man in any stack formation should be concerned with the shield and not concerned with their handgun.

Maneuvering a full size shield or body bunker is really a two hand job. The shield-bearer's job is not to protect himself, it is to provide protection for the *entire team* stacked behind him. If he drops or lowers the shield to return fire, the cover, for not only him but all the guys counting on him to the rear, is lost. (The same consideration does not necessarily apply when using a lightweight shield like the Patriot 3 Minuteman folding shield, which *is* designed for one-hand use and return fire by the shield bearer.)

For this reason, when CPD SWAT deploys a shield, the only responsibility of the shield bearer is protecting the folks behind him. All fire is returned by the guys behind the shield bearer. He stands braced against any bullet impacts, which is a job in and of itself and requires a hell of a lot of nerve.

Not everyone agrees with this philosophy, which is where laser sighted pistols come in. If you are the shield man, and tasked with handling a pistol at the same time, you know that it is a difficult job trying to hold the shield and peer through the shield port to get some sort of sight picture. When you do this, you expose most of your shooting hand and arm. Not so when you have a laser sighted pistol, you only need to expose a portion of your hand at the side of the shield as you activate the laser (one hand operation with a momentary switch system like CTC lasergrips is critical here), watching through the viewport for the dot.

I realized the importance of this system early on. When using a laser-equipped autoloader with a shield remember this: Don't let the slide of the pistol touch the shield, which will cause a malfunction, making your pistol a single shot. No time for tap-rack-bang here, you have to hold the shield, remember? Smith and Wesson answered this potential problem a couple of years ago with a revolver that would work well as a ballistic shield gun for those agencies that want to have the shield bearer deploy a handgun.

Although any revolver can work with CTC grips, Smith and Wesson upped the ante with Model 327 M&P R8, an 8-shot .357 Magnum. Produced in a tactical matte black finish with a 5-inch barrel and a 1913 Rail beneath the muzzle to accommodate a light, the 327 is set up to load its .357/.38 Special rounds conventionally or via a full moon clip. With this revolver and CTC Grips and an

Above: Here, the shield bearer is also operating with a drawn pistol. If you choose to work shields in this fashion, a laser equipped pistol is a must.

Opposite Page: Here, officers carrying lifeline portable shield utilize method recommended by Sgt. John Groom and author. Shield bearer is responsible only for the holding, maneuvering, and positioning of the shield.

227

Insight strobing pistol light up front, the entry man would have a formidable option indeed. Weight is a solid 36 ounces, and the price is a reasonable $1335 MSRP considering the gun is a Performance Center Semi-Custom limited edition piece. The best part though is that the barrel of this gun can be rested tight against the side of the shield and the gun will fire all eight shots without malfunction. If there was a 4-inch version of this, with appropriate security holster available, and I was allowed to carry it, this gun would be my duty weapon of choice.

In any event, if you are going to require your shield bearer to carry a pistol, make sure you practice with the shield and live fire with it. It would also be a good idea to use it in Simunitions Training, to take impacts with it and see if you can still return fire.

In Summary

Laser sighted weapons save lives. SWAT teams are not there to kill people. SWAT exists to apply overwhelming *potential* force and advantage against the criminally-intended, to cause them to cease their actions without the need to fire a shot. Sometimes, just letting a suspect know that SWAT has been called causes him or her to give up even before they get there. In the barricade in Marysville, the last thing we wanted to do was shoot the guy holding himself hostage, or see him shoot himself. Lasers are one way

Kimber Custom Eclipse II showing left grip panel and master off and on switch. Master switch is important in deactivating laser when its use would not be a plus or to prevent accidental activation during storage.

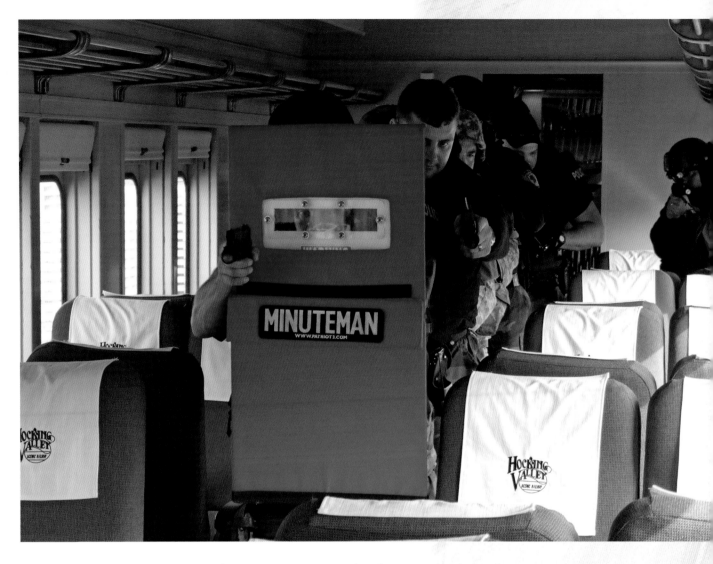

to deter suspects. They may cause the suspect to give up when he knows he is targeted. They allow an officer to define that the person who is targeted is a suspect. They allow you to move rapidly in dynamic situations while maintaining target acquisition as you search for the suspects. They allow you to shoot and save your life from all sorts of unconventional positions without having to use iron sights for alignment. One thing they won't do is make a bad shooter better. But today, they are a necessary component of the weapons system, for SWAT and patrol officers alike. The technology is there, reliable, and documentable. Choose your system wisely, and make good use of it.

This work only a sample of the ever-changing tactical lighting and laser sighting market. As with any electronic product, the specifics and technical aspects are subject to change over time. However, the foundations laid out in this book should hold true for some time to come. Whenever dealing with any new technique or product, research it, try it out for yourself, and make sure the claims made are accurate and that they work for you.

Bus and passenger train assault, using Patriot Minuteman training shield and pistol rifle lights. The shield-bearer's job is to provide protection for the entire team stacked behind him.

229

LIGHTS

SHEFFIELD 1 WATT TACTLITE LUXEON FLASHLIGHT

1 Watt Luxeon LED
6 tooth strike plate
10 times brighter than other LEDS
10,000 hour LED life. Runs continuously for 15 hours
Anodized aluminum non-slip handle
O-ring sealed and water resistant
Up to 35 lumens
1 AA battery included

SUREFIRE 6P

Compact (pocket sized), high-intensity incandescent flashlight for tactical, self-defense, and general use. Produces a smooth, brilliant, pre-focused tactical-level beam with three times the light of a big two-D-cell flashlight—bright enough to temporarily blind and disorient a person by impairing his night-adapted vision. Light output may be nearly doubled with optional P61 lamp.

Features:

Rugged aerospace-grade aluminum body, Type II anodized in glossy black
O-ring sealed, weatherproof
Tempered Pyrex® window
Tailcap switch: press for momentary-on, twist for constant-on
Switch lockout prevents accidental activation during transport or storage
Max Output: 65/120 lumens with optional ultra high-output lamp
Runtime: 60/20 minutes with optional ultra high-output lamp
Length: 5.20 inches
Weight: 5.30 ounces
Battery: Two 123A lithiums

SUREFIRE G2

Compact (pocket sized), high-intensity incandescent flashlight for tactical, self-defense, and general use. Similar to our 6P but with a tough polymer body. Puts out a smooth, brilliant, pre-focused, tactical-level beam with over three times the light of a big two-D-cell

flashlight—bright enough to temporarily blind and disorient a person by impairing his night-adapted vision. Light output may be nearly doubled with optional P61 lamp. Small size, light weight, and high output make it a perfect for camping, backpacking, emergency/disaster-preparedness kits, or everyday carry.

Features:

Rugged, lightweight, corrosion-proof Nitrolon® polymer body, available in black, olive drab, tan, yellow. O-ring sealed, weatherproof. Tailcap switch: press for momentary-on, twist for constant-on. Switch lockout prevents accidental activation during transport or storage.
Max Output: 65/120 lumens with optional ultra high-output lamp
Runtime: 60/20 minutes with optional ultra high-output lamp
Length: 5.10 inches
Weight: 4.10 ounces
Battery: Two 123A lithiums

SUREFIRE E2L-HA-WH

Compact (pocket sized), dual-output LED flashlight with extended runtime. Its virtually indestructible, two-stage light-emitting diode (LED) light source produces a smooth, pre-focused beam that, at maximum output, is three times brighter than that of a big two-D-cell flashlight. At its low setting it produces a useful three lumens of light and continues producing useful light levels for 100 hours on a set of lithium batteries. Small size (it's lightweight enough to clip to hat brim for hands-free operation), dual output, extended runtime, and 10-year battery shelf life make the E2L perfect for camping, backpacking, travel, emergency/disaster preparedness kits, or as an everyday-carry for general use.

Features:

Dual-output LED light source has no filament to burn out or break, lasts for thousands of hours. Rugged aerospace-grade aluminum body, Mil-Spec Type III hard anodized in olive drab. O-ring sealed, weatherproof. Total Internal Reflection (TIR) lens. Pocket clip. Tailcap switch: press for momentary-on, press further to click constant-on. Switch lockout prevents accidental activation during transport or storage.
Max Output: High: 60 lumens; Low: 3 lumens
Runtime: High: 11 hours; Low: 100 hours
Bezel Diameter: 1.0 inch

Length: 5.40 inches
Weight: 3.70 ounces

SUREFIRE G3L-BK

Compact (palm sized), high-intensity LED flashlight for tactical, outdoor, and general use. Puts out a smooth, brilliant beam with four times the light of a two-D-cell flashlight. Produces tactical-level lighting (enough to temporarily blind and disorient an aggressor) for nearly six hours and useful light levels for an impressive 9.4 hours on a single set of batteries. Features a tough, corrosion-proof Nitrolon® body with molded-in grid and a rugged, aerospace-grade aluminum bezel anodized in black. Light weight, compact size, high output, and extended runtime make the G3 LED a great choice for law enforcement, security, military, and self-defense applications; camping, backpacking, and general outdoor use; and emergency/disaster-preparedness.

Features:

Virtually indestructible, microprocessor-controlled LED has no filament to burn out or break; lasts for thousands of hours. Produces tactical-level light for 5.8 hours on a set of batteries; 9.4 hours of useful light. Precision reflector creates smooth beam without spots or rings. Rugged, lightweight, corrosion-proof Nitrolon® polymer body and anodized aluminum bezel in black. O-ring sealed; weatherproof. Tailcap switch: press for momentary-on, twist for constant-on. Patented switch lockout prevents accidental activation.

Max Output: 80 lumens
Runtime: 9.42 hours (5.8 hrs tactical-level light)
Length: 6.50 inches
Weight: 5.50 ounces
Battery: Three 123A Lithium

SUREFIRE G3L-BK-KIT01

Compact (palm sized), high-intensity LED flashlight with an ergonomic holster specially designed for quick deployment of the flashlight—especially when pairing the light with a handgun. Developed for use in law enforcement, where split seconds count, the G3™ LED Holster Kit is also a great choice for anyone who needs a flashlight that produces tactical-level output (enough to temporarily blind an assailant) and an effective, ergonomic way to carry and deploy the light

quickly. The G3 LED runs for 9.4 hours on a single set of batteries. The included rugged polymer holster has an integral magazine that holds three spare batteries, giving the G3 LED the capacity to run for over 18 hours in the field—far longer than a rechargeable flashlight. The reversible, ambidextrous holster is adjustable to accommodate personal preference and to permit maximum ease and speed when drawing the light and pairing it with a handgun, if applicable. The holster accommodates any SureFire flashlight with a 1.25" aluminum bezel. Kit includes flashlight, holster, mounting hardware, manual, and nine SureFire 123A lithium batteries.

SUREFIRE L1

Compact (pocket sized), dual-output LED flashlight for backpacking, camping, and general use. Uses a virtually indestructible, power-regulated light emitting diode (LED) light source plus a two-stage tailcap switch for instant selection of desired output level—extremely long-runtime low beam for close-up work or a long-runtime high beam with over three times the light of a big two-D-cell flashlight. Small size, extended runtime, high output, and 10-year battery shelf life make it perfect for emergency/disaster preparedness kits, the outdoors, or everyday carry.

Features:

LED light source has no filament to burn out or break, lasts for thousands of hours. LED output available in white. Rugged aerospace-grade aluminum body, Mil-Spec Type III hard anodized in olive drab. O-ring sealed, weather proof. Total internal reflection (TIR) lens produces tightly focused beam. Pocket clip. Tailcap switch: press for momentary-on low beam, press further for high beam, twist for constant-on. Switch lockout prevents accidental activation during transport or storage.

Max Output: High: 65 lumens; Low: 10 lumens
Runtime: High: 1.5 hours; Total: 16 hours
Bezel Diameter: 1.0 inch
Length: 4.52 inches
Weight: 2.9 ounces

SUREFIRE OPTIMUS

Eleven settings ensure that the pocket-sized Surefire Optimus is ready for virtually any situation, environment, or circumstance. Set its magnetic selector ring to any of eight preset output levels ranging from two lumens (enough to read a map) to 200 lumens of blinding light that's instantly available by pressing its Max Blast™ tailcap all the way down.

For a tactical advantage that doesn't involve overwhelming an aggressor's eyesight with 200 lumens of electronically regulated LED light, switch the Optimus to its strobe setting and stun him with bright, flickering light designed to disorient and confuse. And should you ever need an emergency beacon, just set the Optimus to its SOS setting and stick it where a passing rescue plane, boat, or vehicle can see it. To help you get the most out of your batteries, the Optimus even features a built-in fuel gauge that lets you know when you should consider switching to a lower output level or changing batteries.

Simply twist its bezel to change the beam's light distribution from spot to flood and any point in between—without any deterioration in beam quality, thanks to SureFire's Vari-Beam™ technology. The Optimus uses precision optics to redistribute the light's energy. The result is a pure beam that's always in focus.

Leave the pocket clip on to carry it in your pocket, or remove it and holster the light. Taking it off also lets you take full advantage of the Optimus' Combat-Grip,™ a stepped-down body that provides a secure hold in any weather and makes it easier to pair the Optimus with a handgun.

Features:

Microprocessor-controlled, virtually indestructible LED

Eight pre-set output levels from 2 to 200 lumens

Vari-Beam™technology changes beam from spot to flood and all points in between —with no degradation in quality

Tactical strobe to disorient an aggressor and flashing SOS beacon for emergency use

Built-in fuel gauge serves as a reminder to power down to a lower output level or change batteries

Attachable/removable pocket clip allows customizable carrying options

CombatGrip™provides one-handed control—especially when pairing flashlight with a firearm (includes two rubber grips: one for use with pocket clip, one for use without pocket clip)

Mil-Spec Type III hard-anodized aerospace-grade aluminum body

Compression-resistant O-ring seals for weatherproofing

Coated, impact-resistant Pyrex® window protects optics and LED and helps maximize light transmission

Tailcap switching: press for momentary-on at output level determined by selector ring, press all the way for momentary-on max output; twist for constant-on at output level set by selector ring, twist further for constant-on max output

Patented lockout tailcap feature prevents accidental activation

Runs on 2 Lithium 123A batteries

SUREFIRE X300

The SureFire X300™ features a solid-state, electronically regulated LED that generates 110 lumens of tactical-level light — enough to overwhelm an aggressor's night-adapted vision. Its specially developed Total Internal Reflection (TIR) lens creates a bright, tightly focused central beam with plenty of reach and enough surround beam to accommodate peripheral vision. A hard-anodized aerospace-grade aluminum body protects the X300's electronics, and O-ring seals and gaskets make the entire unit waterproof to 22 meters. A tempered Pyrex® window protects its LED and, thanks to a thin layer of anti-reflective coating, helps maximize light transmission. The X300 attaches to both Universal and Picatinny rails in moments, via its proprietary Rail-Lock™ system, and comes with adapter plates for both. An ambidextrous toggle/push switch provides convenient, fail-safe operation. Optional SureFire grip switches, which allow precision control without altering one's grip on the weapon, are also available for many handguns.

Features:

Max Output: 110 lumens (5 times the light of a two-D-cell flashlight); continues producing tactical-level light for 2.4 hours

Versatile beam is perfect for longerand close-range applications

Ambidextrous tactical switching enables fail-safe operation under fire

Instantly attaches to most handguns with a Universal rail and handguns/long guns with a Picatinny rail

1.39" high by 1.43" wide by 3.53" long; weighs 3.7 ounces (with batteries)

Batteries — two SF123 3-volt lithiums with 10-year shelf life

Aerospace-aluminum construction with Mil-Spec, Type III hard-anodized finish

O-ring sealed and gasketed; waterproof to 22 meter

Accepts optional pressure-activated switches for precision control without altering grip on weapon

SUREFIRE X400

The X400 is the same unit as the X300, but is also equipped with a 635nm Red Laser.

SUREFIRE E1B BACKUP

Ultra compact (finger length), dual-output LED flashlight with extended runtime and tactical-level output. The E1B was developed as an everyday-carry flashlight for undercover officers and as a backup light for patrol officers — but it's also ideal for outdoor, self-defense, and everyday use by civilians. The Backup features a virtually indestructible, electronically regulated light emitting diode (LED) that, on its "high" setting, produces a smooth, tactical-level beam (enough light to temporarily overwhelm the night-adapted vision of an aggressor) with four times the output, of a two-D-cell flashlight. And it continues generating tactical-light levels for 1.3 hours on a single battery. On its "low" setting, the E1B generates five lumens of light that's perfect for reading a map, checking an ID, or navigating a dark pathway, and generates useful light levels for 37 hours. And the E1B's click-on/off tailcap is programmed to instantly deliver maximum output when its pushbutton is depressed, a critical feature in law enforcement and tactical applications where a lot of light is frequently needed immediately. Rounding out this flashlight's features are its unique "melted" styling — no knurling or sharp edges to catch on clothing — and two-way pocket clip, which lets a user carry the Backup bezel up or down, whichever he or she prefers.

Features:

Virtually indestructible, dual-output light emitting diode has no filament to burn out or break; lasts for thousands of hours. Total Internal Reflection (TIR) lens creates a flawless, bright beam with plenty of reach and enough surround beam to accommodate peripheral vision. Coated Pyrex® window protects the lens and LED and maximizes light transmission. Rugged aerospace-grade aluminum body, Mil-Spec Type III hard anodized in black. Sleek, "melted" body has no knurling or sharp edges to catch on or wear out clothing. O-ring sealed, weatherproof. Two-way pocket clip allows light to be carried bezel up or down. Two-stage tailcap switch: press for momentary-on at high setting, release and press again (within two seconds) for momentary-on at low setting; click for constant-on at high-setting, click off and on again (within two seconds) for constant-on at low setting.

Max Output: 5/80 lumens
Runtime: 37/1.3 hours (low/high settings)
Length: 4.00 inches
Weight: 2.80 ounces
Battery: One 123A lithium

STREAMLIGHT STINGER DS™ LED

The Stinger DS™ LED is a rechargeable flashlight with a fully independent dual switch.

Features:

DUAL SWITCH TECHNOLOGY – Access any of the three variable lighting modes and strobe via the tail cap or the head-mounted switch

Head switch operates independently from the tail cap switch

The combination of a rechargeable battery and a lifetime super high flux LED results in the lowest operating cost of any flashlight made.

Deep-dish parabolic reflector produces a long range targeting beam with optimal peripheral illumination to aid in navigation.

Lumens: 80 typical

Runtime: High – Up to 1.75 hours; Medium – Up to 3.5 hours; Low – up to 6.75 hours; Strobe – Up to 5.5 hours

Optimized electronics provides regulated intensity

Length: 8.85 " (22.48 cm)

Weight: 12.8 oz (364 grams)

6000 series machined aircraft aluminum with non-slip rubberized comfort grip

Unbreakable Polycarbonate with scratch-resistant coating

O-Ring sealed construction

3 watt super high flux LED, impervious to shock

3-cell, 3.6 Volt Nickel cadmium sub-C battery is rechargeable up to 1000 times

Includes Anti-roll Ring

Fits existing Stinger chargers

10 hours to recharge on 100V, 120V, 230V or 240V AC

12V DC 2.5 hour fast charger, 5-bank charger or PiggyBack® charger offered

Safety wands, ring holder, color filters accessories available

STREAMLIGHT STYLUS PRO

Streamlight's new high flux LED light with Proprietary Micro Optical Systems has "Battery-

Booster" electronics to provide a super-bright beam.

Features:

Proprietary Micro Optical System (MOS), for optimized output and runtime

Up to 24 lumens output for up to 7.5 hrs runtime

Super-bright 1/2 watt, 30,000 hour high flux LED

An internal polymer body liner and shock proof switch housing allow for operation under the most extreme conditions

Rubber push button tail cap switch

O-ring sealed

Unbreakable polycarbonate lens

Unbreakable pocket clip

Belt Holster included

Corrosion and water resistant construction

Water resistant per IPX4; in accordance with specification EN 60529:1992

Shock-proof; drop test verified above the industry standard of six feet

Type II MIL-SPEC abrasion and corrosion-resistant anodized aircraft aluminum

Includes (2) "AAA" alkaline batteries and holster

1.64 oz. with battery

5.3" long

Available in Matte Black

Limited Lifetime Warranty

STREAMLIGHT SIDEWINDER

Sidewinder, the most versatile military light in the world. Twenty flashlights in one! Each LED features 4 levels of output intensities: Low (5%), Medium (20%), Medium-High (50%), High (100%) plus a Strobe function (100%)

Features:

One switch for On-Off, dimming and mode selection functions.

Pull-to-turn locking rotary color(4)selector knob with tactile indicator for easy operation with gloves

Double click button to initiate strobe function from "Off" position

Push and hold button for light output levels from "Off" position

Sidewinder Light Output and 2 AA Alkaline Battery Run Time

Also accepts 2 "AA" lithium batteries, which allow extended operation, or extreme

temperatures (-40°F 150°F)

Mounts to MOLLE or ACH for hands-free use

High-impact, super-tough nylon case; drop-test verified from 30 feet

Battery polarity indicators for easy replacement in the dark

Unbreakable, gasket-sealed polycarbonate lens with scratch-resistant coating

O-ring sealed for waterproof operation. Meets MIL-STD-810F, Method 512.4

Tethered tailcap to prevent loss

Cord attachment hole supports up to 25 lbs

Articulating 185° rotating head

Spring steel clip attaches to MOLLE or belt

Clip can be mounted on either side of the light

Dimensions: 4.63" High; 2.31" Wide

Weight: 4.96 ounces

Available in Coyote Tan and Green

US and foreign patents pending

One year limited warranty

STREAMLIGHT THE NANO LIGHT

Truly tiny, the Nanolight® is a weatherproof, personal flashlight featuring a 100,000 hour life LED. Includes a non-rotating snap hook for easy one handed operation when attached to a keychain.

Features:

Easily attaches/detaches to just about anything with convenient pocket clip or key ring

Up to 8 hrs. run time

Machined aircraft-grade aluminum with anodized finish

Powered by 4 alkaline button cells (included)

100,000 hr. lifetime high-intensity LED

LED available in white (10 lumens)

1.47" x .51"

.36 oz.

Available in black

STREAMLIGHT MICROSTREAM

Streamlight's new high-flux LED light with Proprietary Micro Optical Systems has "Battery-Booster" electronics to provide a super-bright beam.

Features:

Proprietary Micro Optical System (MOS), for optimized output and runtime

Up to 20 lumens output for up to 1.5 hrs runtime

Super-bright 1/2 watt, 30,000 hour high flux LED

An internal polymer body liner and shock proof switch housing allow for operation under the most extreme conditions

Rubber push button tail cap switch

O-ring sealed

Unbreakable polycarbonate lens

Corrosion and water resistant construction

Water resistant per IPX4; in accordance with specification EN 60529:1992

Type II MIL-SPEC abrasion and corrosion-resistant anodized aircraft aluminum

Shock-proof; drop test verified above the industry standard of six feet

Unbreakable pocket clip

Key ring and safety lanyard included

Includes (1) "AAA" alkaline battery

1.04 oz with battery

3.5" Long

Available in Matte Black

Limited Lifetime Warranty

STREAMLIGHT SUPER TAC

Gun Mountable and extremely bright

Up to 30,000 peak beam candlepower

C4 LED is 3X brighter than a Super high-flux LED

135 Lumens

Runtime: up to 3.5 hours

Machined Aluminum

Length: 6.62 inches (16.81 cm)

Weight: 7.1 oz (200 g)

Limited Lifetime Warranty

Two 3 Volt CR123A Batteries (included)

Holster Included

STREAMLIGHT TL-2

The brightness of a larger light in a compact size that can be comfortably used with a firearm.

Features:

Team Soldier Certified Gear

Two 3 volt CR123A lithium batteries with a storage life of 10 years (included)

High-pressure xenon gas-filled bi-pin bulb

Up to 7,900 peak beam candlepower (78 lumens)

Adjustable focus

Spare bulb included

1.3 hrs. continuous run time

Pocket clip, adjustable lanyard

Head: 1.25;" Body: .9" x Length 4.9"

4.2 oz. with batteries

Shock-Proof model available. Designed to withstand even the punishing recoil of a 3" 12 gauge magnum slug.

Available in black

STREAMLIGHT SCORPION LED

One of the brightest, lightest personal flashlight ever created, the Scorpion® LED is the only tactical light with a rubberized grip and tailcap switch and anti-roll head. Available with a C4 LED.

Features:

Team Soldier Certified Gear

Anti-roll head

C4 LED is 2X brighter than a Super high-flux LED, delivers 120 lumens

Up to 3.5 hours of runtime to the 10% output level.

5.72"

5.3 oz. with batteries

Two 3 volt CR123A lithium batteries with a storage life of up to 10 years (included)

Machined aluminum covered by a rubber-armored sleeve for a sure grip

O-ring sealed for moisture protection

Available in black

STREAMLIGHT TLR-1 AND TLR-2

Intensly bright, virtually indestructable tactical light, attaches/detaches to almost any gun in seconds. The TLR-2 has the same great features of the TLR-1 with an integrated laser sight for accurate aiming.

Features:

Powered by two 3-volt CR123 lithium batteries with 10-year storage life

Shockproof super high-flux LED with blinding beam (up to 80 lumens) with bright side-light – will not break or burn out

Up to 2.5 hrs runtime

Rail grip clamp system securely attaches/detaches quickly and safely with no tools and without putting your hands in front of muzzle

Fast, Adjustable, Secure Side mounting to 1913 and Glock style Rails

Machined aluminum sealed construction with black anodized finsih

Waterproof to one meter for one hour,

dustproof

Ambidextrous momentary/steady on/off switch

Highly accurate sight repeatability when remounting

Fits existing light bearing holsters

4.18 oz.

Lithium Battery Notice under TECH DOCS

MIL-SPEC 810F Performance Tested

AIMSHOT! HEATSEEKER

HeatSeeker tracks any heat source up to 300 yards!

Technology for the hunt, security or law enforcement! Heatseeker works by detecting heat sources and motion of heat to help find game and bad guys. Temperatures are read as infrared light waves which appear on the digital bar graph display. A "squelch" alert can also be heard through the ear plug. Detects objects as close as 2' and can reach as far as 900' under optimum conditions.

Features:

Built-in laser and infrared sighting makes acquiring targets easier

Infrared laser capability for tracking in total darkness while using night vision

Adjustable volume, for when silence is critical

Runs on one 9V battery (included)

High-impact ABS plastic construction

7" long and weighs just 8-1/4 ozs.

Includes belt pouch, earphone and wrist strap.

AIMSHOT! XENON ILLUMINATOR
TACTICAL FLASHLIGHT TX 125 & TX 75

The Xenon Illuminator is a bright (165 lumen - TX125, 120 lumen TX75) and shatterproof tactical flashlight with a lightweight aluminum bulb base. A new advanced heat dissipation system has been engineered to increase bulb life and resist flashlight burnout in high temperature environments. Used by military and law enforcement agencies around the world. It provides all the light needed to quickly identify any threats hiding in dimly lit areas. With the universal tactical flashlight glove, you can scan an area with the light while remaining firing-ready.

Features:

Dual glass/polycarbonate lens: shatterproof & high-heat resistance

Super-lightweight @ 3 oz

Made of virtually unbreakable Black Delrin® with non-slip rubber body

Advanced aluminum heat dissipation system

2-position end (constant-on, intermittent)

Focusable beam Shatter-proof lens and shock-resistant lamp assembly

Waterproof to 100M

Belt pouch included

AIMSHOT! MT61167
UNIVERSAL MOUNTING SYSTEM

The AimSHOT mounting system will enable you to mount laser sights on virtually any weapon including pistols, revolvers, rifles, and shotguns. Available in both black and silver, constructed of lightweight aluminum, mounts are equipped with shims to accommodate any pistol or revolver including round and square trigger guards. Rifle mounts include various length screws which adjust to any diameter barrel. For shotguns, the rib vent adaptor will fit any double barrel or rib vent shotgun.

BURRIS SHOTCAM

The ShotCam fastens to the picatinny rail of many handguns, shotguns, and carbines. It features three technologies: 120 Lumen Flashlight; Projected Laser Sight; Digital Video Camera, all rolled up into a compact and lightweight package.

One primary application is for law enforcement officers to not only have the benefits of laser and illumination, but to also record on video an entire conflict automatically once a handgun is removed from a holster. Specialized holsters are used with ShotCam which have a special magnet molded into the plastic. A special switch on the ShotCam senses the magnet to put the unit into sleep mode. Once the handgun is removed from the holster the ShotCam is actuated and records up to one hour of video. The video can then be used as evidence to support the officer, department, and government agency. The same could be said for application in a home defense situation.

If a full hour of video is taken, ShotCam stops video recording and goes into a still frame mode capturing a 3.2megapixel photograph of what the gun was pointing at when the shot was fired. The ShotCam can be set to several modes such that any or all of it's features can be activated automatically when unholstering a handgun, or manually. Choose illumination only, laser only, video only, or still frame only, or any combination of these modes. The ShotCam can be quickly removed from a weapon in seconds and used in special situations as an illuminator or camcorder when these features are desired but using a weapon as a pointing devise is inappropriate.

PENTAGON LIGHT X2

Xenon is the best performing bulb filling gas and provides the maximum lumen per watt over the other gases for incandescent lamps. X2's xenon light source generates an amazing 70 lumens of powerful light collimated by their proprietary reflector designed for focusing the light generated into a smooth intensified light beam.

The light beam is pre-focused at the factory for maximal center intensity in achieving the greatest distance. The lamp assembly is completely isolated from the rest of the light while the batteries are compartmentalized to provide X2 with excellent performance against weapon recoil. The "flaming heat-sink" design of the head ensures adequate heat dissipation for thermal management of the xenon bulb in lengthening its bulb life and optimizing its performance. X2 is crafted out of aerospace grade aluminum tube using precision CNC machine in anti-reflective, anti-corrosive, and anti-abrasive military spec Type III hard anodized exterior finish. All connections are sealed with double O-rings for extra protection against water leakage. X2 is not just a limited use incandescent light, since its head is interchangeable for alternate light sources from a diverse selection of conversion heads available separately, so your initial investment for a high quality flashlight is maximized. The removable pocket clip can be taken off easily for carrying the light in a holster. X2 is preconfigured with TC4 push on/off PentagonLight™ signature tail-cap switch. The extended long throw of our tail button switch can easily press slightly for momentary on while allowing click to constant on. The switch is housed in the anti-roll pentagonal shape tail cap making it easy for one-hand operation. Optional tail-caps are available for additional switching functions. Two PentagonLight™ CR-123A lithium batteries with 10-year shelf-life are included. For a similar light but size is the concern, consider X1 Xenon Light. For longer distance and brightness, consider X3 Xenon Light.

Features:

Brightness: 80 Lumens
Run-Time: 60 Minutes
Batteries: Two CR-123A
Bezel Size: 1.25"
Length: 5.5" (140 mm)
Weight: 5.2 oz. (147 g)
Xenon Gas-Filled Lamp
Aerospace Grade Aluminum Body
TC4 Push On/Off Tail Switch
Double O-Ring Sealing
Military Spec Type III Hard Anodized Exterior
Removable Pocket Clip

OPTICS

BURRIS XTR RIFLESCOPES

Burris has gone to extremes to engineer the ultimate in high-performance optics the XTR Xtreme Tactical Riflescopes. Extra-large, ultra-premium lenses produce unsurpassed resolution, clarity, and brightness. Index-matched HiLume multicoating boosts clarity and, enhanced with new StormCoat™, causes water to bead and shed off for a clearer view when water drops are present.

Outer tube walls are 25% thicker for 42% greater strength. Double-force coil spring suspension locks the inner tube in place for unfailing accuracy.

XTRs also feature side turret-mounted parallax adjustment systems. LRS models have a fully integrated side turret-mounted illumination system. The new 1X-4X XTR equipped with the innovative XTR Ballistic 5.56 Reticle represents the state of the art in tactical optics. The whole package is waterproof, fogproof, shockproof and warranted forever.

The XTR-14 1X-4X riflescope features the XTR Ballistic 5.56 Reticle. A true 1X optic, it is shown matched to XTR Rings and a FastFire reflex sight, which is an offering in this fully-assembled configuration (ideal for M4's and AR15's). It covers the tactical bases from entry work to longrange counter-sniper duties.

This all-new addition to the Fullfield line is built for the mobile shooter who keeps weight to a minimum. High-grade lenses finished with Burris' exclusive index-matched HiLume multicoating for minimal light loss and optimal clarity. Low-profile TAC-2 adjustment knobs. Available in the proven Ballistic Plex reticle, which is calibrated perfectly to short magnum cartridges.

Color: Olive Drab. Plex, Ballistic PLex, Ballistic Mil-dot

BURRIS FASTFIRE

Extremely fast, rugged and low profile, the FastFire sight is a sighting solution for pinpoint accuracy on handguns and shotguns. Unlimited field of view and unlimited eye relief. This compact, lightweight red dot has an integrated light sensor that self-adjusts the red dot brightness for optimal performance. Features windage and elevation adjustments, on/off switch and protective sight cover. Operates on CR2032 battery. FastFire Mounts sold separately.

EOTECH HOLOGRAPHIC SIGHTS

The Eotech holographic patterns have been designed to be instantly visible in any light, instinctive to

237

center regardless of shooting angle, and to remain in view while sweeping the engagement zone. Reticles of EOTech HOLOgraphic Weapon Sights are designed as large, see-through patterns to achieve lightning quick reticle to target acquisition without covering or obscuring the point of aim.

The EoTech Holographic Weapon Sight (HWS) employs a true Heads-Up Display that eliminates blind spots, constricted vision, or the tunnel vision associated with tubed sights. All user controls are flush to the Eotech Holographic Weapon Sight's streamline housing with no protruding knobs, battery compartments or mounting rings blocking vision at the target area. True, 2 eyes open shooting is realized with EOTech HWS. Instant threat identification is achieved by maximizing the operator's peripheral vision and ultimately gaining greater control of the engagement zone.

LEUPOLD TACTICAL MARK 4 CQ/T

The fast target acquisition and illuminated reticle of a red dot sight, the utility of a 1x to 3x riflescope, and the ability to function with or without batteries; this is the Leupold® Mark 4® CQ/T®.

The CQ/T riflescope, parts and accessories fall under the jurisdiction of the U.S. Department of State. Unless required State Department license is obtained, this product is for sale in the U.S.A. only.

LEUPOLD MARK 4 1.5-5X20MM MR/T M2 ILLUMINATED RETICLE

The illuminated Mil Dot or Tactical Milling Reticle (TMR™) ensures precision shot placement in even the worst light conditions, and is night-vision compatible. These reticles are ideal in tactical situations, yet also provide greater accuracy of range estimation for hunters and target shooters. The Index Matched Lens System® delivers superior resolution from edge to edge of the visual field, along with peak image brightness and optimal contrast in low light. Finger-adjustable 1⁄2-MOA windage and elevation adjustments with audible, tactile clicks. Engraved Bullet Drop Compensation dial for 5.56mm/.223 Rem, or 7.62mm/.308 win.

LEUPOLD MARK 4 8.5-25X50MM ER/T M1 FRONT FOCAL RIFLESCOPE

Every feature was put in place for one purpose: to help you get the maximum peformance from your long-range firearms, at the range, hunting, or in a tactical environment. The Leupold® Index Matched Lens System® delivers resolution from edge to edge of the visual field – even at 25x – along with peak image brightness and optimal contrast. Side focus parallax adjustment for fast, easy parallax focusing from 75 yards to infinity, from any shooting position.

KONUS M30 4.5X – 16X – 40MM

Engraved reticle technology
Built-in anti-canting bubble system
Locking fast focus ocular
45 degree offset illuminator switch
Flip-Up lens caps
True 30mm tube (throughout)
Fully-multi coated hi-def optics
Locking tactical turret knobs
    (resettable to zero)
Mid-sized parallax wheel for easier
    adjustment and clear visual (down to
    10 yards)
Ultra Blue illumination for dark targets
Precision 1/8 MOA adjustments
Includes 4" sunshade
Magnification/Objective: 4.5-16X40 mm
Power: 4.5-16X
Objective Diameter: 40 mm
Reticle: Mil Dot Engraved Ultra Blue illumination
Parallax Setting: 10 yds.inf.
Waterproof: Yes
FOV (Field Of View): 23.1 ft at 100 Yards
Eye Relief: 4 inches
M.O.A.: Precision 1/8 MOA 85 MOA Max
Optics: Fully Multi-Coated
Color: Matte Black
Weight: 26.7 oz.
Length: 14.9 Inches
Tube Size: 30 mm

KONUS 7281 M30 SERIES 6.5X-25X 44MM

Engraved reticle technology
Built-in anti-canting bubble system
Locking fast focus ocular
45 degree offset illuminator switch
Flip-Up lens caps
True 30mm tube (throughout)
Fully-multi coated hi-def optics
Locking tactical turret knobs (resettable to zero)
Includes 4" sunshade

Magnification/Objective: 6.5-25X44 mm
Power: 6.5-25X
Objective Diameter: 44 mm
Reticle: Mil-Dot I.R. Ultra Blue illumination
Parallax Setting: 10 yds.inf.
Waterproof: Yes
FOV (Field Of View): 17.3ft at 100 Yards
Eye Relief: 4 Inches
M.O.A.: Precision 1/8 MOA 50 MOA Max
Optics: Fully-multi coated hi-def optics
Color: Matte Black
Weight: 30 oz.
Length: 17.7 Inches
Tube Size: 30 mm

KONUS 7282 M30 SERIES 8.5X-32X 52MM

Engraved reticle technology
Built-in anti-canting bubble system
Locking fast focus ocular
45 degree offset illuminator switch
Flip-Up lens caps
True 30mm tube (throughout)
Fully-multi coated hi-def optics
Locking tactical turret knobs
   (resettable to zero)
Mid-sized parallax wheel for easier
   adjustment and clear visual (down
   to 10 yards)
Ultra Blue illumination for dark targets
Precision 1/8 MOA adjustments
Includes 4" sunshade
Magnification/Objective: 8.5-32X52 mm
Power: 8.5-32X
Objective Diameter: 52 mm
Reticle: Mil Dot Engrved Ultra Blue illum
Parallax Setting: 10 yds.inf.
Waterproof: Yes
FOV (Field Of View): 23.1ft at 100 Yards
Eye Relief: 4 inches
M.O.A.: 1/8 MOA adjustments
Optics: Fully Multi Coated
Color: Matte Black
Weight: 26.7 oz.
Length: 14.9 Inches
Tube Size: 30mm

SCHMIDT & BENDER 1.1–4 X 20 SHORT DOT POLICE MARKSMAN II

A separate turret with 11 click stops controls the illumination function of a precise red dot at the center of the reticle. Fully variable illumination levels range from barely visible, for use with night vision equipment, to full bright for quick, accurate shots in bright, harsh daylight. With illumination switched off, the Short Dot functions as a standard scope with nonilluminated crosshairs. This gives the Short Dot "any light, any time" versatility and reliability in any circumstance the shooter may encounter. Four bullet-drop compensators are supplied for 5.56 mm cartridges, including the 62 gr. Green Tip, 75 gr. Hornady TAP, and the SR25 with M118R16 and M118 LR20 loads. Turrets are non-locking.

SCHMIDT & BENDER 1.1–4 X 20 SHORT DOT WITH LOCKING TURRETS

Evolved from the basic Short Dot model, the addition of locking turrets and the CQB reticle results in a highly specialized instrument suitable for high-stress urban and combat situations. You have a choice of rings calibrated for either the M855, 75 gr. TAP or M118LR loads, to cover the popular 5.56 and 7.62 offerings. Locking windage, elevation and illumination turrets insure that the scope's settings will not change even under the most rigorous system.

The reticle is located in the first focal plane, and includes ranging capabilities at higher magnification. At 1.1 power, the skeleton post system virtually disappears for fast, accurate target acquisition. The same highly flexible Flash Dot system as in the standard Short Dot is included.

SCHMIDT & BENDER 1.1–4 X 24 ZENITH SHORT DOT LE

The reticle is located in the second focal plane. At 1.1 power it is more substantial, preferred for quick response when illumination is not required. At 4 power, the illuminated Flash Dot covers only 1.57" at 100 yards (compared to 5.9" for a reticle in the first focal plane). This allows more precise shot placement at longer ranges.

Locking illumination and elevation turrets are standard, calibrated for the M855, 75 gr. TAP or M118LR. Also included is our unique Posicon control, providing a graphic representation of where the reticle lies within its adjustment range. This makes for easier mounting and sighting in. Our Flash Dot illumination system is standard. Offered with reticles FD2 or FD7.

SCHMIDT & BENDER 3–12 X 50 PM II

A versatile scope, allowing precise shot placement to 1000 meters yet still presenting an exceptionally wide field of view at low power. Available with paral-

239

lax adjustment or with parallax adjustment and illuminated reticles.

Two elevation/windage options are offered; Option One has one-centimeter click values with an elevation range of 220cm at 100m. Option Two has a "double turn" elevation knob with increments of 1/4MOA per click. Elevation range is 56MOA at 100m. Windage is also 1/4MOA per click, with a total adjustment of ±14MOA. Offered with P1 or P3 rangefinding reticles.

SCHMIDT & BENDER 3–12 X 50 PM II LP

Combines parallax compensation, illuminated reticle control and 1/4MOA or centimeter clicks. There are two elevation adjustment options: Option One is calibrated to 0.1 Mil click values. Option Two is calibrated in 1/4MOA click values. Color-coded window indicators graphically illustrate the reticle's position within the overall adjustment travel, preventing the shooter from becoming "lost" within the adjustment range. The entire adjustment range can be covered in just two turns of the elevation knob, while the entire 3-12x magnification range is covered in just one-half turn (180 degrees).

Parallax adjustment is located in its own separate turret, as are the illuminated reticle controls. The reticle brightness is fully adjustable with 11 graduated settings allowing precise selection relative to ambient light. As with all Schmidt & Bender illuminated reticles, it turns off between settings saving battery power and allowing you to easily return to a pre-selected illumination level. Available with the P3, P4, or P4 Fine reticles.

SCHMIDT & BENDER 4–16 X 50 PM II

A wide magnification range provides versatility from close range shots to distances beyond 1000 meters. A 50mm objective lens provides outstanding performance even under the poorest light conditions. Available in two configurations; parallax adjustment only and parallax and illuminated-reticle adjustment. The 4-16 x 50 is offered with "double turn" elevation

knob with 1/4 MOA clicks and an adjustment range of 56 MOA. The entire 56-minute adjustment range can be covered in just two turns of the elevation knob, while the IAL window illustrates the adjustment position within the overall range. Windage increments are also 1/4 MOA per click, the total adjustment range ±14 MOA. Offered with P1 or P3 reticles.

SCHMIDT & BENDER 4–16 X 50 PM II LP

The Schmidt and Bender 4–16 x 50 in an illuminated reticle LP model. An illuminated reticle and parallax adjustment are standard, each controlled by a separate turret. The LP system features a color-coded elevation knob that gives the shooter instant reference as to where the elevation is set. Just one turn of the knob provides 28 minutes of elevation. A window within the dial then changes to yellow, and one additional turn provides an additional 28 minutes of adjustment. The entire 56-minute adjustment range can be covered in just two turns of the elevation knob. Click values are 1/4 MOA. P3 or P4 Fine reticles available.

SCHMIDT & BENDER 5-25 X 56 POLICE MARKSMAN II LP

This scope offers true 2000-meter capability. Unlike most long-range variables that offer only a 4x magnification multiple, the 5-25 x 56 provides a full 5x and a wider field of view. Parallax adjustment in a separate turret, completely adjustable from 10 meters to infinity. The illuminated reticle has 11 graduated settings offering precise control relative to ambient light. The scope includes Schmidt & Bender's color-coded "Double Turn" elevation knob that gives the shooter instant reference to where the elevation is set. The entire 100-minute adjustment range can be covered in just two turns of the knob. The user will never become "lost" within the adjustment range. The 5–25 x 56 is offered with 56 MOA of 1/4 MOA clicks, or 273cm (93 MOA) of 1cm clicks. Your choice of P3 or P4 reticles.

YUKON/YUKON-CENTURION SYSTEMS 24025

The NVMT 1x24 Head Gear Kit incorporates the element of hands-free night vision with the quality and value of a 1x24 monocular. The NVMT 1x24 monocular uses no magnification so that users can see a clear image with no distortion or change in depth perception. The small, compact monocular is secured to the head gear by a mounting system that sits easily on the front head strap so that the NVMT can be flipped up when not in use or flipped down when activated; the NVMT head gear is designed to be used with your right eye only and can not be interchanged for the left. The 1x24 also features separately activated Pulse™ system IR illuminator that uses a pulsating infrared beam to enhance night vision viewing capabilities. A simple detaching mechanism allows the monocular to be taken off the mount for hand-held use. Additional

accessories for the NVMT 1x24 are the NVMT IR Flashlight, Riflescope Conversion Kit and Digital Camera Adapter. The NVMT Goggle 1x24 is backed by Yukon's Limited Lifetime Warranty.

YUKON/YUKON-CENTURION SYSTEMS 25025

The Viking 1x24 NV Goggles are a night vision binocular that allows for incredibly detailed observation ability under the darkness of night that includes a head gear accessory for a flip-up, adjustable and hands-free unit. The Viking 1x24 provides clear viewing in total darkness by utilizing a built-in IR infrared illuminator; when in use the illuminator emits a pulsing frequency that is so energy efficient it creates less battery drainage and prolongs battery life. The ergonomically designed rubberized body is surprisingly lightweight and can be taken on long expeditions both easily and comfortably, and is great for prolonged use with the head gear accessory. The Viking utilizes the revolutionary Eclipse™ Lens Cover System which uses flip-up covers that can be easily clipped back against the body of the binoculars and rotated out of the user's viewing area while eliminating lens cap hassles. Pin holes in the lens caps allow the Viking to be used in the daytime when the caps are closed. Also featured is a dual diopter adjustment with central focusing knob, fully multi-coated optics and water and fog resistance. The Viking 1x24 NV Goggles are backed by Yukon's Limited Lifetime Warranty.

YUKON/YUKON-CENTURION SYSTEMS 26013T

The Varmint Hunter 2.5x50 uses enhanced optics, a durable, titanium body and sleek design to separate itself from any other night vision riflescope. The Varmint Hunter incorporates a long mount into its ergonomic design to allow for more comfort during shooting while also enabling the scope to accommodate the widest range of rifles, including bolt action styles. It is also equipped with a powerful 50mm lens to provide higher resolution and light gathering capabilities, and flip-up lens covers open to reveal quality multi-coated optics and an illuminated reticle. A built-in, powerful Pulse™ infrared illuminator is easily activated to enhance image brightness and increase range in total darkness; a precision windage and elevation adjustment and remote are additional features. The Varmint Hunter is also digital camera adaptable with the digital camera accessory; other accessories include a laser pointer, AK adapter, IR flashlight and doubler

lens, which are all sold separately. The Varmint Hunter is backed by Yukon's Limited Lifetime Warranty.

YUKON/YUKON-CENTURION SYSTEMS 26014

The NVRS Tactical 2.5x50 uses enhanced optics, a durable, titanium body and sleek design to separate itself from any other night vision riflescope. The NVRS Tactical 2.5x50 has internal focusing ability and incorporates a long mount into its ergonomic design to allow for more comfort during shooting while also enabling the scope to accommodate the widest range of rifles, including bolt action styles. It is also equipped with a powerful 50mm lens to provide higher resolution and light gathering capabilities, and flip-up lens covers open to reveal quality multi-coated optics and an illuminated reticle. A built-in, powerful Pulse™ infrared illuminator is easily activated to enhance image brightness and increase range in total darkness; a precision windage and elevation adjustment and remote are additional features. The NVRS Tactical 2.5x50 is also digital camera adaptable with the digital camera accessory; other accessories include a laser pointer, AK adapter, IR flashlight and doubler lens, which are all sold separately. The NVRS Tactical 2.5x50 is backed by Yukon's Limited Lifetime Warranty.

YUKON/YUKON-CENTURION SYSTEMS 26021

The NVRS Tactical 2.5x42 Gen 2+ uses enhanced optics, a durable, titanium body and sleek design to separate itself from any other night vision riflescope. The NVRS Tactical 2.5x42 Gen 2+ incorporates a long mount into its ergonomic design to allow for more comfort during shooting while also enabling the scope to accommodate the widest range of rifles, including bolt action styles. It is also equipped with a powerful 50mm lens to provide higher resolution and light gathering capabilities, and flip-up lens covers open to reveal quality multi-coated optics and an illuminated reticle. A built-in, powerful Pulse™ infrared illuminator is easily activated to enhance image brightness and increase range in total darkness; a precision windage and elevation adjustment and remote are additional features. The NVRS Tactical 2.5x42 Gen 2+ is also digital camera adaptable with the digital camera accessory; other accessories include a laser pointer, AK adapter and IR flashlight, which are all sold separately. The NVRS Tactical 2.5x42 Gen 2+ is backed by Yukon's Limited Lifetime Warranty.

APPENDIX A: LIGHT & OPTICS CATALOG

VYUKON/YUKON-CENTURION SYSTEMS 26031

The NVRS Tactical 2.5x42 Gen 3 is the most power-ful riflescope in the Titanium line and uses enhanced optics, a durable, titanium body and sleek design to separate itself from any other night vision riflescope. The NVRS Tactical 2.5x42 Gen 3 incorporates a long mount into its ergonomic design to allow for more comfort during shooting while also enabling the scope to accommodate the widest range of rifles, including bolt action styles. It is also equipped with a powerful 50mm lens to provide higher resolution and light gathering capabilities, and flip-up lens cov-ers open to reveal quality multi-coated optics and an illuminated reticle. A built-in, powerful Pulse™ infrared illuminator is easily activated to enhance im-age brightness and increase range in total darkness; a precision windage and elevation adjustment and remote are additional features. The NVRS Tactical 2.5x42 Gen 3 is also digital camera adaptable with the digital camera accessory; other accessories in-clude a laser pointer, AK adapter and IR flashlight, which are all sold separately. The NVRS Tactical 2.5x42 Gen 3 is backed by Yukon's Limited Lifetime Warranty.

YUKON/YUKON-CENTURION SYSTEMS 26041

A key component to the originality of the new NVMT is that it sheds the burden of a one-dimensional item and evolves into a multi-functional system allowing the scope to be used virtually anywhere. The NVMT 3x42 Laser Riflescope merges a powerful 3x42 mon-ocular with a detachable eyepiece, rifle mount and la-ser pointer to create a truly versatile night vision unit. The adjustable laser pointer's beam acts as a target acquisition guide when the unit is mounted to your riflescope and ensures precision while shooting. As with all monoculars in the NVMT series, the NVMT 3x42 has excellent light amplification performance, amplifying visible light several thousand times, and an exclusive Pulse™ built-in infrared illuminator that ex-pands viewing range and minimizes battery drainage. Fully multi-coated optics decrease glare and improve light transmission to provide an excellent viewing ex-perience while the compact and durable Rubber Ar-mor™ body is small enough to fit in the palm of your hand or in a pocket, yet rugged enough to withstand use. Yukon's NVMT Riflescope is perfect for airsoft, varmint control, paintball or any other night gun sports that require a short range, night vision scope. The NVMT 3x42 Laser Riflescope is backed by Yukon's Limited Lifetime Warranty.

YUKON/YUKON-CENTURION SYSTEMS CS44012

The Centurion Systems BORDER PATROL 3.6x68 Gen.2 Long Range Surveillance Night Vision Viewer has a distinguishable, unique panoramic eyepiece, allowing for an increased observation area for ex-tended durations. The Border Patrol Night Vision Viewer is superior for viewing over long distances with exceptional visual comfort, and helps prevent eye fatigue.

YUKON/YUKON-CENTURION SYSTEMS CS45002

The Centurion Systems DEFENDER 1x24 is the Night Vision Goggle that is the evolved version of the PVS-7 with improved functionality and performance. Available with an extensive choice of image intensi-fiers, the DEFENDER Night Vision Goggle provides exceptional performance in the most unfavorable conditions. The Centurion Systems DEFENDER 1x24 Night Vision Goggle can also accept a 3x mag-nifier lens.

YUKON/YUKON-CENTURION SYSTEMS CS45003

The Centurion Systems DEFENDER 1x24 is the Night Vision Goggles that are the evolved version of the PVS-7 with improved functionality and perfor-mance. Available with an extensive choice of image intensifiers, the DEFENDER Night Vision Goggles provide exceptional performance in the most unfavor-able conditions. The Centurion Systems DEFENDER 1x24 Night Vision Goggles can also accept a 3x mag-nifier lens.

YUKON/YUKON-CENTURION SYSTEMS CS45992

The Centurion Systems GOVERNOR 7x84 Gen.3 Night Vision Binoculars are an extremely effective night vision device designed for long distance obser-vation. These Night Vision Binoculars incorporate a 165mm F/2.0 objective lens system to provide a high 7x magnification allowing the user to conduct surveil-lance up to 800 yards.

YUKON/YUKON-CENTURION SYSTEMS CS47003

The Centurion Systems EXPERT 5-12x83 Day / Night Vision Rifle Scope is deadly accurate at long

ranges, and has a special day/night 23 lens zoom optic system.

YUKON/YUKON-CENTURION SYSTEMS CS12001

The Centurion Systems Sortie™ 7x50 Military Binoculars take a high quality BaK-4 prism, pairs it with incredible, fully multicoated lenses, and transforms them into one of the most extraordinary tactical binoculars ever designed. These military binoculars are reliable to a fault, and provide maximum light transmission and optimal brightness so the user can conduct surveillance and observation in even the most unforgiving terrain.

From early dawn to late dusk, the optimum color fidelity and clarity of image enhance any surveillance mission while a generously long eye relief reduces potential eye strain. Every Centurion Systems Sortie™ 7x50 Military Binoculars incorporate a military grade compass and an approximating distance reticle to give the user the ability to coordinate live field exercises and fire support while keeping his eyes on the target. This battle tough military binoculars are nitrogen purged, waterproof, fogproof and encased in rubber armor, making it the favorite tactical binocular of sniper teams, infantry units and special forces.

YUKON/YUKON-CENTURION SYSTEMS CS45001

The Centurion Systems PVS-7 Night Vision Goggles / Binoculars are engineered to meet MIL-SPEC requirements and standards. The rugged and reliable design ideally accommodates users for extended wear and superior surveillance functions. These Night Vision Goggles have an integrated IR illuminator with an IR "on" indicator, low battery indicator, excess light exposure cut-off sensor and other features. The night nision system is based on the most advanced image intensifiers, with 64-72 lp/mm and a Figure of Merit of no less than 1600. The Centurion Systems PVS-7 Night Vision Goggles / Binoculars also can accept a 3x magnifier lens.

YUKON/YUKON-CENTURION SYSTEMS CS46002

The Centurion Systems MAGNUM 4x68 Gen.2+ Night Vision Weapon Sight is superior for long range shooting, with outstanding accuracy, in the most unfavorable conditions. This Night Vision Weapon Sight is the best in industry power consumption; 120 hours of battery life time.

YUKON/YUKON-CENTURION SYSTEMS CS47052

The Centurion Systems SHARP SHOOTER Gen.2 Day / Night Riflescope is the most advanced portable sniper system, noted for unparalleled accuracy at long ranges and unique versatility.

YUKON/YUKON-CENTURION SYSTEMS CS47092

The Centurion Systems MARKSMAN Gen.3 is a revolutionary THREE in ONE: Day Weapon Sight / Night Vision Weapon Sight / Night Vision Monocular.

The innovative design of this Day and Night Vision Weapon Sight meets specific requirements for a Tactical Weapon Day Sight, advanced Night Vision Weapon Sight and Night Vision Monocular.

SIGHTRON S2 SCOPES

S2 scopes are completely updated with better glass, tighter tolerances and new lens coatings. The S2 was designed to offer maximum light transmission and accuracy. They feature 1/4 MOA adjustments with finger adjustable turrets and are waterproof, fogproof, shockproof and filled with nitrogen. Sightron scopes are covered by a lifetime factory warranty.

SIGHTRON S3 SCOPES

Sightron's S3 scopes are made of quality 6061 T-6 aluminum and are built to take a lifetime of punishment. They also feature ZACT-7 Revcoat™ 7 layer multi-coating process that give an amazing 99% light transmission per lens, so performance under low light is never a problem. The S3 scopes also have Sightron's patented ExacTrack™ windage and elevation system that guarantees that once adjusted, you'll never experience a shift in the point of impact. Both Sightron S3 Scopes are nitrogen charged, waterproof and shockproof and are covered under Sightron's Lifetime Warranty.

SIGHTRON SIIWP750 BINOCULARS

Fully multi-coated lenses, BaK-4 prisms and rubber coated frame allow it to serve in all weather conditions. Water and fogproof. Includes case, neck strap and lifetime warranty.

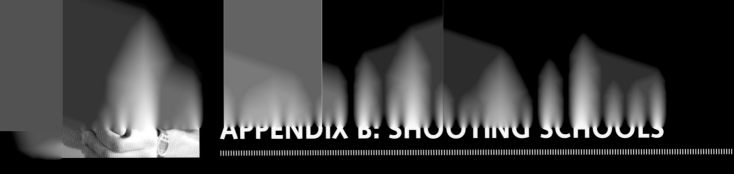

Below is a list of various shooting schools around the country. Typical fees start at about $400 per person for a three- or four-day class and may top out at $2,000 or more depending on the location of the class and the lodging offered.

Most of the people listed here will provide information about firearms and training. If you need a technical advisor for a movie or video project, this is a good place to start. Some folks listed here, like Massad Ayoob of the Lethal Force Institute, also serve as expert witnesses in civil and criminal cases. Some of the better-known schools include the aforementioned Lethal Force Institute, Front Sight, Gunsite, Thunder Ranch and Blackheart International. Some of the instructors listed here have come right from the ranks of the U.S. military Special Operations community.

Absolute Tactical Training
2573 Market St.
San Diego, California 92102
619-858-5832
FAX: 619-692-9408
www.absolutetacticaltraining.com
Keiko Arroyo, Chief Instructor

Academy of Personal Protection and Security
336 Hill Ave.
Suite 102
Nashville, Tennessee 37210
615-360-6002
FAX: 615-366-7374
www.appstraining.com
J. Buford Tune, Director

Advanced Training Assoc.
6136 Mission Gorge Rd #220
San Diego, CA 92120
619-644-1342
Kurt Sawatzky and Lin Henry, Instructors

Advanced Tactical Technologies Inc.
PO Box 51404

Phoenix, AZ 85076
602-706-8010

Advanced Weapons and Tactics
PO Box 6258
Napa, CA 94581
707-253-8926
FAX: 707-253-8927
www.awt-co.com
Walt Marshall, Instructor

Allsafe Defense Systems
1026 N. Tustin Ave.
Orange, CA 92867-5958
714-744-4485
www.allsafedefense.com
T.J. Johnston, Instructor

American Pistol & Rifle Association
(APRA members only)
Firearms Academy Staff
Box USA
Benton, TN 37307
615-338-2328

American Shooting Academy
PO Box 54233
Phoenix, AZ 85078-4233

623-825-7317
www.asa-training.com
James Jarrett, Director

American Small Arms Academy
PO Box 12111
Prescott, AZ 86304
602-778-5623
Chuck Taylor, Instructor

Area 52 Smallarms Training Center
4809 Schley Road
Hillsborough, NC 27278
919-245-0013
area52training@cs.com

Argenbright International Training Institute
(law enforcement, military and corporate security)
4845 Old National Highway, Suite 210
Atlanta, Georgia 30337
800-235-4723

Arizona Defensive Firearms Training
PO Box 44302

Phoenix, Arizona 85064
602-279-3770
FAX: 602-279-0333
www.azccw.com
adft@azccw.com
Rick Barkett, Director

Arkansas Police Trainers
(law enforcement)
212 West Elm Street
Rogers, Arkansas 72756
501-621-1173 or 501-273-9270
FAX: 501-621-1131
Tim Keck, Executive Director

Auto Arms
738 Clearview
San Antonio, TX 78228
512-434-5450

AWARE
(Arming Women Against Rape and
Endangerment)
PO Box 242
Bedford, MA 01730
781-893-0500
877-672-9273 Toll Free
www.aware.org

**Bay Area Professionals for
Firearms Safety & Education**
(Bayprofs)
1600 Saratoga Ave #403-181
San Jose, CA 95129
408-741-5218 (answering machine
only)
www.bayprofs.org
Tom Laye, Training Director

Beretta Training
17601 Beretta Drive
Accokeek, MD 20607
301-283-2191
Russ Logan and Marcel James,
Instructors

Blackheart International, LLC
112 Wood Street
Philippi, WV 26416
877-244-8166
FAX: 304-457-1281
support@bhigear.com
www.bhigear.com

**Blackwater Lodge
and Training Center**
200 Puddin Ridge Rd. Ext.
Moyock, NC 27958
252-435-2488
FAX: 252-435-6388
training@blackwaterlodge.com
www.blackwaterlodge.com
Ken Viera, General Manager

Bob's Tactical
122 Lafayette Road
Salisbury, MA 01952
978-465-5561

Brantly and Associates, Inc.
3001 W. 39th St.
Suite 10
Orlando, FL 32839
407-650-1771
FAX: 407-650-8333
jamesbrantly@cs.com
brantlyandassociates.com

BSR, Inc.
PO Box 190
Summit Point, WV 25446
304-725-6512
FAX: 304-728-7124
office@bsr-inc.com
www.bsrfirearms-training.com

**Burton's Firearm
Instruction**
(for women only)
PO Box 6084

Lynnwood, WA 98036-0084
206-774-7940
Gale Burton, Instructor

Calibre Press
(law enforcement and
military personnel training)
666 Dundee Road, Ste. 1607
Northbrook, IL 60062-2760
708-498-5680

**California Security
& Safety Institute**
706 E. Arrow Hwy, #E
Covina, CA 91722
800-281-1330
Steven Hurd, Director

**Canadian Academy
of Practical Shooting**
C.P. 312
Roxboro, Quebec H8Y 3K4
Canada
514-696-8591
FAX: 514-696-2348
www.caps-inc.com
Dave Young, Director

Canadian Firearms Training
Ottawa, Ontario
Canada
613-443-0749
www.FirearmsTraining.ca
Dave Bartlett, President

**Chapman Academy
of Practical Shooting**
4350 Academy Road
Hallsville, MO 65255-9707
800-847-0588
573-696-5544
FAX: 573-696-2266
www.chapmanacademy.com
John Skaggs, Director

APPENDIX B: SHOOTING SCHOOLS

Chelsea Gun Club of New York City, Inc.
c/o West Side Range
20 W. 20th Street
New York, NY 10011
212-929-7287
James D. Surdo, Instructor

Cirillo's Tactical Handgun Training
1211 Venetian Way
Panama City, FL 32405
Jim Cirillo, Instructor

CivilShield
Los Gatos, CA
408-354-1424
FAX: 408-399-2270
www.civilshield.com

Colorado Firearms Academy
20 S. Potomac Street
Aurora, Colorado 80012
303-360-5400
John Noble and Michael Schaffer, Instructors

Colorado Gun Training
2767 S. Parker Road, #253
Aurora, Colorado 80014
720-435-9964
Rick Vizachero, Director
train@theRange.com
firearmstrainingsite.com

Colorado Weapons Training
PO Box 745504
Arvada, Colorado 80006-5504
303-421-8541
ColoradoWeaponsTraining.com

Combative Concepts
826 Orange Avenue, #518
Coronado, CA 92118
619-521-2855

COMTAC, Ltd.
PO Box 12269
Silver Spring, MD 20908
301-924-4315

FAX: 301-924-3854
comtac@comtac.com
www.comtac.com
Charles A. Davis, Director of Training

Continental Threat Management
507 Owen Drive
Fayetteville, NC 28304
910-485-8805
NCLFI@aol.com
Timothy A. Noe, Director

Cumberland Tactics
PO Box 1400
Goodlettsville, TN 37070
615-822-7779
Randy@guntactics.com
www.guntactics.com/
Randy Cain, Director

Dalton's International Shootists Institute
PO Box 88
Acton, CA 93510
www.isishootists.com
Mike Dalton, Instructor

Dan Mitchell's Clay Target and Wing Shooting School
304 Roosevelt
Nampa, ID 83651
208-467-2793
www.idfishnhunt.com/mitchell.htm

Defense Arts of Texas
214 N. 16th Suite B-6
McAllen, TX
Robert E. Henry, Director
956-682-0388

Defense Associates
PO Box 824
Fairfield, CT 06430
www.defenseassociates.com
203-261-8719

Defensive Firearms Academy
PO Box 615
Iselin, New Jersey 08830

www.dfatactics.com
Larry Mraz, Director
732-283-3314

Defensive Firearms Consultants
PO Box 27431
Towson, MD 21285
410-321-6522

Defensive Solutions
190 Cedar Circle
Powell, TN 37849
865-945-5612
info@defensivesolutions.com
www.defensivesolutions.com

Defensive Training for the Armed Citizen (DEFTAC)
5712 Folkstone Lane
Orlando, FL 32822
407-208-0751
deftac03@aol.com
members.aol.com/deftac03
Jon A. Custis, Instructor

Defense Training International, Inc.
749 S. Lemay Ste. A3-337
Ft.Collins, Colorado 80301
970-482-2520
FAX: 970-482-0548
dti@frii.com
www.defense-training.com
John S. Farnam, President

Defensive Use of Firearms
PO Box 4227
Show Low, AZ 85902-4227
www.spw-duf.info

Denton County Sports Association, Inc.
409 Copper Canyon Road
Denton County, TX 76226
940-241-2376
dcsa@airmail.net
www.dentoncountysports.com
Lonnie Ward, Director

DTOM Enterprises
PO Box 415
Bloomingdale, MI 49026-0415
616-628-5039
DTOM.us
MTS@DTOM.us

**Executive Security Services
International**
Box 5585
Huntsville, Ontario, Canada P1H 2L5
705-788-1957
www.essi.cjb.net

Farris Firearms Training
102 Jeremiah Court
Rockvale, Tennessee 37153
615-907-4892
www.farrisfirearms.com
training@farrisfirearms.com

**Federal Law Enforcement Training
Center** (FLETC)
(law enforcement training)
FLETC
Glynco, GA 31524
800-743-5382
FAX: 912-267-3144
Gerald Brooks, Program Specialist

Firearms Academy of Redding
1530 Market Street
Redding, CA 96001
916-244-2190

Firearms Academy of Seattle
PO Box 400
Onalaska, WA 98570
360-978-6100
FAX: 360-978-6102
www.firearmsacademy.com
Marty Hayes, Instructor

**Firearms International Training
Academy**
5139 Stanart Street
Norfolk, VA 23502
757-461-9153
FAX: 757-461-9155

Gerry Fockler, Director

**Firearms Research &
Instruction, Inc.**
PO Box 732
Abingdon, MD 21009
877-456-5075
www.f-r-i.com
steves02@gte.net
Steven Silverman, President

Firearms Training Associates
PO Box 554
Yorba Linda, CA 92885-0554
714-701-9918
FAX: 714-777-9318
Bill Murphy, Instructor
www.ftatv.com

Firearm Training Center
The Bullet Hole Range
78 Rutgers St
Belleville, NJ 07109
201-919-0414
Anthony P. Colandro, Director
www.FirearmTrainingCenter.com

Firearms Training Center
9555 Blandville Road
West Paducah, KY 42086
502-554-5886

Firearms Training Institute
1044 Desert View Dr
Twin Falls, ID 83301
208-735-1469
scoobys@cyberhighway.net

**Firearmz - Firearms Training and
Defense**
PO Box 344
Temple, Georgia 30179-0344
770-562-8663
www.firearmz.net

**Front Sight Firearms Training
Institute**
PO Box 2619
Aptos, CA 95001

800-987-7719
FAX: 831-684-2137
www.frontsight.com
info@frontsight.com
Dr. Ignatius Piazza, Director

Global Security Complex
5750 Herring Road
Arvin, CA 93203
805-845-7011
FAX: 805-845-7945
global@lightspeed.net

Glock, Inc.
(law enforcement and military
personnel training)
PO Box 369
Smyrna, GA 30081
404-432-1202
Al Bell, Director of Training
Frank DiNuzzo, Assistant
Director of Training

Guardian Group International
21 Warren Street, Suite 3E
New York, NY 10007
212-619-2828

**Gunner Joe's Bullseye
Academy**
12247 Buckskin Trail
Poway, CA 92964-6005
858-486-6201
Joe Vaineharrison, Instructor

GunSafety - TampaBay
PO Box 26393
Tampa, Florida 33623-6393
813-354-2799
Michael Perry, Owner
www.gunsafetytampa.com

Gunsite Academy, Inc.
2900 West Gunsite Road
Pauldin, AZ 86334-4301
520-636-4565
FAX: 520-636-1236
Buz Mills, Owner
www.gunsite.net

247

APPENDIX B: SHOOTING SCHOOLS

Guntek Firearms Training
4400 A Ambassador Caffery
Parkway #310
Lafayette, LA 70508
337-984-8711
FAX: 337-993-1159
identify@bellsouth.net

Halo Group, The
316 California Ave
Suite 748
Reno, NV 89509
888-255-HALO
training@thehalogroup.com

Handgun Instruction
Fresno, CA
209-442-8102 or 209-221-9415
Laurie Anderson and Ken Zachary,
Instructors

Heckler & Koch, Inc.
International Training Division
(law enforcement and military
personnel training)
21480 Pacific Boulevard
Sterling, VA 20166-8903
703-450-1900
FAX: 703-450-8180
John Meyer, Jr., Director

**HomeSafe Protective
Training**
5100 Burchette Rd., #3403
Tampa, FL 33647
813-979-7119
Beeper: 813-673-7016
Bret Bartlett, Director

Illinois Small Arms Institute
3512 Roxford Drive
Champaign, IL 61821
217-356-0704
John W. Bowman, Director

**Insight Firearms Training
Development**
PO Box 12293
Prescott, Arizona 86304-2293
928-708-9208

8662NSIGHT
FAX: 928-776-4668
www.insightfirearmstraining.com

InSights Training Center, Inc.
PO Box 3585
Bellevue, WA 98009
425-739-0133
www.insightstraining.com
Greg Hamilton, Instructor

**Institute of Security
Services**
(tactical response team training)
1205 Banner Hill Rd.
Erwin, TN 37650-9301
800-441-0081
FAX: 615-743-2361

**International Academy of
Tactical Training Systems**
#8 129 2nd Ave. N
Saskatoon, Saskatchewan
Canada S7K 2A9
306-975-1995
Brad Hutchinson, Director
www.attscanada.com
ntc@sk.sympatico.ca

**International Association
of Law Enforcement Firearms
Instructors, Inc.**
IALEFI
25 Country Club Road, Suite 707
Gilford, NH 03246
603-524-8787
FAX: 603-524-8856
Robert D. Bossey, Executive Director
ialefi@lr.net
www.ialefi.com

**International Rescue and
Tactical Consultants** (I.R.T.C.)
(law enforcement and private
security training)
PO Box 1128
Westhampton Beach, NY 11978
516-288-0414
Walter Britton and Gary Gross,
Instructors

**International Tactical Training
Seminars Inc.**
11718 Barrington Court, #506
Los Angeles, CA 90049
310-471-2029
www.intltactical.com
Brett McQueen, Instructor

ISI (Instinctive Shooting nternational)
(law enforcement, military, qualified
civilians)
PO Box 6528
Houston, TX 77265-6528
713-666-0269
FAX: 713-666-9791
isi@wt.net
Hanan Yadin, Head Instructor

**James A. Neal Public Safety
Training Center**
(law enforcement)
PO Box 579
Toccoa, Georgia 30577
706-282-7012
www.jamesanealtraining.com

Ladies Handgun Clinics
2631 New Hope Church Road
Raleigh, NC 27604
919-872-8499

Lane Community College
4000 East 30th Ave.
Eugene, OR 97405-0092
503-726-2252
FAX: 503-726-3958
Michael Steen, Instructor

Law Enforcement Educators
789 F.M. 1637
Valley Mills, Texas 76689
800-527-2403
Carl C. Chandler, Jr., Instructor
www.carlchandler.com

Lethal Force Institute (LFI)
PO Box 122
Concord, NH 03302-0122
603-224-6814

www.ayoob.com
Massad Ayoob, Director

**Loss Prevention Services
of New Jersey**
PO Box 15
Mt. Arlington, NJ 07856
973-347-2002
FAX: 973-347-2321
lpsofnjinc@webtv.com

Malins Defense Systems
2642 W.Javelina Ave., Stuite 207
Mesa, AZ 85202
602-838-8139
defense_systmems@hotmail.com
Darrell Malin, Instructor

Marksman's Enterprise
PO Box 556
Stevensville, Montana 59870
406-777-3557
crews@sprynet.com Jim Crews,
Instructor

**Marksmanship Training
Group, Inc.**
2549 W. Golf Rd. #217
Hoffman Estates, IL 60194
630-205-1369
www.kapnick.net/mtg.html
Brian Kapnick, Primary Instructor

Martial Arts Resource
PO Box 110841
Campbell, CA 95011-0841
408-866-5127
MartialArtsResource.com
Ray Terry, Head Instructor

Massachusetts Firearms Seminars
PO Box 881
Lee, MA 01238
413-243-2195
www.mafseminars.com

Midwest Tactical Training Institute
11311 S. Skunk Hollow Road
Mt. Carroll, IL 61053

815-244-2815
Andrew Casavant, Instructor

Midwest Training Group, Inc
1514 Cortland Drive
Naperville, IL 60565
630-579-0351
andykemp@msn.com
Andy Kemp, Director

**Mid-South Institute of
Self-Defense**
(law enforcement and military
personnel training)
5582 Blythe Road
Lake Cornorant, MS 38641
www.weaponstraining.com
John Shaw, Instructor

**MINDRICK Security Academy
and Shooting School**
Budd Road Box 747
Phillipsport, NY 12769
914-647-4048
www.mindrick.com
Fredrick Vobis, Director

**Modern Warrior Defensive
Tactics Institute**
(law enforcement training)
711 N. Wellwood Ave.
Lindenhurst, NY 11757
800-33-WARRIOR
FAX: 516-226-5454
George Demetriou

**National Law Enforcement
Training Center**
4948 Westwood Road
Kansas City, MO 64112
800-445-0857
FAX: 816-531-3416
www.odinpress.com

National Rifle Association
11250 Waples Mill Road
Fairfax, VA 22030
800-672-3888
www.nra.org

Northeast Training Institute
130 N. Fifth Street, Suite 804
Reading, PA 19601
215-872-3433

NOR-CAL Training Academy
2016 Oakdale Ave.
San Francisco, CA 94124-2098
415-550-8282
Bob Borissoff, Instructor

Oceanside Shooting Academy
618 Airport Road
Oceanside, CA
760-945-8567
Bill Jorgensen, Instructor

OffShoots Training Institute
(law enforcement and military
personnel training)
119 Cotillion
San Antonio, Texas 78213
210-541-9884
FAX: 210-541-9884
www.offshootstraining.com
Jerry Lane, Instructor

**Operational Support
Services, Inc.**
19018 Candleview Drive
Spring, TX 77388
281-288-9190 x205
FAX: 281-288-7019
opsupp@getus.com
David Lee Salmon II,
Law Enforcement Training Director

Options for Personal Security
PO Box 489
Sebring, FL 33871-0489
877-636-4677
www.optionsforpersonalsecurity.com
Andy Stanford, Director

Oregon Firearms Academy
Brownsville, OR
541-451-5532
oregonfirearms.d2g.com

249

APPENDIX B: SHOOTING SCHOOLS

Peregrine Corporation, The
PO Box 170
Bowers, PA 19511
610-682-7147
FAX: 610-682-7158
Emanuel Kapelsohn, President

Personal Defense Institute
2603 NW 13th St., #205
Gainesville, FL 32609
904-378-6425
afn01182@afn.org
Jeff Dissell and W.L. Fisher,
Instructors

Personal Defense Training
5220 Linnadine Way
Norcross, GA 30092
404-403-5739
david@personaldefensetraining.com
www.personaldefensetraining.com
David Blinder, Director

Personal Protection Concepts
PO Box 340485
Dayton, Ohio 45434
937-371-7816
info@ppctraining.com
www.ppctraining.com
Brady Smith, Instructor

Personal Protection Strategies
(specializing in women's training)
9903 Santa Monica Blvd., Suite 300
Beverly Hills, CA 90212
310-281-1762
Paxton Quigley, Instructor

Personal Protection Training
PO Box 2008
Woodland Park, Colorado
719-687-8226
southeops@hotmail.com
A.C. Bowolick, Instructor

Personal Responsibility, Inc
221 Fourth Avenue North
Second Floor
Nashville, TN 37219

615-242-3348
FAX: 615-242-6502
John M.L. Brown, President

Personal Safety Institute
15 Central Way, Suite 319
Kirkland, WA 98033
206-827-2015
Ginny Lyford, Director

Personal Security Consulting
PO Box 8118
Albuquerque, NM 87198-8118
505-255-8610

Personal Security & Safety Training (PSST)
PO Box 381
Eagle, ID 83616
208-939-8051
Bruce and Nancy Priddy,
Instructors

Police Training Institute
(law enforcement only)
University of Illinois
1004 S. 4th St.
Champaign, IL 61820
217-333-7811
John W. Bowman, Instructor

Police Training Division
(law enforcement and military
personnel training)
2 Edgebrook Lane
Monsey, NY 10952
Peter Tarley, Instructor

Plus P Technology, Inc.
Minneapolis, MN
612-660-4263
plusp@plusp.com
www.plusp.com/

Practical Firearms Training
Covington, VA
540-559-3074
FAX: 540-559-4151
pgpft@cfw.com

Practical Shooting Academy, The
PO Box 630
Olathe, Colorado 81425
970-323-6111
www.practicalshootingacad.com
Ron Avery, Instructor

PRO
3953 Indianola Ave
Columbus, OH 43214
614-263-1601
www.peoplesrights.org

Progressive F.O.R.C.E. Concepts
PO Box 336301
N. Las Vegas, NV 89033
702-647-1126
FAX: 702-647-7325
www.PFCtraining.com
Steve Krystek, Director

ProTac Glocal Inc
PMB 233
1208 E. Bethany Dr. Suite 2
Allen, Texas 75002
972-359-0303
www.protacglobal.com
Chris Grollnek, President

Pro-Tek
5154 Cemetery Road
Bainbridge, NY 13733
607-343-9999
Tim Roberts, Chief Instructor
tactical@mkl.com

R & S Protection Services
4401 N. Dogwood Dr.
Kenai, Alaska 99611
907-283-7001
Raymond Carr, Instructor
alaskaknives@alaskaknives.com
www.alaskaknives.com

Remington Shooting School
Remington Arms Company
14 Hoefler Avenue
Ilion, NY 13357

315-895-3574
Dale P. Christie, Director

**Rocky Mountain Combat
Applications Training**
PO Box 535
Lake George, Colorado 80827
FAX: 719-748-8557
www.rmcat.com

Rocky Mountain Gun Safety
3812 E. Pikes Peak Ave
Suites 207-208
Colorado Springs, Colorado 80916
719-638-7406
rockymountaingunsafety@yahoo.
com

Rogers Shooting School
1736 Saint Johns Bluff Rd.
Jacksonville, Florida 32246
904-613-1196
rogers-shooting-school.com

Rural/Urban Tactical Training
17660 N. 35th Street
Phoenix, AZ 85032
602-701-1614

Scott, McDougall & Associates
7950 Redwood Drive
Cotati, CA 94931
707-795-BANG
Mac Scott, Instructor

**Security Awareness & Firearms
Education** (SAFE)
PO Box 864
Post Falls, ID 83854-0864
SAFE-LLC.com
staysafe@SAFE-LLC.com
208-773-3624
Robert B. Smith, Director

Security Training International
PO Box 492
Vista, CA 92085
760-940-6385
Candace Crawford, Instructor

**Self Defense Firearms
Training**
5375 Industrial Drive, Suite 107
Huntington Beach, CA 92649-1545
Greg@firearmstraining.com
714-893-8676
FAX: 714-894-7656
Greg Block

Serious Sportsman, Inc.
100 Middletown Road
Pearl River, NY
914-735-7722
John Perkins, Instructor

Shawnee Hunt Club
PO Box 10531
Blacksburg, VA 24062
civic.bev.net/shawnee
Betty Strauss, Training
Coordinator

Shoot-N-Iron, Inc.
17205 Gaddy Road
Shawnee, OK 74801
si-gun@swbell.net
www.shoot-n-iron.com
405-273-4822
FAX: 405-273-4180
Paul Abel, Instructor

Shooters-Edge
PO Box 3821
Beverly Hills, CA 90212
info@shooters-edge.com
www.shooters-edge.com
Bruce Krell, Instructor

Shootrite Firearms Academy
PO Box 189
Owens Cross Roads
Huntsville, AL 35763
www.shootrite.org
256-721-4602
Ed Aldrich, Instructor
James McKee, Instructor

Sierra Firearms Academy
PO Box 9640

Reno, NV 89507
mike@sierrafirearms.com
www.sierrafirearms.com
702-425-1678
Dave Keller and Mike Robbins,
Instructors

Sierra Firearms Training
2936 South West Street
Visalia, CA 93277
559-734-6150
559-280-5600 (cell)
Edward F. Peterson, Instructor

SIGARMS Academy
233 Exeter Road
Epping, NH 03042
www.sigarmsacademy.com
603-679-2003
Tim Connell, Director

**Smith & Wesson Academy &
Armorers School**
2100 Roosevelt Avenue
Springfield, MA 01102-2208
800-331-0852 extension 255/265
Robert E. Hunt, Director

Southern Police Institute
(law enforcement training)
University of Louisville
Louisville, KY 40292
502-852-6561

**South West Association of
Trainers and COMSAT**
PO Box 51510
Amarillo, Texas 79159
www.traintosurvive.com
806-874-1265
FAX: 806-874-1266
Jerry Holland, Director

**Southwest Defensive Shooting
Institute, L.L.C.**
PO Box 190179-266
Dallas, Texas 75219
214-599-0309
A.W. McBee, Instructor

APPENDIX B: SHOOTING SCHOOLS

Southwest Tactical
4351 Sepulveda Blvd., Suite 450
Culver City, CA 90230
310-838-1275

Spartan Group LLC
PO Box 671
Mamers, NC 27552
877-9SPARTA
www.spartangroup.com

Specialized Training Associates
(NRA Training Counselor
Workshops and NRA
Instructor Certification)
1313 N. Ritchie Ct. Suite 2100
Chicago, IL 60610
312-482-9910
FAX: 312-482-9960
PO Box 453
San Jose, CA 95052
408-985-1311
FAX: 408-985-1311
Lpyle@PaulRevere.org
Leroy Pyle, Director

Specter Tactical
60 River Road
East Haddam, Connecticut
06423-1460
860-526-5528
www.spectertactical.com
Chris Adams, Director

St. James Academy, The
PO Box 700
Birmingham, MI 48012
810-545-9000
Michael St. James, Instructor

Storm Mountain Training Center
Rt. 1 Box 60
Elk Garden, WV 26717
304-446-5526
www.stormmountain.com

Strategic Weapons Academy of Texas
100 N. MacArthur, Suite 120
Irving, TX 75061
972-256-3969
www.weaponsacademy.com
Tim Bulot, Executive Director

Sturm, Ruger & Company
Law Enforcement Division
Lacey Place
Southport, CT 06490
203-259-7843

Suarez International
2517 Sycamore Drive, #352
Simi Valley, CA 93065
805-582-2499 (Office and Fax)
Gabriel Suarez, President
www.gabesuarez.com

Surgical Shooting Inc.
13955 Stowe Drive
Poway, CA 92064
858-668-3453
FAX: 858-668-3457
Gary A. Lakis, COO
www.surgicalshooting.com

Tac One
PO Box 3215
Idaho Springs, Colorado 80452
303-698-4566
FAX: 303-582-3655
tacone@juno.com
Gary Cunningham, President

TACFIRE
(Tactical Firearms
Training Institute)
2426 East Main St.
Ventura, CA 93003
805-652-1345
www.tacfire.com
Dave Manning, Chief Instructor

Tactical Defense Institute
2174 Bethany Ridge Road
West Union, OH 45693

937-544-7228
www.tdiohio.com

Tactical Defense International
5 Rose Lane
Apalachin, NY 13732
607-625-4488
glhblh@sg23.com
Gary Hellmers, Master Instructor

Tactical Edge
Security Consultants
19015 Parthenia Street, Suite 203
Northridge, CA 91324
818-890-3930

Tactical Firearms Training Team
16836 Algonquin St, Suite 120
Huntington Beach, CA 92649
714-846-8065
director@tftt.com
www.tftt.com
Max Joseph, Training Director

Tactical Force Institute
4231 Kodiak
Casper, WY 82604
307-266-1063
FAX: 307-472-5797
tfi0397@aol.com
Michael J. Wallace, Instructor

Tactical Gun
P.O. Box 51404
Phoenix, AZ 85048
480-706-8010

Tactical Handgun Training
PO Box 1817
Kingston, NY 12401
845-339-3440
FAX: 845-339-3451
www.tacticalhandguntraining.com
Ken Cooper, President

Tactical Shooting Academy
7366 Colonial Trail East
Surry, VA 23883

757-357-9881
www.tacticalshooting.com

Talon Enterprises
4 Locust Ave
Exeter, NH
603-772-7981
talon@ultranet.com
Bill Burroughs, Instructor

Talons Firearms Training, Inc.
11645 North Highway 287
LaPorte, Colorado 80535
303-493-2221
Ron Phillips and Kyle Caffey,
Instructors

Team One Network
Law Enforcement Training Only
620 Richards Ferry Road
Fredericksburg, Virginia 22406
540-752-8190
FAX: 540-752-8192

Team Virginia
PO Box 1361
Chesterfield, VA 23832
804-931-4554
teamvirginia.tripod.com
Glenn Blandford, Instructor

Texas Small Arms Academy
Houston, TX
713-561-5335
Tim Oxley, Instructor

The Competitive Edge (TCE)
PO Box 805
Oakville, Ontario
Canada L6J 5C5
905-849-6960
Nick Alexakos, Instructor

Threat Management Institute (TMI)
800 West Napa St.
Sonoma, CA 95476
707-939-0303
FAX: 707-939-8684
tmi@crl.com

Peter Kasler and Peggi Bird,
Instructors

Thunder Ranch, Inc.
HCR 1, Box 53
Mountain Home, TX 78058
830-640-3138
FAX: 830-640-3183
www.ThunderRanchInc.com
Clint Smith, Director

Top Gun Training Centre
1042 N. Mountain Ave. #B
PMB 303
Upland, CA 91786
800-677-4407
FAX: 888-677-4407
www.1topgun1.com
R.J. Kirschner, Director of
Operations

Trident Concepts Research Group
PO Box 11955
Prescott, AZ 86304-1955
928-776-5326
FAX: 928-443-0174
www.tridentconcepts.com
Jeff Gonzales, Instructor

Tugs 'n' Thugs Defensive Training
(specializing in, but not limited to,
women's training)
16818 N. 56th St, #220
Scottsdale, AZ 85254
602-788-3609
KateAlex@aol.com

Turnipseed Stance
610 N. Alma School Road, #18-213
Chandler, AZ 85224
602-802-0346
www.turnipseedstance.com
Kent Turnipseed, Instructor

Universal Shooting Academy
4300 Highway 630 East
Frostpoint, FL 33843
305-688-0262
Frank Garcia, Director

Vital Options Institute
503 Trowbridge Street
Allegan MI 49010
616-686-1321
gbadams@datawise.net
Greg Adams and James Bay,
Instructors

Wallin Video Productions
Deadly Force Division Videos
950 Highway 10 Northeast, Suite 110
Minneapolis, MN 55432
612-786-1486
Shelly Mydra

Weigand Shooting Seminars
685 South Main Road
Mountaintop, PA 18707
www.learntoshootpistol.com
Jack Weigand, Instructor

Whitten Arms
2770 Whitten Road
Memphis, TN 38133
901-386-7002
Jim Littlejohn, Director

**Williams Associates
Protective Services, LLC.**
74 Olivia St., Box 164
Derby, CT 06418
203-924-1784
FAX: 203-924-1784
www.wa-protective.com
Brian S. Williams, President

**Wicklander-Zulawski
& Associates**
(law enforcement training)
555 E. Butterfield Rd. Ste. 302
Lombard, IL
800-222-7789

Yavapai Firearms Academy
PO Box 27290
Prescott Valley, AZ 86312
520-772-8262
www.yfainc.com
Louis Awerbuck, Instructor

253

APPENDIX B: SHOOTING SCHOOLS

Schools, Alpha Sorted by State

Alabama
Shootrite Firearms Academy

Alaska
R & S Protection Services

Arizona
Advanced Tactical Technologies Inc.
American Shooting Academy
American Small Arms Academy
Arizona Defensive Firearms Training
Defensive Use of Firearms
Gunsite Training Center
Insight Firearms Training
Development
Malins Defense Systems
Marksman's Enterprise
Rural/Urban Tactical Training
Tactical Gun
Trident Concepts Research Group
Tugs 'n' Thugs Defensive Training
Turnipseed Stance
Yavapai Firearms Academy

Arkansas
Arkansas Police Trainers

California
Absolute Tactical Training
Advanced Training Assoc
Advanced Weapons and Tactics
Allsafe Defense Systems
Bay Area Professionals for Firearms
Safety & Education (Bayprofs)
California Security & Safety Institute
CivilShield
Combative Concepts
Firearms Academy of Redding
Firearms Training Associates
Front Sight Firearms Training Institute
Global Security Complex
Gunner Joe's Bullseye Academy
Handgun Instruction
International Shootists Institute
International Tactical Training
Seminars Inc.
Martial Arts Resource

NOR-CAL
Oceanside Shooting Academy
Personal Protection Strategies
Scott, McDougall & Associates
Self Defense Firearms Training
Security Training International
Sierra Firearms Training
Shooters-Edge
Southwest Tactical
Specialized Training Associates
Suarez International
Surgical Shooting, Inc.
TACFIRE
Tactical Edge
Tactical Firearms Training Team
Threat Management Institute (TMI)
Top Gun Training Centre

Colorado
Colorado Firearms Academy
Colorado Gun Training
Colorado Weapons Training
Defense Training International, Inc.
Personal Protection Training
Practical Shooting Academy, The
Rocky Mountain Combat
Applications Training
Rocky Mountain Gun Safety
Tac One
Talons Firearms Training, Inc.

Connecticut
Defense Associates
Specter Tactical
Sturm, Ruger & Company
Williams Associates Protective
Services, LLC.

Florida
Brantly and Associates, Inc.
Cirillo's Tactical Handgun Training
Defensive Training for the Armed
Citizen
GunSafety - TampaBay
HomeSafe Protective Training
Options for Personal Security
Personal Defense Institute
Rogers Shooting School
Universal Shooting Academy

Georgia
Argenbright International Training
Institute
Federal Law Enforcement Training
Center (FLETC)
Firearmz
Glock, Inc.
James A. Neal Public Safety Training
Center
Personal Defense Training

Idaho
Dan Mitchell's Clay Target and Wing
Shooting School
Firearms Training Institute
Personal Security & Safety Training
(PSST)
Security Awareness & Firearms
Education (SAFE)

Illinois
Calibre Press
Illinois Small Arms Institute
Marksmanship Training Group, Inc.
Midwest Tactical Training Institute
Midwest Training Group
Police Training Institute
Specialized Training Associates
Wicklander-Zulawski & Associates

Kentucky
Firearms Training Center
Southern Police Institute

Louisiana
Guntek Firearms Training

Maryland
Beretta Training
COMTAC
Defensive Firearms Consultants
Firearms Research & Instruction, Inc.

Massachusetts
AWARE
Bob's Tactical
Massachusetts Firearms Serminars
Smith & Wesson Academy &
Armorers School

Michigan
DTOM Enterprises
St. James Academy, The
Vital Options Institute

Minnesota
Plus P Technology, Inc.
Wallin Video Productions

Missouri
Chapman Academy of Practical
Shooting
National Law Enforcement Training
Center

Montana
Marksman's Enterprise

Nevada
Halo Group
Progressive F.O.R.C.E. Concepts
Sierra Firearms Academy

New Hampshire
International Association of Law
Enforcement Firearms
Instructors, Inc.
Lethal Force Institute (LFI)
SIGARMS Academy
Talon Enterprises

New Jersey
Defensive Firearms Academy
Firearm Training Center
Loss Prevention Serivices of New
Jersey

New Mexico
Personal Security Consulting

New York
Chelsea Gun Club, Inc.
Guardian Group International
International Rescue and Tactical
Consultants
MINDRICK Security Academy and
Shooting School
Modern Warrior Defensive Tactics
Institute
Police Training Division

Pro-Tek
Remington Shooting School
Serious Sportsman, Inc.
Tactical Defense International
Tactical Handgun Training

North Carolina
Area 52 Smallarms Training Center
Blackwater Lodge and Training
Center
Continental Threat Management
Ladies Handgun Clinics
Spartan Group

Ohio
Personal Protection Concepts
PRO
Tactical Defense Institute

Oklahoma
Shoot-N-Iron, Inc.

Oregon
Lane Community College
Oregon Firearms Academy

Pennsylvania
Northeast Training Institute
Peregrine Corporation
Weigand Shooting Seminars

Tennessee
Academy of Personal Protection
and Security
American Pistol & Rifle Association
Cumberland Tactics
Defensive Solutions
Farris Firearms Training
Institute of Security Services
Mid-South Institute of Self-Defense
Shooting
Personal Responsibility, Inc.
Whitten Arms

Texas
Auto Arms
Defensive Arts of Texas
Denton County Sports Association
ISI

Law Enforcement Educators
OffShoots Training Institute
Operational Support Services
ProTac Glocal Inc
South West Association of Trainers
and COMSAT
Southwest Defensive Shooting
Institute
Strategic Weapons Academy of
Texas
Texas Small Arms Academy
Thunder Ranch, Inc.

Virginia
Firearms International Training
Academy
Heckler & Koch, Inc.
Practical Firearms Training
Shawnee Hunt Club
Tactical Shooting Academy
Team One Network
Team Virginia

Washington
Burton's Firearm Instruction
Firearms Academy of Seattle
InSights Training Center, Inc.
Personal Safety Institute

Washington, D.C.
National Rifle Association

West Virginia
Blackheart International
BSR, Inc.
Storm Mountain Training Center

Wyoming
Tactical Force Institute

Canada
Canadian Academy of Practical
Shooting
Canadian Firearms Training
Executive Security Services
International
International Academy of Tactical
Training Systems
The Competitive Edge
(TCE)

255

MANUFACTURER'S DIRECTORY

A

A. Uberti S.p.A., Via Artigiana 1, Gardone Val Trompia, Brescia 25063, ITALY, P: 011 390308341800, F: 011 390308341801, www.ubertireplicas.it
Firearms

A.R.M.S., Inc./Atlantic Research Marketing Systems, Inc., 230 W. Center St., West Bridgewater, MA 02379, P: 508-584-7816, F: 508-588-8045, www.armsmounts.com
Scopes, Sights and Accessories

AA & E Leathercraft, 107 W. Gonzales St., Yoakum, TX 77995, P: 800-331-9092, F: 361-293-9127, www.tandybrands.com
Bags & Equipment Cases; Custom Manufacturing; Hunting Accessories; Knives/Knife Cases; Leathergoods; Shooting Range Equipment; Sports Accessories

ACIGI / Fujiiryoki, 4399 Ingot St., Fremong, CA 94538, P: 888-816-0888, F: 510-651-6188, www.fujichair.com
Wholesaler/Distributor

ACR Electronics, Inc., 5757 Ravenswood Rd., Ft. Lauderdale, FL 33312, P: 800-432-0227, F: 954-983-5087, www.acrelectronics.com
Backpacking; Hunting Accessories; Lighting Products; Sports Accessories; Survival Kits/First Aid; Training and Safety Equipment

Accro-Met, Inc., 3406 Westwood Industrial Drive, Monroe, NC 28110, P: 800-543-4755, F: 704-283-2112, www.accromet.com
Gun Barrels; Wholesaler/Distributor

Accu-Fire, Inc., P.O. Box 121990, Arlington, TX 76012, P: 888-MUZZLEMATE, F: 817-303-4505
Firearms Maintenance Equipment

Accu-Shot/B&T Industries, LLC, P.O. Box 771071, Wichita, KS 67277, P: 316-721-3222, F: 316-721-1021, www.accu-shot.com
Gun Grips & Stocks; Hunting Accessories; Law Enforcement; Scopes, Sights & Accessories; Shooting Range Equipment; Sports Accessories; Training and Safety Equipment

Accuracy International North America, Inc., 35100 North State Highway, Mingus, TX 76463-6405, P: 907-440-4024, www.accuracyinternational.org
Firearms; Firearms Maintenance Equipment; Law Enforcement; Magazines, Cartridge; Scopes, Sights & Accessories; Wholesaler/Distributor

AccuSharp Knife Sharpeners/Fortune Products, Inc., 205 Hickory Creek Road, Marble Falls, TX 78654, P: 800-742-7797, F: 800-600-5373, www.accusharp.com
Archery; Camping; Cooking Equipment/Accessories; Cutlery; Hunting Accessories; Knives/Knife Cases; Sharpeners; Sports Accessories

Action Target, P.O. Box 636, Provo, UT 84603-0636, P: 888-377-8033, F: 801-377-8096, www.actiontarget.com
Law Enforcement; Shooting Range Equipment; Targets; Training & Safety Equipment

AcuSport Corp., One Hunter Place, Bellefontaine, OH 43311, P: 800-543-3150, www.acusport.com
Ammunition; Black Powder Accessories; Firearms; Hunting Accessories; Online Services; Retailer Services; Scopes, Sights & Accessories; Wholesaler/Distributor

ADCO Arms Co., Inc., 4 Draper St., Woburn, MA 01801, P: 800-775-3687, F: 781-935-1011, www.adcosales.com
Ammunition; Firearms; Paintball Accessories, Scopes, Sights & Accessories

ADS, Inc., Pinehurst Centre, 477 Viking Dr., Suite 350, Virginia Beach, VA 23452, P: 800-948-9433, F: 757-481-2039, www.adstactical.com

Advanced Armament Corp., 1434 Hillcrest Rd., Norcross, GA 30093, P: 770-925-9988, F: 770-925-9989, www.advanced-armament.com
Firearms; Hearing Protection; Law Enforcement

Advanced Engineered Systems, Inc., 14328 Commercial Parkway, South Beloit, IL 61080, P: 815-624-7797, F: 815-624-8198, www.advengsys.com
Ammunition; Custom Manufacturing

Advanced Technology International, 2733 W. Carmen Ave., Milwaukee, WI 53209, P: 800-925-2522, F: 414-664-3112, www.atigunstocks.com
Books/Industry Publications; Gun Grips & Stocks; Gun Parts/Gunsmithing; Hunting Accessories; Law Enforcement; Scopes, Sights & Accessories

Advanced Training Systems, 4524 Highway 61 North, St. Paul, MN 55110, P: 651-429-8091, F: 651-429-8702, www.duelatron.com
Law Enforcement; Shooting Range Equipment; Targets; Training & Safety Equipment

Advantage Tactical Sight/WrenTech Industries, LLC, 7 Avenida Vista Grande B-7, Suite 510, Sante Fe, NM 87508, F: 310-316-6413 or 505-466-1811, F: 505-466-4735, www.advantagetactical.com
Scopes, Sights & Accessories

Adventure Lights, Inc., 444 Beaconsfield Blvd., Suite 201, Beaconsfield, Quebec H9W 4C1, CANADA, P: 514-694-8477, F: 514-694-2353

Adventure Medical Kits, P.O. Box 43309, Oakland, CA 94624, P: 800-324-3517, F: 510-261-7419, www.adventuremedicalkits.com

Backpacking; Books/Industry Publications; Camping; Custom Manufacturing; Hunting Accessories; Sports Accessories; Survival Kits/First Aid; Training & Safety Equipment

AE Light/Div. of Allsman Enterprises, LLC, P.O. Box 1869, Rogue River, OR 97537, P: 541-471-8988, F: 888-252-1473, www.aelight.com
Camping; Custom Manufacturing; Hunting Accessories; Law Enforcement; Lighting Products; Wholesale/Distributor

AES Optics, 201 Corporate Court, Senatobia, MS 38668, P: 800-416-0866, F: 662-301-4739, www.aesoutdoors.com
Eyewear

Aetco, Inc., 2825 Metropolitan Place, Pomona, CA 91767, P: 800-982-5258, F: 800-451-2434, www.aetcoinc.com
Firearms; Hearing Protection; Holsters; Law Enforcement; Leathergoods; Lighting Products; Training & Safety Equipment; Wholesaler/Distributor

Aguila Ammunition/Centurion Ordnance, Inc., 11614 Rainbow Ridge, Helotes, TX 78023, P: 210-695-4602, F: 210-695-4603, www.aguilaammo.com
Ammunition

Aimpoint, Inc., 14103 Mariah Court, Chantilly, VA 20151, 877-246-7646, F: 703-263-9463, www.aimpoint.com
Scopes, Sights & Accessories

AimShot/Osprey International, Inc., 25 Hawks Farm Rd., White, GA 30184, P: 888-448-3247, F: 770-387-0114, www.aimshot.com, www.miniosprey.com
Archery; Binoculars; Holsters; Hunting Accessories; Law Enforcement; Lighting Products; Scopes, Sights & Accessories; Wholesaler/Distributor

Aimtech Mount Systems, P.O. Box 223, Thomasville, GA 31799-0223, P: 229-226-4313, F: 229-227-0222, www.aimtech-mounts.com
Hunting Accessories; Scopes, Sights & Accessories

Air Gun, Inc., 9320 Harwin Dr., Houston, TX 77036, P: 800-456-0022, F: 713-780-4831, www.airrifle-china.com
Airguns; Ammunition; Hunting Accessories; Scopes, Sights & Accessories; Wholesaler/Distributor

AirForce Airguns, P.O. Box 2478, Fort Worth, TX 76113, P: 877-247-4867, F: 817-451-1613, www.airforceairguns.com
Airguns; Hunting Accessories; Law Enforcement; Scopes, Sights & Accessories

Aitec Co., Ltd., Export Dept., Rm. 817, Crystal Beach ok, Jung Dong Haeundae-Gu Busan, 612 010, SOUTH KOREA, P: 011 82517416497, F: 011 82517462194, www.aitec.co.kr
Lighting Products

Ajax Custom Grips, Inc./Ajax Shooter Supply, 9130 Viscount Row, Dallas, TX

75247, P: 800-527-7537, F: 214-630-4942, www.ajaxgrips.com
Gun Grips & Stocks; Gun Parts/Gunsmithing; Holsters; Law Enforcement; Lighting Products; Magazines, Cartridge; Wholesaler/Distributor

AKDAL/Ucyildiz Arms Ind./Blow & Voltran, Bostanci Cd. Uol Sk. No: 14/A, Y. Dudullu-Umraniye, Istanbul, 34775, TURKEY, P: 011-90 216527671011, F: 011-90 2165276705, www.akdalarms.com, www.voltranarms.com
Airguns; Firearms

Aker International Inc., 2248 Main St., Suite 6, Chula Vista, CA 91911, P: 800-645-AKER, F: 888-300-AKER, www.akerleather.com
Holsters; Hunting Accessories; Law Enforcement; Leathergoods

Al Mar Knives, P.O. Box 2295, Tualatin, OR 97062, P: 503-670-9080, www.almarknives.com
Custom Manufacturing, Knives/Knife Cases

Alexander Arms, U.S. Army Radford Arsenal, Radford, VA 24141, P: 540-639-8356, F: 540-639-8353, www.alexanderarms.com
Ammunition; Firearms; Magazine, Cartridges; Reloading

Allen Company, 525 Burbank St., P.O. Box 445, Broomfield, CO 80020, P: 800-876-8600, F: 303-466-7437, www.allencompany.net
Archery; Black Powder Accessories; Eyewear; Gun Cases; Hearing Protection; Hunting Accessories; Scopes, Sights & Accessories; Shooting Range Equipment

Alot Enterprise Company, Ltd., 1503 Eastwood Centre, 5 A Kung Ngam Village Rd., Shaukeiwan, HONG KONG, P: 011 85225199728, F: 011 85225190122, www.alothk.com
Binoculars; Compasses; Eyewear; Hunting Accessories; Photographic Equipment; Scopes, Sights, & Accessories; Sports Accessories; Telescopes

Alpen Outdoor Corp., 10329 Dorset St., Rancho Cucamonga, CA 91730, P: 877-987-8379, F: 909-987-8661, www.alpenoutdoor.com
Backpacking; Binoculars; Camping; Hunting Accessories; Scopes, Sights & Accessories; Shooting Range Equipment; Sports Accessories, Wholesaler/Distributor

ALPS Mountaineering, 1 White Pine, New Haven, MO 63068, P: 800-344-2577, F: 573-459-2044, www.alpsouthdoorz.com
Backpacking; Camouflage; Camping; Hunting Accessories; Sports Accessories

ALS Technologies, Inc., 1103 Central Blvd., P.O. Box 525, Bull Shoals, AR 72619, P: 877-902-4257, F: 870-445-8746, www.alslesslethal.com
Ammunition; Firearms; Gun Parts/Gunsmithing; Law Enforcement; Training & Safety Equipment

Altama Footwear, 1200 Lake Hearn Dr., Suite 475, Atlanta, GA 30319, P: 800-437-9888, F: 404-260-2889, www.altama.com
Footwear; Law Enforcement

Altamont Co., 291 N. Church St., P.O. Box 309, Thomasboro, IL 61878, P: 800-626-5774, F: 217-643-7973, www.altamontco.com
Gun Grips & Stocks

AlumaGrips, 2851 N. 34th Place, Mesa, AZ 85213, P: 602-690-5459, F: 480-807-3955
Firearms Maintenance Equipment; Gun Grips & Stocks; Gun Parts/Gunsmithing; Law Enforcement

American COP Magazine/FMG Publications, 12345 World Trade Dr., San Diego, CA 92128, P: 800-537-3006, F: 858-605-0247, www.americancopmagazine.com
Books/Industry Publications; Law Enforcement; Videos

American Cord & Webbing Co., Inc., 88 Century Dr., Woonsocket, RI 02895, P: 401-762-5500, F: 401-762-5514, www.acw1.com
Archery; Backpacking; Bags & Equipment Cases; Custom Manufacturing; Law Enforcement; Pet Supplies

American Defense Systems, Inc., 230 Duffy Ave., Hicksville, NY 11801, P: 516-390-5300, F: 516-390-5308, www.adsiarmor.com
Custom Manufacturing; Shooting Range Equipment; Training & Safety Equipment

American Gunsmithing Institute (AGI), 1325 Imola Ave. West, P.O. Box 504, Napa, CA 94559, P: 800-797-0867, F: 707-253-7149, www.americangunsmith.com
Books/Industry Publications; Computer Software; Firearms Maintenance Equipment; Gun Parts/Gunsmithing; Videos

American Plastics/SEWIT, 1225 N. MacArthur Drive, Suite 200, Tracy, CA 95376, P: 209-834-0287, F: 209-834-0924, www.americanplastics.com
Backpacking; Bags & Equipment Cases; Export/Import Specialists; Gun Cases; Holsters; Hunting Accessories; Survival Kits/First Aid; Wholesaler/Distributor

American Security Products Co., 11925 Pacific Ave., Fontana, CA 92337, P: 800-421-6142, F: 951-685-9685, www.amsecusa.com
Gun Cabinets/Racks/Safes

American Tactical Imports, 100 Airpark Dr., Rochester, NY 14624, P: 585-328-3951, F: 585-328-3749

American Technologies Network, Corp./ATN, Corp., 1341 San Mateo Ave., South San Francisco, CA 94080, P: 800-910-2862, F: 650-875-0129, www.atncorp.com

Binoculars; Law Enforcement; Lighting Products; Photographic Equipment; Scopes, Sights & Accessories; Telescopes

Americase, Inc., 1610 E. Main St., Waxahachie, TX 75165, P: 800-972-2737, F: 972-937-8373, www.americase.com
Bags & Equipment Cases; Custom Manufacturing; Gun Cases; Hunting Accessories

AmeriGlo, 5579-B Chamblee Dunwoody Rd., Suite 214, Atlanta, GA 30338, P: 770-390-0554, F: 770-390-9781, www.ameriglo.com
Camping; Law Enforcement; Lighting Products; Scopes, Sights & Accessories; Survival Kits/First Aid; Training & Safety Equipment

Ammo-Loan Worldwide, 815 D, Lewiston, ID 83501, P: 208-746-7012, F: 208-746-1703

Ammo-Up, 10601 Theresa Dr., Jacksonville, FL 32246, P: 800-940-2688, F: 904-645-5918, www.ammoupusa.com
Shooting Range Equipment

AMT/Auto Mag Co./C.G., Inc., 5200 Mitchelldale, Suite E17, Houston, TX 77092, P: 713-686-3232, F: 713-681-5665

ANXO-Urban Body Armor Corp., 7359 Northwest 34 St., Miami, FL 33122, P: 866-514-ANXO, F: 305-593-5498, www.urbanbodyarmor.com
Men & Women's Clothing; Custom Manufacturing; Law Enforcement

Arc'Teryx, 100-2155 Dollarton Hwy., North Vancouver, British Columbia V7H 3B2, CANADA, P: 604-960-3001, F: 604-904-3692, www.arcteryx.com
Backpacking; Camouflage; Men's Clothing; Custom Manufacturing; Gloves, Mitts, Hats; Law Enforcement; Outfitter

Ares Defense Systems, Inc., P.O. Box 10667, Blacksburg, VA 24062, P: 540-639-8633, F: 540-639-8634, www.aresdefense.com
Firearms; Gun Parts/Gunsmithing; Law Enforcement; Lighting Products; Magazines, Cartridge; Scopes, Sights & Accessories; Shooting Range Equipment; Survival Kits/First Aid

ArmaLite, Inc., 745 S. Hanford St., Geneseo, IL 61254, P: 309-944-6939, F: 309-944-6949, www.armalite.com
Firearms; Firearms Maintenance Equipment

Armament Technology, Inc./ELCAN Optical Technologies, 3045 Robie St., Suite 113, Halifax, Nova Scotia B3K 4P6, CANADA, P: 902-454-6384, F: 902-454-4641, www.armament.com
International Exhibitors; Law Enforcement; Scopes, Sights & Accessories; Telescopes; Wholesaler/Distributor

Armatix GmbH, Feringastrabe. 4, Unterfohring, D 85774, GERMANY,

P: 011 498999228140, F: 011 498999228228, www.armatix.de

Armor Express, 1554 E. Torch Lake Dr., P.O. Box 21, Central Lake, MI 49622, P: 866-357-3845, F: 231-544-6734, www.armorexpress.com
Law Enforcement

Armorshield USA, LLC, 30 ArmorShield Dr., Stearns, KY 42647, P: 800-386-9455, F: 800-392-9455, www.armorshield.net
Law Enforcement

Arms Corp. of the Philippines/Armscor Precision International, Armscorp Ave., Bgy Fortune, Marikina City, 1800, PHILIPPINES, P: 011 6329416243, F: 011 6329420682, www.armscor.com.ph
Airguns; Ammunition; Bags & Equipment Cases; Custom Manufacturing; Firearms; Gun Barrels; Gun Parts/Gunsmithing; International Exhibitors

Arms Tech, Ltd., 5025 North Central Ave., Suite 459, Phoenix, AZ 85012, P: 602-272-9045, F: 602-272-1922, www.armstechltd.com
Firearms; Law Enforcement

Arno Bernard Custom Knives, 19 Duiker St., Bethlehem, 9700, SOUTH AFRICA, P: 011 27583033196, F: 011 27583033196

Arrieta, Morkaiko, 5, Elgoibar, (Guipuzcoa) 20870, SPAIN, P: 011-34 943743150, F: 011-34 943743154, www.arrietashotguns.com
Firearms

Arsenal, Inc., 3300 S. Decatur Blvd., Suite 10632, Las Vegas, NV 89102, P: 888-539-2220, F: 702-643-8860, www.arsenalinc.com
Firearms

Artistic Plating Co., 405 W. Cherry St., Milwaukee, WI 53212, P: 414-271-8138, F: 414-271-5541, www.artisticplating.net
Airguns; Ammunition; Archery; Cutlery; Firearms; Game Calls; Gun Barrels; Reloading

ARY, Inc., 10301 Hickman Mills Dr., Suite 110, Kansas City, MO 64137, P: 800-821-7849, F: 816-761-0055, www.aryinc.com
Cutlery; Knives/Knife Cases

ASAT Outdoors, LLC, 307 E. Park Ave., Suite 207A, Anaconda, MT 59711, P: 406-563-9336, F: 406-563-7315
Archery; Blinds; Camouflage; Men's Clothing; Gloves, Mitts, Hats; Hunting Accessories; Law Enforcement; Paintball Accessories

Ashbury International Group, Inc., P.O. Box 8024, Charlottesville, VA 22906, P: 434-296-8600, F: 434-296-9260, www.ashburyintlgroup.com
Camouflage; Firearms; Law Enforcement; Scopes, Sights & Accessories; Wholesaler/Distributor

ASP, Inc., 2511 E. Capitol Dr., Appleton, WI 54911, P: 800-236-6243, F: 800-236-8601, www.asp-usa.com
Law Enforcement; Lighting Products; Training & Safety Equipment

Atak Arms Ind., Co. Ltd., Imes San. Sit. A Blok 107, Sk. No: 70, Y. Dudullu, Umraniye, Istanbul, 34775 TURKEY, P: +902164203996, F: +902164203998, www.atakarms.com

Airguns; Firearms; Training & Safety Equipment

ATK/ATK Commercial Products, 900 Ehlen Dr., Anoka, MN 55303, P: 800-322-2342, F: 763-323-2506, www.atk.com
Ammunition; Binoculars; Clay Targets; Firearms Maintenance Equipment; Reloading; Scopes, Sights & Accessories; Shooting Range Equipment; Targets

ATK /ATK Law Enforcement, 2299 Snake River Ave., Lewiston, ID 83501, P: 800-627-3640, F: 208-798-3392, www.atk.com
Ammunition; Bags & Equipment Cases; Binoculars; Firearms Maintenance Equipment; Reloading; Scopes, Sights & Accessories

Atlanco, 1125 Hayes Industrial Dr., Marietta, GA 30062-2471, P: 800-241-9414, F: 770-427-9011, www.truspec.com
Camouflage; Men's Clothing; Custom Manufacturing; Law Enforcement; Wholesaler/Distributor

Atlanta Cutlery Corp., 2147 Gees Mill Rd., Conyers, GA 30013, P: 800-883-8838, F: 770-760-8993, www.atlantacutlery.com
Custom Manufacturing; Cutlery; Firearms; Holsters; Knives/Knife Cases; Leathergoods; Wholesaler/Distributor

Atsko, 2664 Russel St., Orangeburg, SC 29115, P: 800-845-2728, F: 803-531-2139, www.atsko.com
Archery; Backpacking; Camouflage; Camping; Custom Manufacturing; Hunting Accessories; Scents & Lures

AuctionArms.com, Inc., 3031 Alhambra Dr., Suite 101, Cameron Park, CA 95682, P: 877-GUN-AUCTION, F: 530-676-2497, www.auctionarms.com
Airguns; Archery; Black Powder Accessories; Black Powder/Smokeless Powder; Camping; Firearms; Online Services

Avon Protection Systems, 1369 Brass Mill Rd., Suite A, Belcamp, MD 21017, P: 888-286-6440, F: 410-273-0126, www.avon-protection.com
Law Enforcement; Training & Safety Equipment

AyA-Aguirre Y Aranzabal, Avda. Otaola, 25-3a Planta, Eibar, (Guipúzcoa) 20600, SPAIN, P: 011-34-943-820437, F: 011-34-943-200133, www.aya-fineguns.com
Firearms

B

B-Square/Div. Armor Holdings, Inc., 8909 Forum Way, Fort Worth, TX 76140, P: 800-433-2909, F: 817-926-7012

BAM Wuxi Bam Co., Ltd., No 37 Zhongnan Rd., Wuxi, JiangSu 214024, CHINA, P: 011-86 51085432361, FL 011-86 51085401258, www.china-bam.com
Airguns; Gun Cases; Scopes, Sights & Accessories

BCS International, 1819 St. George St., Green Bay, WI 54302, P: 888-965-3700, F: 888-965-3701
Bags & Equipment Cases; Camouflage; Men & Women's Clothing; Export/Import Specialists; Leathergoods

B.E. Meyers, 14540 Northeast 91st St., Redmond, WA 98052, P: 800-327-5648, F: 425-867-1759, www.bemeyers.com
Custom Manufacturing; Law Enforcement

B & F System, Inc., The, 3920 S. Walton Walker Blvd., Dallas, TX 75236, P: 214-333-2111, F: 214-333-2137, www.bnfusa.com
Binoculars; Cooking Equipment/Accessories; Cutlery; Gloves, Mitts, Hats; Leathergoods; Scopes, Sights & Accessories; Telescopes; Wholesaler/Distributor

BOGgear, LLC, 111 W. Cedar Lane, Suite A, Payson, AZ 85541, P: 877-264-7637, F: 505-292-9130, www.boggear.com
Binoculars; Firearms; Hunting Accessories; Law Enforcement; Outfitter; Photographic Equipment; Shooting Range Equipment; Training & Safety Equipment

BSA Optics, 3911 S.W. 47th Ave., Suite 914, Ft. Lauderdale, FL 33314, P: 954-581-2144, F: 954-581-3165, www.bsaoptics.com
Binoculars; Scopes, Sights & Accessories; Sports Accessories; Telescopes

B.S.N. Technology Srl, Via Guido Rossa, 46/52, Cellatica (Bs), 25060, ITALY, P: 011 390302522436, F: 011 390302520946, www.bsn.it
Ammunition; Gun Barrels; Reloading

Badger Barrels, Inc., 8330 196 Ave., P.O. Box 417, Bristol, WI 53104, P: 262-857-6950, F: 262-857-6988, www.badgerbarrelsinc.com
Gun Barrels

Badger Ordnance, 1141 Swift St., North Kansas City, MO 64116, P: 816-421-4956, F: 816-421-4958, www.badgerordnance.com
Custom Manufacturing; Firearms; Firearms Maintenance Equipment; Gun Parts/Gunsmithing; Law Enforcement; Magazines, Cartridge; Scopes, Sights & Accessories; Telescopes

BAE Systems/Mobility & Protection Systems, 13386 International Parkway, Jacksonville, FL 32218, P: 904-741-5600, F: 904-741-9996, www.baesystems.com
Bags & Equipment Cases; Black Powder/Smokeless Powder; Gloves, Mitts, Hats; Holsters; Hunting Accessories; Law Enforcement; Scopes, Sights & Accessories; Training & Safety Equipment

Barnaul Cartridge Plant CJSC, 28 Kulagina St., Barnaul, 656002, RUSSIAN FEDERATION, P: 011 0073852774391, F: 011 0073852771608, www.ab.ru/~stanok
Ammunition

Barnes Bullets, Inc., P.O. Box 620, Mona, UT 84645, P: 801-756-4222, F: 801-756-2465, www.barnesbullets.com
Black Powder Accessories; Computer Software; Custom Manufacturing; Hunting Accessories; Law Enforcement; Recoil Protection Devices & Services; Reloading

Baron Technology, Inc./Baron Engraving, 62 Spring Hill Rd., Trumbull, CT 06611, P: 203-452-0515, F: 203-452-0663, www.baronengraving.com
Custom Manufacturing; Cutlery; Firearms; Gun Parts/Gunsmithing; Knives/Knife

Cases; Law Enforcement; Outdoor Art, Jewelry, Sculpture; Sports Accessories

Barrett Firearms Mfg., Inc., P.O. Box 1077, Murfreesboro, TN 37133, P: 615-896-2938, F: 615-896-7313, www.barrettrifles.com
Firearms

Barska Optics, 1721 Wright Ave., La Verne, CA 91750, P: 909-445-8168, F: 909-445-8169, www.barska.com

Bates Footwear/Div. Wolverine World Wide, Inc., 9341 Courtland Dr., Rockford, MI 49351, P: 800-253-2184, F: 616-866-5658, www.batesfootwear.com
Footwear; Law Enforcement

Battenfeld Technologies, Inc., 5885 W. Van Horn Tavern Rd., Columbia, MO 65203, P: 877-509-9160, F: 573-446-6606, www.battenfeldtechnologies.com
Firearms Maintenance Equipment; Gun Grips & Stocks; Gun Parts/Gunsmithing; Hearing Protection; Recoil Protection Devices & Services; Reloading; Shooting Range Equipment; Targets

Battle Lake Outdoors, 203 W. Main, P.O. Box 548, Clarissa, MN 56440, P: 800-243-0465, F: 218-756-2426, www.battlelakeoutdoors.com
Archery; Backpacking; Bags & Equipment Cases; Black Powder Accessories; Camping; Gun Cases; Hunting Accessories; Law Enforcement

Batz Corp., 1524 Highway 291 North, P.O. Box 130, Prattsville, AR 72129, P: 800-637-7627, F: 870-699-4420, www.batzusa.com
Backpacking; Camping; Custom Manufacturing; Hunting Accessories; Knives/Knife Cases; Lighting Products; Pet Supplies; Retail Packaging

Bayco Products, Inc., 640 S. Sanden Blvd., Wylie, TX 75098, P: 800-233-2155, F: 469-326-9401, www.baycoproducts.com

Beamshot-Quarton USA, Inc., 5805 Callaghan Rd., Suite 102, San Antonio, TX 78228, P: 800-520-8435, F: 210-735-1326, www.beamshot.com
Airguns; Archery; Crossbows & Accessories; Hunting Accessories; Law Enforcement; Lighting Products; Paintball Accessories; Scopes, Sights & Accessories

Bear & Son Cutlery, Inc., 1111 Bear Blvd. SW, Jacksonville, AL 36265, P: 800-844-3034, F: 256-435-9348, www.bearandsoncutlery.com
Cutlery; Hunting Accessories; Knives/Knife Cases

Beeman Precision Airguns, 5454 Argosy Ave., Huntington Beach, CA 92649, P: 714-890-4800, F: 714-890-4808, www.beeman.com
Airguns; Ammunition; Gun Cases; Holsters; Lubricants; Scopes, Sights & Accessories; Targets

Beijing Defense Co., Ltd., 18 B, Unit One, No. 1 Building, Linghangguoji, Guangqumen Nanxiao St., Chongwen District, Beijing, 100061, CHINA, P: 011 861067153626, F: 011 861067152121, www.tacticalgear.com
Backpacking; Bags & Equipment Cases; Gun Cases; Holsters; Training & Safety Equipment

Bell and Carlson, Inc., 101 Allen Rd., Dodge City, KS 67801, P: 620-225-6688, F: 620-225-9095, www.bellandcarlson.com
Camouflage; Custom Manufacturing; Gun Grips & Stocks; Gun Parts/Gunsmithing; Hunting Accessories; Shooting Range Equipment

Benchmade Knife Company, Inc., 300 Beavercreek Rd., Oregon City, OR 97045, P: 800-800-7427, F: 503-655-7922, www.benchmade.com
Knives/Knife Cases; Men's Clothing

Benelli Armi S.p.A./Benelli USA, 17603 Indian Head Hwy., Accokeek, MD 20607, P: 301-283-6981, F: 301-283-6986, www.benelli.it, www.benelliusa.com
Firearms

Beretta/Law Enforcement and Defense, 17601 Beretta Dr., Accokeek, MD 20607, P: 800-545-9567, F: 301-283-5111, www.berettale.com
Firearms; Gun Parts/Gunsmithing; Holsters; Law Enforcement; Lighting Products

Beretta U.S.A. Corp., 17601 Beretta Dr., Accokeek, MD 20607, P: 800-636-3420, F: 253-484-3775

Berger Bullets, 4275 N. Palm St., Fullerton, CA 92835, P: 714-447-5456, F: 714-447-5478, www.bergerbullets.com
Ammunition; Custom Manufacturing; Reloading

Berry's Manufacturing, Inc., 401 N. 3050 East, St. George, UT 84790, P: 800-269-7373, F: 435-634-1683, www.berrysmfg.com
Ammunition; Custom Manufacturing; Export/Import Specialists; Gun Cases; Reloading; Wholesaler/Distributor

Beta Company, The, 2137B Flintstone Dr., Tucker, GA 30084, P: 800-669-2382, F: 770-270-0599, www.betaco.com
Law Enforcement; Magazines, Cartridge

Beyond Clothing/Beyond Tactical, 1025 Conger St., Suite 8, Eugene, OR 97402, P: 800-775-2279, F: 703-997-6581, www.beyondtactical.com
Backpacking; Camouflage; Men & Women's Clothing; Custom Manufacturing; Law Enforcement

BFAST, LLC, 10 Roff Ave., Palasades Park, NJ 07650, P: 973-706-8210, F: 201-943-3546, www.firearmsafetynet.com
Law Enforcement; Shooting Range Equipment; Sports Accessories; Training & Safety Equipment

Bianchi International, 3120 E. Mission Blvd. Ontario, CA 91761, P: 800-347-1200, F: 800-366-1669, www.bianchi-intl.com
Backpacking; Bags & Equipment Cases; Gun Cases; Holsters; Hunting Accessories; Knives/Knife Cases; Leathergoods; Sports Accessories

Big Sky Racks, Inc., 25A Shawnee Way, Bozeman, MT 58715, P: 800-805-8716, F: 406-585-7378, www.bigskyracks.com
Gun Cabinets, Racks, Safes; Gun Locks; Hunting Accessories

BigFoot Bag/PortaQuip, 1215 S. Grant Ave., Loveland, CO 80537, P: 877-883-0200, F: 970-663-5415, www.bigfootbag.com

Bags & Equipment Cases; Camping; Hunting Accessories; Law Enforcement; Paintball Accessories; Sports Accessories; Tours & Travel

Bill Wiseman & Co., Inc., 18456 Hwy. 6 South, College Station, TX 77845, P: 979-690-3456, F: 979-690-0156, www.billwisemanandco.com
Firearms; Gun Barrels; Gun Parts/Gunsmithing

BioPlastics Co., 34655 Mills Rd., North Ridgeville, OH 44039, P: 440-327-0485, F: 440-327-3666, www.bioplastics.us

Birchwood Casey, 7900 Fuller Rd., Eden Prairie, MN 55344, P: 800-328-6156, F: 952-937-7979, www.birchwoodcasey.com
Black Powder Accessories; Camping; Firearms Maintenance Equipment; Gun Cases; Gun Parts/Gunsmithing; Hunting Accessories; Lubricants; Targets

Black Hills Ammunition, P.O. Box 3090, Rapid City, SD 57709, P: 605-348-5150, F: 605-348-9827, www.black-hills.com
Ammunition

Black Hills Shooters Supply, Inc., 2875 Creek Dr., Rapid City, SD 57703, P: 800-289-2506, F: 800-289-4570, www.bhshooters.com
Reloading; Wholesaler/Distributor

Black Powder Products Group, 5988 Peachtree Corners East, Norcross, GA 30071, P: 800-320-8767, F: 770-242-8546, www.bpiguns.com
Black Powder Accessories; Firearms; Firearms Maintenance Equipment; Hunting Accessories; Scopes, Sights & Accessories

BlackHawk Products Group, 6160 Commander Pkwy., Norfolk, VA 23502, P: 800-694-5263, F: 757-436-3088, www.blackhawk.com
Bags & Equipment Cases; Men's Clothing; Gloves, Mitts, Hats; Holsters; Hunting Accessories; Knives/Knife Cases; Law Enforcement; Recoil Protection Devices & Services

Blackheart International, LLC, RR3, Box 115, Philippi, WV 26416, P: 877-244-8166, F: 304-457-1281, www.bhigear.com
Ammunition; Gun Parts/Gunsmithing; Holsters; Law Enforcement; Magazines, Cartridge; Scopes, Sights & Accessories; Survival Kits/First Aid; Training & Safety Equipment

Blackwater, P.O. Box 1029, Moyock, NC 27958, P: 252-435-2488, F: 252-435-6388, www.blackwaterusa.com
Bags & Equipment Cases; Men's Clothing; Custom Manufacturing; Gun Cases; Holsters; Law Enforcement; Targets; Training & Safety Equipment

Blade-Tech Industries, 2506 104th St. Court S, Suite A, Lakewood, WA 98499, P: 253-581-4347, F: 253-589-0282, www.blade-tech.com
Bags & Equipment Cases; Custom Manufacturing; Cutlery; Holsters; Hunting Accessories; Knives/Knife Cases; Law Enforcement; Sports Accessories

Blaser Jagdwaffen GmbH, Ziegelstadel 1, Isny, 88316, GERMANY, P: 011

MANUFACTURER'S DIRECTORY

4907562702348, F: 011 4907562702343, www.blaser.de
Firearms; Gun Barrels; Gun Cases; Gun Grips & Stocks; Hunting Accessories

Blauer Manufacturing Co. 20 Aberdeen St., Boston, MA 02215, P: 800-225-6715, www.blauer.com
Law Enforcement; Men & Women's Clothing

Blue Force Gear, Inc., P.O. Box 853, Pooler, GA 31322, P: 877-430-2583, F: 912-964-7701, www.blueforcegear.com
Bags & Equipment Cases; Hunting Accessories; Law Enforcement; Scopes, Sights & Accessories; Sports Accessories

Blue Ridge Knives, 166 Adwolfe Rd., Marion, VA 24354, P: 276-783-6143, F: 276-783-9298, www.blueridgeknives.com
Binoculars; Cutlery; Export/Import Specialists; Knives/Knife Cases; Lighting Products; Scopes, Sights & Accessories; Sharpeners; Wholesaler/Distributor

Blue Stone Safety Products Co., Inc., 2950 W. 63rd St., Chicago, IL 60629, P: 773-776-9472, F: 773-776-9472, www.wolverineholsters.com
Holsters; Law Enforcement

Bluegrass Armory, 145 Orchard St., Richmond, KY 40475, P: 859-625-0874, F: 859-625-0874, www.bluegrassarmory.com
Firearms

Bluestar USA, Inc., 111 Commerce Center Drive, Suite 303, P.O. Box 2903, Huntersville, NC 28078, P: 877-948-7827, F: 704-875-6714, www.bluestar-hunting.com
Archery; Crossbows & Accessories; Hunting Accessories; Law Enforcement; Training & Safety Equipment; Wholesaler/Distributor

BlueWater Ropes/Yates Gear, Inc., 2608 Hartnell Ave., Suite 6, Redding, CA 96002, P: 800-YATES-16, F: 530-222-4640, www.yatesgear.com
Law Enforcement; Training & Safety Equipment; Wholesaler/Distributor

Bobster Eyewear, 12220 Parkway Centre Dr., Suite B, Poway, CA 92064, P: 800-603-2662, F: 858-715-0066, www.bobster.com
Eyewear; Hunting Accessories; Law Enforcement; Shooting Range Equipment; Sports Accessories; Training & Safety Equipment

Body Specs Sunglasses & Goggles, 22846 Industrial Place, Grass Valley, CA 95949, P: 800-824-5907, F: 530-268-1751, www.bodyspecs.com
Eyewear; Law Enforcement; Shooting Range Equipment; Training & Safety Equipment

Boker USA, Inc., 1550 Balsam St., Lakewood, CO 80214, P: 800-992-6537, F: 303-462-0668, www.bokerusa.com
Cutlery; Knives/Knife Cases

Boston Leather, Inc., 1801 Eastwood Dr., P.O. Box 1213, Sterling, IL 61081, P: 800-733-1492, F: 800-856-1650, www.bostonleather.com
Bags & Equipment Cases; Custom Manufacturing; Gun Cases; Holsters;

Knives/Knife Cases; Law Enforcement; Leathergoods; Pet Supplies

Boyds' Gunstock Industries, Inc., 25376 403rd Ave., Mitchell, SD 57301, P: 605-996-5011, F: 605-996-9878, www.boydsgunstocks.com
Custom Manufacturing; Firearms Maintenance Equipment; Gun Grips & Stocks; Gun Parts/Gunsmithing; Hunting Accessories; Shooting Range Equipment

Boyt Harness/Bob Allen Sportswear, 1 Boyt Dr., Osceola, IA 50213, P: 800-685-7020, www.boytharness.com
Gun Cases; Hunting Accessories; Law Enforcement; Men & Women's Clothing; Pet Supplies; Shooting Accessories

Breaching Technologies, Inc., P.O. Box 701468, San Antonio, TX 78270, P: 866-552-7427, F: 210-590-5193, www.breachingtechnologies.com
Law Enforcement; Training & Safety Equipment

Break-Free, 13386 International Parkway, Jacksonville, FL 32218, P: 800-433-2909, F: 800-588-0339, www.break-free.com
Law Enforcement; Lubricants

Brenneke™ of America, L.P., P.O. Box 1481, Clinton, IA 52733, P: 800-753-9733, F: 563-244-7421, www.brennekeusa.com
Ammunition

Brenzovich Firearms & Training Center/dba BFTC, 22301 Texas 20, Fort Hancock, TX 79839, P: 877-585-3775, F: 915-764-2030, www.brenzovich.com
Airguns; Ammunition; Archery; Black Powder Accessories; Export/Import Specialists; Firearms; Training & Safety Equipment; Wholesaler/Distributor

Briley Manufacturing, Inc., 1230 Lumpkin Rd., Houston, TX 77043, P: 800-331-5718, F: 713-932-1043
Chokes, Gun Accessories, Gunsmithing

Brite-Strike Technologies, 26 Wapping Rd., Jones River Industrial Park, Kingston, MA 02364, P: 781-585-5509, F: 781-585-5332, www.brite-strike.com
Law Enforcement; Lighting Products

Broco, Inc., 10868 Bell Ct., Rancho Cucamonga, CA 91730, P: 800-845-7259, F: 800-845-7259, www.brocoinc.com
Law Enforcement

Brookwood/Fine Uniform Co., 1125 E. Broadway, Suite 51, Glendale, CA 91205, P: 626-443-3736, F: 626-444-1551, www.brookwoodbags.com
Archery; Backpacking; Bags & Equipment Cases; Camping; Gun Cases; Hunting Accessories; Knives/Knife Cases; Shooting Range Equipment

Brownells/Brownells MIL/LE Supply Group, 200 S. Front St., Montezuma, IA 50171, P: 800-741-0015, F: 800-264-3068, www.brownells.com
Export/Import Specialists; Firearms Maintenance Equipment; Gun Grips & Stocks; Gun Parts/Gunsmithing; Lubricants; Magazines, Cartridge; Scopes, Sights & Accessories; Wholesaler/Distributor

Browning, 1 Browning Place, Morgan, UT 84050, P: 801-876-2711, F: 801-876-3331, www.browning.com

Browning Outdoor Health and Safety Products, 1 Pharmacal Way, Jackson, WI 53037, P: 800-558-6614, F: 262-677-9006, www.browningsupplies.com
Survival Kits/First Aid

Brunton, 2255 Brunton Ct., Riverton, WY 82501, P: 307-857-4700, F: 307-857-4703, www.brunton.com
Backpacking, Binoculars, Camping, Scopes

Buck Knives, Inc., 660 S. Lochsa St., Post Falls, ID 83854, P: 800-326-2825, www.buckknives.com
Backpacking; Camping; Custom Manufacturing; Cutlery; Hunting Accessories; Knives/Knife Cases; Law Enforcement; Sharpeners

Buffer Technologies, P.O. Box 105047, Jefferson City, MO 65110, P: 877-628-3337, F: 573-634-8522, www.buffertech.com
Gun Parts/Gunsmithing; Law Enforcement; Magazines, Cartridge; Recoil Protection Devices & Services

Bul, Ltd., 10 Rival St., Tel Aviv, 67778, ISRAEL, P: 011 97236392911, F: 011 97236874853, www.bultransmark.com
Firearms; Gun Barrels; Gun Parts/Gunsmithing; Law Enforcement

Bulldog Barrels, LLC, 106 Isabella St., 4 North Shore Center, Suite 110, Pittsburgh, PA 15212, P: 866-992-8553, F: 412-322-1912, www.bulldogbarrels.com
Firearms; Gun Barrels; Gun Parts/Gunsmithing

Bulldog Cases, 830 Beauregard Ave., Danville, VA 24541, P: 800-843-3483, F: 434-793-7504
Bags & Equipment Cases; Camouflage; Gun Cases; Holsters

Bulldog Equipment, 3706 SW 30th Ave., Hollywood, FL 33312, P: 954-581-5510 or 954-448-5221, F: 954-581-4221, www.bulldogequipment.us
Backpacking; Bags & Equipment Cases; Custom Manufacturing; Gloves, Mitts, Hats; Gun Cases; Law Enforcement; Outfitter

Burris Company, Inc., 331 E. 8th St., Greeley, CO 80631, P: 970-356-1670, F: 970-356-8702, www.burrisoptics.com
Binoculars; Scopes, Sights & Accessories; Targets

Bushido Tactical, LLC, P.O. Box 721289, Orlando, FL 32972, P: 407-454-4256, F: 407-286-4416, www.bushidotactical.com
Law Enforcement; Training

Bushnell Law Enforcement/Bushnell Outdoor Products, 9200 Cody St., Overland Park, KS 66214, P: 800-423-3537, F: 800-548-0446, www.unclemikesle.com
Binoculars; Firearms Maintenance Equipment; Gloves, Mitts, Hats; Gun Cases; Holsters; Law Enforcement; Lubricants; Scopes, Sights & Accessories

Business Control Systems Corp., 1173 Green St., Iselin, NJ 08830, P: 800-233-5876, F: 732-283-1192, www.businesscontrol.com
Archery; Computer Software; Firearms; Law Enforcement; Retailer Services;

Shooting Range Equipment; Wholesaler/ Distributor

Butler Creek Corp./Bushnell Outdoor Accessories, 9200 Cody St., Overland Park, KS 66214, P: 800-423-3537, F: 800-548-0446, www.butlercreek.com
Firearms Maintenance Equipment; Gun Barrels; Gun Grips & Stocks; Hunting Accessories; Leathergoods; Scopes, Sights & Accessories

C

CASL Industries/Tanglefree/Remington, P.O. Box 1280, Clayton, CA 94517, P: 877-685-5055, F: 925-685-6055, www.tanglefree.com or www.caslinindustries.com
Bags & Equipment Cases; Blinds; Camouflage; Decoys; Gun Cases; Hunting Accessories

CAS Hanwei, 650 Industrial Blvd., Sale Creek, TN 37373-9797, P: 800-635-9366, F: 423-332-7248, www.cashanwei.com
Custom Manufacturing; Cutlery; Knives/ Knife Cases; Leathergoods; Wholesaler/ Distributor

CCF Race Frames LLC, P.O. Box 29009, Richmond, VA 23242, P: 804-622-4277, F: 804-740-9599, www.ccfraceframes. com
Firearms; Firearms Maintenance Equipment; Gun Parts/Gunsmithing; Law Enforcement

CCI Ammunition/ATK Commercial Products, 2299 Snake River Ave., Lewiston, ID 83501, P: 800-256-8685, F: 208-798-3392, www.cci-ammunition.com
Ammunition

CJ Weapons Accessories, 317 Danielle Ct., Jefferson City, MO 65109, P: 800-510-5919, F: 573-634-2355, www.cjweapons.com
Firearms Maintenance Equipment; Gun Parts/Gunsmithing; Hunting Accessories; Law Enforcement; Magazines, Cartridge; Shooting Range Equipment; Sports Accessories; Wholesaler/Distributor

CMMG, Inc., 620 County Rd. 118, P.O. Box 369, Fayette, MO 65248, P: 660-248-2293, F: 660-248-2290, www.cmmginc.com
Firearms; Law Enforcement; Magazines, Cartridge

CTI Industries Corp., 22160 N. Pepper Rd., Barrington, IL 60010, P: 866-382-1707, F: 800-333-1831, www.zipvac.com
Archery; Backpacking; Bags & Equipment Cases; Camping; Cooking Equipment/ Accessories; Custom Manufacturing; Food; Hunting Accessories

CVA, 5988 Peachtree Corners East, Norcross, GA 30071, P: 800-320-8767, F: 770-242-8546
Black Powder Accessories; Firearms; Firearms Maintenance Equipment; Gun Barrels

CZ-USA/Dan Wesson, 3327 N. 7th St., Kansas city, KS 66115, P: 800-955-4486, F: 913-321-4901, www.cz-usa.com
Firearms

Caesar Guerini USA, 700 Lake St., Cambridge, MD 21613, P: 866-901-1131, F: 410-901-1137, www.gueriniusa.com
Firearms

CALVI S.p.A., Via Iv Novembre, 2, Merate (LC), 23807, ITALY, P: 011 3903999851, F: 011 390399985240, www.calvi.it
Custom Manufacturing; Firearms; Gun Barrels; Gun Locks; Gun Parts/ Gunsmithing

Camelbak Products, 2000 S. McDowell Blvd., Petaluma, CA 94954, P: 800-767-8725, F: 707-665-3844, www.camelbak. com
Backpacking; Bags & Equipment Cases; Gloves, Mitts, Hats; Holsters; Law Enforcement

Camerons Products/CM International, Inc., 2547 Durango Dr., P.O. Box 60220, Colorado Springs, CO 80960, P: 888-563-0227, F: 719-390-0946, www. cameronsproducts.com
Backpacking; Camping; Cooking Equipment/Accessories; Hunting Accessories; Retailer Services; Tours/ Travel; Wholesaler/Distributor

Camfour, Inc., 65 Westfield Industrial Park Rd., Westfield, MA 01085, P: 800-FIREARM, F: 413-568-9663, www. camfour.com
Ammunition; Black Powder Accessories; Computer Software; Export/Import Specialists; Firearms; Hunting Accessories; Law Enforcement; Wholesaler/Distributor

Cammenga Corp., 100 Aniline Ave. N, Suite 258, Holland, MI 49424, P: 616-392-7999, F: 616-392-9432, www.cammenga. com
Magazines, Cartridge; Reloading; Training & Safety Equipment

C-More Systems, 7553 Gary Rd., P.O. Box 1750, Manassas, VA 20109, P: 888-265-8266, F: 703-361-5881, www.cmore.com
Airguns; Archery; Crossbows & Accessories; Custom Manufacturing; Firearms; Hunting Accessories; Law Enforcement; Scopes, Sights & Accessories; Shooting Range Equipment

Camp Technologies, LLC/Div. DHS Technologies, LLC, 33 Kings Hwy., Orangeburg, NY 10962, P: 866-969-2400, F: 845-365-2114, www.camprtv. com
Backpacking; Camping; Hunting Accessories; Law Enforcement; Outfitter; Sports Accessories; Vehicles, Utility & Rec

Cannon Safe, Inc., 216 S. 2nd Ave., Building 932, San Bernardino, CA 92408, P: 800-242-1055, F: 909-382-0707, www.cannonsafe.com
Gun Cabinets/Racks/Safes; Gun Locks

Carl Zeiss Optronics GmbH, Gloelstr. 3-5, Wetzlar, 35576, GERMANY, P: 011 4964414040, F: 011 496441404510, www.zeiss.com/optronics
Law Enforcement; Scopes, Sights & Accessories; Shooting Range Equipment; Targets; Telescopes

Carl Zeiss Sports Optics/Zeiss, 13005 N. Kingston Ave., Chester, VA 23836, P: 800-441-3005, F: 804-530-8481, www. zeiss.com/sports
Binoculars; Scopes, Sights & Accessories

Carlson's Choke Tubes, 720 S. Second St., P.O. Box 162, Atwood, KS 67730, P: 785-626-3700, F: 785-626-3999, www. choketube.com
Custom Manufacturing; Firearms Maintenance Equipment; Game Calls; Gun Parts/Gunsmithing; Hunting Accessories; Scopes, Sights & Accessories; Shooting Range Equipment

Carson Optical, 35 Gilpin Ave., Hauppauge, NY 11788, P: 800-967-8427, F: 631-427-6749, www.carsonoptical.com
Binoculars; Export/Import Specialists; Scopes, Sights & Accessories; Telescopes

Cartuchos Saga, Pda. Caparrela s/n, Lleida, 25192, SPAIN, P: 011 34973275000, F: 011 34973275008
Ammunition

Case Cutlery (W.R. Case & Sons Cutlery Co.), Owens Way, Bradford, PA 16701, P: 800-523-6350, F: 814-358-1736, www. wrcase.com
Cutlery; Knives/Knife Cases; Sharpeners

Caspian Arms, Ltd., 75 Cal Foster Dr., Wolcott, VT 05680, P: 802-472-6454, F: 802-472-6709, www.caspianarms.com
Firearms; Gun Parts/Gunsmithing; Law Enforcement

Cejay Engineering, LLC/InfraRed Combat Marking Beacons, 2129 Gen Booth Blvd., Suite 103-284, Virginia Beach, VA 23454, P: 603-880-8501, F: 603-880-8502, www.cejayeng.com
Lighting Products

Celestron, 2835 Columbia St., Torrance, CA 90503, P: 310-328-9560, F: 310-212-5835, www.celestron.com
Binoculars; Scopes, Sights & Accessories; Telescopes

Center Mass, Inc., 6845 Woonsocket, Canton, MI 48187, P: 800-794-1216, F: 734-416-0650, www.centermassinc.com
Bags & Equipment Cases; Emblems & Decals; Hunting Accessories; Law Enforcement; Men's Clothing; Shooting Range Equipment; Targets; Training & Safety Equipment

Century International Arms, Inc., 430 S. Congress Dr., Suite 1, DelRay Beach, FL 33445, P: 800-527-1252, F: 561-265-4520, www.centuryarms.com
Ammunition; Firearms; Firearms Maintenance Equipment; Gun Parts/ Gunsmithing; Law Enforcement; Magazines, Cartridge; Scopes, Sights & Accessories; Wholesaler/Distributor

Cequre Composite Technologies, 5995 Shier-Rings Rd., Suite A, Dublin, OH 43016, P: 614-526-0095, F: 614-526-0098, www.wearmor.com
Custom Manufacturing; Law Enforcement; Shooting Range Equipment; Targets

Cerakote/NIC Industries, Inc., 7050 Sixth St., White City, OR 97503, P: 866-774-7628, F: 541-830-6518, www. nicindustries.com
Camouflage; Custom Manufacturing; Firearms; Firearms Maintenance Equipment; Knives/Knife Cases; Law Enforcement; Lubricants; Paintball Guns

Chapman Innovations, 343 W. 400 South, Salt Lake City, UT 84101, P: 801-415-

MANUFACTURER'S DIRECTORY

0024, F: 801-415-2001, www.carbonx.
com
*Gloves, Mitts, Hats; Law Enforcement; Men
& Women's Clothing*

Charter Arms/MKS Supply, Inc., 8611A
North Dixie Dr., Dayton, OH 45414, P:
866-769-4867, F: 937-454-0503, www.
charterfirearms.com
Firearms

Cheddite France, 99 Route de Lyon, P.O.
Box 112, Bourg-les-Valence, 26500,
FRANCE, P: 011 33475564545, F: 011
33475563587, www.cheddite.com
Ammunition

Chengdu Lis Business, 4-3-9, 359
Shuhan Rd., Chengdu, SICH 610036,
CHINA, P: 0110862887541867, F: 011
862887578686, www.lisoptics.com
*Binoculars; Compasses; Cutlery; Lighting
Products; Scopes, Sights & Accessories;
Telescopes*

CheyTac Associates, LLC, 363 Sunset Dr.,
Arco, ID 83213, P: 256-325-0622, F: 208-
527-3328, www.cheytac.com
*Ammunition; Computer Software;
Custom Manufacturing; Firearms; Law
Enforcement; Training & Safety Equipment*

Chiappa Firearms-Armi Sport di Chiappa
Silvia e C. SNC, Via Milano, 2, Azzano
Mella (Bs), 25020, ITALY, P: 011
390309749065, F: 011 390309749232,
www.chiappafirearms.com
Black Powder Accessories; Firearms

China Shenzhen Aimbond Enterprises Co.,
Ltd., 19D, Building No. 1, China Phoenix
Building, No. 2008, Shennan Rd., Futian
District, Shenzhen, Guangdong 518026,
CHINA, P: 011 8675582522730812, F:
011 8675583760022, www.sino-optics.
com
*Binoculars; Eyewear; Firearms
Maintenance Equipment; Hunting
Accessories; Lighting Products; Scopes,
Sights & Accessories; Telescopes*

Chip McCormick Custom, LLC, 105 Sky
King Dr., Spicewood, TX 78669, P:
800-328-2447, F: 830-693-4975, www.
cmcmags.com
*Gun Parts/Gunsmithing; Magazines,
Cartridge*

Choate Machine & Tool, 116 Lovers Lane,
Bald Knob, AR 72010, P: 800-972-6390,
F: 501-724-5873, www.riflestock.com
Gun Grips & Stocks; Law Enforcement

Chongqing Dontop Optics Co., Ltd.,
No. 5 Huangshan Ave. Middle Beibu
New District, Chongqing, 401121,
CHINA, P: 011 862386815057, F: 011
862386815100, www.dontop.com
*Binoculars; Custom Manufacturing;
Scopes, Sights & Accessories; Shooting
Range Equipment; Telescopes*

Chongqing Jizhou Enterprise Co., Ltd.,
Rm 8-1, Block A3, Jiazhou Garden,
Chongqing, Yubei 401147, CHINA, P: 011
862367625115, F: 011 862367625121,
www.cqjizhou.com
*Binoculars; Compasses; Scopes, Sights &
Accessories; Telescopes*

Chonwoo Corp./Chonwoo Case & Cover
(Tianjin) Co., Ltd., 4-6, SamJun-Dong
Songpa-gu, Seoul, 138-837, SOUTH
KOREA, P: 011 8224205094, F: 011
8224236154, www.chonwoo.co.kr
*Backpacking; Bags & Equipment Cases;
Gun Cases; Holsters; Hunting Accessories;
Knives/Knife Cases; Leathergoods*

Chris Reeve Knives, 2949 S. Victory View
Way, Boise, ID 83709, P: 208-375-0367,
F: 208-375-0368, www.chrisreeve.com
*Backpacking; Camping; Cutlery; Hunting
Accessories; Knives/Knife Cases; Law
Enforcement; Sports Accessories*

Christensen Arms, 192 E. 100 North,
Fayette, UT 84630, P: 888-517-8855, F:
435-528-5773, www.christensenarms.
com
*Custom Manufacturing; Firearms; Gun
Barrels*

Christie & Christie Enterprises, Inc., 404
Bolivia Blvd., Bradenton, FL 34207, P:
440-413-0031, F: 440-428-5551
*Gun Grips & Stocks; Gun Parts/
Gunsmithing; Magazines, Cartridge;
Scopes, Sights & Accessories; Wholesaler/
Distributor*

Cimarron Firearms Co., 105 Winding Oaks
Rd., P.O. Box 906, Fredericksburg, TX
78624, P: 830-997-9090, F: 830-997-
0802, www.cimarron-firearms.com
*Black Powder Accessories; Firearms; Gun
Cases; Gun Grips & Stocks; Gun Parts/
Gunsmithing; Holsters; Leathergoods;
Wholesaler/Distributor*

Clever SRL, Via A. Da Legnano, 9/A, I-
37141 Ponteflorio, Verona, ITALY, P: 011
390458840770, F: 011 390458840380,
www.clevervr.com
Ammunition

Clymer Precision, 1605 W. Hamlin Rd.,
Rochester Hills, MI 48309, P: 877-
REAMERS, F: 248-853-1530, www.
clymertool.com
*Black Powder Accessories; Books/Industry
Publications; Custom Manufacturing;
Firearms Maintenance Equipment; Gun
Parts/Gunsmithing; Law Enforcement;
Reloading*

Coast Products/LED Lenser, 8033 NE
Holman St., Portland, OR 97218, P:
800-426-5858, F: 503-234-4422, www.
coastportland.com
*Camping; Compasses; Cutlery; Knives/
Knife Cases; Law Enforcement; Lighting
Products; Sharpeners*

Cobra Enterprises of Utah, Inc., 1960 S.
Milestone Dr., Suite F, Salt Lake City, UT
84104, P: 801-908-8300, F: 801-908-
8301, www.cobrapistols.net
Firearms

Codet Newport Corp./Big Bill Work Wear,
924 Crawford Rd., Newport, VT 05855, P:
800-992-6338, F: 802-334-8268, www.
bigbill.com
*Backpacking; Bags & Equipment Cases;
Camouflage; Camping; Footwear; Gloves,
Mitts, Hats; Men's Clothing*

Cold Steel Inc., 3036 Seaborg Ave., Suite A,
Ventura, CA 93003, P: 800-255-4716, F:
805-642-9727, www.coldsteel.com
*Cutlery; Knives/Knife Cases; Law
Enforcement; Sports Accessories; Videos*

Collector's Armoury, Ltd., P.O. Box 1050,
Lorton, VA 22199, P: 800-336-4572, F:
703-493-9424, www.collectorsarmoury.
com
*Black Powder Accessories; Books/Industry
Publications; Cutlery; Firearms; Holsters;
Home Furnishings; Training & Safety
Equipment; Wholesaler/Distributor*

Colonial Arms, Inc. 1504 Hwy. 31 S, P.O.
Box 250, Bay Minette, AL 36507, P:
800-949-8088, F: 251-580-5006, www.
colonialarms.com
*Firearms; Firearms Maintenance
Equipment; Gun Barrels; Gun Parts/
Gunsmithing; Hunting Accessories;
Lubricants; Recoil Protection Devices &
Services; Wholesaler/Distributor*

Colt's Manufacturing Co., LLC, P.O. Box
1868, Hartford, CT 06144, P: 800-962-
COLT, F: 860-244-1449, www.coltsmfg.
com
*Custom Manufacturing; Firearms; Gun
Parts/Gunsmithing; Law Enforcement*

Columbia River Knife and Tool, 18348 SW
126th Pl., Tualatin, OR 97062, P: 800-
891-3100, F: 503-682-9680, www.crkt.
com
Knives/Knife Cases; Sharpeners

Columbia Sportswear Co., 14375 NW
Science Park Dr., Portland, OR 97229, P:
800-547-8066, F: 503-985-5800, www.
columbia.com
*Bags & Equipment Cases; Binoculars;
Footwear; Gloves, Mitts, Hats; Men &
Women's Clothing; Pet Supplies; Scopes,
Sights & Accessories*

Combined Tactical Systems, 388 Kinsman
Rd., P.O. Box 506, Jamestown, PA
16134, P: 724-932-2177, F: 724-932-
2166, www.less-lethal.com
Law Enforcement

Compass Industries, Inc., 104 E. 25th
St., New York, NW 10010, P: 800-
221-9904, F: 212-353-0826, www.
compassindustries.com
*Binoculars; Camping; Compasses; Cutlery;
Export/Import Specialists; Eyewear;
Hunting Accessories; Wholesaler/
Distributor*

Competition Electronics, 3469 Precision
Dr., Rockford, IL 61109, P: 815-
874-8001, F: 815-874-8181, www.
competitionelectronics.com
*Firearms Maintenance Equipment;
Reloading; Shooting Range Equipment;
Training & Safety Equipment*

Condor Outdoor Products, 1866 Business
Center Dr., Duarte, CA 91010, P: 800-
552-2554, F: 626-303-3383, www.
condoroutdoor.com
*Backpacking; Bags & Equipment Cases;
Camouflage; Footwear; Gun Cases;
Holsters; Wholesaler/Distributor*

Condor Tool & Knife, Inc., 6309 Marina Dr.,
Orlando, FL 32819, P: 407-876-0886, F:
407-876-0994, www.condortk.com
*Archery; Camping; Custom Manufacturing;
Cutlery; Gun Cases; Hunting Accessories;
Knives/Knife Cases; Leathergoods*

Connecticut Shotgun Mfg. Co., 100
Burritt St., New Britain, CT 06053, P:
800-515-4867, F: 860-832-8707, www.
connecticutshotgun.com
*Firearms; Firearms Maintenance
Equipment; Gun Cabinets/Racks/Safes;*

Gun Cases; Gun Parts/Gunsmithing; Hunting Accessories; Knives/Knife Cases; Scopes, Sights & Accessories

Consorzio Armaioli Bresciani, Via Matteotti, 325, Gardone V.T., Brescia 25063, ITALY, P: 011 39030821752, F: 011 39030831425, www.armaiolibresciani.org
Firearms; Gun Parts/Gunsmithing; Videos

Consorzio Cortellinai Maniago SRL, Via Della Repubblica, 21, Maniago, PN 33085, ITALY, P: 011 39042771185, F: 011 390427700440, www.consorziocoltellinai.it
Camping; Cutlery; Hunting Accessories; Knives/Knife Cases; Law Enforcement

Cooper Firearms of MT, Inc./Cooper Arms, 4004 Hwy. 93 North, P.O. Box 114, Stevensville, MT 59870, P: 406-777-0373, F: 406-777-5228, www.cooperfirearms.com
Custom Manufacturing; Firearms

CopShoes.com/MetBoots.com, 6655 Poss Rd., San Antonio, TX 78238, P: 866-280-0400, F: 210-647-1401, www.copshoes.com
Footwear; Hunting Accessories; Law Enforcement

Cor-Bon/Glaser/Div. Dakota Ammo Inc., 1311 Industry Rd., P.O. Box 369, Sturgis, SD 57785, P: 605-347-4544, F: 605-347-5055, www.corbon.com
Ammunition

Counter Assault Pepper Sprays/Bear Deterrent, Law Enforcement & Personal Defense, 120 Industrial Court, Kalispell, MT 59901, P: 800-695-3394. F: 406-257-6674, www.counterassault.com
Archery; Backpacking; Camping; Hunting Accessories; Law Enforcement; Sports Accessories; Survival Kits/First Aid; Training & Safety Equipment

Crackshot Corp., 2623 E 36th St. N, Tulsa, OK 74110, P: 800-667-1753, F: 918-838-1271, www.crackshotcorp.com
Archery; Backpacking; Camping; Footwear; Hunting Accessories; Men & Women's Clothing; Training & Safety Equipment

Crest Ultrasonics Corp., P.O. Box 7266, Trenton, NJ 08628, P: 800-273-7822, F: 877-254-7939, www.crest-ultrasonics.com
Custom Manufacturing; Firearms Maintenance Equipment; Gun Parts/Gunsmithing; Law Enforcement; Lubricants; Shooting Range Equipment; Wholesaler/Distributor

Crimson Trace Holdings, LLC/Lasergrips, 9780 SW Freeman Dr., Wilsonville, OR 97070, P: 800-442-2406, F: 503-783-5334, www.crimsontrace.com
Firearms; Gun Grips & Stocks; Hunting Accessories; Law Enforcement; Scopes, Sights & Accessories; Training & Safety Equipment

Crosman Corp., Inc., Routes 5 and 20, East Bloomfield, NY 14443, P: 800-724-7486, F: 585-657-5405, www.crosman.com
Airguns; Airsoft; Ammunition; Archery; Crossbows & Accessories; Scopes, Sights & Accessories; Shooting Range Equipment; Targets

Crye Precision, LLC, 63 Flushing Ave., Suite 252, Brooklyn, NY 11205, P:

718-246-3838, F: 718-246-3833, www.cryeprecision.com
Bags & Equipment Cases; Camouflage; Custom Manufacturing; Law Enforcement; Men's Clothing

Cuppa, 3131 Morris St. N, St. Petersburg, FL 33713, P: 800-551-6541, F: 727-820-9212, www.cuppa.net
Custom Manufacturing; Emblems & Decals; Law Enforcement; Outdoor Art, Jewelry, Sculpture; Retailer Services

Custom Leather, 460 Bingemans Centre Dr., Kitchener, Ontario N2B 3X9, CANADA, P: 800-265-4504, F: 519-741-2072, www.customleather.com
Custom Manufacturing; Gun Cases; Hunting Accessories; Leathergoods

Cutting Edge Tactical, 166 Mariners Way, Moyock, NC 27958, P: 800-716-9425, F: 252-435-2284, www.cuttingedgetactical.com
Bags & Equipment Cases; Binoculars; Eyewear; Footwear; Gun Grips & Stocks; Law Enforcement; Lighting Products; Training & Safety Equipment

Cygnus Law Enforcement Group, 1233 Janesville Ave., Fort Atkinson, WI 53538, P: 800-547-7377, F: 303-322-0627, www.officer.com
Law Enforcement

Cylinder & Slide, Inc., 245 E. 4th St., Fremont, NE 68025, P: 800-448-1713, F: 402-721-0263, www.cylinder-slide.com
Firearms; Gun Barrels; Gun Grips & Stocks; Gun Parts/Gunsmithing; Magazines, Cartridge; Scopes, Sights & Accessories; Wholesaler/Distributor

D

DAC Technologies/GunMaster, 12120 Colonel Glenn Rd., Suite 6200, Little Rock, AR 72210, P: 800-920-0098, F: 501-661-9108, www.dactec.com
Black Powder Accessories; Camping; Cooking Equipment/Accessories; Firearms Maintenance Equipment; Gun Cabinets/Racks/Safes; Gun Locks; Hunting Accessories; Wholesaler/Distributor

DMT-Diamond Machine Technology, 84 Hayes Memorial Dr., Marlborough, MA 01752, P: 800-666-4368, F: 508-485-3924, www.dmtsharp.com
Archery; Cooking Equipment/Accessories; Cutlery; Hunting Accessories; Knives/Knife Cases; Sharpeners; Sports Accessories; Taxidermy

D & K Mfg., Co., Inc., 5180 US Hwy. 380, Bridgeport, TX 76426, P: 800-553-1028, F: 940-683-0248, www.d-k.net
Bags & Equipment Cases; Custom Manufacturing; Emblems & Decals; Law Enforcement; Leathergoods

D.S.A., Inc., 27 W. 990 Industrial Ave. (60010), P.O. Box 370, Lake Barrington, IL 60011, P: 847-277-7258, F: 847-277-7263, www.dsarms.com
Ammunition; Books/Industry Publications; Firearms; Gun Grips & Stocks; Gun Parts/Gunsmithing; Law Enforcement;

Magazines, Cartridge; Scopes, Sights & Accessories

Daisy Manufacturing Co./Daisy Outdoors Products, 400 W. Stribling Dr., P.O. Box 220, Rogers, AR 72756, P: 800-643-3458, F: 479-636-0573, www.daisy.com
Airguns; Airsoft; Ammunition; Clay Targets; Eyewear; Scopes, Sights & Accessories; Targets; Training & Safety Equipment

Dakota Arms, Inc., 1310 Industry Rd., Sturgis, SD 57785, P: 605-347-4686, F: 605-347-4459, www.dakotaarms.com
Ammunition; Custom Manufacturing; Export/Import Specialists; Firearms; Gun Cases; Gun Grips & Stocks; Gun Parts/Gunsmithing; Reloading

Damascus Protective Gear, P.O. Box 543, Rutland, VT, 05702, P: 800-305-2417, F: 805-639-0610, www.damascusgear.com
Archery; Custom Manufacturing; Gloves, Mitts, Hats; Law Enforcement; Leathergoods

Dan's Whetstone Co., Inc./Washita Mountain Whetstone Co., 418 Hilltop Rd., Pearcy, AR 71964, P: 501-767-1616, F: 501-767-9598, www.danswhetstone.com
Black Powder Accessories; Camping; Cutlery; Gun Parts/Gunsmithing; Hunting Accessories; Knives/Knife Cases; Sharpeners; Sports Accessories

Daniel Defense, Inc., 6002 Commerce Blvd., Suite 109, Savannah, GA 31408, P: 866-554-4867, F: 912-964-4237, www.danieldefense.com
Firearms

Darn Tough Vermont, 364 Whetstone Dr., P.O. Box 307, Northfield, VT 05663, P: 877-DARNTUFF, F: 802-485-6140, www.darntough.com
Backpacking; Camping; Footwear; Hunting Accessories; Men & Women's Clothing

Davidson's, 6100 Wilkinson Dr., Prescott, AZ, 86301, P: 800-367-4867, F: 928-776-0344, www.galleryofguns.com
Ammunition; Firearms; Law Enforcement; Magazines, Cartridge; Online Services; Scopes, Sights & Accessories; Wholesaler/Distributor

Del-Ton, Inc., 218B Aviation Pkwy., Elizabethtown, NC 28337, P: 910-645-2172, F: 910-645-2244, www.del-ton.com
Firearms; Gun Barrels; Gun Parts/Gunsmithing; Law Enforcement; Wholesaler/Distributor

Demyan, 10, 2nd Donskoy Ln., Moscow, 119071, RUSSIAN FEDERATION, P: 011 74959847629, F: 011 74959847629, www.demyan.info
Airguns; Firearms

DeSantis Holster and Leather Goods Co., 431 Bayview Ave., Amityville, NY 11701, P: 800-424-1236, F: 631-841-6320, www.desantisholster.com
Bags & Equipment Cases; Gun Cases; Holsters; Hunting Accessories; Law Enforcement; Leathergoods

Desert Tactical Arms, P.O. Box 65816, Salt Lake City, UT 84165, P: 801-975-7272, F: 801-908-6425, www.deserttacticalarms.com
Firearms; Law Enforcement

MANUFACTURER'S DIRECTORY

Diamondback Tactical, 23040 N. 11th Ave., Bldg. 1, Phoenix, AZ 85027, P: 800-735-7030, F: 623-583-0674, www.diamondbacktactical.com
Law Enforcement

Diana/Mayer & Grammelspacher GmbH & Co. KG, Karlstr, 34, Rastatt, 76437, GERMANY, P: 011 4972227620, F: 011 49722276278, www.diana-airguns.de
Airguns; Scopes, Sights & Accessories

Dillon Precision Products, Inc., 8009 E. Dillon's Way, Scottsdale, AZ 85260, P: 800-223-4570, F: 480-998-2786, www.dillonprecision.com
Bags & Equipment Cases; Feeder Equipment; Hearing Protection; Holsters; Hunting Accessories; Reloading

Dimension 3D Printing, 7655 Commerce Way, Eden Prairie, MN 55344, P: 888-480-3548, F: 952-294-3715, www.dimensionprinting.com
Computer Software; Custom Manufacturing; Gun Parts/Gunsmithing; Hunting Accessories; Scopes, Sights & Accessories

Directex, 304 S. Leighton Ave., Anniston, AL 36207, P: 800-845-3603, F: 256-235-2275, www/directex.net
Archery; Backpacking; Bags & Equipment Cases; Custom Manufacturing; Export/Import Specialists; Gun Cases; Holsters; Hunting Accessories

Dixie Gun Works, Inc., 1412 W. Reelfoot Ave., P.O. Box 130, Union City, TN 38281, P: 800-238-6785, F: 731-885-0440, www.dixiegunworks.com
Black Powder Accessories; Book/Industry Publications; Firearms; Gun Parts/Gunsmithing; Hunting Accessories; Knives/Knife Cases

DNZ Products, LLC/Game Reaper & Freedom Reaper Scope Mounts, 2710 Wilkins Dr., Sanford, NC 27330, P: 919-777-9608, F: 919-777-9609, www.dnzproducts.com
Black Powder Accessories; Custom Manufacturing; Gun Parts/Gunsmithing; Hunting Accessories; Scopes, Sights & Accessories

Docter Optic/Imported by Merkel USA, 7661 Commerce Lane, Trussville, AL 35173, P: 800-821-3021, F: 205-655-7078, www.merkel-usa.com
Binoculars; Scopes, Sights & Accessories

DoubleStar/J&T Distributing, P.O. Box 430, Winchester, KY 40391, P: 888-736-7725, F: 859-745-4638, www.jtdistributing.com
Firearms Maintenance Equipment; Gun Barrels; Gun Parts/Gunsmithing; Magazines, Cartridge; Wholesaler/Distributor

DPMS Firearms, LLC, 3312 12th St. SE, St. Cloud, MN 56304, P: 800-578-3767, F: 320-258-4449, www.dpmsinc.com
Firearms; Scopes, Sights & Accessories

DriFire, LLC, 3151 Williams Rd., Suite E, Columbus, GA 31909, P: 866-266-4035, F: 706-507-7556, www.drifire.com
Camouflage; Men & Women's Clothing; Training & Safety Equipment

Du-Lite Corp., 171 River Rd., Middletown, CT 06457, P: 860-347-2505, F: 860-344-9404, www.du-lite.com
Gunsmithing; Lubricants

Dummies Unlimited, Inc., 2435 Pine St., Pomona, CA 91767, P: 866-4DUMMIES, F: 909-392-7510, F: 909-392-7510, www.dummiesunlimited.com
Law Enforcement; Shooting Range Equipment; Targets; Training & Safety Equipment

Duostock Designs, Inc., P.O. Box 32, Welling, OK 74471, P: 866-386-7865, F: 918-431-3182, www.duostock.com
Firearms; Gun Grips & Stocks; Law Enforcement; Recoil Protection Devices & Services

Durasight Scope Mounting Systems, 5988 Peachtree Corners East, Norcross, GA 30071, P: 800-321-8767, F: 770-242-8546, www.durasight.com
Scopes, Sights & Accessories

Dynamic Research Technologies, LLC, 405 N. Lyon St., Grant City, MO 64456, P: 660-564-2331, F: 660-564-2103, www.drtammo.com
Ammunition; Reloading

E

E-Z Mount Corp., 1706 N. River Dr., San Angelo, TX 76902, P: 800-292-3756, F: 325-658-4951, www.ezmountcorp@zipnet.us
Gun Cabinets/Racks/Safes

E-Z Pull Trigger, 932 W. 5th St., Centralia, IL 62801, P: 618-532-6964, F: 618-532-5154, www.ezpulltriggerassist.com
Firearms; Gun Parts/Gunsmithing; Hunting Accessories

E.A.R., Inc./Insta-Mold Div., P.O. Box 18888, Boulder, CO 80303, P: 800-525-2690, F: 303-447-2637, www.earinc.com
Eyewear; Hearing Protection; Law Enforcement; Shooting Range Equipment; Wholesaler/Distributor

ER Shaw/Small Arms Mfg., 5312 Thoms Run Rd., Bridgeville, PA 15017, P: 412-221-4343, F: 412-221-4303, www.ershawbarrels.com
Custom Manufacturing; Firearms; Gun Barrels

ECS Composites, 3560 Rogue River Hwy., Grants Pass, OR 97527, P: 541-476-8871, F: 541-474-2479, www.transitcases.com
Custom Manufacturing; Gun Cases; Law Enforcement; Sports Accessories

EMCO Supply, Inc./Red Rock Outdoor Gear, 2601 Dutton Ave., Waco, TX 76711, P: 800-342-4654, F: 254-662-0045
Backpacking; Bags & Equipment Cases; Blinds; Camouflage; Compasses; Game Calls; Hunting Accessories; Law Enforcement

E.M.F. Co., Inc./Purveyors of Fine Firearms Since 1956, 1900 E. Warner Ave., Suite 1-D, Santa Ana, CA 92705, P: 800-430-1310, F: 800-508-1824, www.emf-company.com
Black Powder Accessories; Firearms; Gun Parts/Gunsmithing; Holsters; Leathergoods; Wholesaler/Distributor

EOTAC, 1940 Old Dunbar Rd., West Columbia, SC 29172, P: 803-744-9930, F: 803-744-9933, www.eotac.com
Tactical Clothing

ESS Goggles, P.O. Box 1017, Sun Valley, ID 83353, P: 877-726-4072, F: 208-726-4563
Eyewear; Hunting Accessories; Law Enforcement; Shooting Range Equipment; Training & Safety Equipment

ETL/Secure Logic, 2351 Tenaya Dr., Modesto, CA 95354, P: 800-344-3242, F: 209-529-3854, www.securelogiconline.com
Firearms; Gun Cabinets/Racks/Safes; Training & Safety Equipment

Eagle Grips, Inc., 460 Randy Rd., Carol Stream, IL, 60188, P: 800-323-6144, F: 630-260-0486, www.eaglegrips.com
Gun Grips & Stocks

Eagle Imports, Inc., 1750 Brielle Ave., Suite B-1, Wanamassa, NJ 07712, P: 732-493-0333, F: 732-493-0301, www.bersafirearmsusa.com
Export/Import Specialists; Firearms; Holsters; Magazines, Cartridge; Wholesaler/Distributor

Eagle Industries Unlimited, Inc., 1000 Biltmore Dr., Fenton, MO 63026, P: 888-343-7547, F: 636-349-0321, www.eagleindustries.com
Backpacking; Bags & Equipment Cases; Camping; Gun Cases; Holsters; Hunting Accessories; Law Enforcement; Sports Accessories

Ear Phone Connection, 25139 Avenue Stanford, Valencia, CA 91355, P: 888-372-1888, F: 661-775-5622, www.earphoneconnect.com
Airsoft; Hearing Protection; Law Enforcement; Paintball Accessories; Two-Way Radios

EarHugger Safety Equipment, Inc., 1819 N. Main St., Suite 8, Spanish Fork, UT 84660, P: 800-236-1449, F: 801-371-8901, www.earhuggersafety.com
Law Enforcement

Easy Loop Lock, LLC, 8049 Monetary Dr., Suite D-4, Riviera Beach, FL 33404, P: 561-304-4990, F: 561-337-4655, www.ellock.com
Camping; Gun Locks; Hunting Accessories; Sports Accessories; Wholesaler/Distributor

E-Z Mount Corp., 1706 N. River Dr., San Angelo, TX 76902, P: 800-292-3756, F: 325-658-4951, www.ezmountcorp@zipnet.us
Gun Cabinets/Racks/Safes

E-Z Pull Trigger, 932 W. 5th St., Centralia, IL 62801, P: 618-532-6964, F: 618-532-5154, www.ezpulltriggerassist.com
Firearms; Gun Parts/Gunsmithing; Hunting Accessories

Eberlestock, P.O. Box 862, Boise, ID 83701, P: 877-866-3047, F: 240-526-2632, www.eberlestock.com
Archery; Backpacking; Bags & Equipment Cases; Gun Grips & Stocks; Hunting Accessories; Law Enforcement

Ed Brown Products, Inc., P.O. Box 492, Perry, MO 63462, P: 573-565-3261, F: 573-565-2791, www.edbrown.com
Computer Software; Custom Manufacturing; Firearms; Gun Barrels; Gun Parts/Gunsmithing; Magazines, Cartridge; Scopes, Sights & Accessories

El Paso Saddlery, 2025 E. Yandell, El Paso, TX 79903, P: 915-544-2233, F: 915-544-2535, www.epsaddlery.com
Holsters; Leathergoods

ELCAN Optical Technologies, 1601 N. Plano Rd., Richardson, TX 75081, P: 877-TXELCAN, F: 972-344-8260, www.elcan.com
Binoculars; Custom Manufacturing; Law Enforcement; Scopes, Sights & Accessories

Eley Limited/Eley Hawk Limited, Selco Way, First Ave., Minworth Industrial Estate, Minworth, Sutton Coldfield, West Midlands B76 1BA, UNITED KINGDOM, P: 011 4401213134567, F: 011-4401213134568, www.eleyammunition.com, www.eleyhawkltd.com
Ammunition

Elite Iron, LLC, 1345 Thunders Trail, Bldg. D, Potomac, MT 59823, P: 406-244-0234, F: 406-244-0135, www.eliteiron.net
Law Enforcement; Scopes, Sights & Accessories

Elite Survival Systems, 310 W. 12th St., P.O. Box 245, Washington, MO 63090, P: 866-340-2778, F: 636-390-2977, www.elitesurvival.com
Backpacking; Bags & Equipment Cases; Custom Manufacturing; Footwear; Gun Cases; Holsters; Knives/Knife Cases; Law Enforcement

Ellett Brothers, 267 Columbia Ave., P.O. Box 128, Chapin, SC 29036, P: 800-845-3711, F: 800-323-3006, www.ellettbrothers.com
Ammunition; Archery; Black Powder Accessories; Firearms; Hunting Accessories; Leathergoods; Scopes, Sights & Accessories; Wholesaler/Distributor

Ellington-Rush, Inc./Cough Silencer/SlingStix, 170 Private Dr., Lula, GA 30554, P: 706-677-2394, F: 706-677-3425, www.coughsilencer.com, www.slingstix.com
Archery; Black Powder Accessories; Game Calls; Hunting Accessories; Law Enforcement; Shooting Range Equipment

Elvex Corp., 13 Trowbridge, Bethel, CT 06801, P: 800-888-6582, F: 203-791-2278, www.elvex.com
Eyewear; Hearing Protection; Hunting Accessories; Law Enforcement; Men's Clothing; Paintball Accessories

Emerson Knives, Inc., 2730 Monterey St., Suite 101, Torrance, CA 90503, P: 310-212-7455, F: 310-212-7289, www.emersonknives.com
Camping; Cutlery; Knives/Knife Cases; Men & Women's Clothing; Wholesaler/Distributor

Energizer Holdings, 533 Maryville University Dr., St. Louis, MO 63141, P: 314-985-2000, F: 314-985-2207, www.energizer.com

Backpacking; Camping; Hunting Accessories; Law Enforcement; Lighting Products; Sports Accessories; Survival Kits/First Aid; Training & Safety Equipment

Enforcement Technology Group, Inc., 400 N. Broadway, 4th Floor, Milwaukee, WI 53202, P: 800-873-2872, F: 414-276-1533, www.etgi.us
Custom Manufacturing; Law Enforcement; Online Services; Shooting Range Equipment; Training & Safety Equipment; Wholesaler/Distributor

Entreprise Arms, Inc., 5321 Irwindale Ave., Irwindale, CA 91706-2025, P: 626-962-8712, F: 626-962-4692, www.entreprise.com
Firearms; Gun Parts/Gunsmithing

Environ-Metal, Inc./Hevishot®, 1307 Clark Mill Rd., P.O. Box 834, Sweet Home, OR 97386, P: 541-367-3522, F: 541-367-3552, www.hevishot.com
Ammunition; Law Enforcement; Reloading

EOTAC, 1940 Old Dunbar Rd., West Columbia, SC 29172, P: 888-672-0303, F: 803-744-9933, www.eotac.com
Gloves, Mitts, Hats; Men's Clothing

Epilog Laser, 16371 Table Mountain Pkwy., Golden, CO 80403, P: 303-277-1188, F: 303-277-9669, www.epiloglaser.com
Custom Manufacturing; Law Enforcement

Essential Gear, Inc./eGear, 171 Wells St., Greenfield, MA 01301, P: 800-582-3861, F: 413-772-8947, www.essentialgear.com
Backpacking; Camping; Hunting Accessories; Law Enforcement; Lighting Products; Sports Accessories; Survival Kits/First Aid; Training & Safety Equipment

European American Armory Corp., P.O. Box 560746, Rockledge, FL 32956, P: 321-639-4842, F: 321-639-7006, www.eaacorp.com
Airguns; Firearms

Extendo Bed Co., 223 Roedel Ave., Caldwell, ID 83605, P: 800-752-0706, F: 208-286-0925, www.extendobed.com
Law Enforcement; Training & Safety Equipment

Extreme Shock USA, 182 Camp Jacob Rd., Clintwood, VA 24228, P: 877-337-6772, F: 276-926-6092, www.extremeshockusa.net
Ammunition; Law Enforcement; Lubricants; Reloading

ExtremeBeam Tactical, 2275 Huntington Dr., Suite 872, San Marino, CA 91108, P: 626-372-5898, F: 626-609-0640, www.extremebeamtactical.com
Camping; Law Enforcement; Lighting Products; Outfitter

F

F&W Media/Krause Publications, 700 E. State St., Iola, WI 54990, P: 800-457-2873, F: 715-445-4087, www.krausebooks.com
Books/Industry Publications; Videos

F.A.I.R. Srl, Via Gitti, 41, Marcheno, 25060, ITALY, P: 011 39030861162, F: 011 390308610179, www.fair.it
Firearms; Gun Barrels; Gun Parts/Gunsmithing; Hunting Accessories

F.A.P. F. LLI Pietta SNC, Via Mandolossa, 102, Gussago, Brescia 25064, ITALY, P: 011 390303737098, F: 011 390303737100, www.pietta.it
Black Powder Accessories; Firearms; Gun Cases; Gun Grips & Stocks; Gun Parts/Gunsmithing; Holsters

F.I.A.V. L. Mazzacchera SPA, Via S. Faustino, 62, Milano, 20134, ITALY, P: 011 390221095411, F: 011 390221095530, www.flav.it
Gun Parts/Gunsmithing

FNH USA, P.O. Box 697, McLean, VA 22101, P: 703-288-1292, F: 703-288-1730, www.fnhusa.com
Ammunition; Firearms; Law Enforcement; Training & Safety Equipment

F.T.C. (Friedheim Tool), 1433 Roosevelt Ave., National City, CA 91950, 619-474-3600, F: 619-474-1300, www.ftcsteamers.com
Firearms Maintenance Equipment

Fab Defense, 43 Yakov Olamy St., Moshav Mishmar Hashiva, 50297, ISRAEL, P: 011 972039603399, F: 011 972039603312, www.fab-defense.com
Gun Grips & Stocks; Law Enforcement; Targets

FailZero, 7825 SW Ellipse Way, Stuart, FL 34997, P: 772-223-6699, F: 772-223-9996
Gun Parts/Gunsmithing

Falcon Industries, P.O. Box 1690, Edgewood, NM 87015, P: 877-281-3783, F: 505-281-3991, www.ergogrips.net
Gun Grips & Stocks; Gun Parts/Gunsmithing; Law Enforcement; Scopes, Sights & Accessories; Sports Accessories

Fasnap® Corp., 3500 Reedy Dr., Elkhart, IN 46514, P: 800-624-2058, F: 574-264-0802, www.fasnap.com
Backpacking; Bags & Equipment Cases; Gun Cases; Holsters; Hunting Accessories; Knives/Knife Cases; Leathergoods; Wholesaler/Distributor

Fausti Stefano s.r.l., Via Martiri dell'Indipendenza 70, Marcheno (BS), 25060, ITALY, P: 011 390308960220, F: 011 390308610155, www.faustistefanoarms.com
Firearms

Federal Premium Ammunition/ATK Commercial Products, 900 Ehlen Dr., Anoka, MN 55303, P: 800-322-2342, F: 763-323-2506, www.federalpremium.com
Ammunition

Fenix Flashlights, LLC/4Sevens, LLC, 4896 N. Royal Atlanta Dr., Suite 305, Tucker, GA 30084, P: 866-471-0749, F: 866-323-9544, www.4sevens.com
Backpacking; Camping; Law Enforcement; Lighting Products

FenixLightUS/Casualhome Worldwide, Inc., 29 William St., Amityville, NY 11701, P: 877-FENIXUS, F: 631-789-2970, www.fenixlightus.com
Camping; Law Enforcement; Lighting Products; Scopes, Sights & Accessories; Shooting Range Equipment; Wholesaler/Distributor

Fiocchi of America, Inc., 6930 N. Fremont Rd., Ozark, MO 65721, P: 800-721-

MANUFACTURER'S DIRECTORY

AMMO, 417-725-1039, www.fiocciusa.
com
Ammunition; Reloading

First Choice Armor & Equipment, Inc., 209
Yelton St., Spindale, NC 28160, P: 800-
88-ARMOR, F: 866-481-4929, www.
firstchoicearmor.com
*Law Enforcement; Training & Safety
Equipment*

First-Light USA, LLC, 320 Cty. Rd. 1100
North, Seymour, IL 61875, P: 877-454-
4450, F: 877-454-4420, www.first-light-
usa.com
*Backpacking; Camping; Firearms; Law
Enforcement; Lighting Products; Survival
Kits/First Aid; Training & Safety Equipment*

Fleming & Clark, Ltd., 3013 Honeysuckle
Dr., Spring Hill, TN 37174, P: 800-
373-6710, F: 931-487-9972, www.
flemingandclark.com
*Bags & Equipment Cases; Footwear; Gun
Cases; Hunting Accessories; Knives/Knife
Cases; Leathergoods; Men's Clothing;
Wholesaler/Distributor*

Flitz International, Ltd., 821 Mohr Ave.,
Waterford, WI 53185, P: 800-558-8611,
F: 262-534-2991, www.flitz.com
*Black Powder Accessories; Firearms
Maintenance Equipment; Gun Barrels; Gun
Grips & Stocks; Gun Parts/Gunsmithing;
Knives/Knife Cases; Lubricants; Scopes,
Sights & Accessories*

Fobus Holsters/CAA-Command Arms
Accessories, 780 Haunted Lane,
Bensalem, PA 19020, P: 267-803-1517,
F: 267-803-1002, www.fobusholsters.
com, www.commandarms.com
*Bags & Equipment Cases; Firearms; Gun
Cases; Gun Grips & Stocks; Gun Parts/
Gunsmithing; Holsters; Law Enforcement;
Scopes, Sights & Accessories*

Force One, LLC, 520 Commercial Dr.,
Fairfield, OH 45014, P: 800-462-7880, F:
513-939-1166, www.forceonearmor.com
Custom Manufacturing; Law Enforcement

Forster Products, Inc., 310 E. Lanark Ave.,
Lanark, IL 61046, P: 815-493-6360, F:
815-493-2371, www.forsterproducts.com
*Black Powder Accessories; Custom
Manufacturing; Firearms Maintenance
Equipment; Gun Parts/Gunsmithing;
Lubricants; Reloading; Scopes, Sights &
Accessories*

Fort Knox Security Products, 993 N.
Industrial Park Rd., Orem, UT 84057, P:
800-821-5216, F: 801-226-5493, www.
ftknox.com
*Custom Manufacturing; Gun Cabinets/
Racks/Safes; Home Furnishings; Hunting
Accessories*

Foshan City Nanhai Weihong Mold Products
Co., Ltd./Xinwei Photo Electricity
Industrial Co., Ltd., Da Wo District,
Dan Zhao Town, Nanhai, Foshan City,
GuangZhou, 528216, CHINA, P: 011
8675785444666, F: 011 8675785444111,
www.weihongmj.net
Binoculars; Scopes, Sights & Accessories

Fox Knives Oreste Frati SNC, Via La
Mola, 4, Maniago, Pordenone 33085,
ITALY, P: 011 39042771814, F: 011
390427700514, www.foxcutlery.com

*Camouflage; Camping; Cutlery; Hunting
Accessories; Knives/Knife Cases; Law
Enforcement; Wholesaler/Distributor*

Fox Outdoor Products, 2040 N. 15th Ave.,
Melrose Park, IL 60160, P: 800-523-
4332, F: 708-338-9210, www.foxoutdoor.
com
*Bags & Equipment Cases; Camouflage;
Eyewear; Gun Cases; Holsters; Law
Enforcement; Men's Clothing; Wholesaler/
Distributor*

FoxFury Personal Lighting Solutions, 2091
Elevado Hill Dr., Vista, CA 92084, P:
760-945-4231, F: 760-758-6283, www.
foxfury.com
*Backpacking; Camping; Hunting
Accessories; Law Enforcement; Lighting
Products; Paintball Accessories; Sports
Accessories; Training & Safety Equipment*

Franchi, 17603 Indian Head Hwy.,
Accokeek, MD 20607, P: 800-264-4962,
www.franchiusa.com
Firearms

Franklin Sports, Inc./Uniforce Tactical
Division, 17 Campanelli Pkwy.,
Stoughton, MA 02072, P: 800-225-8647,
F: 781-341-3220, www.uniforcetactical.
com
*Camouflage; Eyewear; Gloves, Mitts, Hats;
Law Enforcement; Leathergoods; Men's
Clothing; Wholesaler/Distributor*

Franzen Security Products, Inc., 680 Flinn
Ave., Suite 35, Moorpark, CA 93021, P:
800-922-7656, F: 805-529-0446, www.
securecase.com
*Bags & Equipment Cases; Custom
Manufacturing; Gun Cases; Gun Locks;
Hunting Accessories; Law Enforcement;
Shooting Range Equipment; Training &
Safety Equipment*

Fraternal Blue Line, P.O. Box 260199,
Boston, MA 02126, P: 617-212-1288, F:
617-249-0857, www.fraternalblueline.org
*Custom Manufacturing; Emblems &
Decals; Law Enforcement; Men & Women's
Clothing; Wholesaler/Distributor*

Freedom Arms, Inc., 314 Hwy. 239,
Freedom, WY 83120, P: 800-833-4432,
F: 800-252-4867, www.freedomarms.
com
*Firearms; Gun Cases; Holsters; Scopes,
Sights & Accessories*

Freelinc, 266 W. Center St., Orem, UT
84057, P: 866-467-1199, F: 801-672-
3003, www.freelinc.com
Law Enforcement

Front Line/Army Equipment, Ltd., 6 Platin
St., Rishon-Le-Zion, 75653, ISRAEL, P:
011 97239519460, F: 011 97239519463,
www.front-line.co.il
*Bags & Equipment Cases; Gun Cases;
Holsters*

Frost Cutlery Co., 6861 Mountain View Rd.,
Ooltewah, TN 37363, P: 800-251-7768,
F: 423-894-9576, www.frostcutlery.com
*Camping; Cooking Equipment/
Accessories; Cutlery; Hunting Accessories;
Knives/Knife Cases; Retail Packaging;
Sharpeners; Wholesaler/Distributor*

Fujinon, Inc., 10 High Point Dr., Wayne, NJ
07470, P: 973-633-5600, F: 973-694-
8299, www.fujinon.jp.com
Binoculars; Scopes, Sights & Accessories

Fusion Tactical, 4200 Chino Hills Pkwy.,
Suite 820-143, Chino Hills, CA 91709, P:
909-393-9450, F: 909-606-6834
*Custom Manufacturing; Retail Packaging;
Sports Accessories; Training & Safety
Equipment*

G

G24 Innovations, Ltd., Solar Power,
Westloog Environmental Centre, Cardiff,
CF3 2EE, UNITED KINGDON, 011
442920837340, F: 011 443930837341,
www.g24i.com
*Bags & Equipment Cases; Camping;
Custom Manufacturing; Lighting Products*

G96 Products Co., Inc., 85-5th Ave., Bldg.
6, P.O. Box 1684, Paterson, NJ 07544, P:
877-332-0035, F: 973-684-3848, www.
g96.com
*Black Powder Accessories; Firearms
Maintenance Equipment; Lubricants*

GG&G, 3602 E. 42nd Stravenue, Tucson,
AZ 85713, P: 800-380-2540, F: 520-748-
7583, www.gggaz.com
*Custom Manufacturing; Firearms; Gun
Barrels; Gun Grips & Stocks, Gun Parts/
Gunsmithing; Law Enforcement; Lighting
Products; Scopes, Sights & Accessories*

G.A. Precision, 1141 Swift St., N. Kansas
City, MO 64116, P: 816-221-1844, F:
816-421-4958, www.gaprecision.net
Firearms

GT Industrial Products, 10650 Irma Dr.,
Suite 1, Northglenn, CO 80233, P: 303-
280-5777, F: 303-280-5778, www.gt-ind.
com
*Camping; Hunting Accessories; Lighting
Products; Survival Kits/First Aid*

Galati Gear/Galati International, 616
Burley Ridge Rd., P.O. Box 10, Wesco,
MO 65586, P: 877-425-2847, F: 573-
775-4308, www.galatigear.com, www.
galatiinternational.com
*Bags & Equipment Cases; Cutlery; Gun
Cases; Holsters; Knives/Knife Cases; Law
Enforcement; Sports Accessories*

Galileo, 13872 SW 119th Ave., Miami, FL
33186, P: 800-548-3537, F: 305-234-
8510, www.galileosplace.com
*Binoculars; Photographic Equipment;
Scopes, Sights & Accessories; Telescopes*

Gamebore Cartridge Co., Ltd., Great
Union St., Hull, HU9 1AR, UNITED
KINGDOM, P: 011 441482223707, F: 011
4414823252225, www.gamebore.com
Ammunition; Cartridges

Gamehide–Core Resources, 12257C
Nicollet Ave. S, Burnsville, MN 55337, P:
888-267-3591, F: 952-895-8845, www.
gamehide.com
*Archery; Camouflage; Custom
Manufacturing; Export/Import Specialists;
Gloves, Mitts, Hats; Hunting Accessories;
Men & Women's Clothing*

Gamo USA Corp., 3911 SW 47th Ave.,
Suite 914, Fort Lauderdale, FL 33314, P:
954-581-5822, F: 954-581-3165, www.
gamousa.com
*Airguns; Ammunition; Hunting Accessories;
Online Services; Scopes, Sights &
Accessories; Targets*

Geissele Automatics, LLC, 1920 W. Marshall St., Norristown, PA 19403, P: 610-272-2060, F: 610-272-2069, www.ar15trigger.com
Firearms; Gun Parts/Gunsmithing

Gemstar Manufacturing, 1515 N. 5th St., Cannon Falls, MN 55009, P: 800-533-3631, F: 507-263-3129
Bags & Equipment Cases; Crossbows & Accessories; Custom Manufacturing; Gun Cases; Law Enforcement; Paintball Accessories; Sports Accessories; Survival Kits/First Aid

Gemtech, P.O. Box 140618, Boise, ID 83714, P: 208-939-7222, www.gem-tech.com
Firearms; Hearing Protection; Law Enforcement; Training & Safety Equipment; Wildlife Management

General Inspection, LLC, 10585 Enterprise Dr., Davisburg, MI 48350, P: 888-817-6314, F: 248-625-0789, www.geninsp.com
Ammunition; Custom Manufacturing

General Starlight Co., 250 Harding Blvd. W, P.O. Box 32154, Richmond Hill, Ontario L4C 9S3, CANADA, P: 905-850-0990, www.electrooptic.com
Binoculars; Law Enforcement; Photographic Equipment; Scopes, Sights & Accessories; Telescopes; Training & Safety Equipment; Wholesaler/Distributor

Gerber Legendary Blades, 14200 SW 72nd Ave., Portland, OR 97224, P: 800-443-4871, F: 307-857-4702, www.gerbergear.com
Knives/Knife Cases; Law Enforcement; Lighting Products

Gerstner & Sons, Inc., 20 Gerstner Way, Dayton, OH 45402, P: 937-228-1662, F: 937-228-8557, www.gerstnerusa.com
Bags & Equipment Cases; Custom Manufacturing; Gun Cabinets/Racks/Safes; Gun Cases; Home Furnishings; Knives/Knife Cases; Shooting Range Equipment

GH Armor Systems, 1 Sentry Dr., Dover, TN 37058, P: 866-920-5940, F: 866-920-5941, www.gharmorsystems.com
Custom Manufacturing; Law Enforcement; Men & Women's Clothing

Girsan–Yavuz 16, Batlama Deresi Mevkii Sunta Sok. No 19, Giresun, 28200, TURKEY, P: 011 905332160201, F: 011 904542153928, www.yavuz16.com
Firearms; Gun Parts/Gunsmithing

Glendo Corp./GRS Tools, 900 Overlander Rd., P.O. Box 1153, Emporia, KS 66801, P: 800-835-3519, F: 620-343-9640, www.glendo.com
Books/Industry Publications; Custom Manufacturing; Lighting Products; Scopes, Sights & Accessories; Videos; Wholesaler/Distributor

Glock, Inc., 6000 Highlands Pkwy., Smyrna, GA 30082, P: 770-432-1202, F: 770-433-8719, www.glock.com, www.teamglock.com, www.gssfonline.com
Firearms; Gun Parts/Gunsmithing; Holsters; Knives/Knife Cases; Law Enforcement; Men & Women's Clothing; Retailer Services

Goex, Inc., P.O. Box 659, Doyline, LA 71023, P: 318-382-9300, F: 318-382-9303, www.goexpowder.com
Ammunition; Black Powder/Smokeless Powder

Gold House Hardware (China), Ltd., Rm 12/H, 445 Tian He Bei Rd., Guangzhou, 510620, CHINA, P: 011 862038801911, F: 011 862038808485, www.ghhtools.com
Camping; Cutlery; Gun Cases; Hunting Accessories; Knives/Knife Cases; Scopes, Sights & Accessories; Targets

Golight, Inc., 37146 Old Hwy. 17, Culbertson, NE 69024, P: 800-557-0098, F: 308-278-2525, www.golight.com
Camping; Hunting Accessories; Law Enforcement; Lighting Products; Vehicles, Utility & Rec

Gore & Associates, Inc., W.L., 295 Blue Ball Rd., Elkton, MD 21921, P: 800-431-GORE, F: 410-392-9057, www.gore-tex.com
Footwear; Gloves, Mitts, Hats; Law Enforcement; Men & Women's Clothing

Gould & Goodrich, Inc., 709 E. McNeil St., Lillington, NC, 27546, P: 800-277-0732, FL 910-893-4742, www.gouldusa.com
Holsters; Law Enforcement; Leathergoods

Gradient Lens Corp., 207 Tremont St., Rochester, NY 14608, P: 800-536-0790, F: 585-235-6645, www.gradientlens.com
Firearms Maintenance Equipment; Gun Barrels; Gun Parts/Gunsmithing; Scopes, Sights & Accessories; Shooting Range Equipment

Granite Security Products, Inc., 4801 Esco Dr., Fort Worth, TX 76140, P: 817-561-9095, F: 817-478-3056, www.winchestersafes.com
Gun Cabinets/Racks/Safes

Gransfors Bruks, Inc., P.O. Box 818, Summerville, SC 29484. P: 843-875-0240, F: 843-821-2285
Custom Manufacturing; Law Enforcement; Men's Clothing; Wholesaler/Distributor

Grauer Systems, 38 Forster Ave., Mount Vernon, NY 10552, P: 415-902-4721, www.grauerbarrel.com
Firearms; Gun Barrels; Gun Grips & Stocks; Law Enforcement; Lighting Products; Scopes, Sights & Accessories

Green Supply, Inc., 3059 Audrain Rd., Suite 581, Vandalia, MO 63382, P: 800-424-4867, F: 573-594-2211, www.greensupply.com
Ammunition; Camping; Computer Software; Firearms; Hunting Accessories; Online Services; Retailer Services; Scopes, Sights & Accessories; Wholesaler/Distributor

Grizzly Industrial, 1821 Valencia St., Bellingham, WA 98229, P: 800-523-4777, F: 800-438-5901, www.grizzly.com
Firearms Maintenance Equipment; Gun Cabinets/Racks/Safes; Gun Parts/Gunsmithing

Grohmann Knives, Ltd., 116 Water St., P.O. Box 40, Pictou, Nova Scotia B0K 1H0, CANADA, P: 888-7-KNIVES, F: 902-485-5872, www.grohmannknives.com
Backpacking; Camping; Cooking Equipment/Accessories; Custom Manufacturing; Cutlery; Hunting Accessories; Knives/Knife Cases; Sharpeners

GrovTec US, Inc., 16071 SE 98t Ave., Clackamas, OR, 97015, P: 503-557-4689, F: 503-557-4936, www.grovtec.com
Custom Manufacturing; Firearms Maintenance Equipment; Gun Parts/Gunsmithing; Holsters

Gun Grabber Products, Inc., 3417 E. 54th St., Texarkana, AR 71854, P: 877-486-4722, F: 870-774-2111, www.gungrab.com
Gun Cabinets/Racks/Safes; Hunting Accessories

Gun Video, 4585 Murphy Canyon Rd., San Diego, CA 92123, P: 800-942-8273, F: 858-569-0505, www.gunvideo.com
Books/Industry Publications; Gun Parts/Gunsmithing; Law Enforcement; Training & Safety Equipment; Videos

GunBroker.com, P.O. Box 2511, Kennesaw, GA 30156, P: 720-223-2083, F: 720-223-0164, www.gunbroker.com
Airguns; Computer Software; Firearms; Gun Parts/Gunsmithing; Hunting Accessories; Online Services; Reloading; Retailer Services

GunMate Products/Bushnell Outdoor Accessories, 9200 Cody, Overland Park, KS 66214, P: 800-423-3537, F: 800-548-0446, www.unclemikes.com
Gun Cases; Holsters; Hunting Accessories; Leathergoods

Gunslick Gun Care/ATK Commercial Products, N5549 Cty. Trunk Z, Onalaska, WI 54650, P: 800-635-7656, F: 763-323-3890, www.gunslick.com
Firearms Maintenance Equipment; Lubricants

GunVault, Inc., 216 S. 2nd Ave., Bldg. 932, San Bernardino, CA 92408, P: 800-222-1055, F: 909-382-2042, www.gunvault.com
Gun Cabinets/Racks/Safes; Gun Cases; Gun Locks

H

HKS Products, Inc., 7841 Foundation Dr., Florence, KY 41042, P: 800-354-9814, F: 859-342-5865, www.hksspeedloaders.com
Hunting Accessories; Law Enforcement

H & M Metal Processing, 1850 Front St., Cuyanoga Falls, OH 44221, P: 330-928-9021, F: 330-928-5472, www.handmmetal.com
Airguns; Archery; Black Powder Accessories; Custom Manufacturing; Firearms Maintenance Equipment; Gun Barrels; Gun Parts/Gunsmithing

H-S Precision, Inc., 1301 Turbine Dr., Rapid City, SD 57703, P: 605-341-3006, F: 605-342-8964, www.hsprecision.com
Firearms; Gun Barrels; Gun Grips & Stocks; Law Enforcement; Magazines, Cartridge; Shooting Range Equipment

Haix®-Schuhe Produktions-u. Vertriebs GmbH, Aufhofstrasse 10, Mainburg, Bavaria 84048, GERMANY, P: 011

MANUFACTURER'S DIRECTORY

49875186250, F: 011 498751862525,
www.haix.com
Footwear; Law Enforcement; Leathergoods

Haix North America, Inc., 157 Venture Ct.,
Suite 11, Lexington, KY 40511, P: 866-
344-4249, F: 859-281-0113, www.haix.
com
Footwear; Law Enforcement; Leathergoods

Hammerhead Ind./Gear Keeper, 1501
Goodyear Ave., Ventura, CA 93003, P:
888-588-9981, F: 805-658-8833, www.
gearkeeper.com
*Backpacking; Camping; Compasses;
Game Calls; Hunting Accessories; Law
Enforcement; Lighting Products; Sports
Accessories*

Harris Engineering, Inc., 999 Broadway,
Barlow, KY 42024, P: 270-334-3633, F:
270-334-3000
*Hunting Accessories; Shooting Range
Equipment; Sports Accessories*

Harris Publications, Inc./Harris Tactical
Group, 1115 Broadway, 8th Floor, New
York, NY 10010, P: 212-807-7100, F:
212-807-1479, www.tactical-life.com
*Airguns; Books/Industry Publications;
Cutlery; Firearms; Knives/Knife Cases;
Law Enforcement; Paintball Guns; Retailer
Services*

Hastings, 717 4th St., P.O. Box 135,
Clay Center, KS 67432, P: 785-
632-3169, F: 785-632-6554, www.
hastingsammunition.com
Ammunition; Firearms; Gun Barrels

Hatsan Arms Co., Izmir-Ankara Karayolu
26. Km. No. 289, OSB Kemalpasa, Izmir,
35170, TURKEY, P: 011 902328789100,
F: 011 902328789723, www.hatsan.com.
tr
*Airguns; Firearms; Scopes, Sights &
Accessories*

Havaser Turizm, Ltd., Nargileci Sokak No.
4, Mercan, Eminonu, 34450, TURKEY, P:
011 90212135452, F: 011 902125128079
Firearms

Hawke Sport Optics, 6015 Highview Dr.,
Suite G, Fort Wayne, IN 46818, P: 877-
429-5347, F: 260-918-3443, www.
hawkeoptics.com
*Airguns; Binoculars; Computer Software;
Crossbows & Accessories; Scopes, Sights
& Accessories*

Health Enterprises, 90 George Leven Dr., N.
Attleboro, MA 02760, P: 800-633-4243, F:
508-695-3061, www.healthenterprises.com
Hearing Protection

Heckler & Koch, Inc., 5675 Transport Blvd.,
Columbus, GA 31907, P: 706-568-1906,
F: 706-568-9151, www.hk-usa.com
Firearms

Hendon Publishing Co./Law and Order/
Tactical Response Magazines, 130
Waukegan Rd., Suite 202, Deerfield, IL
60015, P: 800-843-9764, F: 847-444-
3333, www.hendonpub.com
*Books/Industry Publications; Law
Enforcement*

Heritage Manufacturing, Inc., 4600 NW
135th St., Opa Locka, FL 33054, P:
305-685-5966, F: 305-687-6721, www.
heritagemfg.com
Firearms

Heros Pride, P.O. Box 10033, Van Nuys, CA
91410, P: 888-492-9122, F: 888-492-
9133, www.herospride.com
*Custom Manufacturing; Emblems &
Decals; Law Enforcement; Men & Women's
Clothing; Wholesaler/Distributor*

Hi-Point Firearms/MKS Supply, Inc., 8611-
A N. Dixie Dr., Dayton, OH 45414, P:
877-425-4867, F: 937-454-0503, www.
hi-pointfirearms.com
*Firearms; Holsters; Law Enforcement;
Magazines, Cartridge*

Hiatt Thompson Corp., 7200 W. 66th
St., Bedford Park, IL 60638, P: 708-
496-8585, F: 708-496-8618, www.
handcuffsusa.com
Law Enforcement

High Standard Mfg., Co./F.I., Inc. ATM–
AutoMag, 5200 Mitchelldale, Suite E17,
Houston, TX 77092, P: 800-272-7816, F:
713-681-5665, www.highstandard.com
*Firearms; Gun Barrels; Gun Grips & Stocks;
Gun Parts/Gunsmithing; Lubricants;
Magazines, Cartridge*

Highgear/Highgear USA, Inc., 145 Cane
Creek Industrial Park Rd., Suite 200,
Fletcher, NC 28732, P: 888-295-4949, F:
828-681-5320, www.highgear.com
*Camping; Compasses; Hunting
Accessories; Lighting Products; Sports
Accessories; Survival Kits/First Aid*

HitchSafe Key Vault, 18424 Hwy. 99,
Lynnwood, WA 98037, P: 800-654-1786,
F: 206-523-9876, www.hitchsafe.com
*Gun Cabinets/Racks/Safes; Gun Locks;
Hunting Accessories; Outfitter; Sports
Accessories; Vehicles, Utility & Rec*

HiViz Shooting Systems/North Pass, Ltd.,
1941 Heath Pkwy., Suite 1, Fort Collins,
CO 80524, P: 800-589-4315, F: 970-416-
1208, www.hivizsights.com
*Black Powder Accessories; Gun Parts/
Gunsmithing; Hunting Accessories;
Paintball Accessories; Recoil Protection
Devices & Services; Scopes, Sights &
Accessories; Sports Accessories*

Hogue, Inc., 550 Linne Rd., Paso Robles,
CA 93447, P: 805-239-1440, F: 805-239-
2553, www.hogueinc.com
Gun Grips & Stocks; Holsters

Homak Manufacturing Co., Inc., 1605 Old
Rt. 18, Suite 4-36, Wampum, PA 16157,
P: 800-874-6625, F: 724-535-1081,
www.homak.com
*Custom Manufacturing; Gun Cabinets/
Racks/Safes; Gun Cases; Gun Locks;
Hunting Accessories; Reloading; Retail
Packaging*

HongKong Meike Digital Technology
Co., Ltd., No. 12 Jiaye Rd. Pinghu St.,
Longgang District, Shenzhen, GNGD
518111, CHINA, P: 011 8613424151607,
F: 011 8675528494339, www.mkgrip.
com
Scopes, Sights & Accessories

Hope Global, 50 Martin St., Cumberland,
RI 02864, P: 401-333-8990, F: 401-334-
6442, www.hopeglobal.com
*Custom Manufacturing; Footwear; Hunting
Accessories; Law Enforcement; Pet
Supplies; Scopes, Sights & Accessories;
Shooting Range Equipment; Sports
Accessories*

Hoppe's/Bushnell Outdoor Accessories,
9200 Cody, Overland Park, KS 66214, P:
800-221-9035, F: 800-548-0446, www.
hoppes.com
*Black Powder Accessories; Firearms
Maintenance Equipment; Hearing
Protection; Law Enforcement; Lubricants;
Shooting Range Equipment*

Horizon Manufacturing Ent., Inc./RackEm
Racks, P.O. Box 7174, Buffalo Grove, IL
60089, P: 877-722-5369 (877-RACKEM-
9), F: 866-782-1550, www.rackems.com
*Airguns; Custom Manufacturing; Firearms;
Firearms Maintenance Equipment;
Footwear; Gloves, Mitts, Hats; Gun
Cabinets/Racks/Safes; Holsters; Hunting
Accessories; Law Enforcement; Shooting
Range Equipment*

Hornady Manufacturing Co., 3625 Old
Potash Hwy., P.O. Box 1848, Grand
Island, NE 68803, P: 308-382-1390, F:
308-382-5761, www.hornady.com
*Ammunition; Black Powder Accessories;
Lubricants; Reloading*

Horus Vision, LLC, 659 Huntington Ave.,
San Bruno, CA 94066, P: 650-588-8862,
F: 650-588-6264, www.horusvision.com
*Computer Software; Law Enforcement;
Scopes, Sights & Accessories; Targets;
Watches*

Howard Leight by Sperian, 900 Douglas
Pike, Smithfield, RI 02917, P: 866-
786-2353, F: 401-233-7641, www.
howardleightshootingsports.com, www.
sperianprotection.com
*Eyewear; Hearing Protection; Hunting
Accessories; Sports Accessories; Training
& Safety Equipment*

Huanic Corp., No. 67 Jinye Rd., Hi-
tech Zone, Xi'an, SHNX 710077,
CHINA, P: 011 862981881001, F: 011
862981881011, www.huanic.com
*Hunting Accessories; Scopes, Sights &
Accessories; Shooting Range Equipment;
Targets*

Hunter Co., Inc./Hunter Wicked Optics,
3300 W. 71st Ave., Westminster, CO
80030, P: 800-676-4868, F: 303-428-
3980, www.huntercompany.com
*Binoculars; Custom Manufacturing; Gun
Cases; Holsters; Hunting Accessories;
Knives/Knife Cases; Leathergoods;
Scopes, Sights & Accessories*

Hunterbid.com/Chiron, Inc., 38 Crosby Rd.,
Dover, NH 03820, P: 603-433-8908, F:
603-431-4072, www.hunterbid.com
*Gun Grips & Stocks; Gun Parts/
Gunsmithing*

HyperBeam, 1504 Sheepshead Bay Rd.,
Suite 300, Brooklyn, NY 11236, P:
888-272-4620, F: 718-272-1797, www.
nightdetective.com
*Binoculars; Hunting Accessories;
Law Enforcement; Lighting Products;
Photographic Equipment; Scopes, Sights &
Accessories; Shooting Range Equipment;
Telescopes*

Hyskore/Power Aisle, Inc., 193 West Hills
Rd., Huntington Station, NY 11746, P:
631-673-5975, F: 631-673-5976, www.
hyskore.com
*Custom Manufacturing; Export/
Import Specialists; Eyewear; Firearms*

Maintenance Equipment; Gun Cabinets/ Racks/Safes; Hearing Protection; Shooting Range Equipment

I

IHC, Inc., 12400 Burt Rd., Detroit, MI 48228, P: 800-661-4642, F: 313-535-3220, www.ihccorp.com
Archery; Backpacking; Camping; Crossbows & Accessories; Firearms; Lighting Products; Magazines, Cartridge; Scopes, Sights & Accessories

i-SHOT/S.E.R.T. System, 16135 Kennedy St., Woodbridge, VA 22191, P: 703-670-8001, F: 703-940-9148, www.ishot-inc.com
Bags & Equipment Cases; Custom Manufacturing; Firearms; Law Enforcement; Training & Safety Equipment; Wholesaler/Distributor

Icebreaker, Inc., P.O. Box 236, Clarkesville, GA 30523, P: 800-343-BOOT, F: 706-754-0423, www.icebreakerinc.com
Camouflage; Footwear; Gloves, Mitts, Hats; Hunting Accessories

Import Merchandiser's Inc./MasterVision Cap Lights, N-11254 Industrial Lane, P.O. Box 337, Elcho, WI 54428, P: 715-275-5132, F: 715-275-5176, www.mastervisionlight.com
Camping; Custom Manufacturing; Gloves, Mitts, Hats; Hunting Accessories; Lighting Products; Sports Accessories

Indo-US Mim Tec. Pvt., Ltd., 315 Eisenhower Pkwy., Suite 211, Ann Arbor, MI 48108, P: 734-327-9842, F: 734-327-9873, www.mimindia.com
Airguns; Archery; Crossbows & Accessories; Gun Locks; Gun Parts/ Gunsmithing; Knives/Knife Cases; Paintball Guns; Scopes, Sights & Accessories

Industrial Revolution/Light My Fire USA, 9225 151st Ave. NE, Redmond, WA 98052, P: 888-297-6062, F: 425-883-0036, www.industrialrev.com
Camping; Cooking Equipment/ Accessories; Cutlery; Knives/Knife Cases; Lighting Products; Photographic Equipment; Survival Kits/First Aid; Wholesaler/Distributor

Indusys Techologies Belgium SPRL (UFA–Belgium), 22 Pas Bayard, Tavier, Liege B-4163, BELGIUM, P: 011 3243835234, F: 011 3243835189, www.indusys.be
Ammunition; Reloading; Shooting Range Equipment; Training & Safety Equipment

INOVA/Emissive Energy Corp., 135 Circuit Dr., North Kingstown, RI 02852, P: 401-294-2030, F: 401-294-2050, www.inovalight.com
Backpacking; Camping; Hunting Accessories; Law Enforcement; Lighting Products; Sports Accessories; Survival Kits/First Aid; Training & Safety Equipment

Insight Tech-Gear, 23 Industrial Dr., Londonderry, NH 03053, P: 877-744-4802, F: 603-668-1084, www.insighttechgear.com
Hunting Accessories; Law Enforcement; Lighting Products; Paintball Accessories; Scopes, Sights & Accessories; Training & Safety Equipment

Instant Armor, Inc., 350 E. Easy St., Suite 1, Simi Valley, CA 93065, P: 805-526-3046, F: 805-526-9213, www.instantarmor.com
Law Enforcement

Instrument Technology, Inc., P.O. Box 381, Westfield, MA 10186, P: 413-562-3606, F: 413-568-9809, www.scopes.com
Law Enforcement

International Cartridge Corp., 2273 Route 310, Reynoldsville, PA 15851, P: 877-422-5332, F: 814-938-6821, www.iccammo.com
Ammunition; Law Enforcement; Reloading; Shooting Range Equipment; Training & Safety Equipment

International Supplies/Seahorse Protective Cases, 945 W. Hyde Park, Inglewood, CA 90302, P: 800-999-1984, F: 310-673-5988, www.internationalsupplies.com
Bags & Equipment Cases; Export/Import Specialists; Eyewear; Gun Cases; Lighting Products; Photographic Equipment; Retailer Services; Wholesaler/Distributor

Interstate Arms Corp., 6 Dunham Rd., Billerica, MA 01821, P: 800-243-3006, F: 978-671-0023, www.interstatearms.com
Firearms

Iosso Products, 1485 Lively Blvd., Elk Grove, IL 60007, P: 888-747-4332, F: 847-437-8478, www.iosso.com
Black Powder Accessories; Crossbows & Accessories; Firearms Maintenance Equipment; Gun Parts/Gunsmithing; Hunting Accessories; Law Enforcement; Lubricants; Reloading

Ithaca Gun Co., LLC, 420 N. Warpole St., Upper Sandusky, OH 43351, P: 877-648-4222, F: 419-294-3230, www.ithacagun.com
Firearms

ITT, 7635 Plantation Rd., Roanoke, VA 24019, P: 800-448-8678, F: 540-366-9015, www.nightvision.com
Binoculars; Scopes, Sights & Accessories

ITW Military Products, 195 E. Algonquin Rd., Des Plaines, IL 60016, P: 203-240-7110, F: 847-390-8727, www.itwmilitaryproducts.com
Backpacking; Bags & Equipment Cases; Camouflage; Cooking Equipment/ Accessories; Custom Manufacturing; Law Enforcement

Iver Johnson Arms Inc./Manufacturing Research, 1840 Baldwin St., Suite 10, Rockledge, FL 32955, P: 321-636-3377, F: 321-632-7745, www.iverjohnsonarms.com
Firearms; Gun Parts/Gunsmithing; Training & Safety Equipment

J

JBP Holsters/Masters Holsters, 10100 Old Bon Air Pl., Richmond, VA 23235, P: 804-320-5653, F: 804-320-5653, www.jbpholsters.com
Gun Cases; Holsters; Hunting Accessories; Law Enforcement; Leathergoods; Sports Accessories; Training & Safety Equipment; Wholesaler/Distributor

JGS Precision Tool Mfg., LLC, 60819 Selander Rd., Coos Bay, OR 97420, P:

541-267-4331, F: 541-267-5996, www.jgstools.com
Firearms Maintenance Equipment; Gun Parts/Gunsmithing

J & J Armory/Dragon Skin/Pinnacle Armor, 1344 E. Edinger Ave., Santa Ana, CA 92705, P: 866-9-ARMORY, F: 714-558-4817, www.jandjarmory.com
Firearms; Law Enforcement; Training & Safety Equipment

J & K Outdoor Products, Inc., 3864 Cty. Rd. Q, Wisconsin Rapids, WI 54495, P: 715-424-5757, F: 715-424-5757, www.jkoutdoorproducts.com
Archery; Hunting Accessories; Law Enforcement; Paintball Accessories; Scopes, Sights & Accessories

J-Tech (Steady Flying Enterprise Co., Ltd.), 1F, No. 235 Ta You Rd., Sung Shang, Taipei, 105, TAIWAN, P: 011 886227663986, F: 011 886287874836, www.tacticaljtech.com
Backpacking; Custom Manufacturing; Gloves, Mitts, Hats; Gun Cases; Holsters; Law Enforcement; Lighting Products; Wholesaler/Distributor

Jack Link's Beef Jerky, One Snackfood Ln., P.O. Box 397, Minong, WI 54859, P: 800-346-6896, F: 715-466-5986, www.linksnacks.com
Custom Manufacturing

Jackson Rifles X-Treme Shooting Products, LLC, Glenswinton, Parton, Castle Douglas, SCOTLAND DG7 3NL, P: 011 441644470223, F: 011 441644470227, www.jacksonrifles.com
Firearms; Gun Barrels; Gun Parts/ Gunsmithing; Wholesaler/Distributor

Jacob Ash Holdings, Inc., 301 Munson Ave., McKees Rocks, PA 15136, P: 800-245-6111, F: 412-331-6347, www.jacobash.com
Camouflage; Gloves, Mitts, Hats; Hunting Accessories; Law Enforcement; Leathergoods; Men & Women's Clothing; Sports Accessories

James River Manufacturing, Inc./James River Armory, 3601 Commerce Dr., Suite 110, Baltimore, MD 21227, P: 410-242-6991, F: 410-242-6995, www.jamesriverarmory.com
Firearms

Japan Optics, Ltd., 2-11-29, Ukima, Kita-ku, Tokyo, 115-0051, JAPAN, P: 011 81359146680, F: 011 81353722232
Scopes, Sights & Accessories

Jeff's Outfitters, 599 Cty. Rd. 206, Cape Girardeau, MO 63701, P: 573-651-3200, F: 573-651-3207, www.jeffsoutfitters.com
Bags & Equipment Cases; Custom Manufacturing; Gun Cases; Hunting Accessories; Knives/Knife Cases; Leathergoods; Scopes, Sights & Accessories

John's Guns/A Dark Horse Arms Co., 1041 FM 1274, Coleman, TX 76834.P: 325-382-4885, F: 325-382-4887, www.darkhorsearms.com
Custom Manufacturing; Firearms; Hearing Protection; Law Enforcement

Jonathan Arthur Ciener, Inc., 8700 Commerce St., Cap Canaveral, FL

MANUFACTURER'S DIRECTORY

32920, P: 321-868-2200, F: 321-868-2201, www.22lrconversions.com
Firearms; Gun Barrels; Gun Parts/ Gunsmithing; Hunting Accessories; Magazines, Cartridge; Recoil Protection Devices & Services; Shooting Range Equipment; Training & Safety Equipment

Joy Enterprises, 1862 Dr., ML King Jr. Blvd., Port Commerce Center III, Riviera Beach, FL 33404, P: 800-500-FURY, F: 561-863-3277, www.joyenterprises.com
Binoculars; Camping; Compasses; Cutlery; Knives/Knife Cases; Law Enforcement; Sharpeners; Sports Accessories

JP Enterprises, Inc., P.O. Box 378, Hugo, NN 55038, P: 651-426-9196, F: 651-426-2472, www.jprifles.com
Firearms; Gun Parts/Gunsmithing; Recoil Protection Devices & Services; Scopes, Sights & Accessories

JS Products, Inc./Snap-on, 5440 S. Procyon Ave., Las Vegas, NV 89118, P: 702-362-7011, F: 702-362-5084
Lighting Products

K

KA Display Solutions, Inc., P.O. Box 99, 512 Blackman Blvd. W, Wartrace, TN 37183, P: 800-227-9540, F: 931-389-6686, www.kadsi.com
Custom Manufacturing; Gun Cabinets/ Racks/Safes; Gun Cases; Home Furnishings; Knives/Knife Cases; Retailer Services; Scopes, Sights & Accessories

K.B.I., Inc./Charles Daly, P.O. Box 6625, Harrisburg, PA 17112, P: 866-325-9486, F: 717-540-8567, www.charlesdaly.com
Ammunition; Export/Import Specialists; Firearms; Hunting Accessories; Law Enforcement; Scopes, Sights & Accessories

Ka-Bar Knives, Inc., 200 Homer St., Olean, NY 14760, P: 800-282-0130, FL 716-790-7188, www.ka-bar.com
Knives/Knife Cases; Law Enforcement

KDF, Inc., 2485 St. Hwy. 46 N, Seguin, TX 78155, P: 800-KDF-GUNS, F: 830-379-8144
Firearms; Gun Grips & Stocks; Recoil Protection Devices & Services; Scopes, Sights & Accessories

KDH Defense Systems, Inc., 401 Broad St., Johnstown, PA 15906, P: 814-536-7701, F: 814-536-7716, www. kdhdefensesystems.com
Law Enforcement

KNJ Manufacturing, LLC, 757 N. Golden Key, Suite D, Gilbert, AZ 85233, P: 800-424-6606, F: 480-497-8480, www. knjmfg.com
Bags & Equipment Cases; Custom Manufacturing; Gun Cases; Holsters; Hunting Accessories; Law Enforcement; Wholesaler/Distributor

KNS Precision, Inc., 112 Marschall Creek Rd., Fredericksburg, TN 78624, P: 830-997-0000, F: 830-997-1443, www. knsprecisioninc.com
Firearms; Gun Grips & Stocks; Gun Parts/ Gunsmithing; Law Enforcement; Lighting Products; Scopes, Sights & Accessories;

Training & Safety Equipment; Wholesaler/ Distributor

KP Industries, Inc., 3038 Industry St., Suite 108, Oceanside, CA 92054, P: 800-956-3377, F: 760-722-9884, www. kpindustries.com
Export/Import Specialists; Law Enforcement; Outfitter; Paintball Accessories; Shooting Range Equipment; Sports Accessories; Training & Safety Equipment

K-VAR Corp., 3300 S. Decatur Blvd., Suite 10601, Las Vegas, NV 89102, P: 702-364-8880, F: 702-307-2303, www.k-var. com
Firearms Maintenance Equipment; Gun Barrels; Gun Grips & Stocks; Magazines, Cartridge; Scopes, Sights & Accessories

Kahr Arms, 130 Goddard Memorial Dr., Worcester, MA 01603, P: 508-795-3919, FL 508-795-7046, www.kahr.com
Firearms; Holsters; Law Enforcement

Kalispel Case Line/Cortona Shotguns, 418641 SR 20, P.O. Box 267, Cusick, WA 99119, P: 509-445-1121, F: 509-445-1082, www.kalispelcaseline.com
Archery; Bags & Equipment Cases; Export/ Import Specialists; Firearms; Gun Cases; Law Enforcement; Wholesaler/Distributor

Kel-Tec CNC Ind., Inc., 1475 Cox Rd., Cocoa, FL 32926, P: 321-631-0068, F: 321-631-1169, www.kel-tec-cnc.com
Firearms

Kelbly's, Inc., 7222 Dalton Fox Lk. Rd., North Lawrence, OH 44666, P: 330-683-4674, F: 330-682-7349, www.kelbly.com
Firearms; Scopes, Sights & Accessories

Keng's Firearms Specialty, Inc./Versa-Pod/ Champion Gun Sights, 875 Wharton Dr. SW, P.O. Box 44405, Atlanta, GA 30336, P: 800-848-4671, F: 404-505-8445, www.versapod.com
Gun Grips & Stocks; Hunting Accessories; Scopes, Sights & Accessories

Kent Cartridge, 727 Hite Rd., P.O. Box 849, Kearneysville, WV, 25430, P: 888-311-5368, F: 304-725-0454, www. kentgamebore.com
Ammunition

Kenyon Consumer Products/KCP Acquisition, LLC, 141 Fairgrounds Rd., West Kingston, RI 02892, P: 800-537-0024, F: 401-782-4870, www. kenyonconsumer.com
Backpacking; Camping; Law Enforcement; Men & Women's Clothing

Kershaw Knives, 18600 SW Teton Ave., Tualatin, OR 97062, P: 800-325-2891, F: 503-682-7168, www.kershawknives.com
Cutlery; Knives/Knife Cases

KG Industries, LLC, 16790 US Hwy. 63 S, Bldg. 2, Hayward, WI 54843, P: 800-348-9558, F: 715-934-3570, www.kgcoatings. com
Camouflage; Custom Manufacturing; Firearms; Firearms Maintenance Equipment; Gun Barrels; Knives/Knife Cases; Law Enforcement; Lubricants

Kick-EEZ Products, 1819 Schurman Way, Suite 106, Woodland, WA 98674, P: 877-KICKEEZ, F: 360-225-9702, www. kickeezproducts.com

Black Powder Accessories; Clay Targets; Gun Grips & Stocks; Gun Parts/ Gunsmithing; Hunting Accessories; Recoil Protection Devices & Services; Targets

Kiesler Distributor of Lewis Machine & Tool Co., 2802 Sable Mill Rd., Jeffersonville, IN 47130, P: 800-444-2950, F: 812-284-6651, www.kiesler.com
Firearms

Kilgore Flares Co., LLC, 155 Kilgore Dr., Toone, TN 38381, P; 731-228-5371, F: 731-228-4173, www.kilgoreflares.com
Ammunition

Kimber Mfg., Inc./Meprolight, Inc., One Lawton St., Yonkers, NY 10705, P: 888-243-4522, F: 406-758-2223
Firearms; Law Enforcement

Kitasho Co., Ltd./Kanetsune, 5-1-11 Sakae-Machi, Seki-City, Gifu-Pref, 501 3253 JAPAN, P: 11 81575241211, FL 011 81575241210, www.kanetsune.com
Knives/Knife Cases

Knight Rifles/Div. Modern Muzzleloading, 715B Summit Dr., Decatur, AL 52544, P: 800-696-1703, F: 256-260-8951, www. knightrifles.com
Firearms

Knight's Manufacturing Co., 701 Columbia Blvd., Titusville, FL 32780, P: 321-607-9900, F: 321-383-2143, www. knightarmco.com
Firearms; Scopes, Sights & Accessories

Kolpin Outdoors/Bushness Outdoor Accessories, 9200 Cody, Overland Park, KS 66214, P: 800-423-3537, F: 800-548-0446, www.kolpin-outdoors.com
Firearms Maintenance Equipment; Gun Cases; Hunting Accessories

Konus USA Corp., 7530 NW 79th St., Miami, FL 33166, P: 305-884-7618, F: 305-884-7620, www.konususa.com
Binoculars; Compasses; Eyewear; Scopes, Sights & Accessories; Sports Accessories; Telescopes; Watches

Kowa Optimed, Inc., 20001 S. Vermont Ave., Torrance CA 90502, P: 800-966-5692, F: 310-327-4177, www.kowa-usa. com
Binoculars; Scopes, Sights & Accessories; Telescopes

Krause Publications/F&W Media, 700 E. State St., Iola, WI 54990, P: 888-457-2873, F: 715-445-4087, www.krausebooks.com
Books/Industry Publications; Videos; DVDs

Krieger Barrels, Inc., 2024 Mayfield Rd., Richfield, WI 53076, P: 262-628-8558, F: 262-628-8748, www.kriegerbarrels.com
Gun Barrels

Kriss-TDI, 2697 International Dr., Pkwy. 4, 140, Virginia Beach, VA 23452, P: 202-821-1089, F: 202-821-1094, www.kriss-tdi.com
Firearms; Law Enforcement; Magazines, Cartridge

Kroll International, 51360 Danview Tech Ct., Shelby TWP, MI 48315, P: 800-359-6912, F: 800-359-9721, www.krollcorp.com
Bags & Equipment Cases; Footwear; Gloves, Mitts, Hats; Holsters; Hunting Accessories; Knives/Knife Cases; Law Enforcement; Wholesaler/Distributor

Kruger Optical, LLC, 141 E. Cascade Ave., Suite 208, P.O. Box 532, Sisters, OR 97759, P: 541-549-0770, F: 541-549-0769, www.krugeroptical.com
Binoculars; Scopes, Sights & Accessories

Kunming Yuanda Optical Co., Ltd./Norin Optech Co. Ltd., 9/F Huihua Bldg. No. 80 Xianlie, Zhong Rd., Guangzhou, 51007, CHINA, P: 011 862037616375, F: 011 862037619210, www.norin-optech.com
Binoculars; Compasses; Scopes, Sights & Accessories; Sports Accessories; Telescopes

Kutmaster/Div. Utica Cutlery Co., 820 Noyes St., Utica, NY 13503, P: 800-888-4223, F: 315-733-6602, www.kutmaster.com
Backpacking; Camping; Cooking Equipment & Accessories; Cutlery; Hunting Accessories; Knives/Knife Cases; Sports Accessories; Survival Kits/First Aid

Kwik-Site Co./Ironsighter Co., 5555 Treadwell, Wayne, MI 48184, P: 734-326-1500, F: 734-326-4120, www.kwiksitecorp.com
Black Powder Accessories; Firearms Maintenance Equipment; Hunting Accessories; Scopes, Sights & Accessories; Sporting Accessories

L

L.P.A. Srl di Ghilardi, Via Vittorio Alfieri, 26, Gardone V.T., 25063, ITALY, P: 011 390308911481, F: 011 390308910951, www.lpasights.com
Black Powder Accessories; Gun Parts/Gunsmithing; Scopes, Sights & Accessories

L-3 Communications-Eotech, 1201 E. Ellsworth Rd., Ann Arbor, MI 48108, P: 734-741-8868, F: 734-741-8221, www.l-3com.com/eotech
Law Enforcement; Scopes, Sights & Accessories

L-3 Electro-Optical Systems, 3414 Herrmann Dr., Garland, TX 75041, P: 866-483-9972, F: 972-271-2195, www.l3nightvision.com
Law Enforcement; Scopes, Sights & Accessories

L.A. Lighter, Inc./Viclight, 19805 Harrison Ave., City of Industry, CA 91789, P: 800-499-4708, F: 909-468-1859, www.lalighter.com
Camping; Cooking Equipment/ Accessories; Lighting Products; Sports Accessories; Training & Safety Equipment; Wholesaler/Distributor

L.A.R. Manufacturing, 4133 W. Farm Rd., West Jordan, UT 84088, P: 801-280-3505, F: 801-280-1972, www.largrizzly.com
Firearms

LEM Products, 109 May Dr., Harrison, OH 45030, P: 513-202-1188, F: 513-202-9494, www.lemproducts.com
Books/Industry Publications; Cooking Equipment/Accessories; Cutlery; Knives/Knife Cases; Sharpeners; Videos; Wholesaler/Distributor

L&R Ultrasonics, 577 Elm St., Kearny, NJ 07032, P: 201-991-5330, F: 201-991-5870, www.lrultrasonics.com
Decoys; Firearms; Firearms Maintenance Equipment; Gun Parts/Gunsmithing; Lubricants; Reloading; Shooting Range Equipment

LRB Arms, 96 Cherry Lane, Floral Park, NY 11001, P: 516-327-9061, F: 516-327-0246, www.lrbarms.com
Firearms; Wholesaler/Distributor

LRI–Photon Micro Light, 20448 Hwy. 36, Blachly, OR 97412, P: 541-925-3741, F: 541-925-3751, www.laughingrabbitinc.com
Backpacking; Camping; Hunting Accessories; Law Enforcement; Lighting Products; Sports Accessories; Survival Kits/First Aid; Training & Safety Equipment

Lachausee/New Lachaussée, UFA Belgium, Rue de Tige, 13, Herstal, Liège B 4040, BELGIUM, P: 011 3242488811, F: 011 3242488800, www.lachaussee.com
Ammunition; Firearms Maintenance Equipment; Reloading; Shooting Range Equipment

Lakeside Machine, LLC, 1213 Industrial St., Horseshoe Bend, AR 72512, P: 870-670-4999, F: 870-670-4998, www.lakesideguns.com
Custom Manufacturing; Firearms; Hunting Accessories; Law Enforcement

Lanber, Zubiaurre 3, P.O. Box 3, Zaldibar, (Vizcaya) 48250, SPAIN, P: 011 34946827702, F: 011 34946827999, www.lanber.com
Firearms

Lancer Systems, 7566 Morris Ct., Suite 300, Allentown, PA, 18106, P: 610-973-2614, F: 610-973-2615, www.lancer-systems.com
Custom Manufacturing; Gun Parts/ Gunsmithing; Magazines, Cartridge

Landmark Outdoors/Yukon Advanced Optics/Sightmark/Mobile Hunter/ Trophy Score/Amacker, 201 Regency Pkwy., Mansfield, TX 76063, P: 877-431-3579, F: 817-453-8770, www.landmarkoutdoors.com
Airsoft; Binoculars; Custom Manufacturing; Feeder Equipment; Hunting Accessories; Law Enforcement; Paintball Accessories; Scopes, Sights & Accessories; Shooting Range Equipment; Treestands; Wholesaler/ Distributor

Lanigan Performance Products/KG Industries, 10320 Riverburn Dr., Tampa, FL 33467, P: 813-651-5400, F: 813-991-6156, www.thesacskit.com
Gun Parts/Gunsmithing

Lansky Sharpeners, P.O. Box 50830, Henderson, NV 89016, P: 716-877-7511, F: 716-877-6955, www.lansky.com
Archery; Camping; Cooking Equipment/ Accessories; Cutlery; Hunting Accessories; Knives/Knife Cases; Law Enforcement; Sharpeners

LaRue Tactical, 850 CR 177, Leander, TX 78641, P: 512-259-1585, F: 512-259-1588, www.laruetactical.com
Custom Manufacturing; Scopes, Sights & Accessories; Targets

Laser Ammo, Ltd., #7 Bar Kochva St., Rishon Lezion, 75353, ISRAEL, P: 682-286-3311, www.laser-ammo.com
Ammunition; Firearms; Law Enforcement; Scopes, Sights & Accessories; Shooting Range Equipment; Training & Safety Equipment

Laser Devices, Inc., 2 Harris Ct., Suite A-4, Monterey, CA 93940, P: 800-235-2162, F: 831-373-0903, www.laserdevices.com
Holsters; Law Enforcement; Lighting Products; Scopes, Sights & Accessories; Shooting Range Equipment; Sports Accessories; Targets; Training & Safety Equipment

Laser Shot, Inc., 4214 Bluebonnet Dr., Stafford, TX 77477, P: 281-240-8241, F: 281-240-8241
Law Enforcement; Training & Safety Equipment

LaserLyte, 101 Airpark Rd., Cottonwood, AZ 86326, P: 928-649-3201, F: 928-649-3970, www.laserlyte.com
Hunting Accessories; Scopes, Sights & Accessories

LaserMax, Inc., 3495 Winton Place Bldg. B, Rochester, NY 14623, P: 800-527-3703, F: 585-272-5427, www.lasermax.com
Airsoft; Crossbows & Accessories; Firearms; Law Enforcement; Paintball Accessories; Scopes, Sights & Accessories; Shooting Range Equipment; Training & Safety Equipment

Lauer Custom Weaponry/Duracoat Products, 3601 129th St., Chippewa Falls, WI 54729, P: 800-830-6677, F: 715-723-2950, www.lauerweaponry.com
Camouflage; Custom Manufacturing; Firearms; Hunting Accessories; Law Enforcement; Lubricants; Magazines, Cartridge; Scopes, Sights & Accessories

Law Enforcement Targets, Inc., 8802 W. 35 W. Service Dr. NE, Blaine, MN 55449, P: 800-779-0182, F: 651-645-5360, www.letargets.com
Eyewear; Gun Cabinets/Racks/Safes; Gun Grips & Stocks; Hearing Protection; Law Enforcement; Targets; Training & Safety Equipment

Law Officer Magazine/Div. Elsevier Public Safety/Elsevier, 525 B St., Suite 1900, San Diego, CA 92101, P: 800-266-5367, F: 619-699-6396, www.lawofficer.com
Books/Industry Publications; Law Enforcement

Lawman Leather Goods, P.O. Box 30115, Las Vegas, NV 89173, P: 877-44LAWMAN, F: 702-227-0036, www.lawmanleathergoods.com
Black Powder Accessories; Books/Industry Publications; Holsters; Law Enforcement; Leathergoods; Wholesaler/Distributor

Lazzeroni Arms Co., 1415 S. Cherry Ave., Tuscon, AZ 85713, P: 888-4-WARBIRD, F: 520-624-6202, www.lazzeroni.com
Ammunition; Firearms

Leapers, Inc., 32700 Capitol St., Livonia, MI 48150, P: 734-542-1500, F: 734-542-7095, www.leapers.com
Airguns; Airsoft; Bags & Equipment Cases; Gun Cases; Holsters; Law Enforcement; Lighting Products; Scopes, Sights & Accessories

MANUFACTURER'S DIRECTORY

Leatherman Tool Group, Inc., 12106 NE Ainsworth Circle, Portland, OR 97220, P: 800-847-8665, F: 503-253-7830, www. leatherman.com
Backpacking; Hunting Accessories; Knives/ Knife Cases; Lighting Products; Sports Accessories

Leatherwood/Hi-Lux Optics/Hi-Lux, Inc., 3135 Kashiwa St., Torrance, CA 90505, P: 888-445-8912, F: 310-257-8096, www.hi-luxoptics.com
Binoculars; Scopes, Sights & Accessories; Telescopes

Legacy Sports International, 4750 Longley Lane, Suite 208, Reno, NV 89502, P: 775-828-0555, F: 775-828-0565, www. legacysports.com
Firearms; Gun Cabinets/Racks/Safes; Gun Cases; Scopes, Sights & Accessories

Leica Sport Optics/Leica Camera Inc., 1 Peart Ct., Unit A, Allendale, NJ 07401, P: 800-222-0118, F: 201-955-1686, www. leica-camera.com/usa
Binoculars; Photographic Equipment; Scopes, Sights & Accessories

LensPen–Parkside Optical, 650-375 Water St., Vancouver, British Columbia V6B 5C6, CANADA, P: 877-608-0868, F: 604-681-6194, www.lenspens.com
Binoculars; Hunting Accessories; Law Enforcement; Photographic Equipment; Scopes, Sights & Accessories; Sports Accessories; Telescopes

Les Baer Custom, Inc., 1804 Iowa Dr., Leclaire, IA 52753, P: 563-289-2126, F: 563-289-2132, www.lesbaer.com
Custom Manufacturing; Export/Import Specialists; Firearms; Gun Barrels; Gun Parts/Gunsmithing

Leupold & Stevens, Inc., 14400 NW Greenbriar Pkwy. 9700, P.O. Box 688, Beaverton, OR 97006, P: 503-646-9171, F: 503-526-1478, www.leupold.com
Binoculars; Lighting Products; Scopes, Sights & Accessories

Level Lok Shooting System/Div. Brutis Enterprises Inc., 105 S. 12th St., Pittsburgh, PA 15203, P: 888-461-7468, F: 412-488-5440, www.levellok.com
Binoculars; Firearms; Gun Grips & Stocks; Hunting Accessories; Photographic Equipment; Scopes, Sights & Accessories; Shooting Range Equipment; Sports Accessories

Lew Horton Distributing Co., Inc., 15 Walkup Dr., P.O. Box 5023, Westboro, MA 01581, P: 800-446-7866, F: 508-366-5332, www.lewhorton.com
Ammunition; Firearms; Hunting Accessories; Knives/Knife Cases; Law Enforcement; Magazines, Cartridge; Scopes, Sights & Accessories; Wholesaler/ Distributor

Lewis Machine & Tool, 1305 11th St. W, Milan, IL 61264, P: 309-787-7151, F: 309-787-7193, www.lewismachine.net
Firearms

Liberty Safe & Security Products, Inc., 1199 W. Utah Ave., Payson, UT 84651, P: 800-247-5625, F: 801-465-5880, www. libertysafe.com
Firearms Maintenance Equipment; Gun Cabinets/Racks/Safes; Gun Locks; Home Furnishings; Hunting Accessories; Law Enforcement; Sports Accessories; Training & Safety Equipment

Lightfield Ammunition Corp., P.O. Box 162, Adelphia, NJ 07710, P: 732-462-9200, F: 732-780-2437, www.lightfieldslugs.com
Ammunition

LightForce USA, Inc/NightForce Optics, 1040 Hazen Ln., Orofino, ID 83544, P: 800-732-9824, F: 208-476-9817, www. nightforceoptics.com
Law Enforcement; Lighting Products; Scopes, Sights & Accessories; Telescopes

LimbSaver, 50 W. Rose Nye Way, Shelton, WA 98584, P: 877-257-2761, F: 360-427-4025, www.limbsaver.com
Archery; Crossbows & Accessories; Hunting Accessories; Men's Clothing; Paintball Accessories; Recoil Protection Devices & Services; Scopes, Sights & Accessories

Linton Cutlery Co., Ltd., 7F, No. 332, Yongji Rd., Sinyi District, Taipei, 110, TAIWAN, P: 011 886227090905, F: 011 886227003978, www.linton-cutlery.com
Cutlery; Export/Import Specialists; Hunting Accessories; Law Enforcement; Sports Accessories; Wholesaler/Distributor

Linville Knife and Tool Co., P.O. Box 71, Bethania, NC 27010, P: 336-923-2062
Cutlery; Gun Grips & Stocks; Knives/Knife Cases

Lipseys, P.O. Box 83280, Baton Rouge, LA 70884, P: 800-666-1333, FL 225-755-3333, www.lipseys.com
Black Powder Accessories; Firearms; Holsters; Hunting Accessories; Magazines, Cartridge; Online Services; Scopes, Sights & Accessories; Wholesaler/Distributor

Little Giant Ladders, 1198 N. Spring Creek Pl., Springville, UT 84663, P: 800-453-1192, F: 801-489-1130, www. littlegiantladders.com
Law Enforcement; Training & Safety Equipment

LockSAF/VMR Capital Group, 2 Gold St., Suite 903, New York, NY 10038, P: 877-568-5625, F: 877-893-4502, www. locksaf.com
Gun Cabinets/Racks/Safes

Lone Wolf Distributors, Inc., 57 Shepard Rd., P.O. Box 3549, Oldtown, ID 83822, P: 888-279-2077, F: 208-437-1098, www.lonewolfdist.com
Books/Industry Publications; Firearms Maintenance Equipment; Gun Barrels; Gun Parts/Gunsmithing; Holsters; Scopes, Sights & Accessories; Videos; Wholesaler/ Distributor

Lone Wolf Knives, 9373 SW Barber St., Suite A, Wilsonville, OR 97070, P: 503-431-6777, F: 503-431-6776, www. lonewolfknives.com
Archery; Backpacking; Camouflage; Camping; Cutlery; Hunting Accessories; Knives/Knife Cases; Law Enforcement

Long Perng Co., Ltd., #16, Hejiang Rd., Chung Li Industrial Zone, Chung Li City, Taoyuan Hsien, 320, TAIWAN, P: 011 88634632468, F: 011 88634631948, www.longperng.com.tw
Binoculars; Scopes, Sights & Accessories; Telescopes

Lothar Walther Precision Tools, Inc., 3425 Hutchinson Rd., Cumming, GA 30040, P: 770-889-9998, F: 770-889-4919, www. lothar-walther.com
Custom Manufacturing; Export/Import Specialists; Gun Barrels

Lou's Police Distributor, 7815 W. 4th Ave., Hialeah, FL 33014, P: 305-822-5362, F: 305-822-9603, www.louspolice.com
Ammunition; Firearms; Gun Grips & Stocks; Hearing Protection; Holsters; Law Enforcement; Scopes, Sights & Accessories; Wholesaler/Distributor

LouderThanWords.US/Heirloom Precision, LLC, 2118 E. 5th St., Tempe, AZ 85281, P: 480-804-1911, www.louderthanwords. us
Firearms; Gun Parts/Gunsmithing; Holsters

Lowrance–Navico, Eagle–Navico, 12000 E. Skelly Dr., Tulsa, OK 74128, P: 800-352-1356, F: 918-234-1707, www.lowrance. com
Archery; Backpacking; Camping; Hunting Accessories; Law Enforcement; Sports Accessories; Survival Kits/First Aid; Vehicles, Utility & Rec

Lowy Enterprises, Inc., 1970 E. Gladwick St., Rancho Dominguez, CA 90220, P: 310-763-1111, F: 310-763-1112, www. lowyusa.com
Backpacking; Bags & Equipment Cases; Custom Manufacturing; Law Enforcement; Outfitter; Paintball Accessories; Sports Accessories; Wholesaler/Distributor

Luminox Watch Co., 2301 Kerner Blvd., Suite A, San Rafael, CA 94901, P: 415-455-9500, F: 415-482-8215, www. luminox.com
Backpacking; Camping; Custom Manufacturing; Hunting Accessories; Law Enforcement, Outdoor Art, Jewelry, Sculpture; Sports Accessories; Watches

LWRC International, LLC, 815 Chesapeake Dr., Cambridge, MD 21613, P: 410-901-1348, F: 410-228-1799, www.lwrifles. com
Ammunition; Custom Manufacturing; Firearms; Firearms Maintenance Equipment; Gun Barrels; Gun Parts/ Gunsmithing; Law Enforcement; Magazines, Cartridge

Lyalvale Express Limited, Express Estate, Whittington, Lichfield, WS13 8XA, UNITED KINGDOM, P: 011-44 1543434400, F: 011-44 1543434420, www.lyalvaleexpress.com
Ammunition

M

MDM/Millennium Designed Muzzleloaders, Ltd., RR 1, Box 405, Maidstone, VT 05905, P: 802-676-331, F: 802-676-3322, www.mdm-muzzleloaders.com
Ammunition; Black Powder Accessories; Black Powder/Smokeless Powder; Custom Manufacturing; Firearms Maintenance Equipment; Gun Barrels; Gun Cases; Scopes, Sights & Accessories

MDS Inc., 3429 Stearns Rd., Valrico, FL 33596, P: 800-435-9352, F: 813-684-5953, www.mdsincorporated.com

Firearms Maintenance Equipment; Gun Parts/Gunsmithing; Law Enforcement

MFI, 563 San Miguel, Liberty, KY 42539, P: 606-787-0022, F: 606-787-0059, www.mfiap.com
Custom Manufacturing; Export/Import Specialists; Firearms; Gun Grips & Stocks; Gun Parts/Gunsmithing; Scopes, Sights & Accessories; Sports Accessories; Wholesaler/Distributor

MGI, 102 Cottage St., Bangor, ME 04401, P: 207-945-5441, F: 207-945-4010, www.mgimilitary.com
Firearms; Gun Barrels; Law Enforcement

MG Arms, Inc., 6030 Treaschwig Rd., Spring, TX 77373, P: 281-821-8282, F: 281-821-6387, www.mgarmsinc.com
Ammunition; Custom Manufacturing; Firearms; Gun Grips & Stocks; Wholesaler/Distributor

MPI Outdoors/Grabber, 5760 N. Hawkeye Ct., Grand Rapids, MI 49509, P: 800-423-1233, F: 616-977-7718, www.warmers.com
Backpacking; Camouflage; Camping; Cooking Equipment/Accessories; Gloves, Mitts, Hats; Hunting Accessories; Lighting Products; Survival Kits/First Aid

MPRI, 10220 Old Columbia Rd., Suites A & B, Columbia, MD 21046, P: 800-232-6448, F: 410-309-1506, www.mpri.com
Ammunition; Gun Barrels; Law Enforcement; Shooting Range Equipment; Targets; Training & Safety Equipment

M-Pro 7 Gun Care/Bushnell Outdoor Accessories, 9200 Cody, Overland Park, KS 66214, P: 800-845-2444, F: 800-548-0446, www.mpro7.com
Black Powder Accessories; Firearms Maintenance Equipment; Gun Parts/Gunsmithing; Hunting Accessories; Law Enforcement; Lubricants

M-Pro 7 Gun Care, 225 W. Deer Valley Rd., Suite 4, Phoenix, AZ 85027, P: 888-YES-4MP7, F: 623-516-0414, www.mpro7.com
Black Powder Accessories; Firearms Maintenance Equipment; Gun Parts/Gunsmithing; Hunting Accessories; Law Enforcement; Lubricants

MSA, 121 Gamma Dr., Pittsburgh, PA 15238, P: 800-672-2222, F: 412-967-3373
Bags & Equipment Cases; Eyewear; Hearing Protection; Law Enforcement; Survival Kits/First Aid; Training & Safety Equipment

MSA Safety Works, 121 Gamma Dr., Pittsburgh, PA 15238, P: 800-969-7562, F: 800-969-7563, www.msasafetyworks.com
Eyewear; Hearing Protection; Shooting Range Equipment; Training & Safety Equipment

MT2, LLC/Metals Treatment Technologies, 14045 W. 66th Ave., Arvada, CO 80004, P: 888-435-6645, F: 303-456-5998, www.mt2.com
Firearms Maintenance Equipment; Shooting Range Equipment

Mace Security International, 160 Benmont Ave., Bennington, VT 05201, P: 800-255-2634, F: 802-753-1209, www.mace.com

Archery; Camping; Hunting Accessories; Law Enforcement; Sports Accessories; Training & Safety Equipment

Mag Instrument, Inc./Maglite, 2001 S. Hellman Ave., Ontario, CA 91761, P: 800-289-6241, F: 775-719-4586, www.maglite.com
Backpacking; Camping; Hunting Accessories; Lighting Products; Sports Accessories; Survival Kits/First Aid; Training & Safety Equipment

Maglula, Ltd., P.O. Box 302, Rosh Ha'ayin, 48103, ISRAEL, P: 011 97239030902, F: 011 97239030902, www.maglula.com
Firearms Maintenance Equipment; Gun Parts/Gunsmithing; Magazines, Cartridge; Shooting Range Equipment

Magnum USA, 4801 Stoddard Rd., Modesto, CA 95356, P: 800-521-1698, F: 209-545-2079, www.magnumboots.com
Footwear; Law Enforcement; Men's Clothing

Magnum Research, Inc., 7110 University Ave. NE, Minneapolis, MN 55432, P: 800-772-6168, F: 763-574-0109, www.magnumresearch.com
Firearms

Magpul Industries Corp., P.O. Box 17697, Boulder, CO 80308, P: 877-462-4785, F: 303-828-3469, www.magpul.com
Firearms; Gun Grips & Stocks; Gun Parts/Gunsmithing; Law Enforcement; Videos

Magtech Ammunition Co., Inc., 248 Apollo Dr., Suite 180, Lino Lakes, MN 55014, P: 800-466-7191, F: 763-235-4004, www.magtechammunition.com
Ammunition; Export/Import Specialists; Law Enforcement; Reloading; Shooting Range Equipment; Wholesaler/Distributor

Mahco, Inc., 1202 Melissa Dr., Bentonville, AR 72712, P: 479-273-0052, F: 479-271-9248
Bags & Equipment Cases; Binoculars; Camouflage; Camping; Hunting Accessories; Knives/Knife Cases; Scopes, Scopes, Sights & Accessories

Majestic Arms, Ltd., 101-A Ellis St., Staten Island, NY 10307, P: 718-356-6765, F: 718-356-6835, www.majesticarms.com
Firearms; Gun Barrels; Gun Parts/Gunsmithing

Mako Group, 74 Rome St., Farmingdale, NY 11735, P: 631-880-3396, F: 631-880-3397, www.themakogroup.com
Custom Manufacturing; Gun Grips & Stocks; Law Enforcement; Lighting Products; Scopes, Sights & Accessories; Targets; Training & Safety Equipment; Wholesaler/Distributor

Mancom Manufacturing Inc., 1335 Osprey Dr., Ancaster, Ontario L9G 4V5, CANADA, P: 888-762-6266, F: 905-304-6137, www.mancom.ca
Custom Manufacturing; Law Enforcement; Shooting Range Equipment; Training & Safety Equipment

Manners Composite Stocks, 1209 Swift, North Kansas City, MO 64116, P: 816-283-3334, www.mannerstock.com
Custom Manufacturing; Firearms Maintenance Equipment; Gun Grips & Stocks; Law Enforcement; Shooting Range Equipment

Dave Manson Precision Reamers/Div. Loon Lake Precision, Inc., 8200 Embury Rd., Grand Blanc, MI 48439, P: 810-953-0732, F: 810-953-0735, www.mansonreamers.com
Black Powder Accessories; Custom Manufacturing; Firearms Maintenance Equipment; Gun Barrels; Gun Parts/Gunsmithing; Recoil Protection Devices & Services; Reloading

Mantis Knives/Famous Trails, 1580 N. Harmony Circle, Anaheim, CA 92807, P: 877-97-SCOPE, F: 714-701-9672, www.mantisknives.com
Binoculars; Camping; Hunting Accessories; Knives/Knife Cases; Law Enforcement; Photographic Equipment; Scopes, Sights & Accessories; Wholesaler/Distributor

Manzella Productions, 80 Sonwil Dr., Buffalo, NY 14225, P: 716-681-8880, F: 716-681-6888
Hunting Accessories; Law Enforcement

Marbles, 420 Industrial Park, Gladstone, MI 49837, P: 906-428-3710, F: 906-428-3711, www.marblescutlery.com
Compasses; Cutlery; Scopes, Sights & Accessories; Sharpeners

Marlin Firearms/H&R, 100 Kenna Dr., P.O. Box 248, North Haven, CT 06473, P: 888-261-1179, F: 336-548-8736, www.marlinfirearms.com
Firearms

Marvel Precision, LLC, P.O. Box 127, Cortland, NE 68331, P: 800-295-1987, F: 402-791-2246, www.marvelprecision.com
Firearms; Wholesaler/Distributor

Masen Co., Inc., John, 1305 Jelmak St., Grand Prairie, TX 75050, P: 972-970-3691, F: 972-970-3691, www.johnmasen.com
Firearms Maintenance Equipment; Gun Grips & Stocks; Gun Parts/Gunsmithing; Magazines, Cartridge; Online Services; Scopes, Sights & Accessories; Wholesaler/Distributor

Maserin Coltellerie SNC, Via dei Fabbri, 19, Maniago, 33085, ITALY, P: 011 39042771335, F: 011 390427700690, www.maserin.com
Cutlery; Hunting Accessories; Knives/Knife Cases; Law Enforcement; Sports Accessories

Maurice Sporting Goods, Inc., 1910 Techny Rd., Northbrook, IL 60065, P: 866-477-3474, F: 847-715-1419, www.maurice.net
Archery; Camping; Firearms Maintenance Equipment; Game Calls; Gloves, Mitts, Hats; Hunting Accessories; Sports Accessories; Wholesaler/Distributor

Maxpedition Hard-Use Gear/Edgygear, Inc., P.O. Box 5008, Palos Verdes, CA 90274, P: 877-629-5556, F: 310-515-5950, www.maxpedition.com
Backpacking; Bags & Equipment Cases; Gun Cases; Holsters; Hunting Accessories; Knives/Knife Cases; Law Enforcement; Sports Accessories

MaxPro Police & Armor, 4181 W. 5800 N, Mountain Green, UT 84050, P: 801-876-3616, F: 801-876-2746, www.maxpropolice.com
Training & Safety Equipment

273

MANUFACTURER'S DIRECTORY

Mayville Engineering Co. (MEC), 800 Horicon St., Suite 1, Mayville, WI 53050, P: 800-797-4MEC, F: 920-387-5802, www.mecreloaders.com
Reloading

McConkey, Inc./ATV Backpacker Cart, P.O. Box 1362, Seeley Lake, MT 59868, P: 308-641-1085, F: 866-758-9896, www.atvbackpackercart.com
Ammunition; Backpacking; Camping; Hunting Accessories; Sports Accessories; Vehicles, Utility & Rec; Wholesaler/ Distributor

McGowan Manufacturing Co., 4854 N. Shamrock Pl., Suite 100, Tucson, AZ 85705, P: 800-342-4810, F: 520-219-9759, www.mcgowanmfg.com
Archery; Camping; Cooking Equipment/ Accessories; Crossbows & Accessories; Cutlery; Hunting Accessories; Knives/Knife Cases; Sharpeners

McKeon Products, Inc./Mack's Hearing Protection, 25460 Guenther, Warren, MI 48091, P: 586-427-7560, F: 586-427-7204, www.macksearplugs.com
Camping; Hearing Protection; Hunting Accessories; Sports Accessories; Training & Safety Equipment

McMillan Fiberglass Stocks, 1638 W. Knudsen Dr., Suite A, Phoenix, AZ 85027, P: 877-365-6148, F: 623-581-3825, www.mcmillanusa.com
Firearms; Gun Grips & Stocks

Mcusta Knives/Mcusta Knives USA, P.O. Box 22901, Portland, OR 97269, P: 877-714-5487, F: 503-344-4631, www.mcustausa.com
Cooking Equipment/Accessories; Cutlery; Hunting Accessories; Knives/Knife Cases; Law Enforcement; Sports Accessories; Wholesaler/Distributor

Mead Industries, Inc., 411 Walnut St., P.O. Box 402, Wood River, NE 68883, P: 308-583-2875, F: 308-583-2002
Ammunition

MEC-GAR SRL, Via Mandolossa, 102/a, Gussago, Brescia, 25064, ITALY, P: 011 390303735413, F: 011 390303733687, www.mec-gar.it
Gun Parts/Gunsmithing; Law Enforcement; Magazine, Cartridge

Meggitt Training Systems/Caswell, 296 Brogdon Rd., Suwanee, GA 30024, P: 800-813-9046, F: 678-288-1515, www.meggitttrainingsystems.com
Custom Manufacturing; Law Enforcement; Shooting Range Equipment; Targets; Training & Safety Equipment

Meopta USA, Inc., 50 Davids Dr., Hauppauge, NY, 11788, P: 800-828-8928, F: 631-436-5920, www.meopta.com
Binoculars; Scopes, Sights & Accessories; Telescopes

Meprolight, 2590 Montana Hwy. 35, Suite B, Kalispell, MT 59901, P: 406-758-2222, F: 406-758-2223
Scopes, Sights & Accessories

Meprolight, Ltd., 58 Hazait St., Or-Akiva Industrial Park, Or-Akiva, 30600, ISRAEL, P: 011 97246244111, F: 011 97246244123, www.meprolight.com
Binoculars; Firearms; Gun Parts/ Gunsmithing; Hunting Accessories; Law Enforcement; Lighting Products; Scopes, Sights & Accessories; Telescopes

Mercury Luggage Mfg. Co./Code Alpha Tactical Gear, 4843 Victory St., Jacksonville, FL 32207, P: 800-874-1885, F: 904-733-9671, www.mercuryluggage.com
Bags & Equipment Cases; Camouflage; Custom Manufacturing; Export/Import Specialists; Law Enforcement

Merkel USA, 7661 Commerce Ln., Trussville, AL 35173, P: 800-821-3021, F: 205-655-7078, www.merkel-usa.com
Binoculars; Firearms; Scopes, Sights & Accessories

Mesa Tactical, 1760 Monrovia Ave., Suite A14, Costa Mesa, CA 92627, P: 949-642-3337, F: 949-642-3339, www.mesatactical.com
Gun Grips & Stocks; Law Enforcement; Scopes, Sights & Accessories

Meyerco, 4481 Exchange Service Dr., Dallas, TX 75236, P: 214-467-8949, F: 214-467-9241, www.meyercousa.com
Bags & Equipment Cases; Camping; Cutlery; Gun Cases; Hunting Accessories; Knives/Knife Cases; Law Enforcement; Sharpeners

Microsonic, 2960 Duss Ave., Ambridge, PA 15003, P: 724-266-9480, F: 724-266-9482, www.microsonic-inc.com
Hearing Protection

Microtech Knives, Inc./Microtech Small Arms Research, Inc., 300 Chestnut St., Bradford, PA 16701, P: 814-363-9260, F: 814-363-9284, www.msarinc.com
Custom Manufacturing; Cutlery; Firearms; Knives/Knife Cases; Law Enforcement; Sports Accessories

Midwest Industries, Inc., 828 Philip Dr., Suite 2, Waukesha, WI 53186, P: 262-896-6780, F: 262-896-6756, www.midwestindustriesinc.com
Gun Cases; Gun Parts/Gunsmithing; Law Enforcement; Lubricants; Magazines, Cartridge; Scopes, Sights & Accessories

Mil-Comm Products Co., Inc., 2 Carlton Ave., East Rutherford, NJ 07073, P: 888-947-3273, F: 201-935-6059, www.mil-comm.com
Black Powder Accessories; Firearms Maintenance Equipment; Gun Cabinets/Racks/Safes; Gun Locks; Gun Parts/Gunsmithing; Law Enforcement; Lubricants; Paintball Guns

Mil-Spec Plus/Voodoo Tactical, 435 W. Alondra Blvd., Gardena, CA 90248, P: 310-324-8855, F: 310-324-6909, www.majorsurplus.com
Bags & Equipment Cases; Eyewear; Footwear; Gloves, Mitts, Hats; Gun Cases; Law Enforcement

Mil-Tac Knives & Tools, P.O. Box 642, Wylie, TX 75098, P: 877-MIL-TAC6, F: 972-412-2208, www.mil-tac.com
Cutlery; Eyewear; Gloves, Mitts, Hats; Gun Parts/Gunsmithing; Hunting Accessories; Knives/Knife Cases; Law Enforcement; Survival Kits/First Aid

Military Outdoor Clothing, Inc., 1917 Stanford St., Greenville, TX 75401, P: 800-662-6430, F: 903-454-2433, www.militaryoutdoorclothing.com
Bags & Equipment Cases; Camouflage; Gloves, Mitts, Hats; Law Enforcement; Men & Women's Clothing

Milkor USA, Inc., 3735 N. Romero Rd., Suite 2M, Tucson, AZ 85705, P: 520-888-0103, F: 520-888-0122, www.milkorusainc.com
Firearms

Millett Sights/Bushnell Outdoor Products, 6200 Cody, Overland Park, KS 66214, P: 888-276-5945, F: 800-548-0446, www.millettsights.com
Black Powder Accessories; Gun Parts/ Gunsmithing; Hunting Accessories; Law Enforcement; Scopes, Sights & Accessories

Minox USA, 438 Willow Brook Rd., Merdien, NH 03770, P: 866-469-3080, F: 603-469-3471, www.minox.com
Binoculars

Mocean, 1635 Monrovia Ave., Costa Mesa, CA 92627, P: 949-646-1701, F: 949-646-1590, www.mocean.net
Custom Manufacturing; Law Enforcement; Men & Women's Clothing; Wholesaler/ Distributor

Montana Rifle Co./Montana Rifleman, Inc., 3172 Montana Hwy. 35, Kalispell, MT 59901, P: 406-755-4867, F: 406-755-9449, www.montanarifle.com
Custom Manufacturing; Firearms; Gun Barrels; Gun Parts/Gunsmithing

Morovision Night Vision, Inc., P.O. Box 342, Dana Point, CA 92629, P: 800-424-8222, F: 949-488-3361, www.morovision.com
Binoculars; Camping; Hunting Accessories; Law Enforcement; Lighting Products; Photographic Equipment; Scopes, Sights & Accessories; Wholesaler/Distributor

Morton Enterprises, 35 Pilot Ln., Great Cacapon, WV, 25422, P: 877-819-7280, www.uniquecases.com
Bags & Equipment Cases; Custom Manufacturing; Gun Cases; Hunting Accessories; Law Enforcement; Sports Accessories

Moteng, Inc., 12220 Parkway Centre Dr., Poway, CA 92064, P: 800-367-5900, F: 800-367-5903, www.moteng.com
Camping; Cutlery; Knives/Knife Cases; Law Enforcement; Lighting Products; Online Services; Training & Safety Equipment; Wholesaler/Distributor

Mountain Corp./Mountain Life, 59 Optical Ave., P.O. Box 686, Keene, NH 03431, P: 800-545-9684, F: 603-355-3702, www.themountain.com
Law Enforcement; Men & Women's Clothing; Outfitter; Retail Packaging; Wholesaler/Distributor

Mounting Solutions Plus, 10655 SW 185 Terrace, Miami, FL 33157, P: 800-428-9394, F: 305-232-1247, www.mountsplus.com
Scopes, Sights & Accessories; Wholesaler/ Distributor

MTM-Multi Time Machine, Inc., 1225 S. Grand Ave., Los Angeles, CA 90015, P: 213-741-0808, F: 213-741-0840, www.specialopswatch.com

Archery; Backpacking; Camouflage; Hunting Accessories; Law Enforcement; Sports Accessories; Watches

Muela, Ctra. N-420, KM 165, 500, Argamasilla De Calatrava, (Ciudad Real) 13440, SPAIN, P: 011 34926477093, F: 011 34926477237, www.mmuela.com
Knives/Knife Cases

Muller Prinsloo Knives, P.O. Box 2263, Bethlehem, 9700, SOUTH AFRICA, P: 011 27824663885, F: 011 27583037111
Knives/Knife Cases

Mystery Ranch, 34156 E. Frontage Rd., Bozeman, MT 59715, P: 406-585-1428, F: 406-585-1792, www.mysteryranch.com
Backpacking; Bags & Equipment Cases; Camping; Law Enforcement; Photographic Equipment

N

Nantong Universal Optical Instruments Co., Ltd., No. 1 Pingchao Industrial Garden, Nantong, Jiangsu 226361, CHINA, P: 011 8651386726888, F: 011 8651386718158, www.zoscn.com
Airguns; Binoculars; Gun Cases; Gun Locks; Scopes, Sights & Accessories; Wholesaler/Distributor

National Rifle Association, 11250 Waples Mill Rd., Fairfax, VA 22030, P: 800-672-3888, F: 703-267-3810, www.nra.org

N-Vision Optics, 220 Reservior St., Suite 26, Neenham, MA 02494, P: 781-505-8360, F: 781-998-5656, www.nvisionoptics.com
Binoculars; Law Enforcement; Scopes, Sights & Accessories

Navy Arms Co./Forgett Militaria, 219 Lawn St., Martinsburg, WV 25405, P: 304-262-1651, F: 304-262-1658, www.navyarms.com
Firearms

New Century Science & Tech, Inc., 10302 Olney St., El Monte, CA 91731, P: 866-627-8278, F: 626-575-2478, www.ncstar.com
Binoculars; Crossbows & Accessories; Custom Manufacturing; Export/Import Specialists; Firearms Maintenance Equipment; Gun Cases; Lighting Products; Scopes, Sights & Accessories

New Ultra Light Arms, 214 Price St., P.O. Box 340, Granville, WV 26534, P: 304-292-0600, FL 304-292-9662, www.newultralight.com
Firearms

Newcon Optik, 105 Sparks Ave., Toronto M2H 2S5, CANADA, P: 877-368-6666, F: 416-663-9065, www.newcon-optik.com
Binoculars; Hunting Accessories; Law Enforcement; Paintballs; Photographic Equipment; Scopes, Sights & Accessories; Shooting Range Equipment

Nextorch, Inc., 2401 Viewcrest Ave., Everett, WA 98203, P: 425-290-3092, www.nextorch.com
Hunting Accessories; Knives/Knife Cases; Lighting Products

Nightforce, (see Lightforce USA, Inc.)

Night Optics USA, Inc., 5122 Bolsa Ave., Suite 101, Huntington Beach, CA 92649, P: 800-30-NIGHT, F: 714-899-4485, www.nightoptics.com
Binoculars; Camping; Hunting Accessories; Law Enforcement; Scopes, Sights & Accessories; Training & Safety Equipment; Wholesaler/Distributor; Wildlife Management

Night Owl Optics/Bounty Hunter/Fisher Research Labs, 1465-H Henry Brennan, El Paso, TX 79936, P: 800-444-5994, F: 915-633-8529, www.nightowloptics.com
Binoculars; Camping; Hunting Accessories; Law Enforcement; Photographic Equipment; Scopes, Sights & Accessories; Sports Accessories; Telescopes

Night Vision Depot, P.O. Box 3415, Allentown, PA 18106, P: 610-395-9743, F: 610-395-9744, www.nvdepot.com
Binoculars; Hunting Accessories; Law Enforcement; Lighting Products; Scopes, Sights & Accessories; Wholesaler/Distributor

Night Vision Systems (NVS), 542 Kemmerer Ln., Allentown, PA 18104, P: 800-797-2849, F: 610-391-9220, www.nighvisionsystems.com
Law Enforcement; Scopes, Sights & Accessories

Nighthawk Custom, 1306 W. Trimble, Berryville, AR 72616, P: 877-268-4867, F: 870-423-4230, www.nighthawkcustom.com
Firearms; Gun Grips & Stocks; Gun Parts/Gunsmithing; Hearing Protection; Holsters

Nikon, Inc., 1300 Walt Whitman Rd., Melville, NY 11747, P: 631-547-4200, FL 631-547-4040, www.nikonhunting.com
Binoculars; Hunting Accessories; Scopes, Sights & Accessories

Ningbo Electric and Consumer Goods I/E. Corp., 17/F, Lingqiao Plaza, 31 Yaohang Street, Ningbo, Zhejiang, 315000 CHINA P: 011 8657487194807; F: 011 8657487296214

Nite Ize, Inc., 5660 Central Ave., Boulder, CO 80301, P: 800-678-6483, F: 303-449-2013, www.niteize.com
Bags & Equipment Cases; Camping; Custom Manufacturing; Holsters; Lighting Products; Pet Supplies

Nite Lite Co., 3801 Woodland Heights Rd., Suite 100, Little Rock, AR 72212, P: 800-648-5483, F: 501-227-4892, www.huntsmart.com
Game Calls; Hunting Accessories; Lighting Products; Men's Clothing; Pet Supplies; Scents & Lures; Scopes, Sights & Accessories; Training & Safety Equipment

Nitrex Optics/ATK Commercial Products, N5549 Cty. Tk. Z, Onalaska, WI 54650, P: 800-635-7656, F: 763-323-3890, www.nitrexoptics.com
Binoculars; Scopes, Sights & Accessories

NiViSys Industries LLC, 400 S. Clark Dr., Suite 105, Tempe, AZ 85281, P: 480-970-3222, F: 480-970-3555, www.nivisys.com
Binoculars; Law Enforcement; Lighting Products; Photographic Equipment; Scopes, Sights & Accessories; Wholesaler/Distributor

Norica Laurona, Avda. Otaola, 16, Eibar, (Guipúzcoa) 20600, P: 011 34943207445, F: 011 34943207449, www.norica.es, www.laurona.com
Airguns; Ammuntion; Firearms; Hearing Protection; Hunting Accessories; Knives/Knife Cases; Scopes, Sights & Accessories

Norma Precision AB/RUAG Ammotec, Jagargatan, Amotfors, S-67040, SWEDEN, P: 044-46-571-31500, F: 011-46-571-31540, www.norma.cc
Ammunition; Custom Manufacturing; Reloading

North American Arms, Inc., 2150 S. 950 E, Provo, UT 84606, P: 800-821-5783, F: 801-374-9998, www.northamericanarms.com
Firearms

Northern Lights Tactical, P.O. 10272, Prescott, AZ 86304, P: 310-376-4266, F: 310-798-9278, www.northernlightstactical.com
Archery; Hunting Accessories; Law Enforcement; Paintball Accessories; Shooting Range Equipment; Targets; Training & Safety Equipment; Vehicles, Utility & Rec

Nosler, Inc., 107 SW Columbia, P.O. Box 671, Bend, OR 97709, P: 800-285-3701, F: 800-766-7537, www.nosler.com
Ammunition; Black Powder Accessories; Books/Industry Publications; Firearms; Reloading

Nova Silah Sanayi, Ltd., Merkez Mah. Kultur Cad. No: 22/14, Duzce, TURKEY, P: 011-90 2125140279, F: 011-90 2125111999
Firearms

Novatac, Inc., 300 Carlsbad Village Dr., Suite 108A-100, Carlsbad, CA 92008, P: 760-730-7370, FL 760-730-7375, www.novatac.com
Backpacking; Camping; Hunting Accessories; Law Enforcement; Lighting Products; Survival Kits/First Aid; Training & Safety Equipment

Numrich Gun Parts Corp./Gun Parts Corp., 226 Williams Ln., P.O. Box 299, West Hurley, NY 12491, P: 866-686-7424, F: 877-GUN-PART, www.e-gunparts.com
Firearms Maintenance Equipment; Gun Barrels; Gun Cases; Gun Grips & Stocks; Gun Parts/Gunsmithing; Hunting Accessories; Magazines, Cartridge; Scopes, Sights & Accessories

Nuwai International Co., Ltd./Nuwai LED Flashlight, 11 FL., 110 Li Gong St., Bei, Tou Taipei, 11261, TAIWAN, P: 011 886228930199, F: 011 886228930198, www.nuwai.com
Camping; Lighting Products; Outfitter

Nylok Corp., 15260 Hallmark Dr., Macomb, MI 48042, P: 586-786-0100, FL 810-780-0598
Custom Manufacturing; Gun Parts/Gunsmithing; Lubricants

O

O.F. Mossberg & Sons, Inc., 7 Grasso Ave., North Haven, CT 06473, P: 203-230-5300, F: 203-230-5420, www.mossberg.com

MANUFACTURER'S DIRECTORY

Firearms; Gun Barrels; Hunting Accesories; Law Enforcement

Odyssey Automotive Specialty, 317 Richard Mine Rd., Wharton, MJ 07885, P: 800-535-9441, F: 973-328-2601, www.odysseyauto.com
Custom Manufacturing; Gun Cabinets/Racks/Safes; Gun Cases; Law Enforcement; Vehicles, Utility & Rec

Oehler Research, Inc., P.O. Box 9135, Austin, TX 78766, P: 800-531-5125, F: 512-327-6903, www.oehler-research.com
Ammunition; Computer Software; Hunting Accessories; Reloading; Shooting Range Equipment; Targets

Oklahoma Leather Products/Don Hume Leathergoods, 500 26th NW, Miami, OK 74354, P: 918-542-6651, F: 918-542-6653, www.oklahomaleatherproducts.com
Black Powder Accessories; Custom Manufacturing; Cutlery; Holsters; Hunting Accessories; Knives/Knife Cases; Law Enforcement; Leathergoods

Old Western Scrounger, Inc., 50 Industrial Pkwy., Carson City, NV 89706, P: 800-UPS-AMMO, F: 775-246-2095, www.ows-ammunition.com
Ammunition; Reloading

Olivon Manufacturing Co., Ltd./Olivon-Worldwide, 600 Tung Pu Rd., Shanghai, China, Shanghai, Jiangsu, CHINA, P: 604-764-7731, F: 604-909-4951, www.olivonmanufacturing.com
Bag & Equipment Cases; Binoculars; Gun Cabinets/Racks/Safes; Gun Cases; Hunting Accessories; Scopes, Sights & Accessories; Telescopes

Olympic Arms, Inc., 624 Old Pacific Hwy. SE, Olympia, WA 98513, P: 800-228-3471, F: 360-491-3447, www.olyarms.com
Firearms; Gun Barrels; Gun Grips & Stocks; Gun Parts/Gunsmithing; Law Enforcement; Training & Safety Equipment

Ontario Knife Co./Queen Cutlery Co./Ontario Knife Co., 26 Empire St., P.O. Box 145, Franklinville, NY 14737, P: 800-222-5233, F: 800-299-2618, www.ontarioknife.com
Camping; Custom Manufacturing; Cutlery; Hunting Accessories; Knives/Knife Cases; Law Enforcement; Training & Safety Equipment

Op. Electronics Co., Ltd., 53 Shing-Ping Rd. 5/F, Chungli, 320, TAIWAN, P: 011 88634515131, F: 011 88634615130, www.digi-opto.com
Scopes, Sights & Accessories; Training & Safety Equipment

Opti-Logic Corp., 201 Montclair St., P.O. Box 2002, Tullahoma, TN 37388, P: 888-678-4567, F: 931-455-1229, www.opti-logic.com
Archery; Binoculars; Crossbows & Accessories; Hunting Accessories; Law Enforcement; Scopes, Sights & Accessories

Optisan Corp., Taipei World Trade Center 4B06, 5, Hsin Yi Rd., Section 5, Taipei, 110, TAIWAN, P: 011 8675785799936, F: 011 862081117707

Bags & Equipment Cases; Binoculars; Lighting Products; Photographic Equipment; Scopes, Sights & Accessories; Telescopes

Optolyth/Sill Optics GmbH & Co KG, Johann-Höllfritsch-Straße 13, Wendelstein, 90530, GERMANY, P: 011 499129902352, F: 011 499129902323, www.optolyth.de
Binoculars; Scopes, Sights & Accessories

Original Footwear Co., 4213 Technology Dr., Modesto, CA 95356, P: 888-476-7700, F: 209-545-2739, www.originalswat.com
Footwear; Law Enforcement; Wholesaler/Distributor

Osprey International Inc./AimShot, 25 Hawks Farm Rd., White, GA 30184, P: 888-448-3247, F: 770-387-0114, www.osprey-optics.com
Binoculars; Hunting Accessories; Law Enforcement; Lighting Products; Scopes, Sights & Accessories; Wholesaler/Distributor

Otis Technology, Inc., 6987 Laura St., P.O. Box 582, Lyon Falls, NY 13368, P: 800-OTISGUN, F: 315-348-4332, www.otisgun.com
Black Powder Accessories; Firearms Maintenance Equipment; Gun Parts/Gunsmithing; Hunting Accessories; Lubricants; Paintball Accessories; Scopes, Sights & Accessories; Training & Safety Equipment

Outdoor Research, 2203 First Ave. S, Seattle, WA 98134, P: 888-467-4327, F: 206-467-0374, www.outdoorresearch.com/gov
Gloves, Mitts, Hats; Law Enforcement

Outers Gun Care/ATK Commercial Products, N5549 Cty. Tk. Z, Onalaska, WI 54650, P: 800-635-7656, F: 763-323-3890, www.outers-guncare.com
Firearms Maintenance Equipment; Lubricants

P

PMC/Poongsan, 60-1, Chungmoro - 3ka, Chung-Gu, Seoul 100-705, C.P.O. Box 3537, Seoul, SOUTH KOREA, P: 011 92234065628, F: 011 92234065415, www.pmcammo.com
Ammunition; Law Enforcement

PSC, Pendleton Safe Co., 139 Lee Byrd Rd., Loganville, GA 30052, P: 770-466-6661, F: 678-990-7888
Gun Safes

PSI, LLC, 2 Klarides Village Dr., Suite 336, Seymour, CT 06483, P: 203-262-6484, F: 203-262-6562, www.precisionsalesintl.com
Gun Parts/Gunsmithing; Law Enforcement; Magazines, Cartridge; Scopes, Sights & Accessories

P.S. Products, Inc./Personal Security Products, 414 S. Pulaski St., Suite 1, Little Rock, AR 72201, P: 877-374-7900, F: 501-374-7800, www.psproducts.com
Custom Manufacturing; Export/Import Specialists; Holsters; Law Enforcement; Sports Accessories; Wholesaler/Distributor

Pacific Tool & Gauge, Inc., 598 Avenue C, P.O. Box 2549, White City, OR 97503, P:

541-826-5808, F: 541-826-5304, www.pacifictoolandgauge.com
Black Powder Accessories; Books/Industry Publications; Custom Manufacturing; Firearms Maintenance Equipment; Gun Parts/Gunsmithing; Law Enforcement; Reloading

Para USA, Inc., 10620 Southern Loop Blvd., Charlotte, NC 28134-7381, P: 866-661-1911, www.para-usa.com
Firearms

Parker-Hale, Bedford Rd., Petersfield, Hampshire GU32 3XA, UNITED KINGDOM, P: 011-44 1730268011, F: 011-44 1730260074, www.parker-hale.co.uk
Firearms Maintenance Equipment; Law Enforcement; Lubricants

Parmatech Corp., 2221 Pine View Way, Petaluma, CA 94954, P: 800-709-1555, F: 707-778-2262, www.parmatech.com
Custom Manufacturing; Gun Parts/Gunsmithing

Passport Sports, Inc., 3545 N. Courtenay Pkwy., P.O. Box 540638, Merritt Island, FL 32953, P: 321-459-0005, F: 321-459-3482, www.passport-holsters.com
Bags & Equipment Cases; Custom Manufacturing; Gun Cases; Holsters; Leathergoods

Patriot3, Inc., P.O. Box 278, Quantico, VA 22134, P: 888-288-0911, F: 540-891-5654, www.patriot3.com
Law Enforcement

Patriot Ordnance Factory, 23623 N. 67th Ave., Glendale, AZ 85310, P: 623-561-9572, F: 623-321-1680, www.pof-usa.com
Custom Manufacturing; Firearms; Gun Barrels; Gun Parts/Gunsmithing; Hunting Accessories; Law Enforcement

PBC, 444 Caribbean Dr., Lakeland, FL 33803, P: 954-304-5948, www.pbccutlery.com
Cutlery; Knives/Knife Cases

Peacekeeper International, 2435 Pine St., Pomona, CA 91767, P: 909-596-6699, F: 909-596-8899, www.peacekeeperproducts.com
Holsters; Law Enforcement; Leathergoods; Targets; Training & Safety Equipment

Peak Beam Systems, Inc., 3938 Miller Rd., P.O. Box 1127, Edgemont, PA 19028, P: 610-353-8505, F: 610-353-8411, www.peakbeam.com
Law Enforcement; Lighting Products

Peca Products, Inc., 471 Burton St., Beloit, WI 53511, P: 608-299-1615, F: 608-229-1827, www.pecaproducts.com
Custom Manufacturing; Firearms Maintenance Equipment; Hunting Accessories; Law Enforcement; Photographic Equipment; Scopes, Sights & Accessories; Sports Accessories; Wholesaler/Distributor

Peerless Handcuff Co., 95 State St., Springfield, MA 01103, P: 800-732-3705, F: 413-734-5467, www.peerless.net
Law Enforcement

Peltor, 5457 W. 79th St., Indianapolis, IN 46268, P: 800-327-3431, F: 800-488-8007, www.aosafety.com

Eyewear; Hearing Protection; Shooting Range Equipment; Two-Way Radios

Pentax Imaging Co., 600 12th St., Suite 300, Golden, CO 80401, P: 800-877-0155, F: 303-460-1628, www.pentaxsportoptics.com
Binoculars; Photographic Equipment; Scopes, Sights & Accessories

Perazzi U.S.A., Inc., 1010 W. Tenth St., Azusa, CA 91702, P: 626-334-1234, F: 626-334-0344
Firearms

Perfect Fit, 39 Stetson Rd., Ruite 222, P.O. Box 439, Corinna, ME 04928, P: 800-634-9208, F: 800-222-0417, www.perfectfitusa.com
Custom Manufacturing; Emblems & Decals; Law Enforcement; Leathergoods; Training & Safety Equipment; Wholesaler/ Distibutor

Permalight (Asia) Co., Ltd./Pila Flashlights, 4/F, Waga Commercial Centre, 99 Wellington St., Central HONG KONG, P: 011 85228150616, F: 011 85225423269, www.pilatorch.com
Camping; Firearms; Hunting Accessories; Law Enforcement; Lighting Products; Training & Safety Equipment; Wholesaler/ Distributor

Petzl America, Freeport Center M-7, P.O. Box 160447, Clearfield, UT 84016, P: 877-807-3805, F: 801-926-1501, www.petzl.com
Gloves, Mitts, Hats; Law Enforcement; Lighting Products; Training & Safety Equipment

Phalanx Corp., 4501 N. Dixie Hwy., Boca Raton, FL 33431, P: 954-360-0000, F: 561-417-0500, www.smartholster.com
Gun Locks; Holsters; Law Enforcement; Training & Safety Equipment

Phoebus Tactical Flashlights/Phoebus Manufacturing, 2800 Third St., San Francisco, CA 94107, P: 415-550-0770, F: 415-550-2655, www.phoebus.com
Lighting Products

Photop Suwtech, Inc., 2F, Building 65, 421 Hong Cao Rd., Shanghai, 200233, CHINA, P: 011 862164853978, F: 011 862164850389, www.photoptech.com
Law Enforcement; Lighting Products; Scopes, Sights & Accessories

Pinnacle Ammunition Co., 111 W. Port Plaza, Suite 600, St. Louis, MO 63146, P: 888-702-2660, F: 314-293-1943, www.pinnacleammo.com
Ammunition

PistolCam, Inc., 1512 Front St., Keeseville, NY 12944, P: 518-834-7093, F: 518-834-7061, www.pistolcam.com
Firearms; Gun Parts/Gunsmithing; Law Enforcement; Photographic Equipment; Scopes, Sights & Accessories; Videos

Plymouth Engineered Shapes, 201 Commerce Ct., Hopkinsville, KY 42240, P: 800-718-7590, F: 270-886-6662, www.plymouth.com/engshapes.aspx
Crossbows & Accessories; Firearms; Gun Barrels; Gun Parts/Gunsmithing

Point Blank Body Armor/PACA Body Armor, 2102 SW 2 St., Pompano Beach, FL 33069, P: 800-413-5155, F: 954-414-8118, www.pointblankarmor.com, www.pacabodyarmor.com
Law Enforcement

Point Tech, Inc., 160 Gregg St., Suite 1, Lodi, NJ 07644, P: 201-368-0711, F: 201-368-0133
Firearms; Gun Barrels; Gun Parts/ Gunsmithing

Police and Security News, 1208 Juniper St., Quakertown, PA 18951, P: 215-538-1240, F: 215-538-1208, www.policeandsecuritynews.com
Books/Industry Publications; Law Enforcement

Police Magazine/Police Recruit Magazine, 3520 Challenger St., Torrance, CA 90503, P: 480-367-1101, F: 480-367-1102, www.policemag.com
Books/Industry Publications; Law Enforcement

PoliceOne.com, 200 Green St., Second Floor, San Francisco, CA 94111, P: 800-717-1199, F: 480-854-7079, www.policeone.com
Law Enforcement

Portman Security Systems Ltd., 330 W. Cummings Park, Woburn, MA 01801, P: 781-935-9288, F: 781-935-9188, www.portmansecurity.com
Custom Manufacturing; Firearms Maintenance Equipment; Gun Parts/ Gunsmithing; Law Enforcement; Pet Supplies; Scopes, Sights & Accessories; Vehicles, Utility & Rec

PowerBelt Bullets, 5988 Peachtree Corners E, Norcross, GA 30071, P: 800-320-8767, F: 770-242-8546, www.powerbeltbullets.com
Ammunition; Black Powder Accessories

PowerFlare, 6489 Camden Ave., Suite 108, San Jose, CA 95120, P: 877-256-6907, F: 408-268-5431, www.powerflare.com
Lighting Products; Survival Kits/First Aid; Training & Safety Equipment; Wholesaler/ Distributor

PowerTech, Inc./Smith & Wesson Flashlights, 360 E. South St., Collierville, TN 38017, P: 901-850-9393, F: 901-850-9797, www.powertechinc.com
Camping; Hunting Accessories; Law Enforcement; Lighting Products; Sports Accessories

Practical Air Rifle Training Systems, LLC, P.O. Box 174, Pacific, MO 63069, P: 314-271-8465, F: 636-271-8465, www.smallarms.com
Airguns; Custom Manufacturing; Law Enforcement; Shooting Range Equipment; Targets; Training & Safety Equipment

Precision Ammunition, LLC, 5402 E. Diana St., Tampa, FL 33610, P: 888-393-0694, F: 813-626-0078, www.precisionammo.com
Ammunition; Law Enforcement; Reloading

Precision Metalsmiths, Inc., 1081 E. 200th St., Cleveland, OH 44117, P: 216-481-8900, F: 216-481-8903, www.precisionmetalsmiths.com
Archery; Custom Manufacturing; Firearms; Gun Barrels; Gun Locks; Gun Parts/ Gunsmithing; Knives/Knife Cases; Scopes, Sights & Accessories

Precision Reflex, Inc., 710 Streine Dr., P.O. Box 95, New Bremen, OH 45869, P: 419-629-2603, F: 419-629-2173, www.pri-mounts.com
Custom Manufacturing; Firearms; Gun Barrels; Law Enforcement; Magazines, Cartridge; Scopes, Sights & Accessories

Premier Reticles, 175 Commonwealth Ct., Winchester, VA 22602, P: 540-868-2044, F: 540-868-2045 www.premierreticles.com
Scopes, Sights & Accessories; Telescopes

Premierlight, 35 Revenge Rd., Unit 9, Lordswood, Kent ME5 8DW, UNITED KINGDOM, P: 011-44-1634-201284, F: 011-44-1634-201286, www.premierlight-uk.com
Backpacking; Camping; Hunting Accessories; Law Enforcement; Lighting Products; Sports Accessories; Training & Safety Equipment; Wholesaler/Distributor

Primary Weapons Systems, 800 E. Citation Ct., Suite C, Boise, ID 83716, P: 208-344-5217, F: 208-344-5395, www.primaryweapons.com
Firearms; Firearms Maintenance Equipment; Gun Parts/Gunsmithing; Law Enforcement; Recoil Protection Devices & Services

Primax Hunting Gear Ltd., Rm. 309, 3/F Jiali Mansion, 39-5#, Xingning Rd., Ningbo, Zhejiang 315040, CHINA, P: 011 8657487894016, F: 011 8657487894017, www.primax-hunting.com
Backpacking; Bags & Equipment Cases; Blinds; Camping; Compasses; Gun Cases; Hunting Accessories; Scopes, Sights & Accessories

Princeton Tec, P.O. Box 8057, Trenton, NJ 08650, P: 800-257-9080, FL 609-298-9601, www.princetontec.com
Backpacking; Camping; Cooking Equipment/Accessories; Lighting Products; Photographic Equipment; Sports Accessories; Training & Safety Equipment

Pro-Shot Products, P.O. Box 763, Taylorville, IL 62568, P: 217-824-9133, F: 217-824-8861, www.proshotproducts.com
Black Powder Accessories; Firearms Maintenance Equipment; Lubricants

Pro-Systems Spa, Via al Corbé 63, ITALY, P: 011 390331576887, F: 011 390331576295, www.pro-systems.it, www.pro-systems.us
Law Enforcement

Pro Ears/Benchmaster, 101 Ridgeline Dr., Westcliffe, CO 81252, P: 800-891-3660, F: 719-783-4162, www.pro-ears.com
Crossbows & Accessories; Custom Manufacturing; Hearing Protection; Hunting Accessories; Law Enforcement; Shooting Range Equipment; Sports Accessories; Training & Safety Equipment

Professionals Choice/G&A Investments, Inc., 2615 Fruitland Ave., Vernon, CA 90058, P: 323-589-2775, F: 323-589-3511, www.theprofessionalschoice.net
Firearms Maintenance Equipment; Gun Parts/Gunsmithing; Lubricants; Wholesaler/ Distributor

Proforce Equipment, Inc./Snugpak USA, 2201 NW 102nd Place, Suite 1, Miami,

MANUFACTURER'S DIRECTORY

FL 33172, P: 800-259-5962, F: 800-664-5095, www.proforceequipment.com
Backpacking; Camping; Hunting Accessories; Knives/Knife Cases; Law Enforcement; Men's Clothing; Survival Kits/First Aid; Watches

ProMag Industries, Inc./Archangel Manufacturing, LLC, 10654 S. Garfield Ave., South Gate, CA 90280, P: 800-438-2547, F: 562-861-6377, www.promagindustries.com
Gun Grips & Stocks; Gun Parts/Gunsmithing; Law Enforcement; Magazines, Cartridge; Retail Packaging; Scopes, Sights & Accessories

Promatic, Inc., 7803 W. Hwy. 116, Gower, MO 64454, UNITED KINGDOM, P: 888-767-2529, F: 816-539-0257, www.promatic.biz
Airguns; Clay Targets; Shooting Range Equipment; Targets; Training & Safety Equipment

Propper International Sales, 520 Huber Park Ct., St. Charles, MO 63304, P: 800-296-9690, F: 877-296-9690, www.propper.com
Camouflage; Law Enforcement; Men's Clothing

Protective Products International, 1649 NW 136th Ave., Sunrise, FL 33323, P: 800-509-9111, F: 954-846-0555, www.body-armor.com
Custom Manufacturing; Export/Import Specialists; Law Enforcement; Men & Women's Clothing; Training & Safety Equipment; Vehicles, Utility & Rec

Pyramex Safety Products, 281 Moore Lane, Collierville, TN 38017, P: 800-736-8673, F: 877-797-2639, www.pyramexsafety.com
Eyewear; Hearing Protection; Training & Safety Equipment

Q

Quake Industries, Inc., 732 Cruiser Ln., Belgrade, MT 59714, P: 770-449-4687, F: 406-388-8810, www.quakeinc.com
Archery; Crossbows & Accessories; Custom Manufacturing; Hunting Accessories; Scopes, Sights & Accessories; Sports Accessories; Treestands

Quantico Tactical Supply, 109 N. Main St., Raeford, NC 28376, P: 910-875-1672, F: 910-875-3797, www.quanticotactical.com
Eyewear; Firearms; Footwear; Holsters; Knives/Knife Cases; Law Enforcement; Survival Kits/First Aid

Quiqlite, Inc., 6464 Hollister Ave., Suite 4, Goleta, CA 93117, P: 866-496-2606, F: 800-910-5711, www.quiqlite.com
Backpacking; Camping; Hunting Accessories; Law Enforcement; Lighting Products; Reloading; Training & Safety Equipment

R

R & R Racing, Inc., 45823 Oak St., Lyons, OR 97358, P: 503-551-7283, F: 503-859-4711, www.randrracingonline.com
Custom Manufacturing; Hearing Protection; Shooting Range Equipment; Targets; Training & Safety Equipment; Wholesaler/Distributor

R & W Rope Warehouse, 39 Tarkiln Pl., P.O. Box 50420, New Bedford, MA 02745, P: 800-260-8599, F: 508-995-1114, www.rwrope.com
Backpacking; Camouflage; Camping; Custom Manufacturing; Hunting Accessories; Law Enforcement; Pet Supplies; Training & Safety Equipment

Radians, 7580 Bartlett Corp. Dr., Bartlett, TN 38133, P: 877-723-4267, F: 901-266-2558, www.radiansinc.com
Camouflage; Eyewear; Footwear; Gloves, Mitts, Hats; Hearing Protection; Hunting Accessories; Sports Accessories; Training & Safety Equipment

Raine, Inc., 6401 S. Madison Ave., Anderson, IN 46013, P: 800-826-5354, F: 765-622-7691, www.raineinc.com
Bags & Equipment Cases; Camping; Custom Manufacturing; Holsters; Knives/Knife Cases; Law Enforcement; Two-Way Radios

Rainer Ballistics, 4500 15th St. E, Tacoma, WA 98424, P: 800-638-8722, F: 253-922-7854, www.rainierballistics.com
Ammunition; Reloading; Wholesaler/Distributor

Ram Mounting Systems, 8410 Dallas Ave. S, Seattle, WA 98108, P: 206-763-8361, F: 206-763-9615, www.ram-mount.com
Hunting Accessories; Law Enforcement; Sports Accessories; Vehicles, Utility & Rec

Ramba, Via Giorgio La Pira, 20 Flero (Bs), Brescia 25020, ITALY, P: 011 390302548522, F: 011 390302549749, www.ramba.it
Ammunition; Reloading

Ranch Products, P.O. Box 145, Malinta, OH 43535, P: 419-966-2881, F: 313-565-8536, www.ranchproducts.com
Gun Parts/Gunsmithing; Scopes, Sights & Accessories

Range Systems, 5121 Winnetka Ave. N, Suite 150, New Hope, MN 55428, P: 888-999-1217, F: 763-537-6657, www.range-systems.com
Eyewear; Law Enforcement; Shooting Range Equipment; Targets; Training & Safety Equipment

Rat Cutlery Co., 60 Randall Rd., Gallant, AL 35972, P: 865-933-8436, F: 256-570-0175, www.ratcutlery.com
Backpacking; Camping; Cutlery; Knives/Knife Cases; Law Enforcement; Survival Kits/First Aid; Tours/Travel; Training & Safety Equipment

Rattlers Brand/Boyt Harness Co., One Boyt Dr., Osceola, IA 50213, P: 800-550-2698, F: 641-342-2703, www.rattlersbrand.com
Camouflage; Sports Accessories

Raza Khalid & Co., 14/8, Haji Pura, P.O. Box 1632, Sailkot, Punjab 51310, PAKISTAN, P: 011 92523264232, F: 011 92523254932, www.razakhalid.com
Bags & Equipment Cases; Gloves, Mitts, Hats; Gun Cases; Hunting Accessories; Law Enforcement; Paintball Accessories; Pet Supplies; Shooting Range Equipment

RBR Tactical Armor, Inc., 3113 Aspen Ave., Richmond, VA 23228, P: 800-672-7667, F: 804-726-6027, www.rbrtactical.com
Custom Manufacturing; Law Enforcement

Recknagel, Landwehr 4, Bergrheinfeld, 97493, GERMANY, P: 011 49972184366, F: 011 49972182969, www.recknagel.de
Gun Parts/Gunsmithing; Scopes, Sights & Accessories

Recognition Services, 8577 Zionsville Rd., Indianapolis, IN 46268, P: 877-808-9400, F: 877-808-3565, www.we-belong.com
Custom Manufacturing; Emblems & Decals; Law Enforcement; Outfitter

ReconRobotics, Inc., 770 W. 78th St., Edina, MN 55439, P: 952-935-5515, F: 952-935-5508, www.reconrobotics.com
Law Enforcement

Redding Reloading Equipment, 1089 Starr Rd., Cortland, NY 13045, P: 607-753-3331, F: 607-756-8445, www.redding-reloading.com
Lubricants; Reloading

Redman Training Gear, 10045 102nd Terrace, Sebastian, FL 32958, P: 800-865-7840, F: 800-459-2598, www.redmangear.com
Law Enforcement; Training & Safety Equipment

Remington Arms Co., Inc., 870 Remington Dr., P.O. Box 700, Madison, NC 27025, P: 800-243-9700
Ammunition; Cutlery; Firearms; Footwear; Gun Parts/Gunsmithing; Hunting Accessories

Rescomp Handgun Technologies/CR Speed, P.O. Box 11786, Queenswood, 0186, SOUTH AFRICA, P: 011 27123334768, F: 011 27123332112, www.crspeed.co.za
Bags & Equipment Cases; Custom Manufacturing; Holsters; Law Enforcement; Scopes, Sights & Accessories; Sports Accessories; Wholesaler/Distributor

Revision Eyewear, Ltd., 7 Corporate Dr., Essex Junction, VT 05452, CANADA, P: 802-879-7002, F: 802-879-7224, www.revisionready.com
Eyewear; Hunting Accessories; Law Enforcement; Paintball Accessories; Shooting Range Equipment; Sports Accessories; Training & Safety Equipment

Rich-Mar Sports, North 7125 1280 St., River Falls, WI 54022, P: 952-881-6796, F: 952-884-4878, www.richmarsports.com
Cooking Equipment/Accessories; Hunting Accessories; Law Enforcement; Sports Accessories; Training & Safety Equipment

Ridge Outdoors U.S.A., Inc./Ridge Footwear, P.O. Box 389, Eustis, FL 32727-0389, P: 800-508-2668, F: 866-584-2042, www.ridgeoutdoors.com
Footwear; Law Enforcement; Men & Women's Clothing; Sports Accessories

Ring's Manufacturing, 99 East Dr., Melbourne, FL 32904, P: 800-537-7464, F: 321-951-0017, www.blueguns.com
Custom Manufacturing; Law Enforcement; Training & Safety Equipment

Rio Ammunition, Fountainview, Suite 207, Houston, TX 77057, P: 713-266-3091,

F: 713-266-3092, www.rioammo.com, www.ueec.es
Ammunition; Black Powder/Smokeless Powder; Law Enforcement

Rite In The Rain, 2614 Pacific Hwy. E, Tacoma, WA 98424, P: 253-922-5000, F: 253-922-5300, www.riteintherain.com
Archery; Backpacking; Camping; Custom Manufacturing; Law Enforcement; Printing Services; Sports Accessories; Targets

River Rock Designs, Inc., 900 RR 620 S, Suite C101-223, Austin, TX 78734, P: 512-263-6985, F: 512-263-1277, www.riverrockledlights.com
Backpacking; Camping; Hunting Accessories; Law Enforcement; Lighting Products; Sports Accessories; Training & Safety Equipment

Rivers West/H2P Waterproof System, 2900 4th Ave. S, Seattle, WA 98134, P: 800-683-0887, F: 206-682-8691, www.riverswest.com
Camouflage; Law Enforcement; Men & Women's Clothing

RM Equipment, 6975 NW 43rd St., Miami, FL 33166, P: 305-477-9312, F: 305-477-9620, www.40mm.com
Firearms; Gun Grips & Stocks; Law Enforcement

Rock Creek Barrels, Inc., 101 Ogden Ave., Albany, WI 53502, P: 608-862-2357, F: 608-862-2356, www.rockcreekbarrels.com
Gun Barrels

Rock River Arms, Inc., 1042 Cleveland Rd., Colona, IL 61241, P: 866-980-7625, F: 309-792-5781, www.rockriverarms.com
Custom Manufacturing; Firearms; Gun Barrels; Gun Grips & Stocks; Gun Parts/Gunsmithing; Law Enforcement; Magazines, Cartridge; Scopes, Sights & Accessories

Rohrbaugh Firearms Corp., P.o. Box 785, Bayport, NY 11705, P: 800-803-2233, F: 631-242-3183, www.rohrbaughfirearms.com
Firearms

Rose Garden, The, 1855 Griffin Rd., Suite C370, Dania Beach, FL 33004, P: 954-927-9590, F: 954-927-9591, www.therosegardendb.com
Export/Import Specialists; Home Furnishings; Outdoor Art, Jewelry, Sculpture; Wholesaler/Distributor

Rossi/BrazTech, 16175 NW 49th Ave., Miami, FL 33014, P: 800-948-8029, F: 305-623-7506, www.rossiusa.com
Black Powder Accessories; Firearms

Rothco, 3015 Veterans Memorial Hwy., P.O. Box 1220, Ronkonkoma, NY 11779, P: 800-645-5195, F: 631-585-9447, www.rothco.com
Bags & Equipment Cases; Camouflage; Hunting Accessories; Knives/Knife Cases; Law Enforcement; Men & Women's Clothing; Survival Kits/First Aid; Wholesaler/Distributor

RSR Group, Inc., 4405 Metric Dr., Winter Park, FL 32792, P: 800-541-4867, F: 407-677-4489, www.rsrgroup.com
Airguns; Ammunition; Cutlery; Firearms; Gun Cases; Holsters; Scopes, Sights & Accessories; Wholesaler/Distributor

RTZ Distribution/HallMark Cutlery, 4436B Middlebrook Pike, Knoxville, TN 37921, P: 866-583-3912, F: 865-588-0425, www.hallmarkcutlery.com
Cutlery; Knifes/Knife Cases; Law Enforcement; Sharpeners

RUAG Ammotec, Uttigenstrasse 67, Thun, 3602, SWITZERLAND, P: 011 41332282879, F: 011 41332282644, www.ruag.com
Ammunition; Law Enforcement

Ruger Firearms, 1 Lacey Pl., Southport, CT 06890, P: 203-259-7843, F: 203-256-3367, www.ruger.com
Firearms

Ruko, LLC, P.O. Box 38, Buffalo, NY 14207, P: 716-874-2707, F: 905-826-1353, www.rukoproducts.com
Camping; Compasses; Custom Manufacturing; Cutlery; Export/Import Specialists; Hunting Accessories; Knives/Knife Cases; Sharpeners

Russian American Armory Co., 677 S. Cardinal Ln., Suite A, Scottsburg, IN 47170, P: 877-752-2894, F: 812-752-7683, www.raacfirearms.com
Firearms; Knives/Knife Cases; Magazines, Cartridge

S

S&K Industries, Inc., S. Hwy. 13, Lexington, MO 64067, P: 660-259-4691, F: 660-259-2081, www.sandkgunstocks.com
Custom Manufacturing; Gun Grips & Stocks

Saab Barracuda, LLC, 608 McNeill St., Lillington, NC 27546, P: 910-893-2094, F: 910-893-8807, www.saabgroup.com
Camouflage; Law Enforcement

Sabre Defence Industries, LLC, 450 Allied Dr., Nashville, TN 37211, P: 615-333-0077, F: 615-333-6229, www.sabredefence.com
Firearms; Gun Barrels

Safety Harbor Firearms, Inc., 915 Harbor Lake Dr., Suite D, Safety Harbor, FL 34695, P: 727-725-4700, F: 727-724-1872, www.safetyharborfirearms.com
Firearms

Sage Control Ordnance, Inc./Sage International, Ltd., 3391 E. Eberhardt St., Oscoda, MI 48750, P: 989-739-7000, F: 989-739-7098, www.sageinternationalltd.com
Ammunition; Firearms; Gun Grips & Stocks; Gun Locks; Law Enforcement; Reloading

Salt River Tactical, LLC/Ost-Kraft, LLC, P.O. Box 20397, Mesa, AZ 85277, P: 480-656-2683, www.saltrivertactical.com
Bags & Equipment Cases; Firearms Maintenance Equipment; Hunting Accessories; Law Enforcement; Scopes, Sights & Accessories; Shooting Range Equipment; Wholesaler/Distributor

SAM Medical Products, P.O. Box 3270, Tualatin, OR 97062, P: 800-818-4726, F: 503-639-5425, www.sammedical.com
Backpacking; Camping; Law Enforcement; Outfitter; Shooting Range Equipment; Survival Kits/First Aid; Training & Safety Equipment

Samco Global Arms, Inc., 6995 NW 43rd St., Miami, FL 33166, P: 800-554-1618, F: 305-593-1014, www.samcoglobal.com
Ammunition; Firearms; Sports Accessories

Samson Mfg. Corp., 110 Christian Ln., Whately, MA 01373, P: 888-665-4370, F: 413-665-1163, www.samson-mfg.com
Firearms; Gun Parts/Gunsmithing; Law Enforcement; Scopes, Sights & Accessories

Sandpiper of California, 687 Anita St., Suite A, Chula Vista, CA 91911, P: 866-424-6622, F: 619-423-9599, www.pipergear.com
Backpacking; Bags & Equipment Cases; Camouflage; Custom Manufacturing; Law Enforcement

Sandviper, 1611 Jamestown Rd., Morganton, NC 28655, P: 800-873-7225, F: 828-584-6326
Law Enforcement

Sarsilmaz Silah San. A.S, Nargileci Sokak, No. 4, Sarsilmaz Is Merkezi, Mercan, Eminonu, Istanbul, 34116, TURKEY, P: 011 902125133507, F: 011 902125111999, www.sarsilmaz.com
Firearms

Savage Arms, Inc., 118 Mountain Rd., Suffield, CT 06078, P: 866-233-4776, F: 860-668-2168, www.savagearms.com
Black Powder/Smokeless Powder; Firearms; Knives/Knife Cases; Law Enforcement; Shooting Range Equipment

Savannah Luggage Works, 3428 Hwy. 297 N, Vidalia, GA 30474, P: 800-673-6341, F: 912-537-4492, www.savannahluggage.com
Backpacking; Bags & Equipment Cases; Custom Manufacturing; Holsters; Law Enforcement; Training & Safety Equipment

SBR Ammunition, 1118 Glynn Park Rd., Suite E, Brunswick, GA 31525, P: 912-264-5822, F: 912-264-5888, www.sbrammunition.com
Ammunition; Firearms; Law Enforcement

Scharch Mfg., Inc/Top Brass, 10325 Cty. Rd. 120, Salida, CO 81201, P: 800-836-4683, F: 719-539-3021, www.scharch.com
Ammunition; Magazines, Cartridge; Reloading; Retail Packaging; Shooting Range Equipment

Scherer Supplies, Inc., 205 Four Mile Creek Rd., Tazewell, TN 37879, P: 423-733-2615, F: 423-733-2073
Custom Manufacturing; Magazines, Cartridge; Wholesaler/Distributor

Schmidt & Bender GmbH, Am Grossacker 42, Biebertal, Hessen 35444, GERMANY, P: 011 496409811570, US: 800-468-3450, F: ++49-6409811511, www.schmidt-bender.de, www.schmidtbender.com
Hunting Accessories; Law Enforcement; Scopes, Sights & Accessories; Sports Accessories; Telescopes

Scopecoat by Devtron Diversified, 3001 E. Cholla St., Phoenix, AZ 85028, P: 877-726-7328, F: 602-224-9351, www.scopecoat.com
Scopes, Sights & Accessories

MANUFACTURER'S DIRECTORY

SDG Seber Design Group, Inc. 2438 Cades Way, Vista, CA 92081, P: 760-727-5555, F: 760-727-5551, www.severdesigngroup.com
Camping; Cutlery; Knives/Knife Cases; Law Enforcement

SecuRam Systems, Inc., 350 N. Lantana St., Suite 211, Camarillo, CA 93010, P: 805-388-2058, F: 805-383-1728, www.securamsys.com
Gun Cabinets/Racks/Safes

Secure Firearm Products, 213 S. Main, P.O. Box 177, Carl Junction, MO 64834, P: 800-257-8744, F: 417-649-7278, www.securefirearmproducts.com
Bags & Equipment Cases; Custom Manufacturing; Gun Cases; Shooting Range Equipment; Targets

Secure Vault/Boyt Harness Co., One Boyt Dr., Osceola, IA 50213, P: 800-550-2698, F: 641-342-2703
Gun Cabinets/Racks/Safes

Security Equipment Corp., 747 Sun Park Dr., Fenton, MO 63026, P: 800-325-9568, F: 636-343-1318, www.sabrered.com
Backpacking; Camping; Custom Manufacturing; Law Enforcement; Training & Safety Equipment

Self Defense Supply, Inc., 1819 Firman Dr., Suite 101, Richardson, TX 75081, P: 800-211-4186, F: 942-644-6980, www.selfdefensesupply.com
Airguns; Airsoft; Binoculars; Camping; Crossbows & Accessories; Cutlery; Lighting Products; Wholesaler/Distributor

Sellier & Bellot, USA, Inc., P.O. Box 7307, Shawnee Mission, KS 66207, P: 913-664-5933, F: 913-664-5938, www.sb-usa.com
Ammunition; Law Enforcement

Sentry Group, 900 Linden Ave., Rochester, NY 14625, P: 800-828-1438, F: 585-381-8559, www.sentrysafe.com
Gun Cabinets/Racks/Safes; Home Furnishings; Hunting Accessories; Law Enforcement

Sentry Solutions, Ltd., 5 Souhegan St., P.O. Box 214, Wilton, NH 03086, P: 800-546-8049, F: 603-654-3003, www.sentrysolutions.com
Firearms Maintenance Equipment; Gun Parts/Gunsmithing; Hunting Accessories; Lubricants; Sharpeners; Sports Accessories

Serbu Firearms, Inc., 6001 Johns Rd., Suite 144, Tampa, FL 33634, P: 813-243-8899, F: 813-243-8899, www.serbu.com
Firearms; Law Enforcement

Sharp Shoot R Precision, Inc., P.O. Box 171, Paola, KS 66071, P: 785-883-4444, F: 785-883-2525, www.sharpshootr.com
Black Powder Accessories; Custom Manufacturing; Firearms Maintenance Equipment; Lubricants; Reloading; Sports Accessories

Sheffield Equipment, 4569 Mission Gorge Pl., San Diego, CA 92120, P: 619-280-0278, F: 619-280-0011, www.sheffieldcuttingequip.com
Bags & Equipment Cases; Camouflage; Custom Manufacturing; Holsters; Leathergoods; Men & Women's Clothing

Sheffield Tools/GreatLITE Flashlights, 165 E. 2nd St., P.O. Box 3, Mineola, NY 11501, P: 800-457-0600, F: 516-746-5366, www.sheffield-tools.com
Backpacking; Camping; Cutlery; Hunting Accessories; Knives/Knife Cases; Lighting Products

Shelterlogic, 150 Callender Rd., Watertown, CT 06795, P: 800-932-9344, F: 860-274-9306, www.shelterlogic.com
Camouflage; Camping; Custom Manufacturing; Hunting Accessories; Law Enforcement; Pet Supplies; Sports Accessories

Shenzhen Champion Industry Co., Ltd., Longqin Rd. No. 13, Shahu, Pingshan, Longgang Shenzhen City, GNGD 518118, CHINA, P: 011 8675589785877, F: 011 8675589785875, www.championcase.com
Bags & Equipment Cases; Cutlery; Gun Cabinets/Racks/Safes; Gun Cases; Gun Locks; Gun Parts/Gunsmithing; Home Furnishings; Knives/Knife Cases

Shepherd Enterprises, Inc., P.O. Box 189, Waterloo, NE 68069, P: 402-779-2424, F: 402-779-4010, www.shepherdscopes.com
Scopes, Sights & Accessories

Sherluk Marketing, Law Enforcement & Military, P.O. Box 156, Delta, OH 43615, P: 419-923-8011, F: 419-923-8120, www.sherluk.com
Firearms; Firearms Maintenance Equipment; Gun Grips & Stocks; Gun Parts/Gunsmithing; Law Enforcement; Wholesaler/Distributor

Shirstone Optics/Shinei Group, Inc., Komagome-Spancrete Bldg. 8F, Honkomagome 5-4-7, Bunkyo-Ku, Toyko, 113-0021, JAPAN, P: 011 81339439550, F: 011 81339430695, www.shirstone.com
Binoculars; Firearms; Scopes, Sights & Accessories

Shocknife, Inc., 20 Railway St., Winnipeg, Manitoba R2X 2P9, CANADA, P: 866-353-5055, F: 204-586-2049, www.shocknife.com
Knives/Knife Cases; Law Enforcement; Training & Safety Equipment

Shooter's Choice Gun Care/Ventco, Inc., 15050 Berkshire Industrial Pkwy., Middlefield, OH 44062, P: 440-834-8888, F: 440-834-3388, www.shooters-choice.com
Firearms Maintenance Equipment; Gun Parts/Gunsmithing; Law Enforcement; Lubricants

Shooters Depot, 5526 Leopard St., Corpus Christi, TX 78408, P: 361-299-1299, F: 361-289-9906, www.shootersdepot.com
Firearms; Gun Barrels

Shooters Ridge/ATK Commercial Products, N5549 Cty. Tk. Z, Onalaska, WI 54650, P: 800-635-7656, F: 763-323-3890, www.shootersridge.com
Bags & Equipment Cases; Gun Cabinets/Racks/Safes; Hunting Accessories; Magazines, Cartridge; Sports Accessories

Shooting Chrony, Inc., 2446 Cawthra Rd., Bldg. 1, Suite 10, Mississauga, Ontario L5A 3K6, CANADA, P: 800-385-3161, F: 905-276-6295, www.shootingchrony.com
Archery; Black Powder Accessories; Computer Software; Hunting Accessories; Lighting Products; Reloading; Shooting Range Equipment; Sports Accessories

Shooting Ranges International, Inc./Advanced Interactive Systems, 3885 Rockbottom St., North Las Vegas, NV 89030, P: 702-362-3623, F: 702-310-6978, www.shootingrangeintl.com
Firearms; Law Enforcement; Shooting Range Equipment

Sierra Bullets, 1400 W. Henry St., Sedalia, MO 65301, P: 888-223-3006, F: 660-827-4999, www.sierrabullets.com
Books/Industry Publications; Computer Software; Reloading; Videos

SIG SAUER, 18 Industrial Dr., Exeter, NH 03833, P: 603-772-2302, F: 603-772-9082, www.sigsauer.com
Bags & Equipment Cases; Firearms; Holsters; Knives/Knife Cases; Law Enforcement; Training & Safety Equipment

Sightron, Inc., 100 Jeffrey Way, Suite A, Youngville, NC 27596, P: 800-867-7512, F: 919-556-0157, www.sightron.com
Binoculars; Scopes, Sights & Accessories

Silencio/Jackson Safety, 1859 Bowles Ave., Suite 200, Fenton, MO 63026, P: 800-237-4192, F: 636-717-6820, www.jacksonsafety.com
Eyewear; Hearing Protection; Law Enforcement

Silma SRL, Via I Maggio, 74, Zanano Di Sarezzo, Brescia 25068, ITALY, P: 011 390308900505, F: 011 390308900712, www.silma.net
Firearms

Silver State Armory, LLC, P.O. Box 2902, Pahrump, NV 89041, P: 775-537-1118, F: 775-537-1119
Ammunition; Firearms

Simmons, 9200 Cody St., Overland Park, KS 66214, P: 913-782-3131, F: 913-782-4189
Binoculars; Hunting Accessories; Law Enforcement; Scopes, Sights & Accessories

Simunition Operations, General Dynamics Ordnance & Tactical Systems, 5 Montée des Arsenaux, Le Gardeur, Quebec J5Z 2P4, CANADA, P: 800-465-8255, F: 450-581-0231, www.simunition.com
Ammunition; Gun Barrels; Law Enforcement; Magazines, Cartridge, Training & Safety Equipment

Sinclair International, 2330 Wayne Haven St., Fort Wayne, IN 46803, P: 800-717-8211, F: 260-493-2530, www.sinclairintl.com
Ammunition; Bags & Equipment Cases; Books; Cleaning Products; Reloading; Scopes, Sights & Accessories; Software; Targets, Videos

SISCO, 2835 Ana St., Rancho Dominguez, CA 90221, P: 800-832-5834, F: 310-638-6489, www.honeywellsafes.com
Gun Cabinets/Racks/Safes; Hunting Accessories

SKB Corp., 1607 N. O'Donnell Way, Orange, CA 92867, P: 800-654-5992, F: 714-283-0425, www.skbcases.com
Archery; Bags & Equipment Cases; Gun Cases; Hunting Accessories; Knives/

Knife Cases; Law Enforcement; Sports Accessories

SKB Shotguns, 4441 S. 134th St., Omaha, NE 68137, P: 800-752-2767, P: 402-330-8040, www.skbshotguns.com
Firearms

Smith & Warren, 127 Oakley Ave., White Plains, NY 10601, P: 800-53-BADGE, F: 914-948-1627, www.smithwarren.com
Custom Manufacturing; Law Enforcement

Smith & Wesson, 2100 Roosevelt Ave., Springfield, MA 01104, P: 800-331-0852, F: 413-747-3317, www.smith-wesson.com
Firearms; Law Enforcement

Smith Optics Elite Division, 280 Northwood Way, P.O. Box 2999, Ketchum, ID 83340, P: 208-726-4477, F: 208-727-6598, www.elite.smithoptics.com
Eyewear; Law Enforcement; Shooting Range Equipment; Training & Safety Equipment

Smith Security Safes, Inc., P.O. Box 185, Tontogany, OH 43565, P: 800-521-0335, F: 419-823-1505, www.smithsecuritysafes.com
Gun Cabinets/Racks/Safes

Sniper's Hide.com/Snipers Hide, LLC, 3205 Fenton St., Wheat Ridge, CO 80212, P: 203-530-3301, F: 203-622-7331, www.snipershide.com
Books/Industry Publications; Firearms; Law Enforcement; Online Services; Training & Safety Equipment

Sog Armory, Inc., 11707 S. Sam Houston Pkwy. W, Suite R, Houston, TX 77031, P: 281-568-5685, F: 285-568-9191, www.sogarmory.com
Firearms; Firearms Maintenance Equipment; Gun Barrels; Gun Grips & Stocks; Law Enforcement; Scopes, Sights & Accessories; Wholesaler/Distributor

SOG Specialty Knives, 6521 212th St. SW, Lynnwood, WA 98036, P: 888-405-6433, F: 425-771-7689, www.sogknives.com
Cutlery; Hunting Accessories; Knives/Knife Cases; Law Enforcement

Solkoa, Inc., 3107 W. Colorado Ave., Suite 256, Colorado Springs, CO 80904, P: 719-685-1072, F: 719-623-0067, www.solkoa.com
Bags & Equipment Cases; Compasses; Hunting Accessories; Law Enforcement; Survival Kits/First Aid; Training & Safety Equipment; Wholesaler/Distributor

Sona Enterprises, 7825 Somerset Blvd., Suite D, Paramount, CA 90723, P: 562-633-3002, F: 562-633-3583
Binoculars; Camouflage; Camping; Compasses; Lighting Products; Survival Kits/First Aid; Wholesaler/Distributor

SOTech/Special Operations Technologies, 206 Star of India Ln., Carson, CA 90746, P: 800-615-9007, F: 310-202-0880, www.specopstech.com
Backpacking; Bags & Equipment Cases; Custom Manufacturing; Gun Cases; Holsters; Law Enforcement; Shooting Range Equipment; Survival Kits/First Aid

Source One Distributors, 3125 Fortune Way, Suite 1, Wellington, FL 33414, P:

866-768-4327, F: 561-514-1021, www.buysourceone.com
Bags & Equipment Cases; Binoculars; Eyewear; Firearms; Knives/Knife Cases; Men's Clothing; Scopes, Sights & Accessories; Wholesaler/Distributor

Southern Belle Brass, P.O. Box 36, Memphis, TN 38101, P: 800-478-3016, F: 901-947-1924, www.southernbellebrass.com
Firearms Maintenance Equipment; Holsters; Law Enforcement; Men's Clothing; Paintball Guns; Targets; Training & Safety Equipment; Wholesaler/Distributor

Southern Bloomer Mfg. Co. & Muzzleloader Originals, 1215 Fifth St., P.O. Box 1621, Bristol, TN 37621, P: 800-655-0342, F: 423-878-8761, www.southernbloomer.com
Ammunition; Black Powder Accessories; Firearms Maintenance Equipment; Gun Parts/Gunsmithing; Hunting Accessories; Law Enforcement; Reloading; Shooting Range Equipment

SPA Defense, 3409 NW 9th Ave., Suite 1104, Ft. Lauderdale, FL 33309, P: 954-568-7690, F: 954-630-4159, www.spa-defense.com
Firearms; Law Enforcement; Scopes, Sights & Accessories; Tactical Equipment

Spartan Imports, 213 Lawrence Ave., San Francisco, CA 94080, P: 650-589-5501, F: 650-589-5552, www.spartanimports.com
Airguns; Firearms; Law Enforcement; Paintball Guns; Scopes, Sights & Accessories; Training & Safety Equipment; Wholesaler/Distributor

Spec.-Ops. Brands, 1601 W. 15th St., Monahans, TX 79756, P: 866-773-2677, F: 432-943-5565, www.specopsbrand.com
Bags & Equipment Cases; Custom Manufacturing; Holsters; Knives/Knife Cases; Law Enforcement; Shooting Range Equipment; Sports Accessories; Training & Safety Equipment

Specialty Bar Products Co., 4 N. Shore Center, Suite 110, 106 Isabella St., Pittsburgh, PA 15212, P: 412-322-2747, F: 412-322-1912, www.specialty-bar.com
Firearms; Gun Barrels; Gun Parts/Gunsmithing

Specter Gear, Inc., 1107 E. Douglas Ave., Visalia, CA 93292, P: 800-987-3605, F: 559-553-8835, www.spectergear.com
Bags & Equipment Cases; Gun Cases; Holsters; Law Enforcement

Speer Ammunition/ATK Commercial Products, 2299 Snake River Ave., Lewiston, ID 83501, P: 800-256-8685, F: 208-746-3904, www.speer-bullets.com
Ammunition; Reloading

Spiewak/Timberland Pro Valor, 463 Seventh Ave., 11th Floor, New York, NY 10018, P: 800-223-6850, F: 212-629-4803, www.spiewak.com
Footwear; Law Enforcement

Spitfire, Ltd., 8868 Research Blvd., Suite 203, Austin, TX 78758, P: 800-774-8347, F: 512-453-7504, www.spitfire.us

Backpacking; Camping; Sporting Range Equipment; Sports Accessories; Training & Safety Equipment

SportEAR/HarrisQuest Outdoor Products, 528 E. 800 N, Orem, UT 84097, P: 800-530-0090, F: 801-224-5660, www.harrisquest.com
Clay Targets; Hearing Protection; Hunting Accessories; Law Enforcement; Scopes, Sights & Accessories; Shooting Range Equipment; Sports Accessories; Training & Safety Equipment

Sporting Supplies International, Inc.®, P.O. Box 757, Placentia, CA 92871, P: 888-757-WOLF (9653), F: 714-632-9232, www.wolfammo.com
Ammunition

Sports South, LLC, 1039 Kay Ln., P.O. Box 51367, Shreveport, LA 71115, 800-388-3845, www.internetguncatalog.com
Ammunition; Binoculars; Black Powder Accessories; Firearms; Hunting Accessories; Reloading; Scopes, Sights & Accessories; Wholesaler/Distributor

Springboard Engineering, 6520 Platt Ave., Suite 818, West Hills, CA 91307, P: 818-346-4647, F: 818-346-4647
Backpacking; Law Enforcement; Lighting Products; Sports Accessories; Survival Kits/First Aid; Training & Safety Equipment; Wholesaler/Distributor

Springfield Armory, 420 W. Main St., Geneseo, IL 61254, P: 800-680-6866, F: 309-944-3676, www.springfield-armory.com
Firearms

Spyderco, Inc., 820 Spyderco Way, Golden, CO 80403, P: 800-525-7770, F: 303-278-2229, www.spyderco.com
Knives/Knife Cases

SRT Supply, 4450 60th Ave. N, St. Petersburg, FL 33714, P: 727-526-5451, F: 727-527-6893, www.srtsupply.com
Ammunition; Export/Import Specialists; Firearms; Law Enforcement; Wholesaler/Distributor

Stack-On Products Co., 1360 N. Old Rand Rd., P.O. Box 489, Wauconda, IL 60084, P: 800-323-9601, F: 847-526-6599, www.stack-on.com
Bags & Equipment Cases; Gun Cabinets/Racks/Safes; Gun Cases; Hunting Accessories; Shooting Range Equipment; Sports Accessories; Training & Safety Equipment

Stag Arms, 515 John Downey Dr., New Britain, CT 06051, P: 860-229-9994, F: 860-229-3738, www.stagarms.com
Firearms; Law Enforcement

Stallion Leather/Helios Systems, 1104 Carroll Ave., South Milwaukee, WI 53172, P: 414-764-7126, F: 414-764-2878, www.helios-sys.com
Bags & Equipment Cases; Holsters; Knives/Knife Cases; Law Enforcement; Leathergoods; Sports Accessories

Stansport, 2801 E. 12th St., Los Angeles, CA 90023, P: 800-421-6131, F: 323-269-2761, www.stansport.com
Backpacking; Bags & Equipment Cases; Camping; Compasses; Cooking Equipment/Accessories; Hunting

MANUFACTURER'S DIRECTORY

Accessories; Lighting Products; Survival Kits/First Aid

Stark Equipment Corp., 55 S. Commercial St., 4th Floor, Manchester, NH 03101, P: 603-556-7772, F: 603-556-7344, www.starkequipment.com
Gun Grips & Stocks; Hunting Accessories; Law Enforcement

Starlight Cases™, 2180 Hwy. 70-A E, Pine Level, NC 27568, P: 877-782-7544, F: 919-965-9177, www.starlightcases.com
Bags & Equipment Cases; Custom Manufacturing; Gun Cabinets/Racks/ Safes; Gun Cases; Hunting Accessories; Law Enforcement; Scopes, Sights & Accessories; Shooting Range Equipment

Steiner Binoculars, 97 Foster Rd., Suite 5, Moorestown, NJ 08057, P: 800-257-7742, F: 856-866-8615, www.steiner-binoculars.com
Binoculars

SteriPEN/Hydro-Photon, Inc., 262 Ellsworth Rd., Blue Hill, ME 04614, P: 888-783-7473, F: 207-374-5100, www.steripen.com
Backpacking; Camping; Cooking Equipment/Accessories; Law Enforcement; Sports Accessories; Survival Kits/First Aid; Training & Safety Equipment

Sterling Sharpener, P.O. Box 620547, Woodside, CA 94062, P: 800-297-4277, F: 650-851-1434, www.sterlingsharpener.com
Backpacking; Camping; Cooking Equipment/Accessories; Hunting Accessories; Knives/Knife Cases; Law Enforcement; Sharpeners; Survival Kits/ First Aid

Stewart EFI, LLC, 45 Old Waterbury Rd., Thomaston, CT 06787, P: 800-228-2509, F: 860-283-3174, www.stewartefi.com
Ammunition; Backpacking; Custom Manufacturing; Firearms Hearing Protection; Law Enforcement; Lighting Products; Magazines, Cartridge

Steyr Arms, Inc., P.O. Box 840, Trussville, GA 35173, P: 205-467-6544, F: 205-467-3015, www.steyrarms.com
Firearms; Law Enforcement

STI International, 114 Halmar Cove, Georgetown, TX 78628, P: 512-819-0656, F: 512-819-0465, www.stiguns.com
Firearms; Gun Barrels; Gun Parts/ Gunsmithing

Stil Crin SNC, Via Per Gottolengo, 12A, Pavone Mella, Brescia 25020, ITALY, P: 011-390309599496, F: 011-390309959544, www.stilcrin.it
Firearms Maintenance Equipment; Gun Cases; Gun Locks; Lubricants

Strangler Chokes, Inc., 7958 US Hwy. 167 S, Winnfield, LA 71483, P: 318-201-3474, F: 318-473-0982
Custom Manufacturing; Firearms; Gun Barrels; Gun Parts/Gunsmithing; Hunting Accessories; Scopes, Sights & Accessories

Streamlight, Inc., 30 Eagleville Rd., Eagleville, PA 19403, P: 800-523-7488, F: 800-220-7007, www.streamlight.com
Hunting Accessories; Law Enforcement; Lighting Products; Training & Safety Equipment

Streamworks, Inc., 3233 Lance Dr., Suite B, Stockton, CA 92505, P: 209-337-3307, F: 209-337-3342, www.hattail.com
Hearing Protection

Streetwise Security Products/Cutting Edge Products, Inc., 235-F Forlines Rd., Winterville, NC 28590, P: 800-497-0539, F: 252-830-5542, www.streetwisesecurity.net
Law Enforcement

Strider Knives, Inc., 120 N. Pacific St., Suite L7, San Marcos, CA 92069, P: 760-471-8275, F: 503-218-7069, www.striderknives.com
Backpacking; Custom Manufacturing; Cutlery; Hunting Accessories; Knives/Knife Cases; Law Enforcement; Training & Safety Equipment

Strike-Hold/MPH System Specialties, Inc., P.O. Box 1923, Dawsonville, GA 30534, P: 866-331-0572, F: 325-204-2550, www.strikehold.com
Black Powder Accessories; Export/Import Specialists; Firearms Maintenance Equipment; Hunting Accessories; Law Enforcement; Lubricants; Paintball Accessories; Wholesaler/Distributor

Strong Leather Co., 39 Grove St., P.O. Box 1195, Gloucester, MA 01930, P: 800-225-0724, F: 866-316-3666, www.strongbadgecase.com
Bags & Equipment Cases; Holsters; Law Enforcement; Leathergoods

Sturm, 430 S. Erwin St., Cartersville, GA 30120, P: 800-441-7367, F: 770-386-6654, www.sturm-miltec.com
Camouflage; Camping; Firearms; Gun Grips & Stocks; Magazines, Cartridge; Men's Clothing; Scopes, Sights & Accessories

Sun Optics USA, 1312 S. Briar Oaks Rd., Cleburne, TX 76031, P: 817-447-9047, F: 817-717-8461
Binoculars; Custom Manufacturer; Gun Parts/Gunsmithing; Hunting Accessories; Scopes, Sights & Accessories

Sunbuster/Gustbuster, 1966-B Broadhollow Rd., Farmingdale, NY 11735, P: 888-487-8287, F: 631-777-4320, www.sunbuster.info
Clay Targets; Custom Manufacturing; Eyewear; Hunting Accessories; Law Enforcement; Shooting Range Equipment; Sports Accessories; Wholesaler/Distributor

Sun Devil Manufacturing, 663 West 2nd Ave. Suite 16 Mesa, AZ 85210, P: 480-833-9876, F: 480-833-9509, www.sundevilmfg.com
Firearms, Accessories, Receivers

Sunlite Science & Technology, Inc., 345 N. Iowa St., Lawrence, KS 66044, P: 785-832-8818, F: 913-273-1888, www.powerledlighting.com
Camping; Hunting Accessories; Law Enforcement; Lighting Products; Sports Accessories; Survival Kits/First Aid; Tours/ Travel; Training & Safety Equipment

Sunny Hill Enterprises, Inc., W. 1015 Cty. HHH, Chilton, WI 53014, P: 920-898-4707, F: 920-898-4749, www.sunny-hill.com

Custom Manufacturing; Firearms; Gun Barrels; Gun Parts/Gunsmithing; Law Enforcement; Magazines, Cartridge

Super Seer Corp., P.O. Box 700, Evergreen, CO 80437, P: 800-645-1285, F: 303-674-8540, www.superseer.com
Law Enforcement

Super Six Classic, LLC, 635 Hilltop Trail W, Fort Atkinson, WI 53538, P: 920-568-8299, F: 920-568-8259
Firearms

Superior Arms. 836 Weaver Blvd., Wapello, IA 52653, P: 319-523-2016, F: 319-527-0188, www.superiorarms.com
Firearms

Superior Concepts, Inc., 10791 Oak St., P.O. Box 465, Donald, OR 97020, P: 503-922-0488, F: 503-922-2236, www.laserstock.com
Gun Grips & Stocks; Gun Parts/ Gunsmithing; Hunting Accessories; Magazines, Cartridge; Scopes, Sights & Accessories

Sure Site, Inc., 351 Dion St., P.O. Box 335, Emmett, ID 83617, P: 800-627-1576, F: 208-365-6944, www.suresiteinc.com
Shooting Range Equipment; Targets

SureFire, LLC, 18300 Mount Baldy Circle, Fountain Valley, CA 92708, P: 800-828-8809, F: 714-545-9537, www.surefire.com
Knives/Knife Cases; Lighting Products; Scopes, Sights & Accessories

Surgeon Rifles, 48955 Moccasin Trail Rd., Prague, OK 74864, P: 405-567-0183, F: 405-567-0250, www.surgeonrifles.com
Firearms; Gun Parts/Gunsmithing; Law Enforcement

Survival Armor, Inc., 13881 Plantation Rd., International Center I, Suite 8, Ft. Myers, FL 33912, P: 866-868-5001, F: 239-210-0898, www.survivalarmor.com
Law Enforcement; Training & Safety Equipment

Survival Corps, Ltd., Ostashkovskoe Shosse, house 48a, Borodino, Moscow Obl, Mitishinski Region, 141031, RUSSIAN FEDERATION, P: 011 74952257985, F: 011 74952257986, www.survivalcorps.ru
Bags & Equipment Cases; Camouflage; Holsters; Law Enforcement; Outfitter

Swarovski Optik North America, 2 Slater Rd., Cranston, RI 02920, P: 800-426-3089, F: 401-734-5888, www.swarovskioptik.com
Bags & Equipment Cases; Binoculars; Knives/Knife Cases; Scopes, Sights & Accessories; Telescopes; Wholesaler/ Distributor

SWAT Magazine, 5011 N. Ocean Blvd., Suite 5, Ocean Ridge, FL 33435, P: 800-665-7928, F: 561-276-0895, www.swatmag.com
Books/Industry Publications; Law Enforcement; Online Services; Retailer Services; Training & Safety Equipment

Swift Bullet Co., 201 Main St., P.O. Box 27, Quinter, KS 67752, P: 785-754-3959, F: 785-754-2359, www.swiftbullets.com
Ammunition

Switch Pack, LLC, 302 NW 4th St., Grants Pass, OR 97526, P: 541-479-3919, F: 541-474-4573
Backpacking; Blinds; Hunting Accessories; Retailer Services; Sports Accessories; Wholesaler/Distributor

SWR Manufacturing, LLC, P.O. Box 841, Pickens, SC 29671, P: 864-850-3579, F: 864-751-2823, www.swrmfg.com
Firearms; Hearing Protection; Law Enforcement; Recoil Protection Devices & Services; Training & Safety Equipment

Systema Co., 5542 S. Integrity Ln., Fort Mohave, AZ 86426, P: 877-884-0909, F: 267-222-4787, www.systema-engineering.com
Airguns; Airsoft; Law Enforcement; Training & Safety Equipment

Szco Supplies, Inc., 2713 Merchant Dr., P.O. Box 6353, Baltimore, MD 21230, P: 800-232-6998, F: 410-368-9366, www.szco.com
Camping; Custom Manufacturing; Cutlery; Hunting Accessories; Knives/Knife Cases; Pet Supplies; Sharpeners; Wholesaler/Distributor

T

T.Z. Case, 1786 Curtiss Ct., La Verne, CA 91750, P: 888-892-2737, F: 909-392-8406, www.tzcase.com
Airguns; Archery; Custom Manufacturing; Firearms; Gun Cases; Hunting Accessories

Tac Force, 8653 Garvey Ave., Suite 202, Rosemead, CA 91733, P: 626-453-8377, F: 626-453-8378, www.tac-force.com
Backpacking; Bags & Equipment Cases; Gloves, Mitts, Hats; Gun Cases; Holsters; Law Enforcement; Paintball Accessories

Tac Wear, Inc., 700 Progress Ave., Suite 7, Toronto, Ontario M1H 2Z7, CANADA, P: 866-TAC-WEAR, F: 416-289-1522, www.tacwear.com
Gloves, Mitts, Hats; Hunting Accessories; Law Enforcement; Men & Women's Clothing; Sports Accessories; Training & Safety Equipment

Tactical & Survival Specialties, Inc. (TSSI), 3900 Early Rd., P.O. Box 1890, Harrisonburg, VA 22801, P: 877-535-8774, F: 540-434-7796, www.tacsurv.com
Bags & Equipment Cases; Custom Manufacturing; Knives/Knife Cases; Law Enforcement; Men & Women's Clothing; Survival Kits/First Aid; Training & Safety Equipment; Wholesaler/Distributor

Tactical Assault Gear (TAG), 1330 30th St., Suite A, San Diego, CA 92154, P: 888-899-1199, F: 619-628-0126, www.tacticalassaultgear.com
Bags & Equipment Cases; Holsters; Men's Clothing

Tactical Command Industries, Inc., 2101 W. Tenth St., Suite G, Antioch, CA 94509, P: 888-990-1600, F: 925-756-7977, www.tacticalcommand.com
Custom Manufacturing; Hearing Protection; Law Enforcement; Training & Safety Equipment; Two-Way Radios

Tactical Innovations, Inc., 345 Sunrise Rd., Bonners Ferry, ID 83805, P: 208-267-

1585, F: 208-267-1597, www.tacticalinc.com
Firearms; Gun Barrels; Gun Grips & Stocks; Holsters; Law Enforcement; Magazines, Cartridge; Wholesaler/Distributor

Tactical Link, 23175 224th Place SE, Suite E, Maple Valley, WA 98038, P: 866-747-2522, F: 425-433-2522, www.tactcallink.com,
Firearms; Slings, Sets and Moounts

Tactical Medical Solutions, Inc., 614 Pinehollow Dr., Anderson, SC 29621, P: 888-TACMED1, F: 864-224-0064
Law Enforcement; Survival Kits/First Aid; Training & Safety Equipment

Tactical Operations Products, 20972 SW Meadow Way, Tualatin, OR 97062, P: 503-638-9873, F: 503-638-0524, www.tacoproducts.com
Airsoft; Backpacking; Bags & Equipment Cases; Camping; Law Enforcement; Lighting Products; Paintball Accessories

Tactical Products Group, Inc., 755 NW 17th Ave., Suite 108, Delray Beach, FL 33445, P: 866-9-TACPRO, F: 561-265-4061, www.tacprogroup.com
Export/Import Specialists; Footwear; Gun Cases; Holsters; Knives/Knife Cases; Law Enforcement; Men's Clothing; Wholesaler/Distributor

Tactical Rifles, 19250 Hwy. 301, Dade City, FL 33523, P: 352-999-0599, F: 352-567-9825, www.tacticalrifles.net
Firearms

Tactical Solutions, 2181 Commerce Ave., Boise, ID 83705, P: 866-333-9901, F: 208-333-9909, www.tacticalsol.com
Firearms; Gun Barrels; Gun Grips & Stocks; Gun Parts/Gunsmithing; Scopes, Sights & Accessories; Wholesaler/Distributor

TacticalTECH1, 251 Beulah Church Rd., Carrollton, GA 30117, P: 800-334-3368, F: 770-832-1676
Bags & Equipment Cases; Eyewear; Law Enforcement; Lighting Products; Training & Safety Equipment

Tagua Gun Leather, 3750 NW 28th St., Miami, FL 33142, P: 866-678-2482, F: 866-678-2482, www.taguagunleather.com
Firearms; Holsters; Hunting Accessories; Law Enforcement; Leathergoods; Wholesaler/Distributor

Talley Manufacturing, Inc., 9183 Old Number Six Hwy., P.O. Box 369, Santee, SC 29142, P: 803-854-5700, F: 803-854-9315, www.talleyrings.com
Black Powder Accessories; Custom Manufacturing; Gun Parts/Gunsmithing; Hunting Accessories; Scopes, Sights & Accessories; Sports Accessories

Tandy Brands Outdoors, 107 W. Gonzales St., Yoakum, TX 77995, P: 800-331-9092, F: 361-293-9127, www.tandybrands.com
Bags & Equipment Cases; Custom Manufacturing; Hunting Accessories; Knives/Knife Cases; Leathergoods; Shooting Range Equipment; Sports Accessories

TangoDown, Inc., 1588 Arrow Hwy., Unit F, La Verne, CA 91750-5334, P: 909-392-4757, F: 909-392-4802, www.tangodown.com

Gun Grips & Stocks; Law Enforcement; Lighting Products; Magazines, Cartridge; Scopes, Sights & Accessories; Targets

TAPCO, Inc.,3615 Kennesaw N. Industrial Pkwy., P.O. Box 2408, Kennesaw, GA 30156-9138, P: 800-554-1445, F: 800-226-1662, www.tapco.com
Custom Manufacturing; Firearms Maintenance Equipment; Gun Grips & Stocks; Gun Parts/Gunsmithing; Law Enforcement; Magazines, Cartridge; Recoil Protection Devices & Services; Wholesaler/Distributor

Target Shooting, Inc., 1110 First Ave. SE, Watertown, SD 57201, P: 800-611-2164, F: 605-882-8840, www.targetshooting.com
Scopes, Sights & Accessories; Shooting Range Equipment

Tasco/Bushnell Outdoor Products, 9400 Cody, Overland Park, KS 66214, P: 800-221-9035, F: 800-548-0446, www.tasco.com
Binoculars; Scopes, Sights & Accessories; Telescopes

Taser International, 1700 N. 85th St., Scottsdale, AZ 85255, P: 800-978-2737, F: 480-991-0791, www.taser.com
Law Enforcement

Task Holsters, 2520 SW 22nd St., Suite 2-186, Miami, FL 33145, P: 305-335-8647, F: 305-858-9618, www.taskholsters.com
Bags & Equipment Cases; Export/Import Specialists; Gun Cases; Holsters; Hunting Accessories; Law Enforcement; Leathergoods; Wholesaler/Distributor

Taurus International Manufacturing, Inc., 16175 NW 49th Ave., Miami, FL 33014, P: 800-327-3776, F: 305-623-7506, www.taurususa.com
Firearms

Taylor Brands, LLC/Imperial Schrade & Smith & Wesson Cutting Tools, 1043 Fordtown Rd., Kingsport, TN 37663, P: 800-251-0254, F: 423-247-5371, www.taylorbrandsllc.com
Backpacking; Camping; Cutlery; Hunting Accessories; Knives/Knife Cases; Law Enforcement

Taylor's & Co., Inc., 304 Lenoir Dr., Winchester, VA 22603, P: 800-655-5814, F: 540-722-2018, www.taylorsfirearms.com
Black Powder Accessories; Firearms; Firearms Maintenance Equipment; Gun Parts/Gunsmithing; Wholesaler/Distributor

Team SD/TSD Sports, 901 S. Fremont Ave., Suite 218, Alhambra, CA 91803, P: 626-281-0979, F: 626-281-0323, www.airsoftsd.com
Airguns; Airsoft; Paintball Guns & Accessories; Scopes, Sights & Accessories; Sports Accessories; Training & Safety Equipment; Wholesaler/Distributor

Team Wendy, 17000 St. Clair Ave., Bldg. 1, Cleveland, OH 44110, P: 877-700-5544, F: 216-738-2510, www.teamwendy.com
Custom Manufacturing; Hunting Accessories; Law Enforcement; Sports Accessories; Training & Safety Equipment

TEARepair, Inc., 2200 Knight Rd., Bldg. 2, P.O. Box 1879, Land O'Lakes, FL 34639,

P: 800-937-3716, F: 813-996-4523, www.tear-aid.com
Camping; Hunting Accessories; Retail Packaging; Sports Accessories; Survival Kits/First Aid; Wholesaler/Distributor

Technoframes, Via Aldo Moro 6, Scanzorosciate Bergamo, 24020, ITALY, P: 866-246-1095, F: 011 39035668328, www.technoframes.com
Ammunition; Bags & Equipment Cases; Gun Cases; Hunting Accessories; Magazines, Cartridge; Reloading; Shooting Range Equipment

Teijin Aramid USA, Inc., 801-F Blacklawn Rd., Conyers, GA 30012, P: 800-451-6586, F: 770-929-8138, www.teijinaramid.com
Law Enforcement

Television Equipment Associates, Inc., 16 Mount Ebo Rd. S, P.O. Box 404, Brewster, NY 10509, P: 310-457-7401, F: 310-457-0023, www.swatheadsets.com
Law Enforcement

Temco Communications, Inc., 13 Chipping Campden Dr., South Barrington, IL 60010, P: 847-359-3277, F: 847-359-3743, www.temcom.net
Hearing Protection; Law Enforcement; Two-Way Radios

Ten-X Ammunition, Inc., 5650 Arrow Hwy., Montclair, CA 91763, P: 909-605-1617, F: 909-605-2844, www.tenxammo.com
Ammunition; Custom Manufacturing; Law Enforcement; Reloading; Training & Safety Equipment; Wholesaler/Distributor

Teton Grill Co., 865 Xenium Lane N, Plymouth, MN 55441, P: 877-838-6643, F: 763-249-6385, www.tetongrills.com
Cooking Equipment/Accessories; Custom Manufacturing; Cutlery; Knives/Knife Cases

Tetra® Gun Care, 8 Vreeland Rd., Florham Park, NJ 07932, P: 973-443-0004, F: 973-443-0263, www.tetraguncare.com
Firearms Maintenance Equipment; Gun Parts/Gunsmithing; Lubricants

Texas Hunt Co., P.O. Box 10, Monahans, TX 79756, P: 888-894-8682, F: 432-943-5565, www.texashuntco.com
Bags & Equipment Cases; Hunting Accessories; Knives/Knife Cases; Vehicles, Utility & Rec; Wholesaler/Distributor

Texsport, P.O. Box 55326, Houston, TX 77255, P: 800-231-1402, F: 713-468-1535, www.texsport.com
Backpacking; Bags & Equipment Cases; Camouflage; Camping; Compasses; Cooking Equipment/Accessories; Lighting Products; Wholesaler/Distributor

Thermacell/The Schawbel Corp., 100 Crosby Dr., Suite 102, Bedford, MA 01730, P: 866-753-3837, F: 781-541-6007, www.thermacell.com
Archery; Backpacking; Camouflage; Camping; Crossbows & Accessories; Holsters; Hunting Accessories; Scents & Lures

Thermore, 6124 Shady Lane SE, Olympia, WA 98503, P: 800-871-6563, www.thermore.com
Gloves, Mitts, Hats; Men & Women's Clothing; Pet Supplies

Thompson/Center Arms, A Smith & Wesson Co., P.O. Box 5002, Rochester, NH

01104, P: 603-332-2333, F: 603-332-5133, www.tcarms.com
Black Powder Accessories; Black Powder/Smokeless Powder; Firearms; Gun Barrels; Hunting Accessories

Thunderbolt Customs, Inc., 7296 S. Section Line Rd., Delaware, OH 43015, P: 740-917-9135, www.thunderboltcustoms.com
Backpacking; Black Powder Accessories; Camping; Firearms; Hunting Accessories; Pet Supplies; Scopes, Sights & Accessories; Shooting Range Accessories

Tiberius Arms, 2717 W. Ferguson Rd., Fort Wayne, IN 46809, P: 888-982-2842, F: 260-572-2210, www.tiberiusarms.com
Airguns; Law Enforcement; Paintball Guns & Accessories; Training & Safety Equipment

Tiger-Vac, Inc., 73 SW 12 Ave., Bldg. 1, Suite 7, Dania, FL 33004, P: 800-668-4437, F: 954-925-3626, www.tiger-vac.com
Shooting Range Equipment; Training & Safety Equipment

Timney Manufacturing, Inc., 3940 W. Clarendon Ave., Phoenix, AZ 85019, P: 866-4TIMNEY, F: 602-241-0361, www.timneytriggers.com
Firearms Maintenance Equipment; Gun Locks; Gun Parts/Gunsmithing

Tinks, 10157 Industrial Dr., Covington, GA 30014, P: 800-624-5988, F: 678-342-9973, www.tinks69.com
Archery; Hunting Accessories; Scents & Lures; Videos

Tisas-Trabzon Gun Industry Corp., Degol Cad. No: 13-1 Tandogan Ankara, 06580, TURKEY, P: 011 903122137509, F: 011 903122138570, www.trabzonsilah.com
Firearms; Gun Barrels

TMB Designs, Unit 11, Highgrove Farm Ind Est Pinvin, Pershore, Worchestershire WR10 2LF, UNITED KINGDOM, P: 011 441905840022, F: 011 441905850022, www.cartridgedisplays.com
Ammunition; Custom Manufacturing; Emblems & Decals; Hunting Accessories; Outdoor Art, Jewelry, Sculpture; Sports Accessories

Toadbak, Inc., P.O. Box 18097, Knoxville, TN 37928-8097, P: 865-548-1283
Camouflage; Men's Clothing

Tony's Custom Uppers & Parts, P.O. Box 252, Delta, OH 43515, P: 419-822-9578, F: 419-822-9578
Custom Manufacturing; Gun Barrels; Gun Parts/Gunsmithing; Wholesaler/Distributor

Tool Logic, Inc., 2290 Eastman Ave., Suite 109, Ventura, CA 93003, P: 800-483-8422, F: 805-339-9712, www.toollogic.com
Backpacking; Compasses; Cutlery; Knives/Knife Cases; Lighting Products; Sports Accessories; Survival Kits/First Aid

TOPS Knives, P.O. Box 2544, Idaho Falls, ID 82403, P: 208-542-0113, F: 208-552-2945, www.topsknives.com
Backpacking; Custom Manufacturing; Hunting Accessories; Knives/Knife Cases; Law Enforcement; Leathergoods; Men's Clothing; Survival Kits/First Aid

Torel, 107 W. Gonzales St., Yoakum, TX 77995, P: 800-331-9092, F: 361-293-9127, www.tandybrands.com
Bags & Equipment Cases; Custom Manufacturing; Hunting Accessories; Knives/Knife Cases; Leathergoods; Shooting Range Equipment; Sports Accessories

Torrey Pines Logic, Inc., 12651 High Bluff Dr., Suite 100, San Diego, CA 92130, P: 858-755-4549, F: 858-350-0007, www.tplogic.com
Binoculars; Law Enforcement; Scopes, Sights & Accessories; Telescopes

Traditions Performance Firearms, 1375 Boston Post Rd., P.O. Box 776, Old Saybrook, CT 06475-0776, P: 800-526-9556, F: 860-388-4657, www.traditionsfirearms.com
Black Powder Accessories; Firearms; Hunting Accessories; Scopes, Sights & Accessories

Transarms Handels GmbH & Co. KG, 6 Im Winkel, Worms, Rheinland Pfalz 67547, GERMANY, P: 011 490624197770, F: 011 4906241977777
Ammunition; Export/Import Specialists; Firearms; Firearms Maintenance Equipment; Gun Barrels; Gun Parts/Gunsmithing; Law Enforcement; Magazines, Cartridge

Traser H3 Watches, 2930 Domingo Ave., Suite 159, Berkeley, CA 94705, P: 510-479-7523, F: 510-479-7532, www.traserusa.com
Custom Manufacturing; Export/Import Specialists; Law Enforcement; Lighting Products; Men's Clothing; Training & Safety Equipment; Wholesaler/Distributor

Trijicon, Inc., 49385 Shafer Ave., P.O. Box 930059, Wixom, MI 48393, P: 800-338-0563, F: 248-960-7725, www.trijicon.com
Scopes, Sights & Accessories

Triple K Manufacturing Co., Inc., 2222 Commercial St., San Diego, CA 92113, P: 800-521-5062, F: 877-486-6247, www.triplek.com
Black Powder Accessories; Gun Parts/Gunsmithing; Holsters; Hunting Accessories; Leathergoods; Magazines, Cartridge; Pet Supplies

Tristar Sporting Arms, Ltd., 1816 Linn St., North Kansas City, MO 64116, P: 816-421-1400, F: 816-421-4182, www.tristarsporting.com
Export/Import Specialists; Firearms

Troy Industries, Inc., 128 Myron St., West Springfield, MA 01089, P: 866-788-6412, F: 413-383-0339, www.troyind.com
Firearms; Gun Grips & Stocks; Gun Parts/Gunsmithing; Law Enforcement; Scopes, Sights & Accessories

TruckVault, Inc., 211 Township St., P.O. Box 734, Sedro Woolley, WA 98284, P: 800-967-8107, F: 800-621-4287, www.truckvault.com
Custom Manufacturing; Gun Cabinets/Racks/Safes; Hunting Accessories; Law Enforcement; Pet Supplies; Sports Accessories; Training & Safety Equipment

True North Tactical, 500 N. Birdneck Rd., Suite 200, Virginia Beach, VA 23451, P:

800-TNT-1478, F: 757-491-9652, www.
truenorthtactical.com
Backpacking; Bags & Equipment Cases; Gun Cases; Holsters; Law Enforcement; Wholesaler/Distributor

TrueTimber Outdoors, 150 Accurate Way, Inman, SC 29349, P: 864-472-1720, F: 864-472-1834, www.truetimber.com
Bags & Equipment Cases; Blinds; Camouflage; Footwear; Gloves, Mitts, Hats; Hunting Accessories; Men & Women's Clothing

Truglo, Inc., 710 Presidential Dr., Richardson, TX 75081, P: 888-8-TRUGLO, F: 972-774-0323, www.truglo.com
Archery; Binoculars; Black Powder Accessories; Crossbows & Accessories; Hunting Accessories; Law Enforcement; Scopes, Sights & Accessories; Watches

Trulock Tool, 113 Drayton St. NW, P.O. Box 530, Whigham, GA 39897, P: 800-293-9402, F: 229-762-4050, www.trulockchokes.com
Ammunition; Custom Manufacturing; Firearms Maintenance Equipment; Gun Parts/Gunsmithing; Hunting Accessories; Recoil Protection Devices & Services; Sports Accessories; Wholesaler/Distributor

Trumark Mfg. Co., Inc., 1835 38th St., Boulder, CO 80301, P: 800-878-6272, F: 303-442-1380, www.slingshots.com
Archery; Backpacking; Crossbows & Accessories; Hunting Accessories; Sports Accessories

TufForce, 1734 Ranier Blvd., Canton, MI 48187, P: 800-382-7989, F: 888-686-0373, www.tufforce.com
Bags & Equipment Cases; Gun Cases; Gun Grips & Stocks; Holsters; Hunting Accessories; Law Enforcement; Scopes, Sights & Accessories; Wholesaler/Distributor

TurtleSkin Protective Products, 301 Turnpike Rd., New Ipswich, NH 03071, P: 888-477-4675, F: 603-291-1119, www.turtleskin.com
Gloves, Mitts, Hats; Hunting Accessories; Law Enforcement; Men & Women's Clothing; Sports Accessories

U

U.S. Armament Corp., 121 Valley View Dr., Ephrata, PA 17522, P: 717-721-4570, F: 717-738-4890, www.usarmamentcorp.com
Firearms

U.S. Armor Corp., 16433 Valley View Ave., Cerritos, CA 90703, P: 800-443-9798, F: 562-207-4238, www.usarmor.com
Law Enforcement; Training & Safety Equipment

U.S. Explosive Storage, LLC, 355 Industrial Park Dr., Boone, NC 28607, P: 877-233-1481, F: 800-295-1653, www.usexplosive.com
Custom Manufacturing; Firearms Maintenance Equipment; Gun Cabinets/Racks/Safes; Law Enforcement; Magazines, Cartridge; Training & Safety Equipment

U.S. Fire-Arms Mfg. Co., Inc., P.O. Box 1901, Hartford, CT 06144-1901, P: 860-296-7441, F: 860-296-7688, www.usfirearms.com
Firearms; Gun Parts/Gunsmithing

U.S. Optics, Inc., 150 Arovista Circle, Brea, CA 92821, P: 714-582-1956, F: 714-582-1959, www.usoptics.com
Custom Manufacturing; Law Enforcement; Scopes, Sights & Accessories

U.S. Tactical Supply, Inc., 939 Pacific Blvd. SE, Albany, OR 97321, P: 877-928-8645, F: 541-791-2965, www.ustacticalsupply.com
Bags & Equipment Cases; Gun Parts/Gunsmithing; Holsters; Hunting Accessories; Knives/Knife Cases; Law Enforcement; Scopes, Sights & Accessories; Wholesaler/Distributor

Uberti, A., 17603 Indian Head Hwy., Accokeek, MD 20607-2501, P: 800-264-4962, F: 301-283-6988, www.uberti.com
Firearms

Ultimate Survival Technologies, LLC, 14428 167th Ave. SE, Monroe, WA 98272, P: 866-479-7994, F: 206-965-9659, www.ultimatesurvival.com
Backpacking; Bags & Equipment Cases; Camping; Hunting Accessories; Law Enforcement; Men's Clothing; Sports Accessories; Survival Kits/First Aid

Ultra Dot Distribution, 6304 Riverside Dr., P.O. Box 362, Yankeetown, FL, 34498, P: 352-447-2255, F: 352-447-2266, www.ultradotusa.com
Scopes, Sights & Accessories

Ultra Lift Corp., 475 Stockton Ave., Unit E, San Jose, CA 95126, P: 800-346-3057, F: 408-297-1199, www.ultralift.com/safes.html
Custom Manufacturing; Gun Cabinets/Racks/Safes; Gun Cases; Retailer Services; Sports Accessories; Training & Safety Equipment

Ultra Paws, 12324 Little Pine Rd. SW, Brainerd, MN 56401, P: 800-355-5575, F: 218-855-6977, www.ultrapaws.com
Backpacking; Hunting Accessories; Law Enforcement; Outfitter; Pet Supplies; Survival Kits/First Aid; Training & Safety Equipment; Wholesaler/Distributor

Ultramax Ammunition/Wideview Scope Mount, 2112 Elk Vale Rd., Rapid City, SD 57701, P: 800-345-5852, F: 605-342-8727, www.ultramaxammunition.com
Ammunition

Ultrec Engineered Products, LLC, 860 Maple Ridge Ln., Brookfield, WI 53045, P: 262-821-2023, F: 262-821-1156, www.ultrec.com
Backpacking; Binoculars; Firearms; Hunting Accessories; Law Enforcement; Photographic Equipment; Shooting Range Equipment; Training & Safety Equipment

Umarex/Umarex, USA/RAM–Real Action Marker, 6007 S. 29th St., Fort Smith, AR 72908, P: 479-646-4210, F: 479-646-4206, www.umarexusa.com, www.trainingumarexusa.com
Airguns; Airsoft; Ammunition; Firearms; Law Enforcement; Paintball Guns; Scopes, Sights & Accessories; Training & Safety Equipment

Uncle Mike's/Bushnell Outdoor Accessories, 9200 Cody St., Overland Park, KS 66214, P: 800-423-3537, F: 800-548-0446, www.unclemikes.com
Bags & Equipment Cases; Gloves, Mitts, Hats; Gun Cases; Holsters; Hunting Accessories

Under Armour Performance, 1020 Hull St., Third Floor, Baltimore, MD 21230, P: 888-427-6687, F: 410-234-1027, www.underarmour.com
Bags & Equipment Cases; Camouflage; Gloves, Mitts, Hats; Law Enforcement; Men & Women's Clothing; Outfitter; Sports Accessories

United Cutlery Corp., 201 Plantation Oak Dr., Thomasville, GA 31792, P: 800-548-0835, F: 229-551-0182, www.unitedcutlery.com
Camping; Compasses; Custom Manufacturing; Cutlery; Knives/Knife Cases; Law Enforcement; Sharpeners; Wholesaler/Distributor

United Shield International, 1606 Barlow St., Suite 1, Traverse City, MI 49686, P: 800-705-9153, F: 231-933-5368, www.unitedshield.net
Law Enforcement

Urban–E.R.T. Slings, LLC, P.O. Box 429, Clayton, IN 46118, P: 317-223-6509, F: 317-539-2710, www.urbanertslings.com
Firearms; Hunting Accessories; Law Enforcement; Paintball Accessories

US Night Vision Corp., 3845 Atherton Rd., Suite 9, Rocklin, CA 95765, P: 800-500-4020, F: 916-663-5986, www.usnightvision.com
Binoculars; Hunting Accessories; Law Enforcement; Paintball Accessories; Scopes, Sights & Accessories; Sports Accessories; Training & Safety Equipment; Wholesaler/Distributor

US Peacekeeper Products, Inc., W245, N5570 Corporate Circle, Sussex, WI 53089, P: 800-428-0800, F: 262-246-4845, uspeacekeeper.com
Bags & Equipment Cases; Gloves, Mitts, Hats; Hunting Accessories; Men & Women's Clothing

Uselton Arms, 390 Southwinds Dr., Franklin, TN 37064, P: 615-595-2255, F: 615-595-2254, www.useltonarms.com
Custom Manufacturing; Firearms; Gun Barrels; Gun Grips & Stocks; Gun Parts/Gunsmithing; Law Enforcement

V

V.H. Blackinton & Co., Inc., 221 John Dietsch Blvd., P.O. Box 1300, Attleboro Falls, MA 02763, P: 800-699-4436, F: 508-695-5349, www.blackinton.com
Custom Manfucturing; Emblems & Decals; Law Enforcement

Valdada Optics, P.O. Box 270095, Littleton, CO 80127, P: 303-979-4578, F: 303-979-0256, www.valdada.com
Binoculars; Compasses; Custom Manufacturing; Law Enforcement; Photographic Equipment; Scopes, Sights & Accessories; Telescopes; Wholesaler/Distributor

MANUFACTURER'S DIRECTORY

Valiant Armoury, 3000 Grapevine Mills Pkwy., Suite 101, Grapevine, TX 76051, P: 877-796-7374, F: 972-539-9351, www.valliantarmouryswords.com
Wholesaler/Distributor

Valley Operational Wear, LLC/OP Wear Armor, P.O. Box 9415, Knoxville, TN 37940, P: 865-259-6248, F: 865-259-6255
Law Enforcement

Valor Corp., 1001 Sawgrass Corporate Pkwy., Sunrise, FL 33323, P: 800-899-VALOR, F: 866-248-9594, www.valorcorp.com
Airguns; Ammunition; Cutlery; Firearms; Knives/Knife Cases; Law Enforcement; Magazines, Cartridge; Wholesaler/Distributor

Vang Comp Systems, 400 W. Butterfield Rd., Chino Valley, AZ 86323, P: 928-636-8455, F: 928-636-1538, www.vangcomp.com
Firearms; Gun Barrels; Gun Parts/Gunsmithing

Vanguard USA, Inc., 9157 E. M-36, Whitmore Lake, MI 48189, P: 800-875-3322, F: 888-426-7008, www.vanguardworld.com
Archery; Bags & Equipment Cases; Binoculars; Gun Cases; Hunting Accessories; Photographic Equipment; Scopes, Sights & Accessories; Shooting Range Equipment

Vector Optics, 3964 Callan Blvd., South San Francisco, CA 94080, P: 415-632-7089, CHINA, P: 011 862154040649, www.vectoroptics.com
Scopes, Sights & Accessories; Sports Accessories; Wholesaler/Distributor

Vega Holster srl, Via Di Mezzo 31 Z.I., Calcinaia (PI), 56031, ITALY, P: 011 390587489190, F: 011 390587489901, www.vegaholster.com
Bags & Equipment Cases; Gun Cases; Holsters; Hunting Accessories; Law Enforcement; Leathergoods; Shooting Range Equipment

Vega Silah Sanayi, Ltd., Tigcilar Sokak No. 1 Mercan, Eminonu, Istanbul, 34450, TURKEY, P: 011 902125200103, F: 011 902125120879
Firearms

Verney-Carron SA, 54 Blvd. Thiers, Boite Postale 72, St. Etienne Cedex 1, 42002, FRANCE, P: 011 33477791500, F: 011 33477790702, www.verney-carron.com
Custom Manufacturing; Firearms; Gun Barrels; Law Enforcement; Wholesaler/Distibutor

Versatile Rack Co., 5232 Alcoa Ave., Vernon, CA 90058, P: 323-588-0137, F: 323-588-5067, www.versatilegunrack.com
Firearms Maintenance Equipment; Gun Cabinets/Racks/Safes; Gun Cases; Gun Locks; Hunting Accessories; Reloading; Shooting Range Equipment; Sports Accessories

VibraShine, Inc./Leaf River Outdoor Products, 113 Fellowship Rd., P.O. Box 557, Taylorsville, MS 39168, P: 601-785-9854, F: 601-785-9874, www.myleafriver.com

Firearms Maintenance Equipment; Hunting Accessories; Photographic Equipment; Reloading

Victorinox Swiss Army, 7 Victoria Dr., Monroe, CT 06468, P: 800-243-4032, F: 800-243-4006, www.swissarmy.com
Camping; Cutlery; Hunting Accessories; Knives/Knife Cases; Lighting Products; Sports Accessories

Virginia Blade, 5177 Boonsboro Rd., Lynchburg, VA 24503, P: 434-384-1282, F: 434-384-4541

Viridian Green Laser Sights/Laser Aiming Systems Corp., 12637 Sable Dr., Burnsville, MN 55337, P: 800-990-9390, F: 952-882-6227, www.viridiangreenlaser.com
Holsters; Law Enforcement; Lighting Products; Scopes, Sights & Accessories

Vixen Optics, 1010 Calle Cordillera, Suite 106, San Clemente, CA 92673, P: 949-429-6363, F: 949-429-6826, www.vixenoptics.com
Binoculars; Scopes, Sights & Accessories; Telescopes; Wholesaler/Distributor

Vltor Weapon Systems, 3735 N. Romero Rd., Tucson, AZ 85705, P: 866-468-5867, F: 520-293-8807, www.vltor.com
Firearms; Gun Grips & Stocks; Gun Parts/Gunsmithing; Law Enforcement; Recoil Protection Devices & Services

Volquartsen Custom, 24276 240th St., P.O. Box 397, Carroll, IA 51401, P: 712-792-4238, F: 712-792-2542, www.volquartsen.com
Custom Manufacturing; Firearms; Gun Barrels; Gun Grips/Stocks; Gun Parts/Gunsmithing

Vortex Optics, 2120 W. Greenview Dr., Middleton, WI 53562, P: 800-426-0048, F: 608-662-7454
Binoculars; Scopes, Sights & Accessories

Vyse-Gelatin Innovations, 5024 N. Rose St., Schiller Park, IL 60176, P: 800-533-2152, F: 800-533-2152, www.vyse.com
Airguns; Ammunition; Firearms; Law Enforcement; Magazines, Cartridge; Paintball Guns & Accessories; Shooting Range Equipment

W

W.R. Case & Sons Cutlery Co., Owens Way, Bradford, PA 16701, P: 800-523-6350, F: 814-368-1736, www.wrcase.com
Cutlery; Knives/Knife Cases; Sharpeners

Walther USA, 2100 Roosevelt Ave., Springfield, MA 01104, P: 800-372-6454, F: 413-747-3317, www.waltheramerica.com
Bags & Equipment Cases; Firearms; Knives/Knife Cases; Law Enforcement; Lighting Products

Watershed Drybags, 2000 Riverside Dr., Asheville, NC 28804, P: 828-252-7111, F: 828-252-7107, www.drybags.com
Backpacking; Bags & Equipment Cases; Camping; Gun Cases; Hunting Accessories; Law Enforcement; Survival Kits/First Aid; Training & Safety Equipment

Weatherby, Inc., 1605 Commerce Way, Paso Robles, CA 93446, P: 800-227-

2016, F: 805-237-0427, www.weatherby.com
Ammunition; Custom Manufacturing; Firearms

Weaver Optics/ATK Commercial Products, N5549 Cty. Tk. Z, Onalaska, WI 54650, P: 800-635-7656, F: 763-323-3890, www.weaveroptics.com
Binoculars; Scopes, Sights & Accessories

Weber's Camo Leather Goods/Wilderness Dreams Lingerie & Swimwear, 615 Nokomis St., Suite 400, Alexandria, MN 56308, P: 320-762-2816, F: 320-763-9762, www.webersleather.com
Bags & Equipment Cases; Camouflage; Footwear; Home Furnishings; Hunting Accessories; Leathergoods; Men & Women's Clothing

Wellco Enterprises, 150 Westwood Circle, P.O. Box 188, Waynesville, NC 28786, P: 800-840-3155, F: 828-456-3547, www.wellco.com
Footwear; Law Enforcement

Wells Creek Outfitters, 803-12 SW 12th St., Bentonville, AR, 72712, P: 479-273-1174, F: 479-273-0137
Camouflage; Hunting Accessories; Men's Clothing

Wenger N.A./Wenger, Maker of the Genuine Swiss Army Knife, 15 Corporate Dr., Orangeburg, NY 10962, P: 800-431-2996, F: 845-425-4700, www.wengerna.com
Backpacking; Camping; Cutlery; Footwear; Hunting Accessories; Knives/Knife Cases; Watches

Western Powders, Inc., P.O. Box 158, Miles City, MT 59301, P: 800-497-1007, F: 406-234-0430, www.blackhorn209.com
Black Powder/Smokeless Powder; Firearms Maintenance Equipment; Lubricants; Reloading; Wholesaler/Distributor

Western Rivers, Inc., 1582 N. Broad St., Lexington, TN 38351, P: 800-967-0998, F: 731-967-1243, www.western-rivers.com
Decoys; Game Calls; Hunting Accessories; Lighting Products; Pet Supplies; Scents & Lures; Scopes, Sights & Accessories

Westfield Outdoor, Inc., 1593 Esprit Dr., Westfield, IN 46074, P: 317-569-0679, F: 317-580-1834, www.westfieldoutdoor.com
Backpacking; Camping

White Flyer Targets/Div. Reagent Chemical & Research, Inc., 115 Route 202/31 S, Ringoes, NJ 08851, P: 800-322-7855, F: 908-284-2113, www.whiteflyer.com
Clay Targets; Firearms; Shooting Range Equipment; Targets

Wilcox Industries Corp., 25 Piscataque Dr., Newington, NH 03801, P: 603-431-1331, F: 603-431-1221, www.wilcoxind.com
Law Enforcement; Scopes, Sights & Accessories

Wild West Guns, LLC, 7100 Homer Dr., Anchorage, AK 99518-3229, P: 800-992-4570, F: 907-344-4005, www.wildwestguns.com
Custom Manufacturing; Firearms; Gun Parts/Gunsmithing; Outfitter; Recoil Protection Devices & Services; Scopes,

Sights & Accessories; Wholesaler/ Distributor

Wildsteer, 9 Avenue Eugene Brisson, Bourges, F-18000, FRANCE, P: 011 33248211380, F: 011 33248211380, www.wildsteer.com
Archery; Knives/Knife Cases; Leathergoods

Wiley X., Inc., 7491 Longard Rd., Livermore, CA 94551, P: 800-776-7842, F: 925-455-8860, www.wileyx.com
Eye Protection

William Henry Studio, 3200 NE Rivergate St., McMinnville, OR 97128, P: 888-563-4500, F: 503-434-9704, www. williamhenrystudio.com
Cutlery; Knives/Knife Cases

Williams Gun Sight Co., 7389 Lapeer Rd., Davison, MI 48423, P: 800-530-9028, F: 810-658-2140, www.williamsgunsight. com
Black Powder Accessories; Books/ Industry Publications; Compasses; Gun Parts/Gunsmithing; Hunting Accessories; Scopes, Sights & Accessories

Wilson Arms Co., 97 Leetes Island Rd., Branford, CT 06405, P: 203-488-7297, F: 203-488-0135, www.wilsonarms.com
Custom Manufacturing; Firearms; Gun Barrels

Winchester Ammunition/Div. Olin Corp., 427 N. Shamrock St., East Alton, IL 62024, P: 618-258-2365, F: 618-258-3609, www. winchester.com
Ammunition

Winchester Repeating Arms, 275 Winchester Ave., Morgan, UT 84050, P: 801-876-3440, F: 801-876-3737, www. winchesterguns.com
Firearms

Wing-Sun Trading, Inc., 15501 Heron Ave., La Mirada, CA 90638, P: 866-944-1068, F: 714-522-6417
Backpacking; Binoculars; Camping; Compasses; Lighting Products; Photographic Equipment; Scopes, Sights & Accessories; Wholesaler/Distributor

Wolf Peak International, 1221 Marshall Way, Layton, UT 84041, P: 866-953-7325, F: 801-444-9353, www.wolfpeak.net
Airguns; Airsoft; Backpacking; Camouflage; Eyewear; Hunting Accessories; Law Enforcement; Shooting Range Equipment

Woolrich, Inc./Elite Series Tactical, 1 Mill St., Woolrich, PA 17779, P: 800-996-2299, F: 570-769-7662, www.woolrich.com, www. woolricheliteseriestactical.com
Footwear; Gloves, Mitts, Hats; Home Furnishings; Law Enforcement; Men & Women's Clothing; Wholesaler/Distributor

X

X-Caliber Accuracy Systems, 1837 First St., Bay City, MI 48708, P: 989-893-3961, F: 989-893-0241, www.xcaliberaccuracy. com
Hunting Accessories

X-Caliber Tactical, 1111 Winding Creek Pl., Round Rock, TX 78664, P: 512-524-2621, www.xcalibertactical.com
Airguns; Airsoft; Custom Manufacturing; Export/Import Specialists; Law Enforcement; Wholesaler/Distributor

Xenonics Holdings, Inc., 2236 Rutherford Rd., Suite 123, Carlsbad, CA 92008, P: 760-448-9700, FL 760-929-7571, www. xenonics.com
Law Enforcement; Lighting Products

Xisico USA, Inc./Rex Optics USA, Inc., 16802 Barker Springs, Suite 550, Houston, TX 77084, P: 281-647-9130, F: 208-979-2848, www.xisicousa.com
Airguns; Ammunition; Binoculars; Scopes, Sights & Accessories

XS Sight Systems, 2401 Ludella St., Fort Worth, TX 76105, P: 888-744-4880, F: 800-734-7939, www.xssights.com
Gun Parts/Gunsmithing; Law Enforcement; Scopes, Sights & Accessories

Y

Yaktrax, 9221 Globe Center Dr., Morrisville, NC 27560, P: 800-446-7587, F: 919-544-0975, www.yaktrax.com
Backpacking; Camping; Footwear; Sports Accessories

Yankee Hill Machine Co., Inc., 20 Ladd Ave., Suite 1, Florence, MA 01062, P: 877-892-6533, F: 413-586-1326, www.yhm.net
Firearms; Gun Barrels; Gun Cases; Gun Parts/Gunsmithing; Law Enforcement; Scopes, Sights & Accessories

Yukon Advanced Optics, 201 Regency Pkwy., Mansfield, TX 76063, P: 817-453-9966, F: 817-453-8770
Archery; Backpacking; Binoculars; Camping; Custom Manufacturing; Hunting Accessories; Scopes, Sights & Accessories; Wholesaler/Distributor

Z

Z-Blade, Inc., 28280 Alta Vista Ave., Valencia, CA 91355, P: 800-734-5424, F: 661-295-2615, www.pfimold.com
Custom Manufacturing; Hunting Accessories; Knives/Knife Cases

Zak Tool, 319 San Luis Rey Rd., Arcadia, CA 91007, P: 615-504-4456, F: 931-381-2568, www.zaktool.com
Law Enforcement; Training & Safety Equipment

Zanotti USA, 7907 High Knoll Ln., Houston, TX 77095, P: 281-414-2184, www. zanottiusa.com
Custom Manufacturing; Firearms

Zarc International, Inc., P.O. Box 108, Minonk, IL 61760, P: 800-882-7011, F: 309-432-3490, www.zarc.com
Law Enforcement; Retail Packaging

Zero Tolerance Knives, 18600 SW Tetaon Ave., Tualatin, OR 97062, P: 800-325-2891, F: 503-682-7168, www.ztknives. com
Knives/Knife Cases; Law Enforcement

Ziegel Engineering Working Designs, Jackass Field Carts, 2108 Lomina Ave., Long Beach, CA 90815, P: 562-596-9481, F: 562-598-4734, www.ziegeleng. com
Archery; Bags & Equipment Cases; Black Powder Accessories; Custom Manufacturing; Gun Cabinets/Racks/Safes; Gun Cases; Law Enforcement; Shooting Range Equipment

Zippo Manufacturing Co., 33 Barbour St., Bradford, PA 16701, P: 814-368-2700, F: 814-362-1350, www.zippo.com
Camping; Knives/Knife Cases; Lighting Products; Sports Accessories

Zistos Corp., 1736 Church St., Holbrook, NY 11741, P: 631-434-1370, F: 631-434-9104, www.zistos.com
Law Enforcement

Zodi Outback Gear, P.O. Box 4687, Park City, UT 84060, P: 800-589-2849, F: 800-861-8228
Archery; Backpacking; Camping; Cooking Equipment/Accessories; Hunting Accessories; Pet Supplies; Sports Accessories; Training & Safety Equipment

ZOLL Medical Corp., 269 Mill Rd., Chelmsford, MA 01824, P: 800-348-9011, F: 978-421-0025, www.zoll.com
Law Enforcement; Survival Kits/First Aid; Training & Safety Equipment

NUMBERS

3Point5.com, 224 South 200 West, Suite 230, Salt Lake City, UT 84101, P: 801-456-6900/2007, F: 801-485-5039, www.3point5.com

5.11 Tactical Series, 4300 Spyres Way, Modesto, CA 95356, P: 866-451-1726/348, F: 209-548-5348, www.511tactical.com
Bags & Equipment Cases; Men & Women's Clothing; Eyewear; Footwear; Gloves, Mitts, Hats; Law Enforcement; Watches

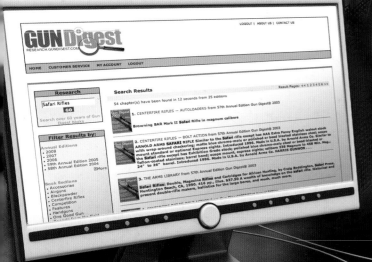